OCR GCSE
Religious Studies

CHRISTIANITY AND ISLAM

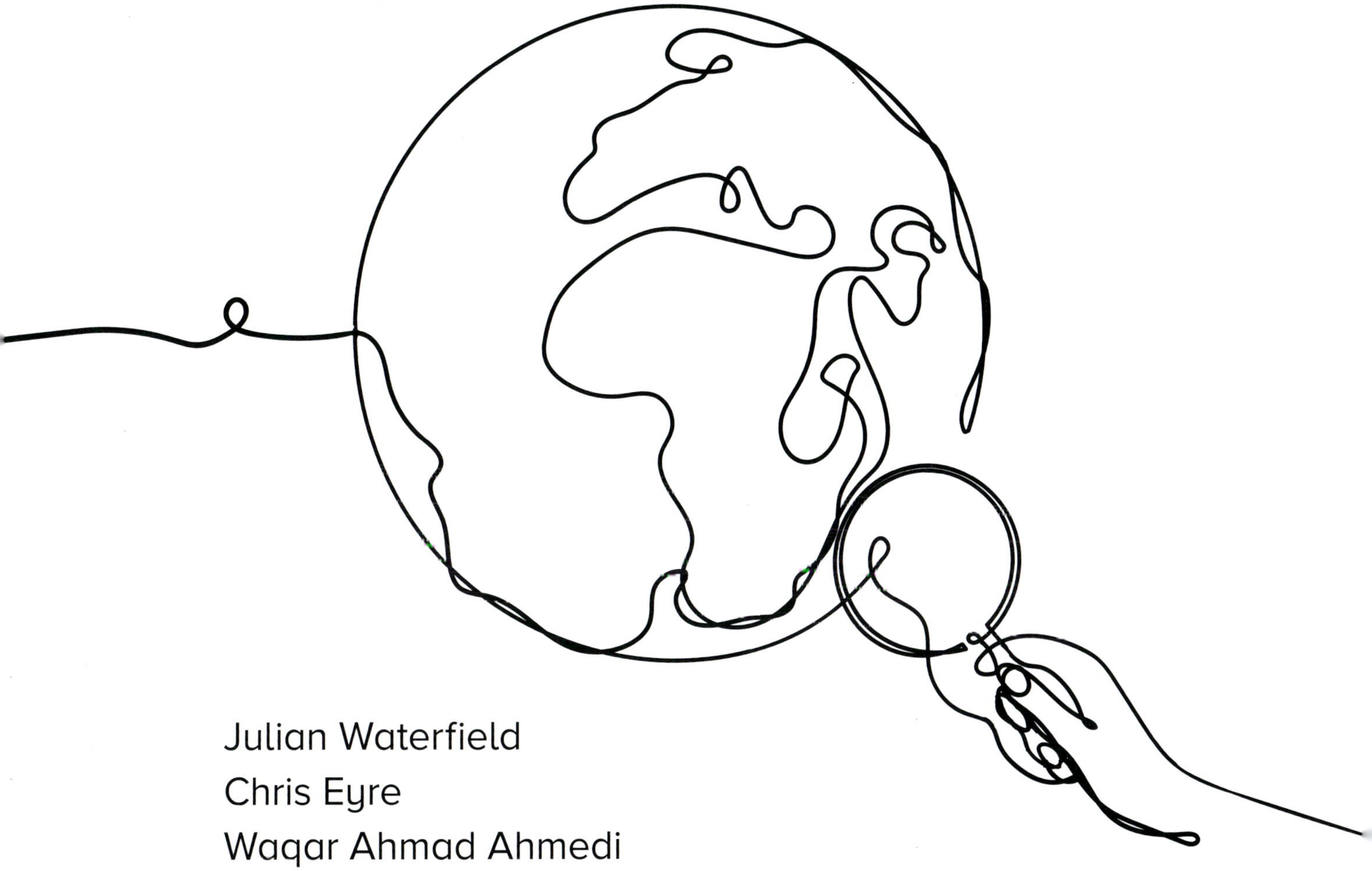

Julian Waterfield
Chris Eyre
Waqar Ahmad Ahmedi

The teaching content of this resource is endorsed by OCR for use with specification GCSE in Religious Studies (9–1) (J625). In order to gain OCR endorsement, this resource has been reviewed against OCR's endorsement criteria. This resource was designed using the most up to date information from the specification. Specifications are updated over time which means there may be contradictions between the resource and the specification, therefore please use the information on the latest specification and Sample Assessment Materials at all times when ensuring students are fully prepared for their assessment.

Any references to assessment and/or assessment preparation are the publisher's interpretation of the specification requirements and are not endorsed by OCR. OCR recommends that teachers consider using a range of teaching and learning resources in preparing learners for assessment, based on their own professional judgement for their students' needs. OCR has not paid for the production of this resource, nor does OCR receive any royalties from its sale. For more information about the endorsement process, please visit the OCR website, www.ocr.org.uk

Acknowledgements

The Publishers would like to thank the following for permission to reproduce copyright material.

p.211 Bertrand Russell quote reprinted with permission of The Bertrand Russell Peace Foundation Ltd; p.71 Source: https://cafod.org.uk/about-us/what-we-doCAFOD used with permission

Translation of sacred texts:

Extracts from the Bible unless otherwise stated are from: THE HOLY BIBLE, NEW INTERNATIONAL VERSION®, NIV® Copyright © 1973, 1978, 1984, 2011 by Biblica, Inc.® Used by permission. All rights reserved worldwide

Extracts from the Qur'an: The Qur'an A new translation by M. A. S. Abdel Haleem © M. A. S. Abdel Haleem 2004, 2005, reprinted with amends 2008, Oxford University Press

Every effort has been made to trace all copyright holders, but if any have been inadvertently overlooked, the Publishers will be pleased to make the necessary arrangements at the first opportunity.

Although every effort has been made to ensure that website addresses are correct at time of going to press, Hodder Education cannot be held responsible for the content of any website mentioned in this book. It is sometimes possible to find a relocated web page by typing in the address of the home page for a website in the URL window of your browser.

Hachette UK's policy is to use papers that are natural, renewable and recyclable products and made from wood grown in well-managed forests and other controlled sources. The logging and manufacturing processes are expected to conform to the environmental regulations of the country of origin.

Orders: please contact Hachette UK Distribution, Hely Hutchinson Centre, Milton Road, Didcot, Oxfordshire, OX11 7HH. Telephone: +44 (0)1235 827827. Email education@hachette.co.uk Lines are open from 9 a.m. to 5 p.m., Monday to Friday. You can also order through our website: www.hoddereducation.co.uk

ISBN: 978 1 3983 7662 5

© Chris Eyre, Julian Waterfield, Waqar Ahmad Ahmedi 2023

First published in 2023 by

Hodder Education,

An Hachette UK Company

Carmelite House

50 Victoria Embankment

London EC4Y 0DZ

www.hoddereducation.co.uk

Impression number 10 9 8 7 6 5 4 3 2 1

Year   2027 2026 2025 2024 2023

All rights reserved. Apart from any use permitted under UK copyright law, no part of this publication may be reproduced or transmitted in any form or by any means, electronic or mechanical, including photocopying and recording, or held within any information storage and retrieval system, without permission in writing from the publisher or under licence from the Copyright Licensing Agency Limited. Further details of such licences (for reprographic reproduction) may be obtained from the Copyright Licensing Agency Limited, www.cla.co.uk

Cover photo © tyasdrawing- stock.adobe.com

Typeset in India

Produced by DZS Grafik, Printed in Slovenia

A catalogue record for this title is available from the British Library.

Contents

Christianity 1

1 Beliefs and teachings 2
- 1.1 Introducing Christianity 2
- 1.2 The nature of God: core characteristics 4
- 1.3 The nature of God: seen in daily life 6
- 1.4 The Trinity 8
- 1.5 Biblical accounts of creation 10
- 1.6 Interpretations of the creation story 12
- 1.7 The Fall and Original Sin 14
- 1.8 The problem of evil 16
- 1.9 The Incarnation 18
- 1.10 The life of Jesus Christ 20
- 1.11 The Sermon on the Mount 22
- 1.12 The death of Jesus Christ 24
- 1.13 The resurrection and ascension of Jesus 26
- 1.14 Salvation 28
- 1.15 Sin and God's grace 30
- 1.16 Eschatology: core beliefs 32
- 1.17 Eschatology: heaven, hell and purgatory 34
- Summary activities 36

2 Practices 38
- 2.1 Worship 38
- 2.2 The structure of church services 40
- 2.3 Prayer 42
- 2.4 The importance of prayer and worship 44
- 2.5 Different types of prayer 46
- 2.6 Sacraments 48
- 2.7 Baptism 50
- 2.8 The Eucharist 52
- 2.9 Pilgrimage 54
- 2.10 Advent and Christmas 56
- 2.11 Lent, Holy Week and Easter 58
- 2.12 Marriage and funerals 60
- 2.13 Families and confirmation 62
- 2.14 Mission 64
- 2.15 New forms of church 66
- 2.16 Ecumenism 68
- 2.17 The Church in the wider world 70
- Summary activities 72

Islam 75

3 Beliefs and teachings 76
- 3.1 Introducing Islam 76
- 3.2 Core beliefs: Sunni Muslims 78
- 3.3 Core beliefs: Shi'a Muslims 80
- 3.4 Core beliefs: comparing Sunni and Shi'a Muslims 82
- 3.5 The nature of Allah: names of Allah 84
- 3.6 The nature of Allah: Tawhid and shirk 86
- 3.7 Prophethood: the role and importance of the prophets 88
- 3.8 Prophethood: prophets before Muhammad 90
- 3.9 Prophethood: Prophet Muhammad 92
- 3.10 Books: books before the Qur'an 94
- 3.11 Books: the Qur'an 96
- 3.12 Angels: the nature of angels 98

iii

- 3.13 Angels: the roles and importance of angels — 100
- 3.14 Eschatological beliefs and teachings: predestination and Allah's plan — 102
- 3.15 Eschatological beliefs and teachings: the free will debate — 104
- 3.16 Life after death: Akhirah and the Day of Judgement — 106
- 3.17 Life after death: heaven and hell — 108
- Summary activities — 110

4 Practices — 112

- 4.1 Importance of the Five Pillars of Islam for Sunni Muslims — 112
- 4.2 Importance of the Ten Obligatory Acts for Shi'a Muslims — 114
- 4.3 Public acts of worship: Salah — 117
- 4.4 Public acts of worship: Salah at home and mosque — 120
- 4.5 Public acts of worship: Shahadah — 122
- 4.6 Private acts of worship — 123
- 4.7 Hajj: origins and importance of Hajj — 126
- 4.8 Hajj: rituals of Hajj — 129
- 4.9 Zakah: the role and importance of giving alms — 132
- 4.10 Zakah: comparing Sunni and Shi'a Muslims — 134
- 4.11 Sawm: the origins of fasting — 136
- 4.12 Sawm: the duties during fasting and its benefits — 138
- 4.13 Festivals and special days: Eid-ul-Adha and Eid-ul-Fitr — 140
- 4.14 Festivals and special days: Eid-ul-Ghadeer and Ashura — 142
- 4.15 Jihad: Greater Jihad — 146
- 4.16 Jihad: Lesser Jihad — 148
- Summary activities — 152

Religion, philosophy and ethics — 155

5 Relationships and families — 156

- 5.1 The role and purpose of a Christian family — 156
- 5.2 What do Christians believe about the purpose and importance of marriage? — 158
- 5.3 What is the significance of the beliefs and teachings reflected in a Christian marriage ceremony? — 160
- 5.4 Is sex something that should only take place within marriage? — 162
- 5.5 Should all Christians marry and have children? — 164
- 5.6 Christian views on same-sex marriage — 166
- 5.7 When relationships end: the ethics of divorce and remarriage — 168
- 5.8 Men and women within Christian families — 170
- 5.9 Men and women within Christian communities — 172
- 5.10 Gender roles in the religious upbringing of children — 174
- 5.11 Christian teachings and beliefs about equality — 176
- 5.12 Christian views on equality, prejudice and discrimination on the basis of gender — 178

5.13 How does culture influence Christian attitudes to equality? 180

Summary activities 182

6 The existence of God 184

6.1 Christian beliefs about God and his goodness 184

6.2 How does a good God relate to the world and to human beings? 186

6.3 What do Christians teach about the relationship between God and human suffering? 188

6.4 Does it matter whether God's existence can be proved? 190

6.5 Does the design argument prove God's existence? 192

6.6 Does the world need a first cause? 194

6.7 What do Christians believe is the purpose of the world? 196

6.8 What does morality show about God and the purpose of human life? 198

6.9 Christian beliefs about revelation and experiencing God 200

6.10 How might God be revealed through scripture and tradition? 202

6.11 How might God be revealed today? 205

6.12 Christian beliefs about experiencing God: conversion and charismatic experiences 208

6.13 Christian beliefs about experiencing God: mystical experiences and visions 211

6.14 Christian beliefs about experiencing God: worship and sacraments 214

Summary activities 216

7 Religion, peace and conflict 218

7.1 Christian teaching about violence in society 218

7.2 Christian responses to terrorism 220

7.3 The just war theory 222

7.4 Can a Christian ever support holy war? 224

7.5 Christian responses to modern warfare 226

7.6 What are the different Christian attitudes to pacifism? 229

7.7 How do Christians show their commitment to peace? 232

7.8 Understanding non-violent action 234

7.9 Understanding reconciliation 236

7.10 Is it always necessary and possible to forgive? 238

7.11 Christian beliefs about justice and injustice 240

7.12 How Christians work for social justice 242

Summary activities 244

8 Dialogue between religious and non-religious views 246

8.1 Christianity in British society 246

8.2 Secularisation 248

8.3 Religious and secular values in education 250

8.4 Marriage and equality 252

8.5 Medical ethics: euthanasia and abortion 254

v

8.6	Medical ethics: genetic manipulation and the creation of life	256	8.11 Dialogue with atheism and agnosticism	266
8.7	Is Christianity the only way to salvation?	258	8.12 Dialogue with humanism	268
8.8	Dialogue between religious groups	260	8.13 Dialogue with secularism	270
8.9	Religion and wider society	262	8.14 Christian views and attitudes	272
8.10	Christian attitudes towards each other	264	Summary activities	274

Glossary 276

Index 280

Christianity

SECTION 1

CHAPTER 1

Beliefs and teachings

1.1 Introducing Christianity

 Aim
To give some broad detail about Christianity that will help you study the course

 Starter
What makes someone a Christian? See how many ideas you can note down.

 Key word
Denomination – a group within a religion

Christian worldviews

Christianity began as part of Judaism around 2000 years ago. The movement was initially a group of followers of the preacher Jesus which eventually became a religious faith in its own right. There are many different types of Christians and the list of views and groups can be bewildering. Rather than thinking about the type of Church (the **denomination**), it may be helpful to think of the ways that Christians see the world as falling into roughly three different types – but of course this is a simplification and it is usually wiser to use words like 'some' or 'most' when describing different views.

■ The Bible is the holy book for all Christians

Christians may see and understand the world through one of the three 'lenses' described below.

Catholic lens | Liberal (Protestant) lens | Evangelical (Protestant) lens

Catholic lens	Liberal (Protestant) lens	Evangelical (Protestant) lens
These Christians tend to be found within the Roman Catholic denomination and take their views from the Bible and the interpretation/ teachings of the Church. They believe that the Church holds the correct interpretation of the Bible and say that human reason is a God-given tool.	These Christians respect the Biblical writings but do not believe that they need to be followed in a precise or literal way. They believe that Christian teachings need to be interpreted for the modern day using Biblical principles.	These Christians believe that the Bible is the only authority that Christians need to decide their beliefs and practices. They tend towards a more literal interpretation of the Bible.

Even within these lenses, there are further lenses linked to how Christians express their views in their life and worship. In this book, we will use the following words:

- **Traditional** – to reflect the lens that a formal approach, which has worked for almost 2000 years, is still the right way to express Christianity.

- **Modern** – to reflect the lens that Christian life should be more reflective of society today and how it has changed.
- **Charismatic** – to reflect the specific approach that believes Christian life should be led by the Holy Spirit in a radical way.

Different denominations

There are lots of different organised Christian groups called denominations. The groups below are five of the most well-known denominations in Britain today. The Catholic Church was the only Christian Church in the Western world until the Reformation. There was a movement in the sixteenth century that said that the Church had lost its way. The churches that emerged from the Reformation 'protested' in different ways against the Catholic Church and so are known as Protestant churches. Each denomination contains a range of different lenses, such as those listed above, which makes it even more challenging to talk about each denomination generally.

Roman Catholic Church | Church of England | Methodist | Baptist | Pentecostal

Catholic	Protestant groups			
Roman Catholic Church	**Church of England**	**Methodist**	**Baptist**	**Pentecostal**
The Catholic Church is the oldest Christian Church, tracing its foundation to St Peter, the disciple of Jesus, who is regarded as the first Pope.	The Church came into being when Henry VIII broke away from Catholicism in the sixteenth century and joined the European Protestant movement. It is the Established Church in England.	The Methodist Church began in the eighteenth century, initially as a group within the Church of England. They tend to have simpler worship services and focus on preaching and social action.	The Baptist Church is a Protestant group which came into being in the sixteenth century. They tend to be largely evangelical, believing in adult baptism by immersion rather than baptism of infants.	The Pentecostal Church is an evangelical group which came into being in the twentieth century. They tend to have lively, modern worship services with a focus on the Holy Spirit's action in the world.

The Bible as a source of authority

The common source of authority for Christians is the Bible. This is a collection of books made up of the Old Testament (Jewish history before the time of Jesus) and the New Testament (stories about Jesus in the Gospels and the early history of the Christian Church).

- Evangelical Christians tend to believe that the Bible was revealed to the world by God and so it has authority for all time. The more liberal the lens of a Christian, the more they see the hand of a human author in these books and also, sometimes, the more they see the need to interpret the teachings for the modern day.
- Catholics believe that the Bible contains all key teachings for life but that the interpretation of the Bible is the role of the Church and so Church teachings hold as much authority as the Bible.

1.2 The nature of God: core characteristics

Aim

To examine some key Christian beliefs about what God is like

Starter

What comes to mind if someone talks about God to you? Make a spider diagram to represent your thoughts.

Key words

Eternal – separate to or outside of time
Omniscient – all-knowing; able to know everything there is to know
Omnipotent – all powerful; able to do anything
Monotheistic – the belief that there is only one God
Transcendent – beyond everyday life; outside the human universe
Immanent – part of everyday life; within the human universe

In order for Christians to believe in and worship God, they need to be clear on what they mean when they describe God.

When God created the universe, the Bible emphasises that God already existed before time began and that God's creation was of all material things. Throughout the story of the Bible, God intervenes in the story of humanity, knows what is happening on Earth and is able to perform miracles but is, in some way, always separate to human activity and therefore human experiences of time.

Characteristic	Christian belief
Eternal	God was not created alongside us or the universe. God cannot have been created by anything, otherwise, there would be something greater than God.
	By emphasising that God is eternal, Christians also understand that God is outside of time. This means that God can see something going wrong and can intervene to help out.
Omniscient	God knows everything that there is to know.
	Logically, this links to the belief that God is outside of time but it also means that God has knowledge of the past and future as well as the present.
Omnipotent	God can do anything.
	This emphasises that God is the greatest being – able to help Christians, whatever they need.

All of these elements are found in the creation story in Genesis 1:

- Eternal: God is outside of time when creating the universe out of nothing. 'In the beginning God created the heavens and the earth': it was God's creation that created time, so God must be separate to what we know of as time.
- Omniscient: at each stage of creation, God sees everything that God is making. God must therefore be able to see (and know) differently to us.
- Omnipotent: the very fact that God is able to create the universe and everything on Earth in careful order demonstrates ultimate power.

The Bible emphasises that there is just one supreme God.

Source of authority

'I am the LORD your God … you shall have no other gods before me…' (Exodus 20:2–3)

■ Winchester Cathedral's design (top) emphasises different aspects of the nature of God to Liverpool Metropolitan Cathedral (bottom)

Characteristic	Christian belief
Monotheism	If God is so separate to the universe and to humans, how can God be close enough to be worshipped?
	The belief in one supreme God could be emphasised in the Bible because when the Bible was put together, other religions accepted many gods and this unique Jewish idea needed to be explained.
	It is clearly one God who creates the universe; this God is revealed as guiding humanity and is named Yahweh (often written as 'the LORD' in Bibles).
	The ultimate guide for life, the Ten Commandments, devotes the first four commandments to the greatness of God, especially his oneness.
Transcendent Immanent	Christians often talk about God being both beyond the world (transcendent) and also within the world (immanent).
	For some Christians, being able to focus on the greatness of God is important and, for others, it is the closeness of God that is important. Indeed, most Christians would say that being able to focus on these two aspects at different times is the key.
	Christians understand God's transcendence to mean that God is beyond anything that a human could fully describe or understand. God's immanence means that God can be known in some way and it is a focus on God's immanence that means that humans can pray.
	This is seen in forms of worship within Christianity: • Traditional worship emphasises the mystery of God either through the choice of language or how formal the service is. Some traditional Catholics prefer to worship God in Latin which might emphasise transcendence. • Modern worship tries to bring God into the midst of the people. In charismatic worship, such as in the Pentecostal Church, God's ability to speak through the people during a service emphasises immanence.

Analyse and evaluate

Does it matter if God is eternal, omniscient or omnipotent?

Yes	No
God cannot be worthy of worship if God is anything but the greatest possible being.	Christians should focus on daily life rather than trying to understand God, who is beyond human understanding.
If God cannot know when and where to intervene for the good of humans, then there seems little point to Christianity.	As long as God is greater than humans, it does not matter whether or not God is completely all-powerful or all-knowing.

Many Christians would argue that what is important is an understanding of a range of different aspects of the nature of God.

Activities

Review

1. Write three bullet points to show you understand God's eternity.
2. What is the difference between calling God transcendent and calling him immanent?

Develop

3. Look at these Gospel passages and link them to the aspects of the nature of God you have studied on these pages: Matthew 6:8, Matthew 19:26, Matthew 25:46, Mark 12:29, Luke 2:14 and John 3:16.

Link

4. How do Christian beliefs about Jesus Christ link to the words studied on these pages?

Debate

5. Do you agree that real Christianity focuses on God's work in the world more than God's transcendence?

Stretch

6. If God knows the future, can humans really claim that they are free to make decisions in their lives?

1.3 The nature of God: seen in daily life

 Aim

To consider aspects of God that relate to daily life

 Starter

Look at the two pieces of artwork on this spread. In your opinion which represents better the Christian God?

 Key words

Benevolent – loving, compassionate, kindly
Personal – able to be related to as a person, not an invisible force
Judge – someone who has the authority to decide right from wrong or make decisions about a person
Forgiving – able to move on from feeling angry or from wishing to punish

 Top tip

For each of the four key words relating to the nature of God, make sure you can say three different things about them and link your points to something from the Bible.

Source of authority

'God so loved the world that he gave his one and only Son, that whoever believes in him shall not perish but have eternal life.' (John 3:16)

Characteristic	Christian belief
Benevolent	God's benevolence is a way of describing God's love for creation.
	It is important for Christians to understand what is meant by love when describing God or the Christian life. The term used for this is *agape*, which is a Greek word that means a specific sort of love, which is: • selfless and sacrificial • centred on justice • unconditional.
	Understanding love in these terms gives a better view of what God's love might be like. God's love is expressed through the idea of 'grace' – the unconditional gift of love that God gives. This is shown in many ways but for Christians, ultimately, through the Jesus story: God comes to Earth to work with humanity and to give the gift of self-sacrifice to save humans for eternity.
	God's benevolence is also shown in the Genesis creation story, where the special place humanity has in creation shows God's love for it.
Personal	The Christian belief that God loves humans leads to another important aspect of God's nature: that God is personal.
	There is little point for Christians in worshipping a God who is remote or with whom it is impossible to have a relationship. This is what worshipping a personal God is all about: the ability to enter into a relationship.
	Some Christians emphasise the gap between humans and God but others focus on the nature of the relationship with God as a friend or parent.
	In the Lord's Prayer ('Our Father'), given by Jesus in Matthew 6:9–13, Jesus uses the word for 'Dad' to describe God.
Judge **Forgiving**	As Christianity has so much emphasis on living the right way and on the afterlife in either heaven or hell, it is natural for there to be a focus on God as judge and on how forgiving God is.
	Some Christians emphasise the gap between humans and God but others focus on the nature of the relationship with God as a friend or parent.

■ Stefan Lochner's *Last Judgement*

Biblical evidence

The Lord's Prayer teaches Christians to pray daily for God's forgiveness and Jesus' teachings often explore these themes. In the Parable of the Lost (Prodigal) Son (Luke 15:11–32), Jesus teaches that:

- However bad a person's sins are (the son wished his father was dead and he lived a very bad life), God forgives them before they even have to ask (the father ran to greet his son before the son even said sorry).
- Every story of forgiveness is a cause for real celebration (the father says his son was dead and now is alive again).

In the Parable of the Sheep and the Goats (Matthew 25:31–46), it is assumed that God judges somebody's actions and whether they go to heaven of hell. In this parable, somebody's actions towards those in need decide whether they go to heaven or hell.

In other parables, such as that of the wise and foolish builders (Matthew 7:24–27), judgement is based on our response to the entire message of God.

Different Christians emphasise God's forgiveness in different ways:

- Protestant Christians tend to say that God's forgiveness was won for all time by Jesus' sacrifice on the cross. When God judges, it is by a person's faith and if they have given their lives to being true followers of Jesus, they will go to heaven.
- Catholic Christians say that their faith requires an active decision to turn to God, away from their sins. In Catholic practice, there are different ways to help people to do this, such as going to Confession. For Catholics, they are judged based on their actions and their faith.

Rembrandt's *The Return of the Prodigal Son*

Analyse and evaluate

Should Christians think of God as a friend?

Yes	No
The Bible teaches that human relationships with God should be close, for example, in the Lord's Prayer.	God is too great to be thought of as a friend. If humans think of God in these terms, they will end up devaluing God.
God's benevolence emphasises God's willingness to be a sacrifice for humans: much like close friendship.	It is not relevant to think of a judge as a friend and the Bible is clear that God will judge humanity.
Many Christians would argue that there are times to focus on their closeness to God and times to remember their unworthiness in the face of the creator of the universe.	

Activities

Review

1. What do Christians understand by the description of God as benevolent?
2. What do different Bible passages teach about God as a judge?

Develop

3. Look at these Gospel passages and link them to the aspects of the nature of God you have studied on these pages: Matthew 5:43–48, Matthew 7:7–11, Luke 8:4–15 and Luke 10:25–37.

Link

4. Should Christians in modern Britain focus on faith or on actions in their daily lives?

Debate

5. Does it really matter whether Christians fully understand God?

Stretch

6. Research the debate about whether humans are justified (saved) by their faith alone or by their actions (works). Prepare three to five key points.

1.4 The Trinity

Aim
To examine the concept of God as a Trinity of persons

Starter
Water can come in three different forms but is still ultimately H_2O. Is it fair to say that it is still the same thing, whatever form it takes?

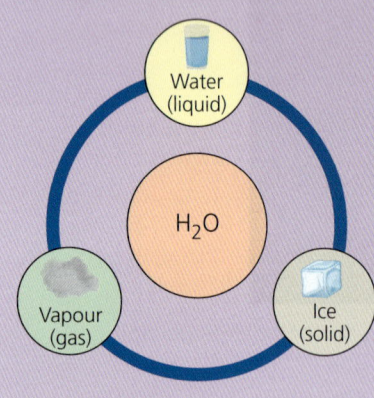

Key word
Trinity – the Christian concept of God as one God in three persons: Father, Son and Holy Spirit

■ A traditional icon of the Trinity

Father, Son and Holy Spirit

The vast majority of Christians believe that God has been revealed to the world in three persons: the **Trinity**. Christians also believe that the understanding of the Trinity is a mystery that cannot be fully understood by humans.

By describing the Father, Son and Holy Spirit as persons, Christians emphasise the possibility of having a relationship with God in different ways and at different times but always with the same God.

Christians are clear that the Father, Son and Holy Spirit are not the same as each other but are all God. They are also not subdivisions of God: each one is fully God on its own. So great is the mystery that many Christians describe the relationship as a 'communion of love'. If any of the persons were not fully God, they would not logically be able to fulfil their purpose properly.

Father	Son	Holy Spirit
Creator	Saviour	Guide
Transcendent	Immanent	Comforter
Protector	Incarnate	Inspiration
Eternal	Resurrected	Active in daily life
Judge	Ascended	Power

Biblical evidence

Christians see the presence of the Trinity from the moment of creation: God the Father as creator, the Son as the Word (who was made flesh – see John 1) who speaks at creation and the Spirit hovering over the face of the waters:

In the beginning God created the heavens and the earth ... and the Spirit of God was hovering ... And God said... (Genesis 1:1–3)

Jesus' final words in Matthew's Gospel are a clear statement of the Trinity, even though the word 'Trinity' is not used anywhere in the Bible. Paul, in his letters, also makes clear references to all three persons of the Trinity: by the time he was writing (10–20 years after Jesus), the Trinity seems to be being discussed.

Sources of authority

'Go and make disciples of all nations, baptising them in the name of the Father and of the Son and of the Holy Spirit...' (Matthew 28:19)

'Grace and peace to you from God our Father ... we have heard of your faith in Christ Jesus ... your love in the Spirit.' (Colossians 1:1–8)

Key words

Polytheism – the idea that there are many gods
Creed – a statement of beliefs

Other interpretations

Some Christians reject the idea of the Trinity as being too difficult or not fully evidenced in the Bible. They believe that the wording of views on the Trinity ends up as **polytheism** and that belief in one God is ultimately the most important to preserve. The debate goes back to the early Church. The hard work in the first 400 years of the Church to establish basic Christian beliefs can be found in the early **creeds**, such as the Apostles' Creed and the Nicene Creed, which are still used in worship today.

Some examples of these views are:

- The belief that Jesus is the Son of God but only the Father is God. The Holy Spirit is the active force that God uses to make things happen on Earth. This is the view, for example, of Christadelphian and Jehovah's Witness communities.
- The belief that the Father, Son and Holy Spirit are united in their purpose but are separate to each other, each with distinct roles. This is the view of the Church of Jesus Christ of Latter-day Saints (also known as the Mormon Church).

Analyse and evaluate

Does it matter if Christians understand the concept of the Trinity?

Yes	No
Christians need to understand God if they are going to be true followers.	God is a mystery and it would be wrong of humans to claim they could understand God fully.
It is in the Bible and so should be understood by Christians.	As long as Christians understand that Jesus saved the world, that is all that matters.

Christians could argue that they will understand the different persons of the Trinity at different times in their lives and that as long as they can access this belief when they need to, this is all that matters.

Activities

Review

1. Write three bullet points to explain the Trinity.
2. Give details of one Christian group that rejects the concept of the Trinity.

Develop

3. Look up either the Apostles' Creed or the Nicene Creed as a further source of authority and make notes on what it says about each person of the Trinity.

Link

4. What does studying the Trinity add to our understanding of the nature of God? Review and develop your notes from spreads 1.2 and 1.3.

Debate

5. To what extent can only people who believe in the Trinity call themselves Christians?

Stretch

6. Some people believe that Paul did not fully believe in the Trinity as Christians do now. Look at these passages and decide what you think the evidence points towards – and whether it matters: Romans 8:9–11, 1 Corinthians 12:3, 2 Corinthians 13:13, Galatians 4:4–6, 2 Thessalonians 2:13–14 and 1 Timothy 1:17.

1.5 Biblical accounts of creation

Aim

To analyse the text of Genesis 1 and 2

Starter

Is a creator God more like a magician or a potter?

Day 1 — Earth, space, time and light

Day 2 — Sea and sky

Day 3 — Dry land and plants

Day 4 — Sun, moon and stars

Day 5 — Sea and flying creatures

Day 6 — Land animals and humans

■ The first creation account

Top tip

Genesis 1 and 2 are set texts. This means that you need to be able to write about them in detail.

Key words

Sabbath – a day of rest and focus on God
Pinnacle – the high point of something
Steward – someone who takes care of something

First creation account: Genesis 1:1–2:3

The first creation account divides the process of creation into six days where God works to create order and observes that the work is good. On the seventh day, God rests and this leads to teachings about observing a **Sabbath** day.

The text portrays God as the creator, powerful enough to create by only word. The emphasis is on God's ability to create something out of nothing. God's creation has a purpose and it is perfect (represented by the word 'good' on each day).

The image of God changes when humankind is created. No longer is God simply creating as a remote figure but God seems to be personally interested in the creation of people. God seems to shift from being a creator to a Father who gives blessings and gifts to the people. Creation here is described as *very* good.

God's two agents of creation are God's Word and the Spirit. The Spirit brings order to the chaos in verse 2. The word for 'Spirit' in the Hebrew text is the same as 'wind' or 'breath'. Jesus is often associated with the Word (which we will examine in spread 1.6). Breath makes us able to speak words and so some Christians see the Trinity as being named and united in this verse.

Thinking about God's Spirit as breath or wind reminds some Christians of the power of the Holy Spirit in the world today; able to move freely around the world and also being identified with the life force in each human being.

The role and purpose of humans in this passage is:

○ to be honoured as the **pinnacle** of creation: they are created last
○ to rule over all animals: good rulership is about being **stewards** and taking care of everything
○ with God's blessing, to be fruitful and increase in number: God's first command to humans is to populate the world.

Second creation account: Genesis 2:4–25

The second creation account develops the story further, focusing in on humankind. Some Christians believe that the second account is an alternative version to the first, which was brought together by the editor of Genesis; others believe that the second acts like a magnifying glass on the first. We see the following features in this section:

- Parts of the Earth already existed.
- Man is created from the dust of the ground and God's breath (Spirit) is breathed into his nostrils.
- Man is placed in the Garden of Eden and his purpose is to look after it.
- God allows the man to eat from anything except the tree of knowledge of good and evil; otherwise he will die.
- God wishes to make a helper for the man and so makes all animals, none of which is suitable.
- The man (now named Adam) is therefore caused to sleep and one of his ribs is used to create woman (who is not named until Chapter 3).
- This physical unity between Adam and Eve is used to represent the need for absolute unity between husband and wife.
- Both Adam and Eve are naked and feel no shame.

Having humans created first in this text emphasises their special role in the world.

Different Christian views

- Some Christians, such as some evangelicals, believe that Adam being created before Eve and Eve being described as a helper to Adam means that men should be in charge of women in a marriage.
- Some, such as Catholics, say that this text simply emphasises the difference between the two genders.
- Others say that the text is outdated.

Analyse and evaluate

Do the two creation accounts contradict each other?

Yes	No
The order of creation is clearly different between the two accounts.	They are two views on the same complex issue. The different words for God emphasise this.
The two accounts use different words for God ('God' in Chapter 1 and 'Yahweh' in Chapter 2) and so are clearly completely different.	The second account is like a spotlight on humanity's early days. This is seen by the fact that creation already exists at the start of the chapter.
Some Christians might argue that the question does not matter because what is important is not the historical accuracy but the religious truths behind the stories.	

Activities

Review

1. What is learned about God and humanity in *each* of the two creation accounts?
2. Create a table or diagram to show the similarities and differences between the two creation accounts.

Develop

3. What are the implications of saying that God created matter out of nothing? Think about what is true for science as well as for religion.

Link

4. Does anything in the two creation accounts contradict the understanding of God studied in the previous pages in this book?

Debate

5. Is there anything useful about the role of humans found in Genesis 1–2 for Christians today?

Stretch

6. There have been different attempts to identify where the Garden of Eden might have actually been located. Research this on the internet and summarise two different views.

1.6 Interpretations of the creation story

Aim

To explore interpretations of the creation story

Starter

Discuss: is being told something using a story with a meaning better or worse than simply being told something?

- For Christians, the Incarnation is where heaven touches Earth. Michaelangelo represented the creation of Adam as a deliberate act of God. Christians consider the Incarnation to be another deliberate act of God the creator, renewing the world

Top tip

John 1 is a set text and you need to understand verses 1–18 in detail.

Key word

Incarnation – the term used to describe God becoming a human being in Jesus

Source of authority

'The Word became flesh and made his dwelling among us.' (John 1:14)

John 1:1–18

John's Gospel is shaped very differently to the other three Gospels. For many Christians, this is because Matthew, Mark and Luke focus on the stories about Jesus' time on Earth, whereas John, writing later than the others, shapes his Gospel symbolically to present truths. For other Christians, the Holy Spirit inspired this writer in a different way.

John's opening verses deliberately recall the Genesis creation accounts and use the symbolism of Genesis to explain some of the truths of Christianity. The key points are:

- The phrase 'in the beginning' echoes Genesis 1:1.
- The 'Word' is a reference to the words that God spoke when creating the world: John emphasises that God's words at creation were a way of understanding the 'Word' who then became human in Jesus.
- The Greek for 'word' (*logos*) also echoes the idea of logic or reason: this reminds Christians that the Word is more than just a word.
- The Word was a part of the creation of the whole universe. It pre-existed the universe and was not just an aspect of God but was God.
- Life and light are given a new meaning as representing more than just the life and light of Genesis but also the life and light that is needed in the darkness of a world of sin.
- As divine light, nothing can overcome it.
- The prophet John the Baptist (a different John to the one who wrote the Gospel) was sent by God to point the world to the light.
- True light came into the world and, despite being the creator of the world, was not recognised and was rejected.
- Those who had faith in the true light became children of God – like the new Adam and Eve.
- The Word (i.e. God) became a human being in the **Incarnation** and Jesus as the Son is clearly being identified alongside the Father (rather than as lower than the Father in some way).
- The Word (i.e. Jesus) replaced the temporary ways of the Old Testament by coming to Earth as God-made-man to restore the close personal relationship with God seen at the start of Genesis.

Therefore, John not only links Jesus to creation but makes a direct claim that Jesus is God, who created the universe and became a human in order to bring light in the darkness. This sets up a very different understanding of what Jesus then went on to do. This clear link and sophisticated thinking is one of the reasons many Christians consider John's Gospel to be so different to the other Gospels.

Christian interpretations of Genesis

Key word
Metaphorical – figurative or symbolic or not literally the case

As we have seen, many Christians understand Genesis symbolically. They might believe that the text contains religious truth but not literal or scientific truth. They might understand the text **metaphorically**. For example, the seven days of creation could be understood to represent seven long periods of time.

While some evangelicals take Genesis to be literally true, there are also some Christians who simply reject the truth of the account on the basis that it was written by people who were trying to understand why the Earth existed.

Analyse and evaluate

Are the Genesis accounts literally true?

Yes	No
The whole Bible is directly revealed by God. God works through humans in many ways and so it is reasonable to believe that God revealed the Bible to humans.	Similar stories from other religious traditions near to the Holy Land exist, suggesting that this is not a genuine account from God.
Any contradictions between the accounts are explained by them being different perspectives on the same thing.	Modern scientific discoveries have demonstrated that better explanations exist for creation, such as the Big Bang and evolution.
The possible issue of the Sun and moon being created only on day four is solved by remembering that the universe existed before the Sun: God created light in general at the start and created the Sun later on.	Day four of the first creation story does not make sense. The idea that humans were created first from dust and then from a rib also does not make sense.
We should not apply our worldview to the Bible. For example, there are three days with no Sun or moon so we need to understand literal truth differently.	John's Gospel shows that even at the time of Jesus, metaphorical truth was seen as a valid type of truth. John does not seem to have read Genesis literally.
Many Christians wonder whether God could simply have used evolution as a tool for the creation of life.	
Many Christians feel that the attempt to reject Christianity on the basis of Genesis being possibly inaccurate is an excuse by those who do not wish to be challenged by the Christian lifestyle.	

Activities

Review
1. Summarise what is learnt about the Word from John 1.
2. What are the strongest arguments for and against whether Genesis is literally true? Why did you choose these?

Develop
3. Do you think a Christian's daily life is affected by whether or not the creation story is literally true? Give at least one argument to agree and one to disagree.

Link
4. What are the possible implications of the different viewpoints given in this spread when it comes to understanding the death and resurrection of Jesus?

Debate
5. 'Symbolism is too difficult. If something is worth saying, then it should be presented at face value.' Is this a valid view? Make sure you use examples from Christianity in your discussion.

Stretch
6. Look at some of the miracles of Jesus. How could they be explained if they are not literally true? Think about alternative explanations and metaphorical understandings. Does it matter? You could start with the bleeding woman (Mark 5:25–34), the centurion's servant (Matthew 8:5–13) and the exorcism of a demon-possessed man (Luke 8:26–39).

Beliefs and teachings 1.6 Interpretations of the creation story

13

1.7 The Fall and Original Sin

Aim

To explore the text of Genesis 3

Starter

Is it ever right to punish someone for what someone else has done?

Key words

Free will – the ability to make choices for ourselves
Original Sin – the first sin of Adam and Eve that is passed on to humans
Good – something that is approved of or is of a high standard
The Fall – the moment when Adam and Eve permanently broke the relationship with God

Top tip

Genesis 3:1–19 is a set text. You could also be asked about the narrative in Chapters 1–3 as a whole.

Genesis 3:1–19

Whether this passage is read metaphorically or literally, it describes a moment of absolute change for the human race. This change came about by Eve and then Adam using their **free will** to be tempted and then act on the advice of the serpent, rather than follow the instructions of God.

If taken literally, the passage shows us that there was a moment when the first humans disobeyed the direct instruction from God (in Chapter 2). All descendants of Adam and Eve – the whole human race – were punished by God for this moment of **Original Sin**.

If taken metaphorically, the passage could be interpreted as saying that human nature turns us away from the perfect idea of **good** that God offers. Alternatively, it could be seen as a story that represents just how far humans are from God. The remainder of the Bible could be about the human quest to become united with God and how God has helped humanity with this.

Some key features to note about the passage are:

- The snake or serpent represents the Devil or Satan, who some Christians believe to be a real figure, perhaps a fallen angel. Other Christians believe the Devil to be symbolic of all the temptation that humans are subject to.

- God had told Adam and Eve not to eat from the tree in the centre of the garden and they would die if they did this. Adam and Eve clearly do not die and some feel that this is a lie told by God. However, Christians would respond by saying that God has not lied but is talking about the death of Adam and Eve's innocence. We see this idea that innocence and the pure relationship with God is destroyed because Adam and Eve are ashamed they are naked.

- Some Christians believe that the idea of God walking in the garden shows that the passage is to be understood in a metaphorical way; others believe that the relationship was different in the Garden of Eden and so we can understand God's presence differently.

- The punishment given by God is to have to struggle to work for success (Adam) and for childbirth to become difficult (Eve). The serpent is also given a hard future.

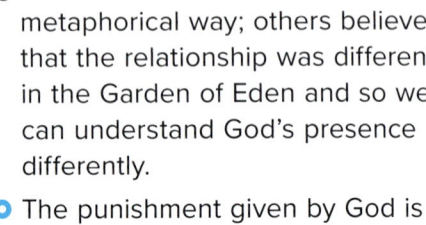

■ **The Fall** of humanity

Source of authority

'Be perfect, therefore, as your heavenly Father is perfect.' (Matthew 5:48)

The concept of good

Christians consider God to be the ultimate source of goodness. This goodness is first revealed in the creation of the universe, which God sees is 'good'. God then shows goodness by guiding creation (by giving them guidelines, such as not eating from the tree of knowledge, and later on by giving the Ten Commandments and other guides to life) and then ultimately sending Jesus as a gift to the Earth.

Christian interpretations

Christians believe that God is the perfect standard of goodness. Christians should try to be like God and if they fail to be like God, this is a sin. Sin is the use of free will to reject God's goodness.

- Catholics describe sin as a failure in humans' love for God; it is a turning away from God's law. It is always possible to turn back to God.
- Many Protestants believe that Original Sin has broken this relationship with God permanently and it is only through God's grace that humans can be saved from this sin.

Analyse and evaluate

Are humans being punished for the sins of Adam and Eve?	
Yes	No
The punishment given by God to Adam and Eve is clear. They broke the relationship between God and humans and it remains broken.	As God is benevolent, punishing all humans for the sins of two people so long ago does not seem likely.
Adam and Eve may not be the first humans but perhaps they were chosen to represent the human race and their punishment therefore can be given to all humans.	The Adam and Eve story is not literally true. Christians learn that each time they sin, they are separating themselves from God.
Even if the passage is symbolic, it is symbolic of the permanent gap between God and humans which humans need to work to overcome.	

Activities

Review

1. Explain how the Adam and Eve story might be understood both by someone who takes the Bible literally and through a more liberal lens.
2. What do Christians understand by the word 'good'?

Develop

3. Take the arguments in the Analyse and evaluate box above and write a counterargument for each one.

Link

4. Which of the aspects of the nature of God are challenged and which are strengthened by understanding that the Adam and Eve story is literally true or symbolically true?

Debate

5. Do you think Christianity spends too long thinking about the Genesis story and not enough time on more important aspects of faith?

Stretch

6. Some might argue that the fact that Eve ate the fruit first has led to poor treatment of women for thousands of years. Adam was, of course, created first in this account. Read Genesis 2–3 again and write an analysis from a feminist viewpoint.

1.8 The problem of evil

Aim

To understand Christian responses to the problem of evil and suffering

Starter

Make a list of evil things. What is the cause of each one? Which are caused by people and which are not?

■ What causes suffering?

Key words

Evil – the opposite of good; something that brings suffering
Moral evil – evil that is a result of human free choices
Natural evil – evil that comes from nature or natural sources
Suffering – pain or harm experienced as a result of evil
Righteous – morally good

Source of authority

'Do not resist an evil person. If anyone slaps you on the right cheek, turn to them the other cheek also.' (Matthew 5:39)

'For my thoughts are not your thoughts, neither are your ways my ways.' (Isaiah 55:8)

The concept of evil

The word '**evil**' tends to be used for things that are completely opposed to the goodness and perfection of God. It is a reality that we all encounter in different ways in our lives and Christians try to combat it through prayer and right living.

The possible causes of evil are varied. They could be linked to:

- a particular situation (for example, the relationship between two people)
- the mindset of a person (for example, if they are angry or ignorant or they have been through a trauma)
- the actions of a person directly involved or more distant (for example, war)
- natural forces (for example, earthquakes).

It is usual to divide the idea of evil into two types:

- **Moral evil** is evil that is the result of other people and their own free choices. There has been a moral decision at the heart of it. For example: murder or violence.
- **Natural evil** is evil that has come from natural sources and humans do not seem to be directly linked to it. For example: earthquakes or volcanoes.

One thing is for certain: evil leads to **suffering**. Whether it is mental or physical suffering for one person or many – or for animals or the environment – suffering refers to the pain or harm that results from evil.

Christian responses

Evil is a challenge for Christians for two broad reasons:

1. There is so much evil in the world and some of it is so extreme that it is hard to explain why God would want to watch the suffering of people who were created out of love.
2. It does not make logical sense for an omnipotent and benevolent God to allow creation to suffer through evil.

There have been many attempts to explain evil. Three broad responses are offered here:

1. Catholic: a response based on the idea of evil as a punishment because God is **righteous** and God's benevolence is not just about love.
2. Evangelical: a response based on having faith in God's plan.
3. Liberal: a response based on developing our characters towards perfection.

Catholic response	Evangelical response	Liberal response
Catholics argue that the ultimate cause of evil and suffering is the Fall. Not only was the good order of the world messed up by Original Sin but also the ongoing human misuse of free will means that suffering continues. Catholics try to explain the issue broadly by saying: • Evil is defined as an absence of goodness or a lack of perfection. It is often caused by people being tempted by the Devil. • Through Adam and Eve (literally or symbolically), humanity chose to turn away from God and broke the relationship with God. • Humans deserve to be punished but God sent Jesus to bring them through this punishment. • Natural evil comes as a result of the Fall and moral evil comes through the ongoing use of our free will.	Evangelical responses to evil focus around the Fall and how all disobedience to God is the responsibility of humans. Evangelical Christians might argue that Christians should focus on having faith that God has a plan for them. This is why God might allow natural evil to cause suffering: God could prevent it but God's ways are sometimes beyond human understanding.	One possible liberal response to the problem of evil is that life is an opportunity to perfect our virtues. Some Christians argue that at the Fall, humans broke the perfect relationship that they had with God and as a result humans need to do all they can to perfect themselves in order to come back into a perfect relationship with God. Somebody's response to suffering can help them to become a better person with better virtues. This approach is often associated with some liberal Christians. It is clear that some people do not achieve perfection before they die and so some versions of this theory say that humans continue the process of perfection in the afterlife, until we all return to the perfect state and we all go to heaven. Traditional Christians would not accept that all people go to heaven.

Analyse and evaluate

Is there a purpose to suffering?

Yes	No
Suffering is a tool given by God to help humans to repair the damage caused by human disobedience.	There cannot be a purpose to suffering when innocent babies suffer or bad people do not seem to suffer.
Suffering is part of God's plan: as humans we may not understand it but why should we understand the creator of the universe?	There is no purpose but suffering is the fault of humans who disobeyed God and God cannot remove suffering without removing free will.
Some Christians could argue that it does not matter if there is a purpose to suffering; what matters is people's response in terms of both their faith and their action.	

Activities

Review
1. What is the difference between moral evil and natural evil? Which is more challenging for Christians and why?
2. For each of the three possible responses to the problem of evil, explain how free will is central to understanding why God allows evil and suffering in the world.

Develop
3. Research the Old Testament story of Job. How is this man's story a possible solution to the problem of evil? Does it work?

Link
4. How is the problem of evil seen differently by those who understand God's benevolence in different ways?

Debate
5. How far is it true to say that suffering is simply the price that humans pay for free will?

Stretch
6. Would Christianity survive if Christians had to change their understanding of God's benevolence or omnipotence in order to try to explain the problem of evil?

1.9 The Incarnation

Aim

To understand the terms Incarnation, Messiah and Son of God

Starter

What elements of the Christmas story can you recall? What is the significance of each part of the story?

Key words

Messiah – the awaited Jewish promised one; anointed one
Son of God – title used to refer to Jesus being God

■ The Christmas story

Source of authority

[Jesus asked:] '"Who do you say I am?" Simon Peter answered, "You are the Messiah, the Son of the living God."' (Matthew 16:15–16)

Top tip

Further evidence for Jesus being the Son of God can be found over the next few pages.

The birth of the Messiah

The Christmas story begins with the angel appearing to Jesus' mother, Mary, to say that she would conceive, despite being a virgin, by the power of the Holy Spirit. An angel appeared to her betrothed, Joseph, to say that he should not divorce her. They travelled to Bethlehem because a census demanded their presence there. Mary went into labour but there was no regular place to stay and so Jesus was born in the animal area and placed in a manger. He was visited by shepherds who had been summoned by angels and by wise men who had followed a star from a distant land.

This well-known story is actually a combination of the accounts in Matthew and Luke. For Christians, it is the culmination of the whole process since the Fall: the process of God setting out to repair the damage created by humans. The Old Testament prepared the Jewish people for a figure who would:

- be born in Bethlehem (and therefore be from the same family as King David, the great king)
- bring about peace
- restore those who were poor or outcasts
- give sight to the blind
- suffer for his people
- restore God's people and their relationship with God.

The Hebrew term used for this figure is '**Messiah**', which means 'anointed one'. The Greek word for 'Messiah' is 'Christ'. Three different groups of people were anointed in Old Testament times: prophets, priests and kings. The Messiah brings together all three of these roles:

- Prophets speak the Word of God to the people and deliver those in need.
- Priests sacrifice on behalf of the people to take prayers to God.
- Kings represent the people and hold authority.

The Son of God

However, from the start of the Gospels, Jesus' role seems to go beyond the expectations of the Messiah. In the Christmas story, it is not just a human that is born: Jesus is conceived by the Holy Spirit and angels celebrate his birth.

Calling Jesus the **Son of God** does not necessarily mean that he is separate to God. Culturally, the term 'son of' can also be used more symbolically, perhaps suggesting someone is like someone else. It primarily shows that Jesus has a close relationship to God. The idea that it was a statement that Jesus *was* God developed later in the Christian teaching about the Incarnation – the belief that God became a human being and so Jesus was both God and man.

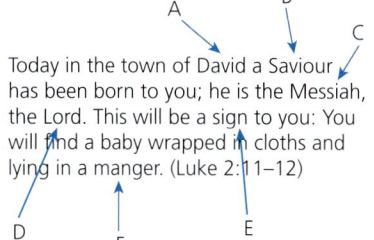

Key:
A – Bethlehem: indicating the Messiah
B – the deliverer of God's people and more
C – the chosen one
D – a title used for God
E – the proof is…
F – a baby in an animal trough

The central Christian belief that Jesus was *fully* God and *fully* human, in a way that cannot be completely understood by humans but which was possible for the creator of the universe to achieve, is summed up in the message of the angels to the shepherds in Luke 2:11–12, where both the human and divine aspects of Jesus come together.

Relevance for Christians today

For most Christians, the Christmas story and the terms 'Messiah' and 'Son of God' show that God's grace is active in the world and that God did all he could to repair the damage caused by sin. A core aspect of belief in the Trinity is the understanding that Jesus was incarnated as both fully God and fully man. In spread 1.4, we examined the views of some Christians who do not believe that Jesus is fully God, which are also relevant here.

Analyse and evaluate

Is the Incarnation relevant to Christians today?

Yes	No
The Incarnation is a huge indicator of God's grace. It sets in motion events that would change and save the world: without the Incarnation, Jesus could not have died.	The Incarnation may be important but other aspects, such as Jesus' teaching on how to live, as well as his death, are actually relevant for modern Christians.
The Christmas story reminds people that Jesus is for all people, even shepherds – considered outcasts at the time – and foreigners like the wise men.	Titles such as 'Messiah' and 'Son of God' are meaningless for modern Christians and so the idea of the Incarnation is outdated.
The Incarnation has become a commercialised Christmas. The Christmas that we see each year is not Biblical so while the Incarnation is important, it is not relevant as expressed in modern society.	

Activities

Review

1. What do Christians understand by describing Jesus as the Messiah?
2. What is the Incarnation?

Develop

3. How does the baptism of Jesus (Matthew 3:13–17) develop Christian understandings of the terms 'Messiah' and 'Son of God'?

Link

4. Look again at John 1:1–18. This is John's version of the Christmas story. What points is John making about the Incarnation and Jesus as the Messiah and Son of God?

Debate

5. Can Jesus ever be fully understood from his various titles?

Stretch

6. Matthew and Luke's Christmas stories are very different. Mark (the earliest Gospel) has no Christmas story. John's is symbolic. Research different explanations for why the Gospels have been developed in this way and present one approach you agree with and one you disagree with.

1.10 The life of Jesus Christ

Aim
To explore the ministry of Jesus Christ

Starter
Make a list of things that Jesus (a) said and (b) did. Can you sort these lists into any categories?

■ An icon of Jesus

Key word
Agape – Greek word for 'love' emphasising unconditional love; the Greek word used to describe God's love for the universe

Top tip
Studying Christianity will hopefully encourage you to get to know the story of Jesus in detail. You could read a Gospel or a children's Bible or watch a film version of his life.

■ The parable of the Good Samaritan is one of Jesus' best-known teachings

Jesus' work

According to the Gospels, Jesus moved around the Holy Land for about three years, spreading his message. Jesus' work on Earth took a number of different forms:

- As a preacher, his sayings were memorable and inspirational, and his teaching challenged the society of his time.
- As a teacher, he taught partly in parables. These stories with meanings were designed to be easily remembered and relevant to his audience.
- As a religious guide, he taught people that their relationship with God was of vital importance and that God could be approached as a friend. He emphasised that what was important on the inside was more important than what was seen on the outside.
- As a miracle-worker, he demonstrated that God's love was unconditional and offered to all, including outcasts. This love is known as *agape* love.

Jesus withstood challenges from religious authorities who felt challenged by what he represented. He never undermined them, however; he simply encouraged them to think carefully about what their priorities were.

Different Christian views

Christians today have much they can learn from Jesus' life:

- Most Christians believe that stories from the Gospels sometimes need to be applied to their lives in order to understand them.
- The majority of Christians believe that there is something to learn from all the Gospel stories, although some liberal Christians might consider some of the passages to be outdated because Jesus was speaking into a cultural context that is very different from our own.
- Evangelical Christians might emphasise the idea that the Gospels are directly revealed by the Holy Spirit and provide direct guidance for their lives.
- More liberal Christian lenses might focus on the broad approaches that the Gospels teach and encourage people to be inspired to apply these to their lives. When faced with a difficult situation, some Christians often ask, 'What would Jesus do?'

Agape love

Jesus' coming to Earth was a sign of God's grace. Jesus' teachings were designed to show people how to live lives full of *agape* when dealing with others. *Agape* love is unconditional, sacrificial and selfless, and focused on justice. The table gives some examples of how Christians might lead the ideal life and the next spread focuses on one specific example.

Teaching	Reference	Possible example for Christians today
Healing of the Bleeding Woman	Mark 5:25–34	Christians should demonstrate *agape* to sidelined members of society.
Healing of the Centurion's Servant	Matthew 8:5–13	Non-Christians are as welcome to be shown *agape* as anyone else.
Parable of the Sower	Luke 8:4–15	People need to receive and work with God's message of *agape* properly.
Parable of the Good Samaritan	Luke 10:25–37	Christians must show neighbourly love to anyone, even those they don't like.
Parable of the Lost Son	Luke 15:11–32	*Agape* demands unconditional forgiveness by humans as well as by God.
Parable of the Sheep and the Goats	Matthew 25:31–46	People will be judged based on how they have shown *agape* to those in need.
Great Commission	Matthew 28:16–20	Christians must take on Jesus' role of spreading the good news of *agape* to the world.

Some Christians are nervous about the emphasis on *agape* love because they believe that good living needs more structure. Catholics, for example, would emphasise that the specific teachings of the Church are necessary in order to make decisions about what is right and what is wrong.

Analyse and evaluate

Does the life of Jesus have much to teach Christians today?

Yes	No
Jesus' examples used in his teachings are timeless and easy to understand in the twenty-first century.	Jesus' parables are full of examples from the first century which are not useful for Christians today.
Jesus' miracles demonstrate that God's love is available for everyone and this is a message that is relevant in any time.	Jesus was a unique person and so how he lived his life is not relevant to people today.

Some Christians might argue that it is important to be inspired by Jesus but to live their lives in their own ways.

Activities

Review
1. List the different ways in which Jesus taught.
2. What is meant by *agape* love? Give examples to illustrate your answer.

Develop
3. Look at Luke 4:16–21. Here, Jesus is saying that he is fulfilling the prophecies about the Messiah. Why might Christians argue that Jesus went far beyond everything Jewish people might have hoped for?

Link
4. Different Christians might read the Gospel stories through different lenses. What might be the impact of doing this? Think about literal and metaphorical lenses as well as others of interest.

Debate
5. 'Jesus' parables are more helpful to Christians than his miracles.' How true would you say this is?

Stretch
6. Look at Matthew 16:13–20. The passage ends with an example of the Messianic Secret – when Jesus insists that people do not tell others who he is. Why might Jesus have asked for this?

21

1.11 The Sermon on the Mount

Aim

To examine the Christian ideal as found in the Sermon on the Mount

Starter

Can being good ever be too difficult to do?

Top tip

The Sermon on the Mount is in Matthew 5–7. You have already met some of the text in earlier spreads.

The Christian ideal

Many Christians believe that the Sermon on the Mount expresses the ideal way to live a Christian life. Some believe Jesus preached it as one sermon; others think that it is a collection of Jesus' teachings over time. Understanding the Sermon on the Mount gives a further insight into *agape*, morality and religious life.

To understand the Sermon on the Mount, it is important to understand that Jesus was teaching in a Jewish society where people tried carefully to follow the Jewish law at all times. Jesus felt that some people sometimes took the law too far and were so careful to follow the rules that they forgot to look after the people around them.

The other thing to look out for throughout the text is Jesus' emphasis on intention rather than action. Being a good Christian is not just about doing things to impress others or even because a Christian has to do them: it is about wanting to and meaning it from the heart.

■ Jesus teaching at the Sermon on the Mount

Different Christian views

- Some Christians might observe that while the issues in the text are timeless, there are some aspects that are specific to a Jewish audience and there are many modern issues that are not covered here (or anywhere in the Bible). They might therefore reject a more evangelical approach to using the Bible as the sole authority when deciding how to live.

- Other Christians would argue that the Sermon on the Mount gives enough information to allow a person to be a good Christian and to respond to whatever situation presents itself.

- The Catholic Church reminds us that the human desire for true happiness comes from God and this is at the heart of the Sermon.

Summary of the text

The Sermon starts with the Beatitudes (5:3–12), a list of groups who are blessed or happy in God's sight. These are not the expected people – they are those who are kind or on the fringes of society. It goes on to encourage people to be proud of their good deeds to make the world a better place (5:13–16).

After insisting that what he teaches does not contradict the Jewish law but instead focuses on intention and true righteousness (5:17–20), Jesus continues:

- Murder is wrong but so is anything that could ever lead to murder: anger or cursing someone, for example (5:21–26).
- Adultery is wrong but so is lusting after someone (5:27–30).
- Old rules about divorce and taking oaths need to be tightened up so that society does not become too loose with its morals (5:31–37).
- Always be the bigger person: turn the other cheek and go the extra mile – and even love your enemies: the Christian should be perfect, just like God is (5:38–48).
- Give to those in need, and pray and fast as if they are private moments between you and God: don't be a hypocrite and make it all about yourself (6:1–18).
- Store up treasures in heaven, not on Earth: don't prioritise money or image (6:19–34).
- Don't be a hypocrite and judge others (7:1–6).
- Ask God for what you need (7:7–12).
- Christian life is a challenge but you need to be good from the inside – and then you can hope to enter the kingdom of heaven (7:13–23).
- Get the foundations right in order for the rest to follow on (7:24–27).

Top tip
It is important to know a range of points from the text, backed up by quotations.

Analyse and evaluate

Is the Christian ideal as found in the Sermon on the Mount realistic for today?

Yes	No
The Sermon emphasises that people's hearts must be pure, which is a timeless ideal.	The sermon was intended for people living in a Jewish community 2000 years ago. It can inspire but not totally guide Christians today.
The Sermon covers religious life, moral decisions and relationships with others, which can be applied to modern situations.	Most Christians accept that violence is sometimes needed and that anger and impure thoughts are natural – it is what they do next in those situations that matters.
The Sermon on the Mount is helpful in some circumstances but does not give guidance on every aspect of modern life.	

Activities

Review
1. Collate three to five short quotations that illustrate the range of teachings in the Sermon on the Mount.
2. Which do you think are the two most relevant teachings in the Sermon on the Mount to Christians today and why?

Develop
3. Look back over spreads 1.1–1.10 and identify where other quotations from the Sermon on the Mount have been used. How does this develop your understanding of the Christian ideal?

Link
4. Draw together all learning on *agape* from this and earlier spreads and present a Christian understanding of the concept in a creative way.

Debate
5. Is it better to aim to be perfect and to fail or to aim to be good and succeed?

Stretch
6. Should Christians decide what is right and what is wrong based on the Bible alone or should they use a combination of the Bible, Church teachings and their reasoning?

1.12 The death of Jesus Christ

Aim

To examine the significance of the death of Jesus for Christians

Starter

Can someone's death ever be good?

The Good Friday story

The **crucifixion** account starts before **Good Friday** as Jesus, knowing what is to come, enters Jerusalem in great triumph. He encounters his opponents, is betrayed by one of his disciples and then is arrested, put on trial, flogged to the point of death, humiliated and then sent to be crucified.

While on the cross, Jesus continued to demonstrate his characteristic virtues of forgiveness and kindness. Many of the events surrounding his death allow the prophecies of the Old Testament to be fulfilled, emphasising further that the Messiah would be a Saviour.

Crucifixion was the punishment of choice for the Romans who ruled over the Holy Land at the time and they were experts at ensuring a prisoner's death was as painful and public as possible. But for Christians today, the emphasis is on the willingness to suffer that Jesus demonstrated, which emphasised his *agape* love for all.

Christian practices

- On Good Friday, churches are often stripped bare and the worship is simple. Many traditional Christians hold back from celebrating the **Eucharist** or from worshipping with too much music. Local communities often celebrate with a walk of witness around their area, often doing this alongside Christians from other denominations.
- For some modern Christians, the focus is not so much on the suffering of Jesus but on the idea that the crucifixion saved humanity. Their worship may emphasise thanksgiving and praise.

One depiction of Jesus's crucifixion

Jesus as Saviour

This title given to Jesus is hardly found in the Bible but it is an important one for Christians today because the understanding that Jesus saved the world through his death on the cross is central to Christian belief. We have already seen the title used by the angels during the Christmas story; the other mention is at the end of a long discussion in John's Gospel during which those who had heard Jesus' message said: 'We know that this man really is the Saviour of the world' (John 4:42).

Different Christian views

- Some Christians might argue that the lack of Biblical references to this title means that we should focus on other titles of Jesus.
- Others would respond that it is so fundamental to the work of Jesus that it is acceptable to use this title for Jesus in prayer and worship.

Key words

Crucifixion – the death of Jesus on the cross
Good Friday – the day in the year when Jesus' crucifixion is remembered
Eucharist – one of the central Christian church services where bread and wine are used to remember the body and blood of Jesus

- For some Christians, when considering Jesus as Saviour, it is more than just about his crucifixion. These Christians might emphasise his incarnation and his teachings or, indeed, his part within the whole history of God's work to save humanity from Original Sin.

Top tip

Understanding the crucifixion fully requires study of the material in the next few spreads.

Analyse and evaluate

Is the story of the crucifixion of Jesus helpful to Christians today?	
Yes	**No**
It demonstrates true *agape* through the emphasis on Jesus' willingness to suffer for all humans.	Crucifixion is an outdated punishment and so Christians cannot fully understand what Jesus went through.
It reminds Christians that God has saved the world from the terrible sin of Adam and Eve.	Christians should focus more on other aspects of Jesus which are more relevant today, such as his teachings.
Some Christians might argue that the crucifixion story is helpful to Christians in the context of the whole of God's plan or the whole of the life of Jesus. We should not single it out.	

Activities

Review

1. Give at least two ways that Good Friday is marked by Christian churches.
2. Where in the Gospels is Jesus described as a Saviour?

Develop

3. Read one of the Gospel accounts of Jesus' crucifixion, such as Mark 15:21–41. Make a list or storyboard of what happened. What is the significance of each aspect?

Link

4. What do you think is the significance of Jesus' death, given the belief that he was both fully God and fully human?

Debate

5. Could it be true to say that the crucifixion is the one part of the Jesus story that simply has to be literally true?

Stretch

6. Research further how Good Friday is celebrated in two different denominations and give at least three similarities and three differences between the two.

25

1.13 The resurrection and ascension of Jesus

Aim

To explore the significance of the resurrection and ascension of Jesus

Starter

What evidence would you need to believe in a miracle?

Key words

Easter – the festival when Christians celebrate the resurrection
Resurrection – rising from the dead; having been completely dead and then coming back to life again
Ascension – Jesus being taken up into heaven

Source of authority

'The angel said to the women, "Do not be afraid, for I know that you are looking for Jesus, who was crucified. He is not here; he has risen, just as he said. Come and see the place where he lay."' (Matthew 28:5–6)

A painting of the empty tomb

The Easter story

After Jesus' crucifixion, he was placed in a tomb, a stone was rolled in front of the entrance and guards were placed in front of the tomb. Early on the Sunday morning, some of the women went to perform the ritual anointing of his body and found the tomb empty. The accounts in the four Gospels differ at this point but the tradition seems clear that Jesus was found to have risen from the dead and his body was changed in a heavenly way. He appeared to some of his followers and then after some time (tradition says 40 days) he ascended into heaven. The **Easter** story, therefore, begins on Easter Day, the day of the **resurrection**, and continues on to celebrate the **ascension** and then, for many Christians, the gift of the Holy Spirit at Pentecost. Celebrations at Easter are full of joy for all Christians.

The resurrection

For most Christians, the resurrection of Jesus is the reason they have a religion and the reason Jesus was more than just an inspirational preacher. The resurrection is a sign that God is greater than death and that death is not necessarily the end. The Gospels, despite not agreeing in their accounts or even giving much space to the account, are careful to demonstrate their belief in the truth of the resurrection. For example:

- They refer to the measures the Romans took to guard the tomb in order to show that Jesus' body was not stolen.
- They make the point that Jesus' body was the same body, just glorified in some way: his body had the marks of the crucifixion, and he could eat but he could also pass through walls.

The ascension

Source of authority

'He was taken up before their very eyes, and a cloud hid him from their sight.' (Acts 1:9)

The New Testament talks about Jesus gathering his disciples and being taken up to heaven in some way. Many Christians interpret this not as Jesus literally floating upwards but in some way transitioning from being on Earth to being in heaven. This is because Christians generally do not literally believe that heaven is up (and hell is down). In Matthew's Gospel, the ascension is not the focus of the final passage; instead the focus is on the necessary work of the disciples:

'...go and make disciples of all nations, baptising them in the name of the Father and of the Son and of the Holy Spirit...' (Matthew 28:19)

Jesus as Lord

Source of authority

'If you declare with your mouth, "Jesus is Lord," and believe in your heart that God raised him from the dead, you will be saved.' (Romans 10:9)

The title 'Lord' is used frequently of Jesus throughout the Gospels. People call him Lord in their conversation with him and it seems to mean 'sir' or 'teacher' or 'wise one'. However, for many Christians, some uses of the title have particular significance. This is because at the time of the New Testament, readers would have realised that Jewish people used the word 'Lord' instead of speaking God's name. The title therefore is seen as a direct claim to Jesus being God. Like all the titles of Jesus, the significance comes from how Christians use the title as much as how it is used in the New Testament.

Analyse and evaluate

Is the ascension important to Christians today?

Yes	No
It shows that Jesus' resurrection was not just so that he could die again in the future: Jesus really had beaten death.	Christians understand now that heaven is not 'up' and so the story is too difficult to believe literally.
It is important to know that Jesus has gone 'up' to heaven so that people can be with him when they die.	There is very little focus on the ascension in the Bible.
Many Christians believe that the ascension is important in a symbolic sense but as long as they believe that Jesus is in heaven, having beaten death, the detail does not matter as much.	

Activities

Review

1. What is the significance of the resurrection and ascension for Christians?
2. Why do some Christians prefer to call Jesus 'Lord'?

Develop

3. Read the accounts of the resurrection (start with Matthew 28 and Luke 24) and comment on (a) how the Gospels show Jesus to be the same but different and (b) how the Gospels try to give evidence of the truth of the story.

Link

4. You have studied four titles of Jesus: Son of God, Messiah, Saviour and Lord. Which might be most relevant for Christians today and why?

Debate

5. In 2017, a survey of British adults found that about a quarter of those who call themselves Christians do not believe in the resurrection of Jesus. Can they still call themselves Christians if they do not believe in this?

Stretch

6. Research further the impact of the death and resurrection of Jesus to Christians today and present five bullet points to illustrate your findings.

1.14 Salvation

Aim
To understand the concepts of salvation and atonement

Key words
Salvation – being saved from sin or sin's consequences
Ransom – a price paid for the release of someone or something

Starter
From what you know so far, how does this image represent salvation?

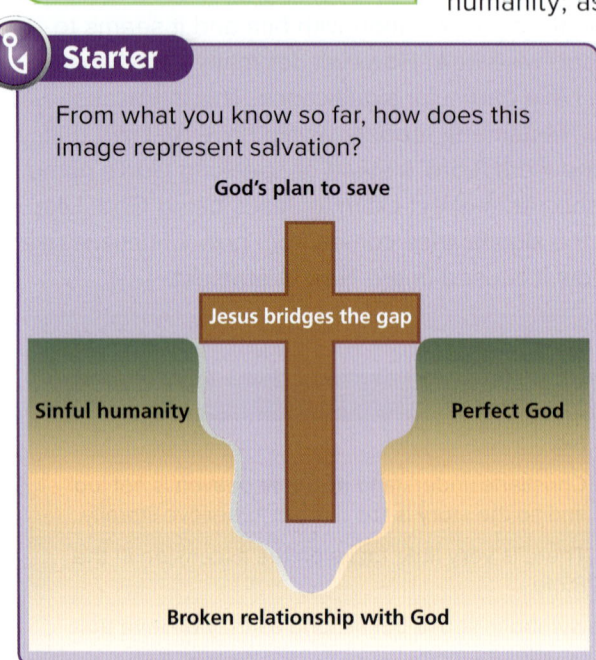

Top tip
The material in this spread and the next one is linked.

Source of authority
'The Son of man did not come to be served, but to serve, and to give his life as a ransom for many.' (Mark 10:45)

Key word
Atonement – repairing the relationship between God and humankind

The sacrifice of Christ

Christian belief is centred around the sacrifice of Jesus on the cross, given ultimate meaning through his resurrection when death was defeated. The role of Christ in **salvation** is expressed through the idea of Jesus being a **ransom**. Jesus paid the price for the sins of humanity through his death. Christians believe that the relationship between humans and God is broken through sin and, by willingly giving his life for the world, Jesus paid the price that was due. As the incarnate Son of God, only Jesus was good enough to pay this price: as a human, Jesus was able to represent humanity; as God, Jesus was able to demonstrate God's grace.

Jesus' sacrifice was made 'once and for all'. In Jewish custom, repayment for sin was made annually through sacrifice by the High Priest; Jesus as the eternal High Priest made the sacrifice for all time.

- Christians believe that humanity plays a part in salvation too, through its belief in this sacrifice of Jesus.
- Christians who read the Bible literally say that humans accept Christ's salvation through their faith.
- Some evangelical Christians say that all that is needed to receive God's forgiveness is to declare that Jesus is Lord.
- Other Christians, such as Catholics, say that it is through good deeds and repentance (e.g. through the sacrament of Confession) that salvation is accepted into a person's life. Catholics remember that the relationship between God and humanity is broken through sin, whereas other Christians might think of the broken relationship of all humanity, represented by Adam and Eve.

Atonement

The diagram at the start of the spread demonstrates Christian beliefs about **atonement**. The relationship between God and humanity needed to be fixed and atonement (at-one-ment) brings together the broken pieces into a whole once more. The Bible teaches Christians:

> '…it was not with perishable things such as silver or gold that you were redeemed from the empty way of life handed down to you from your ancestors but with the precious blood of Christ, a lamb without blemish or defect.' **(1 Peter 1:18–19)**

This suggests that the sacrifice had to be made by God in order to make up for Original Sin, handed down through the generations.

Different Christian views

As we have seen, Christians have different focuses to their beliefs about salvation, depending on a number of things, such as:

- whether the focus should be on their present salvation (for example, repenting from current sin) or their future salvation (for example, having faith in the power of Jesus' sacrifice)
- whether the story of the Fall and Original Sin should be taken literally (so Jesus' sacrifice atoned for the Fall) or metaphorically (so Jesus' sacrifice atones for the ongoing sins of humanity)
- whether the role of humans is primarily to have faith (and believe that Jesus is the risen Lord) or to do good deeds (and to work for the good of the universe).

Analyse and evaluate

Is salvation gained through faith alone?

Yes	No
The Bible teaches: 'If you declare with your mouth, "Jesus is Lord," and believe in your heart that God raised him from the dead, you will be saved.' (Romans 10:9) This seems very clear.	In the Parable of the Sheep and the Goats (Matthew 25:31–46), Jesus teaches that human judgement will be based on how they have treated those in need.
In John's Gospel, Jesus himself teaches: 'I am the way and the truth and the life. No one comes to the Father except through me' (John 14:6) and 'God so loved the world that he gave his one and only Son, that whoever believes in him shall not perish but have eternal life' (John 3:16).	When Jesus encounters the tax-collector Zacchaeus (Luke 19:1–10), it is because of his repentance that he is saved. Jesus states his mission as being 'to seek and to save the lost'.

Some Christians might argue that true faith leads to good deeds and repentance from everyday sin. In the letter of James, the Bible teaches 'faith by itself, if it is not accompanied by action, is dead' (James 2:17).

Activities

Review

1. What is the link between salvation and atonement? Try to refer to sources of authority in your answer.
2. Link the different Christian views in this spread to different lenses and worldviews and denominations of Christians. (See spread 1.1 for a list if you need it.)

Develop

3. How are beliefs about salvation and atonement found in the accounts of the crucifixion and resurrection stories?

Link

4. This spread gives more information that will help you explore the title of Jesus as Saviour. Write three bullet points with evidence to explain this title fully.

Debate

5. Should Christians think about salvation in their daily lives or are there more important things to focus on?

Stretch

6. If faith is needed to be saved, can good people who are not Christians can go to heaven? Research the debate about this.

1.15 Sin and God's grace

Aim

To understand the role of sin, grace, law and the Spirit in the concept of salvation

Starter

What are the five worst sins you can think of?

What is sin?

We have seen that the idea of **sin** can refer to day-to-day actions of people as well as to Original Sin at the Fall. Christians are clear that all humans sin and fall short of the expectations God gives and that sin is what keeps us distant from God's glory. This view was a particular **Pauline** focus (it was very commonly referred to by Paul in his letters).

Different Christian views

- Catholics define different levels of sin: mortal sin is a deliberate breaking of one of God's laws where the person turns their back on God; venial sin also wounds a relationship with God but is not as deliberate in nature. Catholics believe that a person must go to Confession to repent of mortal sin.
- Most Christians believe that human capacity to sin has been inherited from Adam and Eve but some modern Christians will focus on Original Sin being a symbol of human nature. The Bible is clear, however, that humans are inclined to be sinful.

In the Sermon on the Mount, Jesus said that doing sinful things was as bad as being inclined to do sinful things; for example, when talking about murder and anger (see Matthew 5 and spread 1.11).

■ God gives Moses the Ten Commandments

Key words

Sin – actions against God's law
Pauline – referring to St Paul, an Apostle of Jesus who wrote many letters in the New Testament
Grace – the unconditional gift God gives of love

God's grace

God's **grace** is an unconditional gift of *agape* love to the universe.

Different Christian views

- Christians believe that this grace is part of God's plan to redeem the world – a gift to allow the world to get back to the perfection lost by the Fall. Christians emphasise that humans do not deserve this grace and that it is seen most clearly in the decision to become incarnate and to save the world through the crucifixion and resurrection.
- Catholics believe that the freedom of God's gift requires a free response from humans and that this is shown through membership of the Church and through carrying out the work of the Church. The Church exists to be the middle way between God and humanity and to help humans to access God's grace. The worship of the Church, especially in the seven sacraments (see spread 2.6), is a way in which humans can access God's grace.

Top tip

Keep in mind the divergent views of Christians studied in the previous spread.

Source of authority

'All have sinned and fall short of the glory of God, and all are justified freely by his grace through the redemption that came by Christ Jesus.' (Romans 3:23–24)

'I do not do the good I want to do, but the evil I do not want to do – this I keep on doing.' (Romans 7:19)

- For Protestants, access to God's grace tends to focus on an individual's response, rather than the work of the institution of the Church. They focus on the need to accept Jesus as Lord into their lives, generally through baptism.

God's grace is an aspect of God's goodness or benevolence, which is also seen in the giving of laws, such as the Ten Commandments or the Beatitudes. God's desire to guide humanity to make good choices and to know what is sinful allows Christians to make the choices that ensure salvation. The laws are given to make sure people know what is sin and what is not.

Now that Jesus has ascended into heaven, Christians believe that the work of the Holy Spirit is to channel God's grace to believers. The Holy Spirit is God's presence on Earth now; the Spirit inspires and prompts people and it is by the Spirit that people are converted. The Holy Spirit helps people to follow the laws God gives.

Analyse and evaluate

Is God's law too difficult for people to follow?

Yes	No
Humans are sinful beings and the ideals that are given through the Commandments and the Sermon on the Mount can only ever be aspirational.	God only requires that humans try and that they ask for forgiveness when they get things wrong. This is seen, for example, in the Parable of the Lost Son (Luke 15:11–32).
Humans can never fully understand the ways of an omnipotent and omniscient God and so can never be good enough for salvation.	Humans can also never understand fully the benevolence of God. They were created out of God's love and God will ensure that they are looked after.
Some Christians might argue that the law is there to guide people but that faith is all that is actually needed for salvation.	

Activities

Review
1. How does God's grace overcome sin?
2. What is the role of the Holy Spirit in salvation?

Develop
3. Look at these passages and explain how each gives further evidence to this topic: Romans 5:12–21, Romans 6:23 and Ephesians 2:8–9.
What passages from earlier in the course also help with this topic?

Link
4. Many of the themes on these pages have been running through the course. Make a mind map or revision aid to try to draw them together.

Debate
5. Do you think God's grace lays a requirement on Christians to live their lives in a particular way?

Stretch
6. Research different views (religious and non-religious) on whether human nature is generally good or bad. Is the Christian view on Original Sin too pessimistic? Is the Christian view on grace too optimistic?

1.16 Eschatology: core beliefs

Aim
To explore core eschatological beliefs

Starter
What do members of your class think will happen from the moment of death onwards? What is their evidence for their beliefs?

Key words
Parousia – the second coming of Christ
Eschatology – the aspect of belief to do with death, judgement and the afterlife
Apocalyptic – beliefs about the complete destruction of the world at the end of time

The Parousia

Christians believe that when the world as we know it comes to an end, Jesus will return in some form: the **Parousia**. This aspect of **eschatology** will often focus on the teachings in the book of Revelation – the last book of the New Testament which contains prophecies of the end of time. The book is so different to others in the Bible that Christians have interpreted it in many different ways.

Different Christian views

- Evangelical approaches might focus on the time of difficulties and **apocalyptic** descriptions before considering the second coming of Jesus, when a new age is brought about and a new world order established – one of peace, as initially prophesied in the Old Testament (for example, Micah 4:3: 'they will beat their swords into ploughshares').
- Some literalist approaches use the numbers in Revelation and through the Bible to try to work out exactly when the world might end.
- Other Christians believe the numbers might be symbolic (for example, mentions of 'thousand years' in Revelation 20).
- Some Christians focus on the belief that Jesus will return, will judge the world and take the righteous to eternal happiness (for example, the Sheep and the Goats in Matthew 25:31–46). The Catholic Church emphasises that only God knows when this will happen.

The early Church

In the early Church, beliefs were focused on the understanding that the Parousia would occur soon. Early Christians were not expecting to die before Jesus returned and the end times would be characterised by the destruction of the Temple and dramatic apocalyptic events. Early Christians sold their possessions and lived as a community and Paul suggested there was no need to bother getting married. However, beliefs changed as the meaning of Jesus' commandment to preach the good news (Matthew 28:19) was understood and the centrality of preparing for one's personal death and personal judgement was established.

Judgement and resurrection

The Christian belief that humans have immortal souls underpins beliefs about life after death. Having a soul means that humans can survive death and what this looks like is seen in the resurrection of Jesus: his body is glorified and changed. For many Christians, something similar will happen at a person's resurrection: their bodies will be glorified in some way. Other Christians believe it is the soul that goes on to the afterlife as the body is no longer needed.

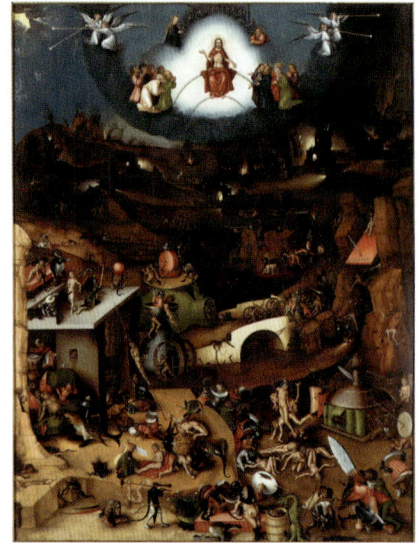

Hieronymus Bosch's *Last Judgement*

Source of authority

'"Why do you stand looking into the sky? This same Jesus, who has been taken from you into heaven, will come back in the same way you have seen him go into heaven."' (Acts 1:11)

'The LORD God formed a man from the dust of the ground and breathed into his nostrils the breath of life, and the man became a living being.' (Genesis 2:7)

Different Christian views

Christian beliefs about judgement centre around when they will be judged and what they will be judged on.

- Christians believe that their judgement will be based on either their faith or their deeds or a combination of the two: it depends on the human response to God's offer of salvation.
- Most Christians believe in a last judgement: a time when all will be gathered together and judged (as seen in the Sheep and the Goats (Matthew 25:31–46) as well as in Revelation).
- For many Christians, such as Catholics, there will be a time of happiness or punishment before the Final Judgement, which is decided in an individual's particular judgement.
- Other Christians believe the soul sleeps from the moment of death until the last judgement.

Analyse and evaluate

Is the body needed for the afterlife?

Yes	No
Our identity comes from both our body and our soul and so we need to be judged and rewarded or punished based on our full identity – including our bodies.	The need for a body comes out of old-fashioned views on the afterlife which included the idea that heaven was up and hell was down.
Jesus' body was changed, not destroyed, at death and so his resurrection can be seen as a model for human resurrection.	The afterlife is not a physical place and so physical things, such as our bodies, are not needed.
Some Christians believe that the afterlife is simply a symbol of how they've lived their lives on Earth and so they should not focus so much on the body or on heaven and hell.	

Activities

Review

1. Explain the terms 'Parousia' and 'apocalyptic'.
2. What are the different Christian views on judgement after death?

Develop

3. Examine the text of 1 Corinthians 15:12–58. What does this text add to Christian eschatological beliefs? How might the text be seen by someone with a literal or a non-literal lens on the Bible?

Link

4. Draw up arguments for different views about what somebody will be judged on: their faith alone, their good deeds or both. Use material from earlier in the course, especially on salvation.

Debate

5. Jesus teaches that we must be ready for judgement: we do not know when it will happen. Is this a good way for modern Christians to lead their lives?

Stretch

6. Revelation is a long example of apocalyptic literature. A shorter example from the New Testament is Matthew 24. How well does this literature fit in the New Testament? Should it have been included?

1.17 Eschatology: heaven, hell and purgatory

Aim

To examine beliefs in heaven, hell and purgatory

Starter

Is it fair that quite good people might go to heaven and quite bad people might go to hell?

Key words

Heaven – a place of eternal happiness and reward
Hell – a place of eternal punishment or separation from God

■ An artist's representation of heaven

Top tip

There are several misconceptions about purgatory. Once someone gets there, they know they are going to heaven; it is not a waiting room before judgement.

Heaven and hell

While **heaven** and **hell** are universally used Christian terms, the understanding of them differs between different groups.

- Heaven has traditionally been seen as a place of paradise, 'with' God in some sense, where those who have been judged righteous exist for all eternity. It is the place of salvation offered by Jesus.
- Hell, by contrast, is a place of agony and torture where those who have been judged as falling short are punished for all eternity.

The images of reward and punishment were embraced by medieval artists in Christianity.

Different Christian views

Modern Christians often feel that the emphasis on punishment is not in line with a benevolent God and this suggestion has led to different interpretations of heaven and hell.

- Heaven is sometimes viewed as symbolic of good deeds done on Earth, an eternal feeling of happiness in the soul or a mystery that cannot quite be understood by humans. One thing is common to different beliefs: the happiness or reward is total – it is paradise.
- Interpretations of hell include:
  - the kingdom of the Devil: hell is a place of punishment where Satan rules
  - a place where people or souls go where God is completely absent: hell is a place of complete separation from God
  - the complete destruction of our souls: if we are judged to go to hell, we do not continue to exist after death.

Key Biblical texts

Heaven	Hell
'They will be his people, and God himself will be with them and be their God. He will wipe every tear from their eyes. There will be no more death or mourning or crying or pain, for the old order of things has passed away.' (Revelation 21:3–4)	'Death and Hades were thrown into the lake of fire. The lake of fire is the second death. Anyone whose name was not found written in the book of life was thrown into the lake of fire.' (Revelation 20:14–15)
'Truly I tell you, today you will be with me in Paradise.' (Luke 23:43)	'…there will be weeping and gnashing of teeth.' (Matthew 25:30)

Purgatory

Different Christian views

- A mainly Catholic eschatological view is that people who are judged ready to go to heaven generally need a time of final cleansing or preparation before being ready to meet God face-to-face – in the way that you might smooth your uniform before going in to see the headteacher. Catholics believe that this is **purgatory**. A person is sent to purgatory after their particular judgement and this place is described as a place of a purifying fire, although some Catholics understand this symbolically. The idea of a purifying fire is referred to in the New Testament (for example, 1 Peter 1:7). There is also the teaching of Jesus that almost anything can be forgiven (Matthew 12:31) – so there must be a way to make up for these sins after death. The book of Revelation says that nothing impure will ever enter God's city (Revelation 21:27). Catholics also pick up on the custom at the time of Jesus to pray for those who have died: if it is possible to pray for those who have died to get to heaven faster, wherever they are must be a temporary place.

- Protestants generally object to purgatory because it is not directly found in the Bible and the passage on praying for the dead comes from a section of the Old Testament that only Catholics think is a part of the Bible. Protestants might also object on the grounds that God knows humans completely and so knows they can never be fully perfect – this is the point of grace.

Key word

Purgatory – a place of cleansing to prepare a soul for heaven

Analyse and evaluate

Does it matter if heaven and hell are real places?

Yes	No
If they are not real places then the truth of the Bible is challenged, the truth of Jesus' sacrifice is challenged and so the very need for reward is challenged!	What matters is how a person lives their life, nothing more. They should never be good because of what might happen to us but because being good is simply the right way to be.
A real place is needed to make up for the effects of the Fall and to bring people back into a perfect relationship with God.	What matters is the fact that God rewards (and punishes) humans – not where or how.

Some Christians argue that heaven and hell are real but just as God is outside of space and time, so too can heaven and hell be seen as states of being rather than real places.

Activities

Review

1. What do Christians understand by the concept of heaven?
2. What is the mainly Catholic view about purgatory?

Develop

3. Read the parable of the workers in Matthew 20:1–16. What does it add to the discussion on these pages?

Link

4. Look at the Nicene Creed. What beliefs about the afterlife can be found in it? What beliefs about Christianity that we have studied are found in this statement that many Christians recite weekly?

Debate

5. To what extent can a benevolent God ever allow eternal punishment?

Stretch

6. Research the Apocrypha – the books of the Old Testament that Catholics accept but Protestants do not. Why is there disagreement? Does it matter?

Summary activities

CHECK YOUR NOTES

STAGE 1

Check that you have detailed notes that cover the following:

- [ ] Different aspects of the nature of God including benevolent, omniscient, omnipotent, monotheistic, judge, eternal, transcendent, immanent, personal, forgiving
- [ ] How Christians understand God as Trinity and issues arising from the idea of the Trinity
- [ ] What Christians learn from the Biblical accounts of creation, for example, the role of the three persons in the Trinity, role of human beings, the Fall
- [ ] Different Christian interpretations of the Biblical accounts of creation, for example literal and metaphorical
- [ ] The problem of evil and suffering and why this is a problem for an omnipotent and benevolent God
- [ ] What is meant by different titles for Jesus Christ including Messiah, Son of God, Lord and Saviour
- [ ] The key teachings of Jesus such as *agape* love and the Sermon on the Mount
- [ ] Key events in the life of Jesus: the Incarnation, crucifixion, resurrection and ascension and how these are understood by different Christians
- [ ] What Christians mean by Salvation including ideas of atonement, law, sin, grace and Spirit
- [ ] The role of Jesus Christ in Salvation: sacrifice and ransom for sins
- [ ] Eschatological beliefs and teachings on death, heaven and hell, purgatory and the second coming of Christ
- [ ] How apocalyptic ideas developed in the early church and reasons for different beliefs today

GETTING READY

STAGE 2

Quick quiz

1. What does monotheistic mean?
2. What Biblical evidence might a Christian have that God is forgiving?
3. What does the word Messiah mean?
4. State two things that John 1:1 says about the Word (Jesus)
5. What does the word 'omniscient' mean?
6. What is meant by Original Sin?
7. What Greek word is used to describe the idea of Christian love?
8. What does the word 'Grace' mean for Christians?
9. What beliefs about God are stated in the Apostles' Creed?
10. What is the Parousia?

Quick quiz answers can be found online at www.hoddereducation.co.uk/ocr-gcse-rs-answers

ACTIVITIES

1. Create a mind map showing what Christians believe about the nature of God. For each key term, aim to add a definition and a source of wisdom or authority to illustrate the point.
2. Use a printed copy of Genesis 1–3 and John 1. Annotate the text in different colours to show what the texts have to say about God the Father, the Spirit, the Word (Jesus), the role of human beings and the Fall.

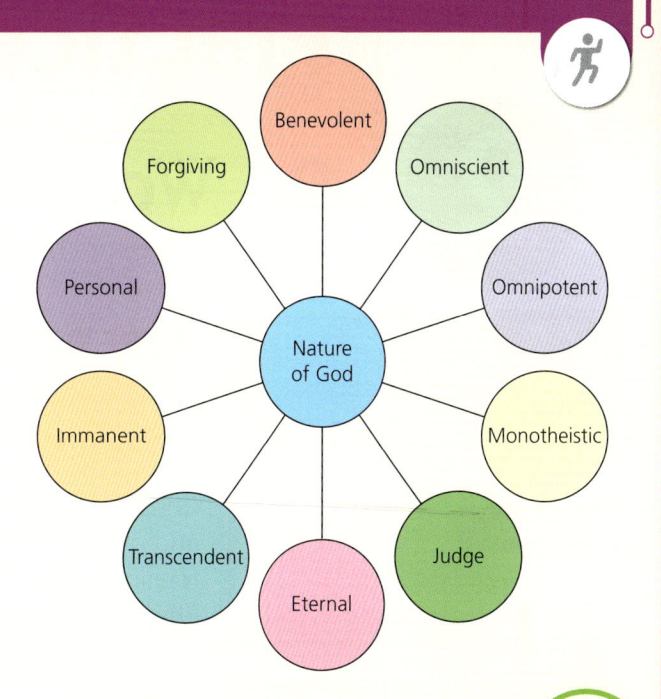

Nature of God: Benevolent, Omniscient, Omnipotent, Monotheistic, Judge, Eternal, Transcendent, Immanent, Personal, Forgiving

GET PRACTISING

Use this section to help you develop your understanding of how to answer questions on this section.

Ask the expert

Every mark counts, every second counts

Tyra writes:

I was surprised that I didn't do as well as I hoped on practice papers. We had practised some longer questions in class and I did OK on those, but I seemed to lose marks on some of the shorter questions. My teacher said that I was losing easy marks. What does he mean?

Expert comment

The shorter questions are worth 3 marks. They can trip people up at times. Sometimes they will ask for quite specific information so it is really important to read the question carefully – BUG the question. It is also worth pointing out that they are intended to be answered briefly – lists or key phrases are usually fine. You do not need to write several sentences as this costs time that could be spent elsewhere. Every mark counts and every second counts.

Thou shalt answer the question

One key problem when answering both shorter and longer questions is when answers miss the point of the question. It is very important that you look at questions carefully so you are sure what is being asked. BUG the question:

Box around the command word

Underline any key words

Glance through checking you've not missed anything

This takes just a few seconds and prevents you straying off question.

CHAPTER 2

Practices

2.1 Worship

Aim
To understand the Christian concept of worship

Starter
How do you show devotion to things or people you love?

■ A modern expression of worship

Key words
Worship – the expression of love and praise for God
Liturgical worship – formal worship using set words, forms and processes
Informal worship – worship that has no set structure
Charismatic worship – worship that draws on the Holy Spirit's presence

Top tip
Many Christians take part in and appreciate a mixture of different types of worship.

Why do Christians worship?

Worship is the term used to describe anything that shows love and praise to God or confirms someone as God's follower. It covers everything from a quick prayer while on the move, to a weeklong Christian conference. Christians worship because God's greatness and glory and gifts to humanity lead them to want to develop their relationship with and thank God for what humans have received. They also might want to ask for things in prayer or for forgiveness for sins. The key focus is the connection with God that they want to develop so that they can work out what God wants them to do. Romans 12:1 describes worship as the giving of our whole selves to God so part of worship is obeying God's request for humans to do it – such as that request found in the first three of the Ten Commandments.

Christians inherited the tradition of worship from Judaism and it evolved over time. The early Church worshipped together in houses, led by local families and visited by the Apostles. As Christianity spread and became recognised, churches and institutions followed and a formal structure for worship emerged. However, Christians have always focused on the importance of individual prayer and worship alongside church worship.

Source of authority
'God is spirit and his worshippers must worship in Spirit and in truth.' (John 4:24)

The role and importance of different types of worship

Source of authority
'To each one the manifestation of the Spirit is given for the common good ... to another miraculous powers, to another prophecy ... to another speaking in different kinds of tongues and to still another the interpretation of tongues.' (1 Corinthians 12:7, 10)

Liturgical worship	The main type of worship over the 2000 years of Church history has been **liturgical worship**. This is worship that follows a set pattern with set words. For example, the Catholic Mass – the Eucharist service, which is the main form of public worship for Catholics – has the same outline with readings from the Bible and prayers changing each day. Advantages of this type of worship include: ○ knowing what is happening so that a worshipper does not lose focus on prayer and also can join in worship in any church of that denomination ○ being able to delve into the deep significance of the words over the course of time ○ the feeling that the set structure is dignified and that within the structure there is plenty of choice and the ability to have some variety in worship (for example, the types of hymns sung). Within liturgical forms of worship, there are those who express themselves traditionally and those who do so using modern hymns.
Informal worship	Many Christians from Protestant churches do not follow such a strict structure but still have an overall framework to their services, with a lot of flexibility within those. There is a wide range of how informal this worship is. The term **informal worship** is also used for any Christians gathering together to worship – for example, in prayer groups or Bible study groups. Christians value the opportunity to express themselves in individual ways, to pray for what they need to pray for and also not to be bound by the rules of the Church. They might feel that they should allow the Holy Spirit to tell them what to pray for.
Charismatic worship	**Charismatic worship** is the term used to describe worship that draws directly on the Holy Spirit's presence. Worship is very informal. It is lively and prayers call the Holy Spirit to be present in the worship. Prayers are usually spoken from the heart often by any member of the congregation (extempore – without planning). The focus is on praise and members of the congregation might raise their hands, clap, dance or express themselves differently to others around them. People feel free to express themselves however they want and they believe the Holy Spirit can be particularly visible in the worship, for example: ○ speaking in tongues: the language of heaven being given as a gift to someone in church ○ laughing in the Spirit: being so filled with the joy of God that you laugh uncontrollably ○ healing in the Spirit: people receive the healing blessings of God, often in dramatic ways. In this type of worship, Christians are focusing on the idea that 'those who are led by the Spirit of God are children of God.' (Romans 8:14).

Analyse and evaluate

Should worship be formal?

Yes	No
Having formal worship set by the church ensures that Christians don't worship in a way that is too narrow.	Formal worship is too repetitive and does not allow the Spirit to lead the church and the Christian people.
Jesus gave us set words for the Eucharist at the Last Supper so perhaps he intended worship to be formal.	Praising God should always come from the heart, not from the words of others. King David danced before God in 2 Samuel 6:14.
Many Christians would argue that what is important is that the individual feels in the heart that they have worshipped God alongside other Christians, however this has happened.	

Activities

Review
1. What might a Christian say is the purpose of worshipping God?
2. What are two key arguments for each of the different approaches to worship?

Develop
3. Research different forms of worship on the internet – perhaps look for videos of some of the forms. Make notes about what you discover for each one.

Link
4. How are the different terms used to describe God (see spreads 1.2–1.3) expressed or found in worship?

Debate
5. Could it be true that charismatic worship is too narrow and ends up being about the church leader's interests rather than God's?

Stretch
6. Find out how Quakers worship and evaluate their approach.

2.2 The structure of church services

Aim

To explore two contrasting Sunday church services

Starter

Which is more spiritual? Formal or informal/charismatic worship? What is a counterargument to your view?

Top tip

There are many other forms of worship for Catholics but the weekly focus is on the Mass.

Key words

Liturgy – a formula for formal public worship
Rite – a formal religious action

■ A Catholic Mass

Catholic Mass

For Catholics, the focus for worship is the Mass – the Eucharist service. Catholic churches try to celebrate the Mass daily if they can because it is the ultimate prayer to God. They believe that the prayers of the whole church – present and not – are offered to God as Jesus' sacrifice takes place once again on the altar. Catholics are expected to worship at Mass every Sunday and on certain other special days in the year.

The Mass is a formal service with a set order. Some prayers and Bible readings change, depending on the day and/or season of the year. Hymns may be sung and some of the regular parts of the Mass can also be sung.

Introductory rites
Welcome, forgiveness of sins, opening prayer

The Liturgy of the Word
Readings from the Old and New Testament
Gospel reading
Sermon
Prayers of the faithful

The Liturgy of the Eucharist
Offering the bread and wine
Prayers over the bread and wine
The Our Father prayer
Holy Communion

Concluding rites
Concluding prayer, blessing, dismissal

■ The structure of the Mass

The opening and concluding prayers and the readings change according to the day and season – the same ones are used across the world. The sermon and prayers of the faithful are particular to the individual church and the majority of the rest are set forms (with some options within them) that all Catholics use and which come from the same tradition for most of the 2000-year history of the Church.

Charismatic services

As charismatic worship is informal, there is no way of describing what all charismatic services are like. Charismatic worship also remains open enough for the Spirit to change the direction of a service. However, a typical structure might include:

- **Time of praise and worship:** songs mixed with Bible verses or prayers, sometimes spoken over a song to prepare people to hear the guidance of the Spirit. A song could be repeated or have instrumental interludes especially if the Spirit moves someone to speak during the song.
- **Time of preaching:** the theme of the Bible passage and sermon linked to it will be chosen locally and the sermon will be the main focus of this part of the service.

Holy Communion might be celebrated a few times a year when the account of the Last Supper might be read out and bread and wine (or grape juice to avoid negative links with alcohol) is passed around the community so that everyone can drink and eat at the same time to show they are united.

Analyse and evaluate

Is charismatic worship a more genuine way of worshipping?

Yes	No
The early Church worshipped informally and under the power of the Spirit – as seen through the New Testament.	The Catholic Mass traces itself back to the early Church – many of the prayers used are almost 2000 years old.
Anything that comes from the heart is more genuine because it is personal.	Formal liturgy allows a person to go deeper over time and to have good days and bad days in terms of their connection to worship.

Some Christians might observe that there is a charismatic movement within the Catholic Church and that many Christians worship in a variety of ways.

Activities

Review

1. What are the similarities and differences between a Catholic Mass and charismatic worship?
2. Pick at least one point of agreement and one point of disagreement from the table above and give a counterargument for those points.

Develop

3. Research the structure of a Church of England Eucharist and present it in a similar way to the material on this spread.

Link

4. How might each of the two approaches to worship try to attract new followers to their Sunday worship?

Debate

5. Could a Catholic approach to worship be better because it does not allow an individual minister's preferences to become the focus of the worship?

Stretch

6. Two denominations that sit between the two extremes of the worship here are the Methodist Church and the Baptist Church. Research the worship of each.

2.3 Prayer

Aim

To explore the concept of prayer

Starter

What makes a good relationship with a close friend?

What is prayer?

For Christians, **prayer** is communication with God, but it is a two-way communication. Christians must listen for God's inspiration either in the moment or perhaps for the day ahead, but also it is an opportunity to express their love for God and ask for things.

As Christians see God as a parent, it is natural to turn to God for advice or guidance. Prayer is important because the relationship with God is entirely spiritual and not physical and so many aspects of a close human relationship need to be adjusted.

The Bible teaches that God knows what people need without them having to mention it (for example, Psalm 139:1–4) but it also encourages Christians to turn to God in prayer. For many Christians, prayer is important because it is for human benefit more than God's. Humans were created to worship God and people's lifelong quest should include a greater understanding of God's nature.

Some Christians try to spend time alone with God – just like we might spend time with a friend. There is no need to find words in this situation but simply enjoy the awareness of God being present. Other Christians use particular structures in their prayers or aids to prayer. Many Christians, especially those who believe the Bible is the inspired Word of God, use the Bible as a way into prayer by reading a passage and trying to focus or meditate on the words. Most Christians would emphasise the importance of people feeling the need to pray in words and forms that are relevant to them and not to feel that there is a set way of doing things. It is not a church leader's relationship with God – it belongs to the person who is praying.

■ Prayer develops one's relationship with God and others

Key word

Prayer – communicating with God in one of many different ways

Source of authority

'Do not be anxious about anything but in every situation, by prayer and petition, with thanksgiving, present your requests to God.' (Philippians 4:6)

The Lord's Prayer

Common to all Christians is the prayer that Jesus taught, the 'Our Father'. Jesus said: 'This, then is how you should pray' and taught the prayer which can be found in Matthew 6:9–13. The form has changed slightly for some Christians because Protestant Christians tend to add the ending 'for thine is the kingdom, the power and the glory, for ever and ever'. This is a traditional ending to many prayers found in the Bible and was combined with the Lord's Prayer. The wording of the prayer in the Bible depends on the translation used; the liturgical prayer in English has a form using traditional words and a form using contemporary words.

The Lord's Prayer is used in both individual prayer and worship and in almost all forms of public or communal worship. It is a sign of unity among Christians that they share the same basic desires as other Christians and it is, of course, a direct instruction from Jesus.

In traditional public worship, such as in the Catholic Mass, the prayer is one of the final acts before the significant moment of receiving Communion, which underlines its significance to Christians.

In Matthew 6:5–14, Jesus explains that the prayer is fundamentally about forgiveness, which could be argued to be the heart of Jesus' entire message. The table explains the different parts of the prayer.

Phrase	Possible Meaning
'Our Father'	'Dad' – an approachable parent.
'Who art in heaven, hallowed be thy name'	A reminder of the greatness of God. 'Hallowed' means 'made holy'.
'Thy Kingdom come, thy will be done, on earth, as it is in heaven'	May the time come when God and God's ways rule on Earth, just like in heaven.
'Give us this day our daily bread.'	Asking for the essentials for daily life. Some link this to Communion. Others say it is spiritual as well as physical.
'And forgive us our trespasses as we forgive those who trespass against us.'	We should forgive those who sin against us as much as we want God to forgive us for what we have done wrong.
'And lead us not into temptation but deliver us from evil.'	Sin comes from falling into temptation, brought about by evil (the Devil) – the prayer is to avoid this.
'For thine is the kingdom, the power and the glory for ever and ever.'	A repeat of God's glory and power.

Analyse and evaluate

Is prayer the most important duty of a Christian?

Yes	No
Humans were created to worship God and so worship, of which prayer is a major part, should be central to their lives.	Christians should first and foremost engage with social justice issues – such as through charity work.
Prayer makes Christians think about the needs of others.	Christians should not be selfish and it could be seen as selfish to pray before spending time with those around them.

Many Christians might argue that all people are called by God to different priorities and so what might be the most important duty for some is not the top priority for others.

Activities

Review

1. How might you explain prayer to someone who was a new Christian?
2. Which section of the Lord's Prayer do you think is the most important to the Church in the twenty-first century and why?

Develop

3. How do the following passages develop an understanding of Christian approaches to prayer: Matthew 6:1–8, Mark 11:22–24, Luke 5:16, Romans 8:26 and 1 Thessalonians 5:16–18?

Link

4. How might the concept of prayer link to the problem of evil?

Debate

5. Is the Lord's Prayer really the only prayer Christians need?

Stretch

6. Would it matter if someone prayed to 'Our Mother' or 'Our Parent'? Give reasons for your answer. You could research alternative forms of the Lord's Prayer to help you decide.

Practices 2.3 Prayer

2.4 The importance of prayer and worship

Aim

To examine the role and importance of public and private prayer

Starter

Can a person be a Christian without going to church?

The rosary is a common devotion for Catholics

Key word

Devotion – a type of religious observance

Source of authority

'This is the confidence we have in approaching God: that if we ask anything according to his will, he hears us.' (1 John 5:14)

Private prayer

Christians believe that individual prayer can have an impact in many ways:

- **To become closer to God:** Christians believe that an individual relationship with God is central to their life.
- **To get God's help in particular situations:** Christians believe that God works in ways people cannot understand as well as, occasionally, through miracles.
- **To get guidance from God:** Christians believe that God speaks through others and situations as well as, occasionally, more directly.
- **To align more with God's will and the example of Jesus:** Christians believe prayer can help them to refocus on how God is revealed to the world.
- **To improve mental wellbeing:** Christians believe prayer can have a positive impact on mental health and emotional wellbeing.

Different Christian views

- For many Christians, private, individual prayer means taking time out of the day, especially in the morning and/or the evening, to pray in a way that is familiar to them.
- For some, the focus is on speaking to God and asking for things; for others, it is about creating silence and listening.
- Some might read a section of the Bible and meditate on it, others might focus their prayer through a formal liturgy – some denominations have set forms of morning, evening and night prayer.
- Some Christians use particular **devotions**, such as the rosary or reading books by Christian writers.

Public worship

Christians like to gather on a Sunday. The Sabbath day (the day God rested in the first creation account) was Saturday for Jewish people but as Jesus rose on a Sunday, Christianity moved the Sabbath to a Sunday. In the UK, the weekend is shaped around Sundays as a day of rest. Gathering on a Sunday is important because:

- It reminds Christians that trying to live a good, Christian life is not something they need to do alone.
- It obeys the command of Jesus to gather and worship.
- It provides the opportunity to be taught by the church leader or priest to understand the Bible or Christian life more fully.

Source of authority

'[Jesus] said, "Where two or three gather in my name, there am I with them."' (Matthew 18:20)

Top tip

The course talks about public worship, worship for communities and communal worship all meaning the same thing. In the same way, individual and private prayer mean the same.

- It allows the church community to work together on other aspects of Christian life (for example, social justice).
- It was the custom of Christians right from the start of the Church to gather together.

Different Christian views

- For Catholics, receiving Holy Communion is a particular devotion that is important to do regularly.
- For many Christians, the opportunity to praise with music is also an important devotion.
- For charismatic Christians, the Spirit is more keenly felt and is shown more in public worship.
- Some Christians might also emphasise the idea that the Fall has damaged all of humanity and so it is important not to battle against this alone.

Outside of Sunday worship, Christians might gather midweek in church or at someone's home for formal or informal worship, prayer groups or Bible study. This gives the opportunity for particular groups to get together – such as women's groups, youth groups, groups for those new to the faith and so on. These opportunities are important because it is through acting as a community that Christianity will grow.

Analyse and evaluate

Is private prayer more important than public worship?

Yes	No
An individual's personal relationship with God should be the goal of their life. This is best done as an individual.	Worship is far more than just praying. Christian worship in public is an important expression of faith.
Everybody approaches prayer differently and so private prayer allows a person to be themselves with God.	Most people struggle with private prayer and public worship helps them to connect with God better.

Most Christians would argue that a combination of private prayer and public worship is best but the balance between the two will be different for different people and at different times.

Activities

Review

1. What is the importance of Christians praying as individuals?
2. Give two similarities and two differences between private and public worship.

Develop

3. Why is the rosary an important devotion for some Catholics? Research further to find out.

Link

4. Why do Christians believe there is an important link between prayer and their salvation? Try to answer from the perspective of different Christian lenses.

Debate

5. Some Christians like to pray while focusing on icons or a cross or crucifix. Other Christians think this is idolatry (worshipping the object rather than God). Does it matter?

Stretch

6. Christians believe that God can and does speak to individuals very occasionally when they pray. If someone claimed that they have met God through a vision, what would make you believe them?

Practices 2.4 The importance of prayer and worship

2.5 Different types of prayer

Aim
To examine a range of types of prayer

Starter
When praying alone, should a Christian use set prayers?

Some Christians use chants that date back hundreds of years

Top tip
It is important to view the types of prayer named as a sample, not a complete list.

Key words
Liturgical prayer – using prayers that are in set forms
Intercessions – prayers for others

Examples of types of prayer

Personal prayer

Some Christians use different aids to their personal prayer to help them to move from one way of praying to the next. This can also help people leading prayers in communities or public worship. One method, called ACTS, highlights four different types of prayer, which most Christians would say should be a regular part of prayer.

Adoration	Prayers that focus on the greatness of God – the Christian shows how much they love and want to worship God.
Confession	Time taken to call to mind the times a person has sinned and to ask for forgiveness.
Thanksgiving	Thanksgiving both for God's forgiveness and areas in life where they have seen or experienced God's blessings.
Supplications	Prayers asking for God's help in particular situations for other people or for themselves.

Of course, these prayers do not all have to be simply words thrown to God:

- Some charismatic Christians might use modern worship music as part of their adoration.
- Some informal worship within the community might ask people to share thanksgivings (or supplications).
- Some more traditional Christians might use set **liturgical prayers** at each stage.

Public prayer

In public worship, where a member of the community prays for things on behalf of the others, the set of prayers is often known as **intercessions** or intercessory prayer. During a Catholic Mass, the intercessions are a set part of the service that come at the end of the Liturgy of the Word.

A common prayer used by many Christians, which is Biblical in origin, is 'The Grace'. This is often used as a conclusion to a series of prayers, a time of prayer or a whole service. It draws together the time of prayer and focuses attention back on the Trinity.

'May the grace of our Lord Jesus Christ, and the love of God, and the fellowship of the Holy Spirit be with us all, evermore. Amen.' ('The Grace')

Some Christians use music or chants to pray. Meditation requires a believer to focus in on themselves and chants that are simple in tone or repetitive (such as chants from the community of Taizé) can help someone to be freed from distractions. An ancient meditational prayer in Christianity is the Jesus prayer: 'Lord Jesus Christ, Son of God,

Key word

Extempore prayer – using own words for prayer; prayer where the words are unplanned

have mercy on me, a sinner.' Music in general lifts a person's heart and, in a Christian context, some prefer traditional music or chants and others, modern hymns and songs. There is often a repetitive element in these, which features especially in charismatic worship.

Different approaches to prayer

As we have seen, many Christians think it is important to pray in their own words and this is known as **extempore prayer**. Not all Christians have opportunities to pray extempore during public worship but it is more of a focus in Protestant churches that have modern worship. Christians might argue that this is important in public worship because it allows people to express themselves before God in their own way. Christians who prefer extempore prayer might reject more formal intercessions in public worship because no one person in the church will know what people want to pray for.

Other Christians prefer set liturgical prayer even when praying individually. They might use the church's format for morning, evening or night prayer, for example. They might use the prayers of the church or of church leaders while praying. This has the advantage of knowing that they are praying alongside others in the Christian community and using the words of famous people or the Church as a whole might inspire them. Others might say it is too rigid and not really an expression of the person's own heart.

Some Christians talk about 'praying in the Spirit'. In many ways, this is simply the ideal to which all Christians should aspire. It is what John's Gospel means when seeking to worship God in Spirit (John 4:24) and describes an approach to prayer where the person prays with God's help. They do not focus on their own words as much as accepting that they do not always know the best way to pray (Romans 8:26). Praying in the Spirit is not a type of prayer as much as an approach to prayer.

Analyse and evaluate

Is ACTS a helpful model for prayer?

Yes	No
It helps someone through the four main types of prayer and allows them to focus on the prayers rather than what should come next.	ACTS could be unhelpful because it does not give the person time to listen to God in contemplation or meditation.
The model rightly places God first, then somebody's unworthiness, then their gratitude and then what they want. This helps Christians not to become selfish.	It is quite a burdensome model which might not be practical for all Christians.

Some Christians might argue that models for prayer are helpful for those with particular needs in their spiritual journey. They might prefer other models, such as TSP (Thank you – Sorry – Please).

Activities

Review

1. Write an example of each type of prayer from ACTS.
2. Why is extempore prayer preferred to set liturgical prayer by some Christians in both individual and communal worship?

Develop

3. Apart from prayers with words, what other aspects of church services might be prayers for a worshipper?

Link

4. Using a range of types and approaches to prayer from recent spreads, explain how different types of prayer help Christians to focus on different aspects of the nature of God.

Debate

5. Set prayer is the right form to use in public worship because a person can pray alone at any time; something different is needed when Christians gather together. Do you agree with this?

Stretch

6. The philosopher Søren Kierkegaard (1813–1855) said that prayer 'does not change God, but it changes the one who offers it'. What do you think he meant by this?

Practices 2.5 Different types of prayer

47

2.6 Sacraments

Aim

To explore different views on sacraments

Starter

In what different ways might Christians get particularly close to God?

The role and meaning of the sacraments

Most Christians speak about **sacraments**, although the precise definition can vary. The majority of Christians use the word to describe rites that:

- are particularly important to Christian life
- were started by Jesus (or given by God)
- are particular channels for God's grace.

The idea of a service channelling God's grace is that at particular services, Christians can enter into a particular closeness with God. Some Christians talk about the sacraments as being symbols of God being real and present on Earth.

Many Christians, including Catholics, describe sacraments as 'outward signs of inward graces'. This emphasises the idea that they are symbols of something divine and special going on in a less obvious way. For example, baptism uses outward signs, such as water, to show deep inward meaning, such as having sins washed away.

Sacraments are signs that a particular moment is being given special religious significance. For some Christians, they mark special life events as well as blessing daily events (for example, the Eucharist). On the inward side, they develop a Christian's relationship with God and/or the Church as a whole and they hope to bring particular help to someone's life.

■ Baptism is a universal sacrament

Key word

Sacrament – a Christian religious ceremony or ritual that is seen as a special way of accessing God's grace

What rites are sacraments?

Christians are split when it comes to answering this question. Although there are some less common variations, broadly there are two approaches:

- **There are two sacraments:** baptism and the Eucharist. Many Protestant Christians take this approach. These are the two rites that Jesus directly commanded people to do and they can be found in the Gospels. Many Protestant Christians who take this approach do not use the word 'sacrament' frequently.

- **There are seven sacraments:** each one is an outward sign of something more significant taking place. This is the Catholic view, as well as that of other Christians. For Catholics, the sacraments not only channel God's grace but also, through this, lead a person to salvation. Examples of this are shown in the table.

■ Sharing bread and wine in the Eucharist

Sacrament	Explanation	Outward sign	Inward grace
Baptism	Welcomed into the church through water	Water poured on a person's head	Being washed away from Original Sin
Eucharist	Commemoration of Jesus' Last Supper before his death	Bread and wine shared among the people	Sharing in the body and blood of Christ
Confirmation	Point where a Catholic becomes an 'adult' Christian	Being anointed with oil	Confirms and seals the graces of baptism for the person themselves
Penance	Confessing sins to God	The words of the person confessing	Restoration of the relationship with God
Anointing the sick	Being anointed with oil when unwell	Being anointed with oil	Closeness with God
Ordination	Becoming a deacon, priest or bishop	Laying on of hands	Becomes able to act as a representative of Christ
Marriage	Marrying one person in a church for life	The vows	Unity between the couple in the eyes of God

Catholics do not believe that everyone has to take part in every sacrament but they do attach special importance to baptism (which is required for all the other sacraments to become accessible) and the Eucharist (which is available through a person's life, not just at special moments).

Analyse and evaluate

Are sacraments needed to come close to God?

Yes	No
God has given the sacraments as gifts to help Christians and so it is important to use them for accessing God's grace.	God's grace is a gift freely given. Christians should not need specific ways to access it.
They are direct commands of God and so it is necessary to obey God.	God is revealed in many ways, including the Bible and creation – these are the ways people should come close to God.
Some Christians would emphasise that humans desperately need God's grace and the sacraments should be part of this but that they need to seek God in every moment of their lives, not just at specific times.	

Activities

Review

1. What do Christians believe the sacraments are for?
2. Why do some Christians believe there are seven sacraments and other believe that there are two?

Develop

3. Draw up a table of arguments for and against the views about the number of sacraments there are.

Link

4. At the Incarnation, Christians believe that heaven and Earth were united. Some Christians note that in the sacraments, the physical and the spiritual are united. How might this make sacraments more significant for Christians?

Debate

5. Do you think that too much emphasis on the sacraments might lead to Christians forgetting to emphasise individual prayer?

Stretch

6. Quakers do not believe there is a need for the sacraments. How do they believe that God's grace can be accessed? What is your response to this view?

Practices 2.6 Sacraments

49

2.7 Baptism

> **Aim**
>
> To understand the practice and meaning of baptism

> **Starter**
>
> How were you welcomed into your current school? How were you welcomed into other communities you are a part of?

A believer's baptism

> **Source of authority**
>
> 'People went out to John the Baptist from … all Judea … Confessing their sins, they were baptised by him in the Jordan River.' (Matthew 3:5–6)

> **Key word**
>
> **Infant baptism** – the baptism of babies

The meaning of baptism

Christians agree that a person's baptism is their initiation or welcome into the church community. Those Christians who teach about sacraments all include baptism in that list of sacraments. For all Christians, it is far more than just about membership of the Christian community.

In the time of Jesus, washing was used in Judaism to make a person ready to worship and there were some examples of full immersion where a person went in and out of the water to signify purification and a fresh start. This is likely to be the baptism that John the Baptist offered and which Jesus received.

For many Christians, baptism is a cleansing from Original Sin. By being baptised, the person can enter the Christian life and is able to be saved. This is why Christians are only baptised once and after their baptism they must work to turn away from their day-to-day sins (for example, Catholics teach about the importance of Confession; many Protestants focus on the need to pray for forgiveness). Some liberal Christians do not focus as much on Original Sin but instead focus on the fresh start of a Christian when they are baptised.

Baptism takes place in a font that is often placed near the entrance to the church so that people are reminded of their own baptism as they enter the church as well as emphasising that baptism is the point where people enter the church family. Where baptism takes place by immersion, fonts are often shaped like tombs to emphasise the idea that at baptism people die with Christ and rise to new life.

Some Christians have rites during services where they are sprinkled with holy water to remind them of their baptism and Catholic churches have blessed water at the entrance to the church so that people can use it to remind themselves as they enter. Many Christians also have services, especially around Easter, where they renew the promises made at baptism – to turn towards Christ and away from sin. A regular reminder of baptism offers Christians the opportunity to reflect on their commitment as disciples of Jesus.

Different approaches to baptism

There are two main approaches to baptism within Christianity.

Infant baptism

Infant baptism is practised by Catholics and some Protestants and is often the approach taken by Christians who emphasise the need to be cleansed from Original Sin in order to be saved. These Christians would not want to wait for baptism because they would not want to risk the child dying before being cleansed. The promises to be a Christian are made by parents and godparents and the child then takes part in confirmation when they are old enough to make the decision to be a disciple of Jesus for themselves. Of course, people of any age can be baptised if they were not baptised as babies. Many Christians focus less on Original Sin and more on the idea that it is important to be a full member of the Christian family from infancy onwards.

Believer's baptism

This is practised by some Protestants who believe that baptism should be the decision of the person themselves. A **believer's baptism** service often includes a testimony from the candidate: a statement of how Jesus has touched their lives and why they want to commit their future to following him. Babies of families in these traditions are welcomed in a **dedication service**. A dedication service gathers the family and friends, and the parents thank God for the gift of their child and promise to do their best to raise their child as a Christian. They also ask for help from a small group of adults (as well as the wider church) to do this.

Key words

Believer's baptism – baptising someone who has decided for themselves to follow Jesus

Dedication service – a service that dedicates a baby to the church community

Analyse and evaluate

Should people be baptised as infants?	
Yes	**No**
It is important for someone to be a full part of the Christian family and fully saved from as early as possible in life.	It is important that becoming a Christian is a free choice – more than most things, their faith needs to be something they decide for themselves.
It is possible to make a personal commitment to Christianity at confirmation.	The earliest Christians were baptised as adults and so this practice should continue.
Some Christians might ask what happens after death to an innocent baby or a Christian who has not yet been baptised. As a result, they might say that baptism is more symbolic than some Christians make out.	

Activities

Review

1. Why do some people believe in infant baptism rather than believer's baptism?
2. How is baptism important to Christians after their day of baptism?

Develop

3. Look up a typical service for a dedication service, infant baptism and believer's baptism. What symbolism is found in each one that shows different Christian beliefs about baptism?

Link

4. How might different interpretations of the Genesis 3 account lead to different beliefs about baptism?

Debate

5. Should families who do not go to church be allowed to have their babies baptised?

Stretch

6. Could God possibly save people who are not baptised? Research the idea of salvation further. You could look up the ideas of limited and unlimited election to start you off.

2.8 The Eucharist

Aim
To understand the practice and meaning of the Eucharist

Starter
What is the significance of a meal for different people and cultures?

Source of authority

'The Lord Jesus, on the night he was betrayed, took bread, and when he had given thanks, he broke it and said, "This is my body, which is for you; do this in remembrance of me." In the same way, after supper he took the cup, saying, "This cup is the new covenant in my blood; do this, whenever you drink it, in remembrance of me." For whenever you eat this bread and drink this cup, you proclaim the Lord's death until he comes.' (1 Corinthians 11:23–26)

The meaning of the Eucharist

Christians share the belief that they take part in the Eucharist because they are re-enacting the Last Supper, when Jesus took bread and wine and instructed the disciples to continue the tradition. The word 'Eucharist' comes from the Greek for 'thanksgiving'.

Different Christian views

Catholics

The Eucharist (or Mass, which comes from the Latin for 'being sent out') is the centre of Catholic practice. They must attend Mass every Sunday and they believe that by gathering for Mass they are fulfilling the specific commandment of Jesus to his church. Catholics believe that at the Mass, God changes the bread and wine into the body and blood of Jesus. The Eucharist is the moment where, for everyday believers, heaven and Earth meet and people can come as close to God as possible, by consuming Jesus' body and blood itself. At the altar, the sacrifice of Jesus is present each time the Eucharist is celebrated. The priest takes on the role of Jesus.

Bread that has previously been blessed and changed into the body of Christ is a focal point for prayer outside of the celebration of Mass. Catholics also believe that it is important to be free from serious sin before receiving Communion and so may try to attend Confession before going to Mass. Young people tend to receive Communion for the first time around seven or eight years old and this Mass is a big celebration for the community.

Protestants

Some Protestant Christians have a different focus. They might call the service the Lord's Supper or Holy Communion and emphasise that the bread and wine are symbols that unite a community. The bread and wine are shared among the people and they might all eat and drink it at the same time. These Christians often do

■ A traditional Eucharist

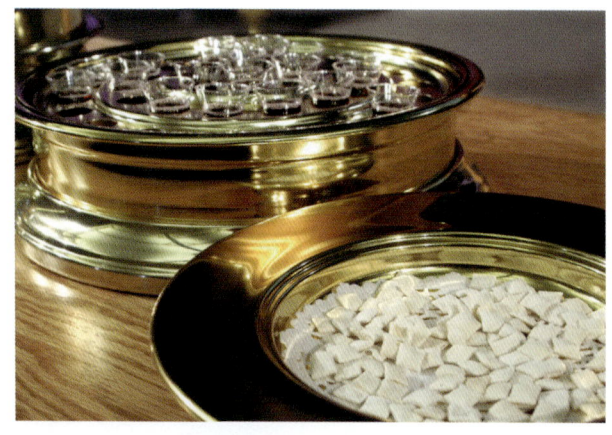

■ A modern Eucharist

not celebrate Holy Communion very often – sometimes just a few times a year. The focus for their worship is on hearing and understanding God's word and praising God. These Protestants (such as Baptists or Methodists) believe that Communion has powerful symbolism because it is done at the instruction of Jesus and it reminds the community that Jesus works in and through his people. Different members of the Church of England hold different views – some closer to the Catholic views and some closer to Baptist views.

The practice of the Eucharist

> **Top tip**
>
> Study this material alongside the work in spread 2.2.

Catholics

The Liturgy of the Eucharist in a Catholic Mass is divided into four sections, to mirror the actions of Jesus at the Last Supper – take, bless, break, give. At Mass, bread and wine are taken by the priest who then gives thanks for it, breaks the bread and then gives it to the people to receive at Communion. The Mass is essentially the same around the world.

Protestants

Protestants who do not celebrate the Eucharist frequently might simply conduct a normal weekly service and, at the end, the bread and wine are placed on a table at the front, the words of Jesus are read out and the bread and wine are shared among the people.

There are many other approaches to beliefs about the celebration of the Eucharist within the range of Protestant Christianity, depending on whether the approach is traditional or not as well as what the essential beliefs about the Eucharist are.

Analyse and evaluate

Is the Eucharist the most important form of Christian worship?

Yes	No
It is what Jesus commanded his disciples to do in his memory before he died.	The Eucharist is outdated and worship should appeal to modern needs more.
It brings humans closer to God in a unique way.	Asking for a person's own personal needs in different types of prayer is more important.

Some Christians might suggest that the Eucharist should be celebrated frequently, alongside other forms of worship.

Activities

Review

1. Outline the beliefs, teachings and practices of the Catholic Church about the Eucharist.
2. Why do some Christians call the Eucharist the Lord's Supper and celebrate it less frequently?

Develop

3. Look up typical services for the two approaches discussed in this spread. What does the symbolism teach about Christian beliefs about the Eucharist?

Link

4. How does this spread, as well as the spread on baptism (2.7), contribute to an understanding of the idea of sacraments?

Debate

5. Should bread and wine be replaced by biscuits and cola in the celebration of the Eucharist?

Stretch

6. As the Eucharist is such a central part of Christian life, take time to research it further and present your findings to the class.

Practices 2.8 The Eucharist

53

2.9 Pilgrimage

Aim
To explore the purpose and impact of pilgrimage

Starter
What places have special meaning or significance for you and/or your family?

Key word
Pilgrimage – a journey to a place of significance

Top tip
You need to understand the purpose of pilgrimage to each of the four locations discussed in this spread in the same amount of detail.

Source of authority
'Every year Jesus' parents went to Jerusalem for the Festival of the Passover.' (Luke 2:41)

■ A pilgrimage is as much about the journey as the destination

Why go on pilgrimage?

Humans have always had special places that they go to for reflection, peace and inner healing. Often, the journey to that place is long and the journey itself is a time of renewal as much as the arrival at the destination. This is the concept of **pilgrimage**, which in the Christian tradition is a journey to anywhere significant for the faith.

Ultimately, Christians go on pilgrimage to become closer to God and to strengthen their faith. They see it as having a long-term impact. Some places of pilgrimage, such as Lourdes, Jerusalem, Rome and Walsingham, are visited with the possibility of more than just a spiritual impact: sick people can be taken there in the hope that healing them is a part of God's plan.

Pilgrimage is not meant to be an easy time: a hard journey or difficult schedule helps show commitment. It is also a time of community: pilgrimage usually happens in a group and this reinforces the communal nature of Christianity, sometimes expanding an individual Christian's horizons in terms of the size of the Church. Individuals or communities can return from a pilgrimage with a renewed sense of commitment or the resolution to move in a new direction. For some people, visiting a place of pilgrimage makes them commit to becoming a Christian – either through a spiritual experience or through the experience of seeing many people worshipping together.

Places of pilgrimage

Pilgrimage can be to a place of significance for Jesus or for the Church as a whole, or it can be to the place of a miracle. Some Christians reject aspects of pilgrimage for being idolatry or for focusing on a saint or living person when Christians should focus on God.

Jerusalem, Holy Land	Rome, Italy
 ● Jesus went on pilgrimage here. ● He spent the final week of his life here and many of the places he visited are key stops on a pilgrimage to Jerusalem. ● Christians from all denominations come on pilgrimage to worship where he died and rose.	 ● This is historically the centre of the Church and now the home of the Catholic Church. ● It is a place full of history for Christians to unite with their past. ● The Pope lives here and often preaches here. It is a place of amazing art and architecture to emphasise the glory of God.

Christianity

Walsingham, England

- Mary appeared in a vision to a widow in the eleventh century, instructing her to build a holy house, which took place miraculously.
- A spring of water was discovered here and people go to drink from the spring for healing (spiritual or physical).
- Worship is quite traditional and traditional members of the Church of England and Catholics attend.

Lourdes, France

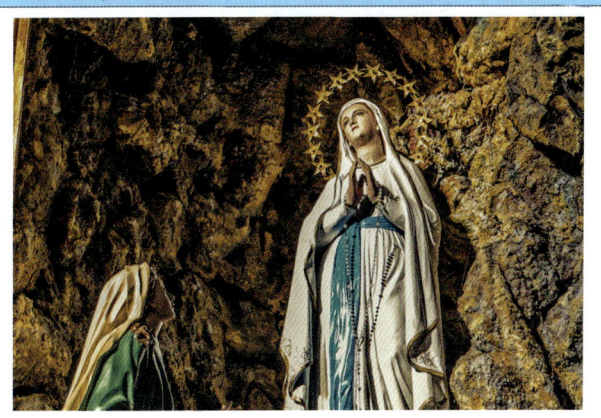

- Mary appeared in a vision to a young girl who discovered a spring in the nineteenth century.
- People visit to bathe in the baths and some go on pilgrimage to help the sick there.
- It is a Catholic site and some reject its importance because it has become very commercialised.

Analyse and evaluate

Are pilgrimages actually important to a Christian's life?

Yes	No
A pilgrimage is such a great commitment that it is an important event for a Christian to go through to show their dedication.	People are saved through their faith not through their deeds. Pilgrimage is a deed.
Any opportunity to draw a person closer to God should be accepted by Christians – even if it is not helpful for all Christians.	The good things that people get from pilgrimage could be achieved through church worship or individual prayer.
Some Christians might support pilgrimages to places like Jerusalem but reject pilgrimages to places that focus on Mary or the Pope.	

Activities

Review

1. Why do many Christians support the idea of pilgrimage? Use examples to justify your points.
2. Why do some Christians think that pilgrimage is not a good use of time for Christians?

Develop

3. In groups of four, take one of the four places of pilgrimage each, research it and share your findings.

Link

4. Think about work you have completed on salvation and worship. Is pilgrimage a form of worship that will help someone get into heaven?

Debate

5. 'The time and money spent on pilgrimages would be better spent helping those in need or the work of the local church.' How fair is this view?

Stretch

6. Find out about arguments for and against healing miracles that some Christians say take place at Lourdes. What are the strongest arguments for and against these miracles being real?

Practices 2.9 Pilgrimage

2.10 Advent and Christmas

Aim

To examine the impact and importance of Advent and Christmas celebrations

Starter

What comes to mind when you think about Christmas?

■ The wreath is a common Advent symbol

Key words

Advent – the season of preparation for Christmas
Christmas – the celebration of the Incarnation

Advent

For most Christians, **Advent** starts four Sundays before Christmas Day (25 December). It is a time of preparation to celebrate the Incarnation, the time when heaven and Earth united in the birth of Jesus. For many Christians, it is also the start of the new church year. It is helpful to think about Advent as preparing for **Christmas** in three ways:

- **Christmas past:** to remember the birth of Jesus. Some Christians, especially Catholics, focus on the role of Mary in the Christmas story. Many might reflect on the journey that Mary and Joseph took to Bethlehem. Many reflect on how God's plan worked to set humanity free from the effects of the Fall through sending great leaders and prophets.
- **Christmas present:** to reflect on the significance of the Incarnation for life today. Some Christians use the time to make resolutions or to go to Confession.
- **Christmas future:** to prepare for the second coming of Jesus. Christians might reflect on the teachings in the Bible about being ready for Jesus to come again.

As Christmas has become so commercialised, many Christians use the season to try to step away from the focus on money. Churches are sometimes decorated less (for example, flowers are generally not used for decoration) and prayers may be said around the Advent wreath. Some Christians, who do not follow a strict pattern for the church's year, might not place as much emphasis on Advent as a season and instead focus on Christmas itself.

Christmas

Most Christians embrace the non-religious aspects of Christmas celebrations and churches will often have Christmas trees and other decorations. However, the focus spiritually is on God's gift of himself to become human to teach the world how to live and,

Key word

Nativity – the story of Jesus' birth

Top tip

Be prepared to use learning about the Incarnation for questions on this topic.

ultimately, to save the world. Christians might reflect on Bible passages that show that God promised to send the Messiah to save humanity a long time before Jesus.

At Christmas, Christians will often have a children's service focused around a crib scene in the church or a **nativity** play or a carol service. Many churches have a service at midnight, to start Christmas Day (traditionally called Midnight Mass) as well as services on the day which are full of joy. Just like the focus in the readings is on the family of Jesus, Christmas is seen as a time of family celebration for Christians. Churches often hold events for those without families or in other need, such as giving Christmas lunch to the local community.

The Christmas season extends for some until Epiphany (6 January, but sometimes celebrated on the nearest Sunday) and for others until Candlemas (2 February). Epiphany remembers the wise men's visit to Jesus (Matthew 2:1–12) and Candlemas remembers the presentation of Jesus in the temple 40 days after his birth (Luke 2:22–40). The season as a whole emphasises that Jesus came for all people (the shepherds represent the lowly and the wise men represent the whole world).

Analyse and evaluate

Should Christians separate themselves from the commercial side of Christmas?

Yes	No
Christmas has become too commercialised and many people do not even reflect on the birth of Jesus.	Christians can use Christmas to witness to the world about the importance of the gift of God in Jesus.
The significance of Christmas is primarily the Incarnation and its spiritual significance and commercialism will get in the way of a person's focus on this.	Christians are called to live within the world and not separate to it.
The shared values of family, love and joy are relevant to both Christians and non-Christians. Christians simply need to take a different perspective to non-Christians.	

Activities

Review

1. What is the significance of Advent within Christianity?
2. How is Christmas a celebration of the Incarnation?

Develop

3. Research two different denominations' celebrations of Advent and Christmas and create a poster for each to invite people to their churches.

Link

4. How do the seasons of Advent and Christmas demonstrate Christian beliefs about: the Fall, the titles of Jesus, the Incarnation?

Debate

5. Debate the idea that Advent should be as important in the life of a Christian as Christmas.

Stretch

6. Read the Christmas stories in Matthew Chapters 1–2 and Luke Chapters 1–2. Find out why different scholars think the stories are so different and see if you can find a reason you agree with.

2.11 Lent, Holy Week and Easter

Aim
To explore the impact and importance of Lent, Holy Week and Easter

Starter
Should Easter be a bigger celebration than Christmas for Christians?

Key words
Lent – the period of preparation for Easter
Holy Week – the week before Easter, remembering Jesus' time in Jerusalem

Source of authority
'Jesus was led by the Spirit into the wilderness to be tempted by the devil. After fasting forty days and forty nights, he was hungry.' (Matthew 4:1–2)

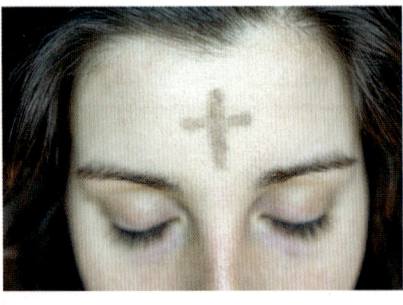

Lent begins on Ash Wednesday

Top tip
See spread 1.12 for more details about Good Friday worship.

Lent

Lent is a period of 40 days which was traditionally when Christians were strict with their lifestyle to prepare for the celebrations of Easter. The 40 days do not include Sundays because all Sundays are days of celebration. Lent is mainly observed by Christians with a more traditional, structured approach, such as Catholics. Many Protestant churches do not focus on it in their church year. Lent begins on Ash Wednesday when Christians traditionally receive the mark of ashes on their forehead as a reminder of their mortality and the need to repent for sin.

A traditional way of understanding Lent comes from the Sermon on the Mount's teaching in Matthew 6:1–18:

- **Prayer:** a time to develop and renew a person's relationship with God. A Christian might go to additional services at church or spend more time in private prayer. Some choose this time to read a Christian book and develop their understanding of their faith.
- **Fasting:** to commemorate the 40 days Jesus spent in the desert before he began his ministry, many Christians choose to hold back an element of their diet. Some give up something (for example, chocolate); others reduce the amount they eat on certain days. Others interpret fasting as giving up their time for something else (for example, taking up exercise or additional prayer). In the desert, Jesus was tempted and Christians focus on trying to build up their spiritual tools to resist temptation in their lives. Catholics might try to go to Confession during Lent.
- **Almsgiving:** giving to the needy. Christians try to develop their relationship with God by increasing their charitable work at this time.

Holy Week

At the end of Lent, Christians remember Jesus' entry into Jerusalem on Palm Sunday (the Sunday before Easter) when he was greeted as a triumphant king, coming to save the people. Many Christians see the journey through **Holy Week** as a kind of personal pilgrimage. They might see significance in moving from the joy of Palm Sunday to the sadness of the crucifixion.

The early part of the week sees Christians reflect on Jesus turning the tables in the Temple, angered that the Temple had become a place of selling more than a place of prayer. They also reflect on the decision of Judas to betray Jesus.

On Maundy Thursday, Christians remember the Last Supper and the start of the Eucharist. The service in the evening often includes the washing of feet to remember Jesus commanding his disciples to serve each other after he had gone. At the end of the Last Supper, Jesus went out into the Garden of Gethsemane, where he prayed and was arrested. Some Christians wait in silence in church, praying and trying to imagine what Jesus went through.

Good Friday is a very simple day with the focus on the sacrifice Jesus went through. Many churches remain bare on Holy Saturday with no service, to remember when Jesus was in the tomb.

Easter

Easter celebrations are full of joy. Churches are richly decorated and the worship is celebratory. In addition to usual Sunday worship, some of the following may happen:

- a night-time service called the Easter Vigil, which charts the story of humanity from the Fall to Jesus as well as celebrating the first Eucharist of Easter
- a dawn service with a new fire to focus on the idea of Christ the light of the world rising out of the darkness of death
- baptisms
- people may renew their baptismal promises
- people may be sprinkled with holy water.

The Easter season continues for 50 days until Pentecost, the celebration of the coming of the Holy Spirit. During this season, the mood is still very festive and there is a focus on renewal and new life (in the northern hemisphere, Easter is a springtime festival).

Analyse and evaluate

Is Easter the ultimate celebration for Christians?

Yes	No
God has shown power over death, light has conquered darkness and the effects of the Fall have been reversed.	The whole of the Christian message should be seen as equally important – Christmas, the teachings of Jesus, and his death and resurrection.
God has fulfilled the promises made throughout the Old Testament.	Every Sunday is a celebration of the resurrection, so Easter should not be singled out.
Some Christians might argue that they need to be careful of the emerging commercialism at Easter and make sure that they do not lose sight of the true meaning of the season.	

Activities

Review

1. Why do many Christians take Lent so seriously?
2. Make a timeline of the events of Holy Week and Easter and include how Christians remember them today.

Develop

3. In small groups, divide up how Christians mark Lent, Holy Week and Easter and research how specific churches or denominations celebrate them. Present your findings to the class.

Link

4. What do the celebrations of Lent, Holy Week and Easter teach about who Jesus was and about the nature of God?

Debate

5. Should Lent be a time of physical struggle for Christians, or should the focus be spiritual?

Stretch

6. Find out about how Christians celebrate Pentecost and state what this shows about beliefs in the Holy Spirit.

2.12 Marriage and funerals

Aim
To explore the impact and importance of two key rites of passage

Starter
What do you already know about how Christians talk about God's love?

Key words
Rite of passage – a ceremony that marks the transition from one stage of life to the next
Ritual – a series of rites brought together in a ceremony

Top tip
Marriage is further studied later in the course – see Chapter 5.

Key word
Vow – a promise made at a wedding

■ A church wedding

Rites of passage

When describing **rites of passage**, Christians refer to key **rituals** that mark significant changes in the journey of life and affect both individuals and communities, such as baptism and marriage. For many, the local church might gather together because, as Christians, they feel that it is important to accompany each other on their individual journeys.

Marriage

For Christians, marriage is a sign of love between the couple. God's eternal love is reflected in the union of the two people. Some Christians believe that marriage can only be between men and women because God deliberately created two genders with the purpose of procreation. Others believe that all love is a gift from God and gender does not matter.

There are some areas that are common to all Christian wedding rituals:

- The ceremony is a time of prayer with Bible readings and a sermon to remind everyone of the religious significance of the marriage and that God is the one who ultimately unites the couple. Just like God's love is sacrificial, so married people must put the other partner first.
- The **vows**, which commit the couple to looking after each other until death, are made in the eyes of God. In traditional Christian churches, the woman might promise to obey the man as part of these promises.
- Rings are exchanged which, by being of precious metal and circular, symbolise the precious and eternal love of the two people.
- There are also legal aspects, depending on the country where the marriage takes place: in the UK, the marriage register is completed.

For Catholics, who believe that marriage is a sacrament, the service often takes place within the celebration of Mass. More modern liberal Protestants might have a free service, although legal aspects, such as the vows, might still need to be more formal.

Funeral rites

The local church community plays an important role in funerals because these are rites of passage from this stage of life to the next. Communities support those who mourn and some Christians, such as Catholics, also pray for those who have died so that they can pass from purgatory to heaven quickly.

The Bible readings, sermon and prayers at a funeral focus on giving thanks for the life of the person who has died as well as on Christian beliefs about the salvation won by Jesus. There are prayers for those left behind. Some Christians, wishing to emphasise that their bodies will be raised at the final judgement, do not agree with cremation after the ceremony. Most others that allow cremation require the ashes to be buried in one place, rather than scattered. During a funeral, there is a formal rite of **commendation** and another of **committal**.

> **Top tip**
>
> Study this spread alongside spread 1.16–1.17 on eschatology.

> **Key words**
>
> **Commendation** – the part of a funeral service where the person who has died is handed over (commended) to God's love
>
> **Committal** – the part of a funeral service where the body of the person who has died is given (committed) to burial or cremation

Analyse and evaluate

Is a funeral more for the living than for the dead person?

Yes	No
Funerals are a chance to say goodbye to the person who has died and to help people come to terms with the death.	At the funeral, the person is commended to God, which is an important rite of passage for them.
Protestants generally believe that the person has already gone to heaven (or not) and so the funeral cannot affect the dead person.	Catholics believe in purgatory and so it is important for everyone to gather to pray for the dead person so that they can move to heaven.
Some would argue that funerals serve both the living and the dead and that this can be seen in the rituals.	

Activities

Review

1. How might weddings and funerals differ between Christians? Why are there these differences?
2. What is the role of the local church community in Christian rites of passage?

Develop

3. How might the following passages relate to marriage and funerals: Genesis 1:27–28, Genesis 2:7, Matthew 5:31–32, Matthew 25:31–46 and Ephesians 5:21–33?

Link

4. Look up the words of a Christian funeral service. How does it reflect the teachings found in earlier topics from this course?

Debate

5. Should rites of passage focus on the individuals, the family/friends or the local church community? Discuss the importance of each group in baptism, marriage and funerals.

Stretch

6. Do you think some feminists are right that texts like Ephesians 5:21–33 show that Christianity can never accept men and women as equal? Research feminism in Christianity to help you decide.

2.13 Families and confirmation

Aim

To examine how church communities nurture and support families

Starter

Why do you think a church community might be important to families?

Ways to support families

A local church community is often like an extended family for Christians and many Christians talk about their church family. Each community is different and there are often differences between how churches approach things depending on their context (for example, if they are in a city centre or a rural village). Christians believe that families are important because they are a sign that Christians are fulfilling God's instruction to fill the Earth. They are an ongoing sign of God's love in the world. Examples of what church community activities might look like include:

- **Parent and baby/toddler/child groups:** supporting each other through community and providing friendship for the parents as well as allowing the children to get used to being around other children.
- **Sunday schools:** often at the same time as the 'adult' church service, Sunday schools help to teach children about their faith.
- **Youth clubs:** providing teenagers the opportunity to interact with other Christians of their age as well as developing their commitment as disciples of Jesus.
- **Marriage preparation classes or groups:** to help people to understand the Christian importance of marriage.
- **Family worship:** some Sunday services might be aimed at families in particular.
- **Visiting the elderly and sick:** ensuring that all members of the community are fully welcome, even if they cannot attend church. Some Christians might visit and offer Holy Communion in the home or hospital.

Source of authority

'Just as a body, though one, has many parts, but all its many parts form one body, so it is with Christ. For we were all baptised by one Spirit so as to form one body.' (1 Corinthians 12:12–13)

Key word

Confirmation – the service when someone takes on the responsibilities of their faith for themselves

Confirmation

A particular rite of passage often occurs when someone is in their mid-teenage years. **Confirmation** is the point for some Christians (for example, Catholics and traditional Protestants) where the promises made by parents and godparents at baptism are taken on by themselves: they become 'adult Christians'. It is generally thought of by these Christians as a sacrament. Those Christians who practise believer's baptism do not have the practice of confirmation.

Confirmation services are usually led by the local bishop, showing that the person is joining a community that is beyond the local church. The promises made at baptism are repeated: belief in the Trinity and a promise to follow the ways of Jesus. Prayers are offered that the person will be given the power of the Holy Spirit in their lives.

■ A teenager being confirmed

The symbol at all confirmations is:

- **the laying on of hands:** this is the ancient method in the Church of symbolising not only the giving of the Holy Spirit but the joining of someone to years of tradition. Jesus laid his hands on his disciples and so any bishop who lays their hands on someone can claim a direct link back to Jesus.

Other common symbols are:

- **anointing with oil:** ancient practice reminds us that anointing took place at key moments to signify that someone is particularly chosen. Christians believe that, at confirmation, they are emphasising that the Holy Spirit is sealed within them and they are called by name to be a follower of Jesus
- **taking a saint's name:** Catholics often take on the name of a saint who will be a special role model for them.

Analyse and evaluate

Is confirmation an important rite of passage?

Yes	No
The Holy Spirit is a vital guide for all Christians and it is important for a person to ask for and accept the Spirit at confirmation.	The symbolism of becoming a disciple of Jesus is at baptism. Confirmation is not needed.
It is important to recognise that by becoming a Christian, someone is joining a worldwide community that stretches back 2000 years.	A person can become a Christian without a Bishop laying hands on their head.
Many Christians accept both of the 'yes' points above but feel that this can be achieved without confirmation – for example, through baptism, prayer and charismatic worship.	

Activities

Review

1. What is the importance of the local church community for Christians?
2. Why do some Christians wish to be confirmed?

Develop

3. Look up 'Messy Church' services. How are these an example of local church communities supporting families?

Link

4. How does a confirmation service reflect Christian beliefs about the Holy Spirit?

Debate

5. Should people need to go to confirmation classes before they are confirmed?

Stretch

6. Find out about the Alpha movement. What role might it play in the local church and beyond?

63

2.14 Mission

Aim
To consider the importance of mission in the modern Church

Starter
Why do Christians believe it is important to spread their message?

Missionary work is about listening as well as talking

Key words
Evangelism – the process of spreading the message of Christianity
Missionary – someone who spreads the message of Christianity

Source of authority
'I am not ashamed of the gospel, because it is the power of God that brings salvation to everyone who believes.' (Romans 1:16)

The importance of mission

Christians believe that their faith is a gift from God that is worth sharing with the world. The promise of being saved has great significance for them and they want to ensure that others hear this message, as well as the teachings of Jesus, which they believe will lead the world to be a better place. In twenty-first-century Britain, many Christians would argue that there is a particular need for **evangelism** and for Christians to act as **missionaries** in their daily lives because of the numbers of people who have turned away from or do not have a Christian faith.

Different Christian views

- For many Christians, the emphasis is on setting an example of what it means to be a Christian and interacting with people as Jesus would have wanted, without pre-judging what their circumstances are. For this reason, Christian charity work is not limited to the Christian community. People might work against injustice, care for God's creation and simply make sure that those they meet see their Christian way of life as being a reflection of God's goodness.

- Other Christians argue that it is important to actively share the message of Jesus and some denominations emphasise the need to invite people to Sunday worship where they can witness to visitors and where visitors can hear the teaching given in the sermon or join an Alpha group. Others actively seek out opportunities to speak in public about the good news, such as by being street evangelists. Christians might refer to the Parable of the Sheep and the Goats (Matthew 25:31–46) to justify care for those in need or to Jesus' command at his ascension for Christians to actively preach and baptise (Matthew 28:19–20).

Christians hope to be inspired by the Holy Spirit and believe that God will guide them to make the right choices. Missionaries take courage from this in their work, remembering Jesus' words in the

Acts version of the ascension story: 'you will receive power when the Holy Spirit comes on you; and you will be my witnesses...' (Acts 1:8).

Different Christian approaches to evangelism

Christian approaches to evangelism also differ based on their views about the importance of making people convert to Christianity. For those who believe that a person must be a Christian to be saved, they will make every effort to bring people into the Church and to make them active disciples of Christ. They might argue that John's Gospel teaches that it is only through active faith in Jesus that anyone can come to God. They might also refer to John 3:16: 'whoever believes in him shall not perish but have eternal life'. This would be the approach of evangelical Christians and many Catholics.

Other, more liberal, Christians might argue that those who live a good life in their own way can be saved and so they should not pressure people to become Christians. They might focus their own work on caring for those in need as well as looking after their spiritual life. Some liberal Christians believe that a loving God would never condemn creation to hell and they would place very little emphasis on evangelism.

Source of authority

'Jesus said, "I am the way and the truth and the life. No one comes to the Father except through me."' (John 14:6)

Analyse and evaluate

Should Christians care for those in need before evangelism?

Yes	No
It is potentially offensive or intolerant to try to convert people to Christianity.	Salvation is too important for Christians not to try to offer it to as many people as they can.
Christians are judged on their work for others (for example, Matthew 25:31–46), not their preaching (for example, Matthew 6:1).	Missionary work was the final command of Jesus and even if it is difficult to go far from home, his command should be respected.

Some Christians might observe that caring for those in need is a form of evangelism because it demonstrates the values of Christianity.

Activities

Review

1. Why might some Christians choose to become missionaries?
2. Why do some Christians choose charity work as their main priority?

Develop

3. Find out how the Gideons, the Salvation Army and Street Pastors approach evangelism and make notes about each.

Link

4. How do different beliefs about salvation affect Christian attitudes to evangelism?

Debate

5. Should Christians try to evangelise using social media and TV channels or should they focus on the people they meet in daily life?

Stretch

6. Find out about the Anglican Church's 'Five Marks of Mission'. What do they suggest about Anglican beliefs about evangelism and do you agree with this approach?

2.15 New forms of church

Aim

To explore the growth of new forms of church

Starter

Discuss what you think a twenty-first-century teenager wants from their experience of a church.

Reasons for the growth of new forms of church

As society moves forward, many traditions in British life are being challenged or are changing. Local communities are less the focus for many because people are exposed to the whole world through the media and the ability to travel. There is a move away from institutions and more focus on freedom of choice. For some Christians, it is important for the Church to reflect this in how it looks. While there seems to be a decline in attendance at Catholic and Church of England churches, for example, there is an increase in worship in modern forms of church with a freer approach to worship and sometimes with charismatic worship.

Outside Europe, Christianity is often growing in its traditional form and this leads some Christians to argue that these churches are still relevant. The charitable work of the Catholic Church, for example, is encouraging more people to become disciples of Jesus in South America and Africa.

For some, new forms of church are about changing the approach to worship. One example might be Holy Trinity Brompton Church in London, which has founded other churches around the UK. This approach is called church planting. Even within established churches, new approaches to worship, such as Messy Church worship, have moved Christians away from set liturgies and brought new people to the faith.

■ Do you recognise this as a church service?

Many churches combine their worship with social activities, shared meals or high-quality contemporary music, which attracts people. They might argue that this is a better reflection of the earliest Christian communities, which focused on being led by the Spirit and community life. Some churches have reordered their buildings to be more like cafés and others use commercial cafés to provide a more relaxed way to gather and to have some prayer and teaching alongside cake. This is known as the café church movement.

Source of authority

'All the believers were together and had everything in common. They sold property and possessions to give to anyone who had need … they broke bread in their homes and ate together with glad and sincere hearts, praising God … And the Lord added to their number daily those who were being saved.' (Acts 2:44–47)

Debate around accepting new forms of church

Christians might suggest that at the heart of their faith is the need to worship God with all their heart. They might say that modern music and engaging teaching, influenced by society, achieves this better than traditions that go back hundreds of years. They might argue that some Christians have got caught in traditions and liturgy and lost sight of a genuine relationship with God. For example, they might reject those Catholics who still like to worship in Latin.

Some might argue that the focus needs to be community over everything else. Some new forms of church do not even have buildings and worship takes place online with people from around the world. This has increased since the COVID-19 pandemic when churches were forced to close. Christian leaders have been forced to engage their churches with new and innovative methods, such as through online worship.

Christians could also argue that in order to encourage young people to come to church, they need to appeal to them more. Their worship might be more like Messy Church for younger children or like youth groups for teenagers.

New churches could also reject the focus on leadership in some denominations, such as the Catholic Church. They might argue that new forms of church allow local people to share their passion for Christ.

Others could reject this approach and argue that Christianity should embrace 2000 years of tradition and that, when worshipping, we are joining in prayer over the centuries as well as across the world. They might say that loud, charismatic worship goes against the dignity required to worship a transcendent creator and that it goes against Jesus' instruction not to pray like the hypocrites who just want to be seen at prayer (Matthew 6:5).

Analyse and evaluate

Are new forms of church a positive step for Christianity?

Yes	No
They are growing the number of Christians, which must be an important step forward.	There is too much focus on 'quick fixes' in worship and not enough time to reflect on the greatness of God.
They acknowledge that Christianity lives within society which is very different now than in the past.	Without any clear structure or leadership, these churches may not teach the message of Jesus accurately.

Some might argue that new forms of church have lots to teach traditional denominations, which could learn to adapt and express themselves in a more relevant way.

Activities

Review

1. Outline, with examples, some of the features of new forms of church.
2. What is the strongest argument for and the strongest argument against new forms of church? Why have you chosen these arguments?

Develop

3. Find out about Hillsong. This is a church that has grown globally. Is it a sign that new forms of church are positive forces within Christianity?

Link

4. What might some Christians argue might be lost from their worship if they embrace new forms of church?

Debate

5. 'Christianity should never stand still. It should move with the times.' Do you think this is a valid argument?

Stretch

6. The passage in Matthew 6:5–7 could be used by both traditional and modern Christians. What does this tell you about how the Bible is understood and used by Christians? What lessons can be learned from this?

Practices 2.15 New forms of church

2.16 Ecumenism

Aim
To examine Christian relationships with other denominations

Starter
Make a list of things that Christians have in common and things that divide them. Are any of these things deal-breakers for good relations?

The Catholic Pope meeting with the Church of England's Archbishop of Canterbury

What is the Church?

Christianity is divided into many different denominations and the relationships between them have not always been calm. Divisions about what is required for salvation get to the heart of how Christianity exists in the world and sometimes seem insurmountable.

- Some Christians believe that other denominations themselves will not get their followers to heaven.
- Catholics believe that Catholicism itself is the only guaranteed way to salvation – though it does not rule out the salvation of other Christians, including other faiths. They see dialogue with other Christians as part of the process of evangelism.
- Others believe that following Jesus is enough and they will allow anyone who joins in a Eucharist to receive Communion and value the gifts that it brings. Many Christians are saddened by the image that the outside world is given through the divided Church.

Ecumenism

Top tip
This topic also comes up later in the course. See spread 8.10 for more details.

While the word 'church' relates both to the building or an individual community (lower case 'c') and the people of God (upper case 'C'), some Christians divide up the concept of the Church further, between the people of God alive currently (**Church temporal**) and those who have gone before and entered heaven (the saints: **Church spiritual**). The work to unite Christians on Earth is known as **ecumenism** and Christians often refer to ecumenical work as being any work designed to bring denominations together in some way. This can be through trying to understand differences in belief, **reconciling** past divisions or simply carrying out activities together, such as worship or charity work.

Ecumenical groups

Key words

Church temporal – the Church on Earth
Church spiritual – the Church in heaven
Ecumenism – work for Christian unity
Reconcile – to restore a broken relationship, often as the step after forgiveness

The World Council of Churches exists to try to bring about the visible unity of Christians, seen through the sharing of the Eucharist. It unites Christian denominations and groups from around the world and focuses on what Christians have in common (for example, a common desire to witness and evangelise). It focuses on the

Christian work of serving others, aiming for justice and looking after God's creation. Rather than ignoring what has gone before, it seeks to work through a process of reconciliation.

The 'Churches Together' movement is an organisation that brings together churches on a national level – for example, the Churches Together in England group, or the Churches Together in Britain and Ireland group. It tries to work on a national, regional and local level to help Christians to 'share a common life'.

Specific ecumenical communities also exist around the world and have their own communities as well as welcoming pilgrims. Some examples are:

- **Taizé:** a village in France where a community of monks live with a focus on meditation, especially through simple chants, and prayer. The monks come from both Catholic and Protestant backgrounds. The community focuses on the importance of reconciliation, celebrating diversity and living faithful lives of joy.
- **Iona:** this community was established on an island in Scotland and focuses on the importance of relationships, especially as the world feels less united. It is a community committed to prayer in action and members of the community now live around the world. They believe only community can change lives.
- **Corrymeela in Northern Ireland:** this community believes that 'Together is better'. It was founded after the Second World War showed how a divided humanity was a bad prospect and the tensions within Christianity in Northern Ireland showed the need for reconciliation and a desire for shared commitment.

Analyse and evaluate

Is ecumenism necessary?

Yes	No
The early Church was united and that was the desire of Jesus. Christians today have strayed from this but need to return to it.	Christians should be free to choose to worship God in any way they wish and there is no need to try to bring them together.
There is always a space for reconciliation and always a need for working together for common goals, changing God's world for the better.	The unity of all people is something too perfect ever to achieve in this life and so Christians should focus on the needs of the area around them instead.
Some might argue that it is not necessary because it is pointless: different denominations have too many points of faith they disagree on.	

Activities

Review

1. What are the different meanings of the word 'church'?
2. What is meant by the word 'ecumenism'?

Develop

3. How do these Bible passages contribute to the discussion about ecumenism: Matthew 25:31–46, John 17:20–23, 1 Corinthians 1:10–17 and 1 Corinthians 12:12–13?

Link

4. Look back over previous spreads and identify which topics discuss the Church as the people of God on Earth (Church temporal) and which discuss the Church as the Church spiritual.

Debate

5. Are the ecumenical groups too small to make any real difference to the world and to Christianity?

Stretch

6. Find out more about the groups and movements discussed in this spread. What specific examples of current work can you find? What happens in Britain in Christian Unity Week? Is ecumenism a positive force in Britain?

2.17 The Church in the wider world

Aim

To explore the Church's work in the wider world

Starter

Discuss what sorts of charities you think Christians should be most involved in. Why did you come up with that list?

Christian Aid seeks to do Christian work in the wider world

Key word

Persecution – bad treatment of a group, perhaps because of religious beliefs

Top tip

You need to know about the work of one of these three agencies in detail, including a recent campaign.

Supporting the persecuted Church

Around the world, Christians do not always enjoy the religious freedoms that we take for granted in this country. The Universal Declaration of Human Rights says that people have the right to freedom of religion, including the freedom to change belief. Christians can be persecuted for:

- trying to convert people
- not following the religion of the country they live in
- challenging injustice and speaking out against those in power.

Persecution might involve not being allowed to go to church in public, being attacked, imprisoned or killed, or being denied basic rights, such as medical care or education. Churches might be damaged and Bibles might be forbidden.

Christians in China are monitored because the Chinese government does not allow anything to be said against it because it believes that would challenge the unity of the country. In North Korea, the leadership wishes to be seen as a god themselves and so Christians are seen as their enemy. In India, Christians are sometimes seen as rejecting the national identity.

Christians might refer to the Sermon on the Mount's teaching to love our enemies (Matthew 5:44) or the Parable of the Good Samaritan (Luke 10:25–37), which teaches that we must treat everyone as a neighbour, including those we are brought up to hate. In the Parable of the Sheep and the Goats (Matthew 25:31–46), visiting people in prison, such as those wrongly imprisoned, is seen as a duty. Christians might also refer to teachings on forgiveness.

Christian responses to these issues include praying for those in need or supporting charities that work with persecuted Christians by giving their time or money. They might also use their influence in their workplaces and with those around them to change attitudes.

Christian aid agencies

A number of charities use Christian values to underpin the work they do in the world to bring an end to poverty and persecution or to care for God's creation. They might work both in this country and abroad and work not only to raise funds for projects abroad but to educate people in this country about global needs. Christians can support with fundraising, either as individuals or as a church community. They might volunteer to be a spokesperson for a charity and might choose to give a charitable gift as a present to someone instead of a regular gift.

Agency	Christian Aid	Tearfund	CAFOD
Description	An agency that fights poverty which prevents people from their God-given right to dignity. It combats discrimination and provides help after natural disasters. It promotes fair trade.	An agency that wants to tackle the complex issue of poverty by reacting to disasters, developing communities and influencing people to challenge injustice.	A Catholic agency that seeks to bring about global change by influencing local communities and changing structures in society as well as enabling Catholics to learn to act in solidarity.
Quotation from website	'We are the changemakers, the peacemakers, the mighty of heart.'	'Poverty is not God's plan. You are.'	'When we unite and make a stand for what we believe in, we can achieve remarkable things.'

Analyse and evaluate

Should Christians support global charities?

Yes	No
God's creation includes the whole world and not simply local communities. Christians must bring love to all.	Christians should be responsible for their local communities first so that they are not overlooked.
The only way to create harmony in the world is to tackle areas of the most concern, which are currently away from Britain.	Christians would be better using their influence on governments rather than supporting aid agencies.
Some Christians would argue that everyone has a different calling from God: some will focus on prayer, some on local charities, some on global agencies and so on.	

Activities

Review
1. How and why might a Christian be persecuted?
2. Why might Christians support one of the Christian aid agencies on these pages?

Develop
3. How do these Bible passages influence Christian beliefs about charity work: Matthew 6:1–4, Matthew 25:31–46, Mark 12:29–31 and Luke 16:19–31?

Link
4. How might Christian work abroad link to your previous learning on evangelism, creation and salvation?

Debate
5. 'There can never be a true definition of what makes a Christian.' How valid is this view?

Stretch
6. Find out about Liberation theology. Is there ever an excuse for Christians to tackle injustice by breaking the law or even supporting violence?

Summary activities

CHECK YOUR NOTES

STAGE 1

Check that you have detailed notes that cover the following:

- ☐ The purposes of different types of worship including liturgical worship and informal/charismatic worship
- ☐ The features of different types of church service
- ☐ Understanding the idea of sacrament including different understandings of baptism
- ☐ Understanding different approaches to the meaning of the Eucharist
- ☐ The role and importance of private prayer and devotion
- ☐ The different types of prayer in public worship, including the Lord's Prayer
- ☐ The idea of pilgrimage and the purpose of pilgrimage to Lourdes, Jerusalem, Walsingham and Rome
- ☐ The importance of festivals such as Advent, Christmas, Lent, Holy Week and Easter for different Christians
- ☐ The role of the Church in the local community in providing rituals to mark rites of passage such as baptism, marriage and funerals
- ☐ The role of the local church in supporting families in the community, for example through Sunday schools, youth clubs and visiting the elderly
- ☐ Mission and evangelism in the Church
- ☐ The role of the Church in the wider world including ecumenical movements and communities
- ☐ The role of the Church in supporting those who are persecuted or in need

GETTING READY

STAGE 2

Quick quiz

1. Name two sacraments that are observed by both Catholics and Protestants.
2. Give one difference between Catholic and Protestant understandings of the Eucharist/Mass.
3. Give one difference between liturgical worship and charismatic worship.
4. What different types of prayer might Christians use in public worship? (Clue ACTS)
5. What places might a Roman Catholic Christian go to on pilgrimage?
6. What different events in the life of Jesus are marked during Holy Week?
7. What is the difference between a dedication and infant baptism?
8. What term is used for the process of sharing the Christian message with others?
9. Give the name of one agency that may provide aid to those suffering hardship.
10. What does the bible suggest about the mission of the Church?

Quick quiz answers can be found online at www.hoddereducation.co.uk/ocr-gcse-rs-answers

ACTIVITIES

STAGE 2

1. Create a set of flashcards for this chapter to help you learn key terms. The key term should be on one side and a definition on the other. You could add a source of wisdom and authority if that is appropriate.
2. **AO2 focus:** Think about some of the possible discussion questions that could be asked on this topic. Generate a list of pros and cons similar to the example below.

Is a believer's baptism better than an infant baptism?	
For	Against
• Person decides for themselves • In the Bible people converted then were baptised	• Baptism cleanses from sin so why wait? • Part of teaching of the Church (Catechism)

GET PRACTISING

STAGE 3

Use this section to help you develop your understanding of how to answer questions on this topic.

Ask the expert

Amina writes:

I try my best to revise, but the more I read my notes, the less things seem to go in. Do I just need to work harder or am I doing something wrong?

Expert answer:

It is not necessarily a matter of working harder, although it is worth regularly reviewing topics rather than leaving it until the end. Some revision techniques are better than others. Reading and re-reading notes or highlighting is quite a passive strategy. Think about more active strategies such as covering and checking, rewriting or quizzing. There are a couple of methods listed below.

Three stages of revision

There is a danger that the word 'revision' suggests we can leave this until we have finished the course. This is unwise. There are three stages of revision.

- **Stage 1:** Check your notes at the end of each topic – make sure you have enough. Where are the extra sources that your teacher hasn't covered in class?
- **Stage 2:** Active and regular review of each of your topics – this could be making flashcards, mind maps, retrieval boxes, or covering and rewriting/summarising. It is important that it is active not passive.
- **Stage 3:** Practising – medium and long questions in timed conditions (this could be paragraphs or essay plans if short of time).

Spaced study

One technique for the later stages of revision is called spaced revision:

1. Spend some time reviewing a topic in detail.
2. Then do something to transform your notes, e.g. make mind maps.
3. Write yourself a quiz.
4. Then do something else for a couple of hours to give yourself time to forget the material.
5. Attempt the quiz you wrote earlier. If you do well, proceed to 6. If not, have a further review before carrying on.
6. Have a go at a longer question – perhaps even a 6-mark and a 15-mark. This will test whether you have retained the material.

Islam

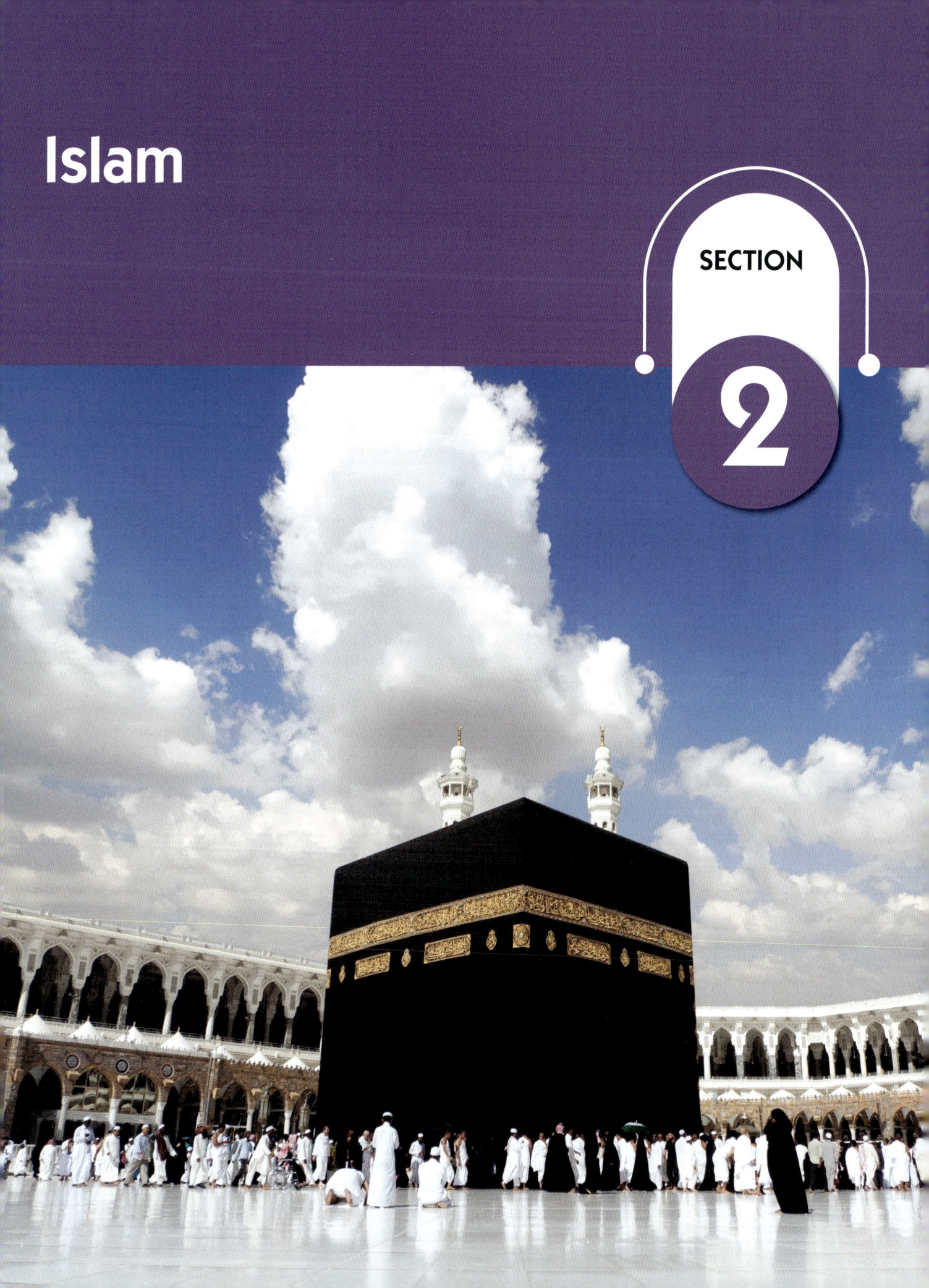

SECTION 2

CHAPTER 3

Beliefs and teachings

3.1 Introducing Islam

Aim
To give some broad detail about Islam and Muslims that will help you study the course

Starter
What makes someone a Muslim? Note down as many ideas as you can.

Key words
Islam – 'peace' and 'submission to Allah'; Allah's chosen religion for humanity
Muslim – a believer in Islam
Allah – Arabic name for God
Ummah – worldwide community of Muslims

Muslim worldviews

Islam is the religion that **Muslims** believe **Allah** (God) has chosen for humanity. Muslims believe that all prophets, beginning with Adam, had taught Islam in some form for many centuries, and the religion was completed and made perfect in the time of Muhammad in seventh-century Arabia.

Within Muhammad's lifetime, Islam had spread throughout the Arabian Peninsula. Less than three decades after his death, it had become established in other parts of Asia, North Africa and Europe. It is estimated that there are 1.8 billion Muslims today, making up almost a quarter of the world's population. This makes Islam the world's largest religion after Christianity.

A Muslim is mainly identified as someone who believes in the declaration of faith, known as the Shahadah, which is the first pillar of Islam: 'There is no god except Allah; Muhammad is the messenger of Allah'. Muslims are also required to believe in the core beliefs.

As with Christians, Muslims are very diverse. There are many different types of Muslims who make up the **ummah** and they may see and understand the world through one of the three 'lenses' below. These lenses are a simplification, so it is wise to use words like 'some' or 'most' when describing these different views.

Sunni lens	Shi'a lens	Ahmadiyya lens
These Muslims make up the largest group in the ummah. Sunni Muslims believe that after the death of the Prophet Muhammad, leadership was given to four Rightly Guided Khalifahs (successors) – Abu Bakr, Umar, Uthman and Ali – who were chosen on the basis of their spiritual devotion, knowledge and other qualities. There are four main schools of thought within the Sunni tradition – Hanafi, Maliki, Hanbali and Shafi – and also sub-groups such Barelwi, Deobandi and Salafi.	These Muslims make up the second main group. Shi'a Muslims believe that after Muhammad, leadership should have been given to the Ahl al-Bayt (the Prophet's family) starting with Ali. They believe in Imams who were appointed by Allah. There are two main schools of thought within the Shi'a tradition – Jafari and Zaydiyyah – and also sub-groups such as Ithna 'Ashari (**Twelver Shi'a Muslims**) and Isma'ili.	These Muslims are a more recently founded community originating in the nineteenth century. They believe in true Islam being revived by their founder, Mirza Ghulam Ahmad, who they believe to be the Messiah and Mahdi (guided leader) promised in the scriptures. In addition, they believe him to be an ummati (follower) prophet under the authority of the Qur'an and Muhammad. They also believe in divinely appointed Khalifahs (successors) who have been leading their community after Ahmad.

Even within these lenses, there are further lenses linked to how Muslims express their views in their life and worship. An example of this are Sufis, many of whom observe particular types of practices

> **✓ Top tip**
>
> The meaning of the term 'imam' depends on the context. In Sunni Islam, it refers to a prayer leader ('imam'), while in Shi'a Islam it refers to the infallible (never wrong) leaders following the death of the Prophet Muhammad ('Imam').

> **✓ Top tip**
>
> Some Muslims see the Sunnah as part of the Hadith.

including ritualised devotional acts that help them remember and connect with Allah. Sufis are not usually seen as a separate sect but are found across different branches and denominations.

Where do Muslims look for guidance?

The primary source of guidance (also known as source of authority) for the majority of Muslims is the Qur'an. It is believed to be the complete and final revelation of Allah, guiding human beings on how to live their lives. Other sources include:

- **Sunnah** – actions of Muhammad
- **Hadith** – sayings of Muhammad
- **Sira** – biographies of Muhammad.

Muslims may see and understand sources of authority through one of the three 'lenses'.

Sunni lens	Shi'a lens	Ahmadiyya lens
In addition to the primary sources, Sunni Muslims also use: - **ijma'** – an agreement within the Muslim community about a particular matter that might not be directly covered by the Qur'an, Sunnah and Hadith - **qiyas** – analogical reasoning where Muslims reach judgements on new situations (e.g. mortgages, use of certain drugs) based on the primary sources - **ijtihad** – an intellectual struggle by an individual (e.g. scholar) to work out what is right and wrong when there is no obvious answer in the Qur'an, Sunnah and Hadith.	Shi'a Muslims believe that the Qur'an, Prophet Muhammad and Imams have equal importance, as the Imams are infallible (do not sin) and cannot teach anything other than the Qur'an. The Imams are from the Ahl al-Bayt (the Prophet's family), a pure line of descendants of the Prophet Muhammad.	For Ahmadiyya Muslims, the Qur'an is followed by Sunnah, then the Hadith and then the teachings of their founder, Mirza Ghulam Ahmad, and his Khalifahs, who are all believed to be guided by Allah.

> **🔑 Key words**
>
> **Twelver Shi'a Muslims** – group in Shi'a Islam who believe that there were 12 Imams after Muhammad's death. Twelvers believe that the twelfth Imam is still alive somewhere on Earth and will one day make himself known and bring equality to all
>
> **Shari'a** – linguistically means 'the way to water'; the Islamic legal system

Muslims also follow a legal code known as **shari'a**. The shari'a for each branch and denomination is based on the sources that they use, which shows that their understanding of what is and isn't allowed in Islam may sometimes differ.

Sources of authority

'You who believe, obey God and the Messenger, and those in authority among you. If you are in dispute over any matter, refer it to God and the Messenger, if you truly believe in God and the Last Day: that is better and fairer in the end.' (Surah 4:59)

'God has made a promise to those among you who believe and do good deeds: He will make them successors (Khalifahs) to the land, as He did those who came before them; He will establish the religion He has chosen for them; He will grant them security to replace their fear.' (Surah 24:55)

3.2 Core beliefs: Sunni Muslims

Aim

To explore the key beliefs in Sunni Islam

Starter

What do Muslims believe? Write down any three examples that you might already know.

Key words

Six Articles of Faith – the key beliefs of Sunni Muslims
Tawhid – the oneness of Allah

■ Muslim pilgrims gather to perform Hajj at the Haram Mosque in Makkah (Mecca), Saudi Arabia

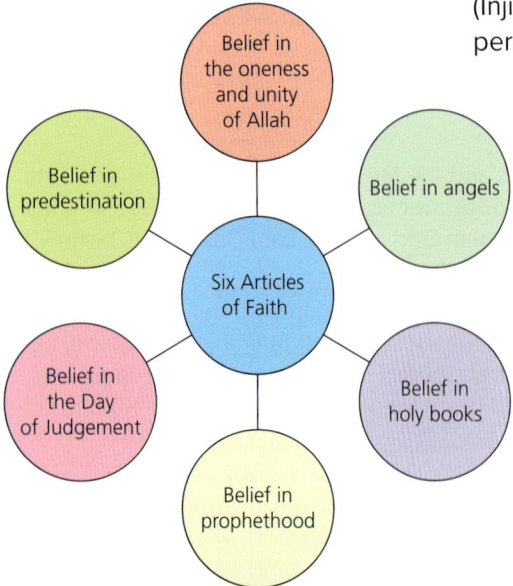

■ The Six Articles of Faith that Sunni Muslims believe in

Core beliefs

Many Muslims follow a set of core beliefs which make up the most important aspects of their religion. These are largely shared by the majority of Muslims, although there can be differences between them. This is the reason there are various groups in Islam. The two main groups are Sunni Muslims and Shi'a (also called Shi'ite) Muslims, who base their beliefs on the Qur'an, the Hadith and other sources of authority.

Six Articles of Faith

Sunni Muslims believe in the **Six Articles of Faith**. These are from the Qur'an and the Hadith:

1 **Belief in Allah as the one and only God** (see spread 3.6) – this is known as **Tawhid** and is the most important belief. Allah is the supreme being, creator and sustainer of the universe without whom nothing and nobody would exist.

2 **Belief in angels** (see spreads 3.12 and 3.13) – these are heavenly beings created to perform various tasks for Allah, for instance, delivering his messages to prophets and recording the actions of every individual. They act as intermediaries between Allah, the prophets and other people. Prominent angels include Jibril, Mika'il and Israfil.

3 **Belief in holy books** (see spreads 3.10 and 3.11) – these are sacred texts which contain Allah's messages and teachings for people. These texts offer guidance about how to live a moral life. Books that were originally revealed by Allah included the Scrolls (Sahifah), Torah (Tawrat), Psalms (Zabur) and Gospel (Injil), before the revelation of the Qur'an as the final and perfect scripture for humanity.

4 **Belief in the Prophets** (see spreads 3.7–3.9) – prophets are special people appointed by Allah to teach and guide others to the right path. More than 124,000 prophets have been sent to the world, including Adam, Ibrahim, Musa, Isa and Muhammad. Some prophets (also called messengers) were given a holy book.

5 **Belief in the Day of Judgement** (see spread 3.16) – this refers to an ultimate time in the afterlife when the dead will be resurrected and held accountable for their lives. Each individual will be rewarded with heaven or punished with hell.

6 **Belief in predestination** (see spread 3.14) – this relates to Allah having a master plan for everything, while also giving humans free will so that they take responsibility for their choices.

Each of the Six Articles of Faith is linked to one another. For instance, belief in holy books would not be possible without belief in Allah and the angels, who reveal Allah's commandments to humanity. For this, belief in prophets is also essential as they are the ones who receive Allah's revelations directly. When these teachings are passed on to other people, they can decide to obey Allah or not; whatever they choose, they will be answerable to it on the Day of Judgement.

Importance of the Six Articles of Faith

The core beliefs have great importance to Sunni Muslims because:

- Recognising Allah as the creator encourages them to be grateful for the life they have been granted and to express thanks through prayer. This is often done in Salah (prayer, also spelt 'Salat' – see page 117).
- By obeying Allah and the Prophet Muhammad, they will remain on the right path and earn the pleasure of Allah. This will be rewarded in the afterlife with a place in heaven.
- They can set an example to others and inspire them to live a good life in accordance with the will of Allah and the Sunnah of the Prophet Muhammad. This will create more peace in society.

Sources of authority

'You who believe, believe in God and His Messenger and in the scripture He sent down to His Messenger, as well as what He sent down before. Anyone who does not believe in God, His angels, His Scriptures, His messengers, and the Last Day has gone far, far astray.' (Surah 4:136)

'While we were one day sitting with the messenger of Allah, there appeared before us a man dressed in extremely white clothes and with very black hair. No traces of travel were visible on him, and none of us knew him. He sat down close by the Prophet … [and] he went on to say, "Inform me about faith." The messenger of Allah answered, "It is that you believe in Allah, and his angels, and his books, and his messengers, and in the Last Day, and in the decree of Allah" … [Later,] the man went off. I waited a while, and then the messenger of Allah said, "Umar, do you know who that questioner was? … That was Jibril (Gabriel). He came to teach you your religion."' (Hadith, Sahih Muslim, Kitab al-Iman 1:4)

Analyse and evaluate

Are all Six Articles of Faith equally important?

Yes	No
All six Articles are mentioned in the Qur'an and the Hadith and so are equally important.	Holy books before the Qur'an are not reliable, so this belief is not as important as the other articles.
Belief in all Six Articles of Faith is compulsory to be a Sunni Muslim, therefore, each one is equally important. Belief is incomplete without them.	Without holy books, there would be no record of the teachings Allah gave to prophets through the angels, therefore, no way of knowing right or wrong, and so holy books are more important.

Some Sunni Muslims may consider particular Articles to have more importance and relevance in their lives, while others treat all as having equal value.

Activities

Review
1. What are the two main groups in Islam?
2. Identify any three of the Six Articles of Faith.

Develop
3. Summarise the Hadith of Jibril (Gabriel) (Sahih Muslim, Kitab al-Iman 1:4) in your own words.

Link
4. Explain how Muslims understand the importance of the core beliefs.

Debate
5. 'It is difficult to follow some of the Articles of Faith today.' To what extent is this conclusion fair? Discuss and note down reasons for and against this view.

Stretch
6. Research these additional Sunni Muslim sources of authority: ijma', qiyas, ijtihad.

3.3 Core beliefs: Shi'a Muslims

Aim

To explore the key beliefs in Shi'a Islam

Starter

What do you already know about Shi'a Muslims? Write down any three points.

Top tip

The 'Day of Resurrection' and 'Day of Judgement' are two ways of describing the same event in the afterlife when every person will be raised and judged by Allah.

Key word

'Usul ad-Din – 'Principles of Faith'; the key beliefs of Shi'a Muslims

Sources of authority

'We made all of them leaders, guiding others by Our command, and We inspired them to do good works, to keep up the prayer, and to give alms: they were Our true worshippers.' (Surah 21:73)

'Today I have perfected your religion for you, completed My blessing upon you, and chosen as your religion *islam* [total devotion to God].' (Surah 5:3)

'I leave you two weighty things. If you stick to both you will never go astray after me: the Book of Allah, and my progeny (Ahl al-Bayt).' (Hadith al-Thaqalayn)

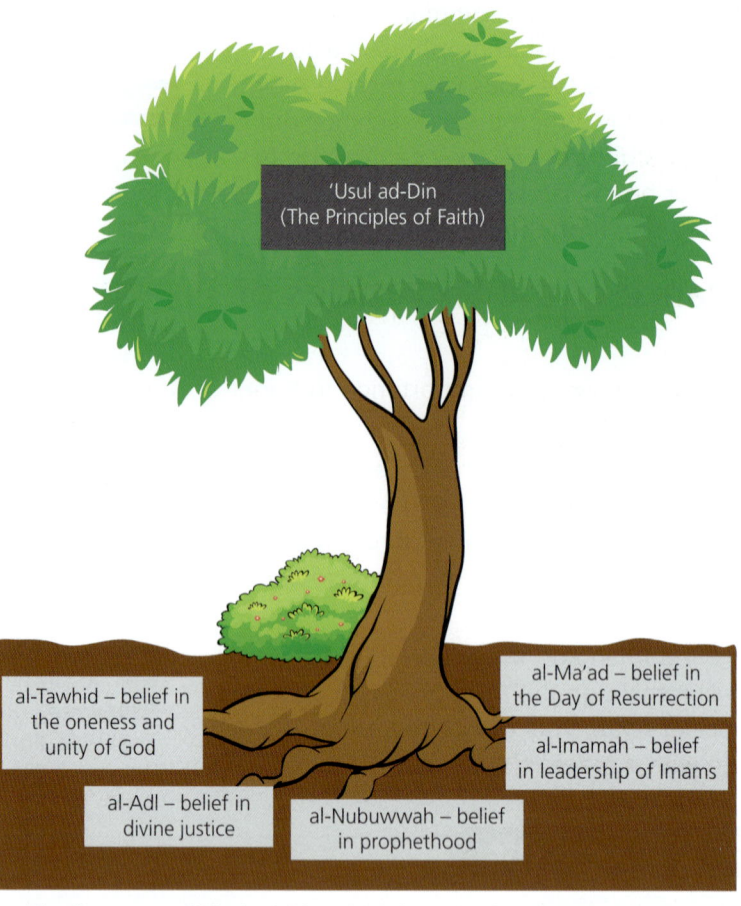

- The five roots of 'Usul ad-Din, which form the foundation of Shi'a Muslim beliefs

Core beliefs

Shi'a Muslims make up the second largest group in Islam. Shi'a Muslims follow a set of core beliefs called the five roots of **'Usul ad-Din** (Principles of Faith).

Five roots of 'Usul ad-Din

The five roots of 'Usul ad-Din are based on the Qur'an, the Hadith and teachings of early Shi'a Muslim leaders and scholars who are seen to be best placed to understand the beliefs. The five roots are:

1. **Belief in the oneness and unity of God (al-Tawhid)** – Allah is perfect, unique, indivisible, has no equals and possesses infinite power and knowledge (see spread 3.6).

2. **Belief in divine justice (al-Adl)** – Allah is just (fair) and possesses perfect wisdom. Justice is the framework within which Allah acts, and it is completely against his nature to be unjust. Allah will bring about justice in the afterlife.

3. **Belief in prophethood (al-Nubuwwah)** – Allah appointed a long chain of prophets and messengers from Adam to Muhammad who appeared in various places of the world during different points in history to pass on Allah's guidance to people (see spreads 3.7–3.9).

The shrine of one of the infallible Imams, Imam Hussein, in Karbala, Iraq

4 **Belief in Imams (Al-Imamah)** – after Muhammad's death, according to Twelver Shi'as, Allah appointed 12 pure and infallible Imams to guide Muslims. These Imams are members of the Ahl al-Bayt (the Prophet's family).

5 **Belief in the Day of Resurrection (al-Ma'ad)** – this is a time of reckoning in the afterlife when Allah will decide the fate of all people. Allah will punish the evil and reward the good.

Importance of the five roots of 'Usul ad-Din for Shi'a Muslims

These beliefs have utmost importance to Shi'a Muslims because by following them:

- They are following Allah, the Prophet Muhammad and the Imams. These are the three central authorities for Shi'a Muslims.
- They will stay rightly guided and live the life Allah wills. This is known through the Qur'an, the Hadith and the teachings of early Shi'a leaders.
- They will be rewarded by Allah for making the right choices in life. This will lead them to heaven.
- They can be models of excellent conduct, reflecting some of the qualities of the Imams who inspire Shi'a Muslims.

Each of the five roots is linked to one another. For instance, belief in divine justice and belief in the leadership of Imams would not be possible without faith in Allah. This is because without Allah, there would be no justice, nor would there be any Imams.

Analyse and evaluate

Are all of the five roots of 'Usul ad-Din equally relevant?

Yes	No
Each links to the others. For example, Allah has sent prophets (al-Nubuwwah) who teach about the afterlife (al-Ma'ad).	Everything Muslims do in this life is in preparation for the afterlife, therefore, al-Ma'ad is the most relevant.
Shi'a scholars have worked hard to establish the five roots as the most important aspects of faith.	Without al-Tawhid, the other roots would not be possible, therefore al-Tawhid is the most relevant.
Some Shi'a Muslims may consider particular roots to have more relevance in their lives, while others treat all five roots as having the same worth.	

Activities

Review

1. Identify three of the five roots of 'Usul ad-Din.
2. What are they based on?

Develop

3. Why is the Hadith al-Thaqalayn important to Shi'a Muslims?

Link

4. Which of the five roots of 'Usul al-Din are similar and which are different to the Sunni Six Articles of Faith?

Debate

5. 'The Ahl al-Bayt are the best people to be Imams.' To what extent is this conclusion fair? Discuss and note down reasons for and against this view.

Stretch

6. Look at Surah 5:3. How and why do Shi'a Muslims believe it refers to Ali?

3.4 Core beliefs: comparing Sunni and Shi'a Muslims

Aim
To explore similarities and differences between Sunni and Shi'a Islam

Starter
Why are there different groups within the same religion? Write down two possible reasons.

Top tip
Two ways that Shi'a Islam differs from Sunni Islam are about beliefs regarding justice and imamate. In Shi'a Islam, Allah can only operate within the boundaries of justice, and the Imams are seen as an extension of Allah's authority and are respected as much as the Prophet Muhammad. These beliefs are not shared by Sunni Muslims.

Key word
Khalifah (Caliph) – successor or leader after the Prophet Muhammad; representative of Allah on Earth

Top tip
Shi'a Muslims also believe in angels and holy books, but these are not included in the 'Usul ad-Din. Similarly, Sunni Muslims believe in divine justice but consider this part of the oneness of Allah.

Core beliefs

Sunni and Shi'a Muslims share many of the same key beliefs, but there are some differences too.

Six Articles of Faith (Sunni Muslims)
- Belief in angels
- Belief in predestination
- Belief in holy books

Shared
- Belief in the oneness and unity of Allah
- Belief in prophethood
- Belief in the Day of Judgement

Five roots of 'Usul ad-Din (Shi'a Muslims)
- Belief in divine justice
- Belief in the leadership of Imams

■ Similarities and differences between the Six Articles of Faith (Sunni Islam) and the five roots of 'Usul ad-Din (Shi'a Islam)

Why are there differences between Sunni and Shi'a Muslims?

After the death of the Prophet Muhammad, his followers disagreed about who should lead the Muslim community:

- The majority accepted the choice of Abu Bakr, the Prophet's father-in-law, who became known as the first Rightly Guided **Khalifah**. This group of people came to be known as Sunni Muslims.
- Others believed that Ali, the Prophet's son-in-law, should have been given authority and that all leaders should be from the Ahl al-Bayt (the Prophet's family), such as Ali, who was raised in the Prophet's house. Those who hold this view are known as Shi'a Muslims.

Disagreements about leadership eventually led to the early Muslim community splitting and the two groups developing their own beliefs and understanding about Islam.

Sources of authority

'If I were to take a Khalil (friend) other than my Lord, I would have taken Abu Bakr as such.' (Hadith, Sahih Bukhari)

'Abu Bakr is the best among people except if a prophet is born.' (Hadith)

'Whoever took me as his mawla [authority, guide], Ali is his mawla.' (Hadith)

'God wishes to keep uncleanness away from you, people of the [Prophet's] House, and to purify you thoroughly.' (Surah 33:33)

✓ Top tip

For Sunni Muslims, the Qur'an is the most important source of authority and wisdom because it is the direct word of Allah. This is followed by the Hadith, which are the words of the Prophet. For Shi'a Muslims, the Qur'an, Prophet Muhammad and Ahl al-Bayt are equally important as the Ahl al-Bayt are pure and sinless, and are able to follow the teachings of the Qur'an perfectly.

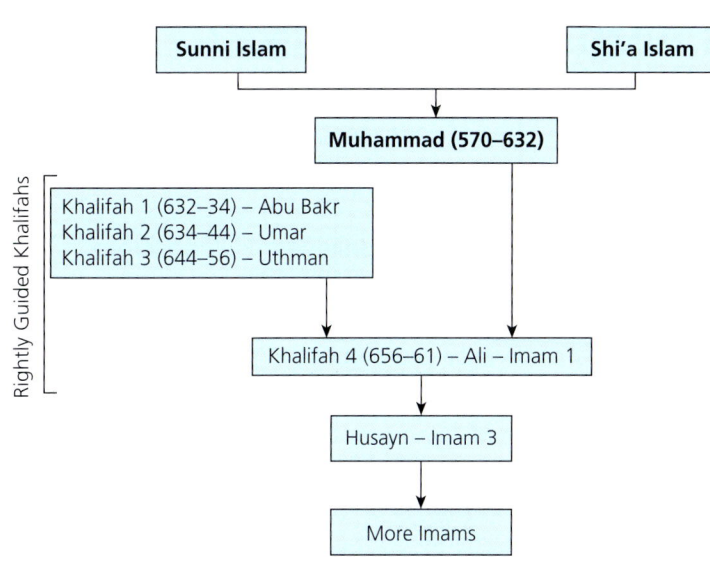

```
Sunni Islam        Shi'a Islam
         ↓           ↓
        Muhammad (570–632)
         ↓
Rightly Guided Khalifahs:
  Khalifah 1 (632–34) – Abu Bakr
  Khalifah 2 (634–44) – Umar
  Khalifah 3 (644–56) – Uthman
         ↓
  Khalifah 4 (656–61) – Ali – Imam 1
         ↓
  Husayn – Imam 3
         ↓
  More Imams
```

■ Sunni and Shi'a Muslims believe in different leaders after the Prophet Muhammad, with Sunnis calling theirs Khalifahs and Shi'as calling theirs Imams

Issues related to core beliefs in Sunni Islam and Shi'a Islam

Shi'a Muslims believe that although Ali believed himself to be Muhammad's legitimate successor, for the sake of maintaining unity, he pledged loyalty to the first three Khalifahs – Abu Bakr, Umar and Uthman.

Sunni Muslims argue that the Qur'an instructs believers to be true to their promises (Surah 17:34) and that Ali would have offered his allegiance to the three before him sincerely. He supported them fully and offered prayers with them, therefore this is seen as evidence that Ali accepted them as Khalifahs.

Analyse and evaluate

Are Muslims united?

Yes	No
The basic beliefs of all Muslims, such as Tawhid, holy books and the Day of Judgement, are the same.	Only Shi'a Muslims believe in the centrality of divine justice (al-Adl) and belief in the leadership of Imams (al-Imamah).
Muslims have read the same Qur'an for centuries and follow the teachings of the Prophet Muhammad.	Sunni and Shi'a Muslims do not believe in Ahmadiyya Muslim leaders as sources of authority.
Muslims will recognise that although there are many commonalities between them, such as their acceptance of the same primary sources like the Qur'an and the Hadith, they will also refer to different sources to support their beliefs.	

Activities

Review

1. Identify three beliefs that are shared by Muslims.
2. Which two beliefs are not the same for different Muslims?

Develop

3. How is the Shi'a Islam belief in divine justice (al-Adl) and belief in the leadership of Imams (al-Imamah) different from Sunni Islam?

Link

4. Are the reasons why divisions occurred in Christianity and Islam the same or different?

Debate

5. 'There are more similarities than differences between different Muslims.' To what extent is this conclusion fair? Discuss and note down reasons for and against this view.

Stretch

6. Are the sources of wisdom and authority used to support Sunni and Shi'a arguments contradictory? Justify your answer.

3.5 The nature of Allah: names of Allah

Aim

To explore the nature of Allah and his names as understood by different Muslims

Starter

What is God like? Write down three ideas religious believers may have about a divine being.

Key words

Merciful – compassionate
Just – fair

Who is Allah? What is he like?

Belief in Allah is central in Islam. Muslims believe Allah is timeless and beyond all space. He has always existed. He created everything and is eternal. He also acts in the world and wants to have a relationship with humanity.

Allah is not a physical being. Muslims believe it is impossible to picture him and most say that any attempt to depict him is disrespectful, and therefore prohibit this. This contrasts with other faiths in which images of divinity are common.

Instead of pictures, Muslims use language and art to try to make sense of Allah. Descriptions of Allah appear frequently in the Qur'an and Hadith. There are 99 attributes or 'beautiful names' of Allah. Some of these are captured in calligraphy in mosques. The Qur'an and Hadith collectively contain more than 100 characteristics of Allah. Some of these include:

Characteristic	Explanation
Al-Wahid	Allah is described as al-Wahid which means the One who is unique and nothing can compare to him. Belief in the oneness of Allah is at the core of Islam and encompasses all other descriptions. Muslims believe all religions originally had Tawhid at their heart.
Merciful	Allah is described as merciful or compassionate. His kindness knows no limits. One of the ways Allah's mercy is demonstrated is through giving guidance to humankind. Teaching people what is right and wrong helps them navigate their way through life in order to earn Allah's pleasure. The words 'In the name of God, the Lord of Mercy, the Giver of Mercy' (known as 'tasmiyyah') appear in the Qur'an 114 times, making it one of the most recited characteristics of Allah in Qur'anic readings and prayer.
Omnipotent	Muslims believe that Allah is omnipotent. This means that he has the power to create everything from nothing and can do as he wills, including performing miracles. He is the only authority in the universe and has control over everything. Omnipotence is also shown through Allah's role as creator and judge. He has the right to hold humans to account in the afterlife and send them to heaven or hell.
Benevolent	Several of the 99 names of Allah highlight his loving and benevolent nature. These include al-Ghaffar (the Most Forgiving), al-Wahhab (the Giver of Gifts), al-Razzaq (the Provider of Sustenance), al-Tawwab (the Acceptor of Repentance) and al-Afuww (the Pardoner). He answers people's prayers and gives guidance as he wants everyone to live a peaceful life.
Fair and Just	As Allah is omniscient (all-seeing) and knows everything, he is fair and just in dealing with humans. Divine justice (al-Adl) is one of the five roots of 'Usul ad-Din in Shi'a Islam. God will not put an impossible burden on anyone, because he is fair to all. Allah decides the fate of people on the Day of Judgement by weighing up their good and bad deeds. This offers comfort to Muslims who know that if justice is not experienced in this life, it will be in the next.
Transcendent and Immanent	Muslims believe that Allah is both far and near. One belief is that he is transcendent, which means that he is above and beyond creation. This links to his omnipotence. Another belief is that he is immanent which means that Allah acts within the universe and remains close to humans, so that their relationship is more personal. This links to his benevolence. This characteristic demonstrates Allah's concern with humankind and intervention when he wills.

Common and divergent attitudes

While all Muslims declare belief in Allah and his attributes, there are different understandings about some aspects of his nature. Sunni and Shi'a Muslims believe that after the revelation of the Qur'an and the death of the Prophet Muhammad, there is no need for Allah to communicate to human beings, as Islam has been completed. In contrast, Ahmadiyya Muslims believe that all of Allah's characteristics are eternally active, therefore he continues to speak to people that he chooses. Whatever is revealed can only be a reminder of what is in the Qur'an and Hadith. This shows that Allah is a living God and that Islam is a living religion.

Muslim worldviews

Many Sunni Muslims use prayer beads to offer 'tasbih' or glorification of Allah's characteristics. There are 99 beads which correspond to the 99 names of Allah.

Twelver Shi'a Muslims believe that Allah appointed all 12 Imams to lead the Muslim community after the death of the Prophet Muhammad. As they speak on behalf of Allah, they cannot make any mistakes. This makes them infallible, and they have divine protection. They are also responsible for protecting belief in oneness (al-Tawhid).

Ahmadiyya Muslims believe that as Allah's attributes are eternal, he continues to communicate to human beings and grant them revelation if he wills.

Top tip
Sometimes when Muslims pray, they address Allah by the attributes that are relevant to what is being prayed for. For instance, someone with financial worries may focus on Allah's attribute of being the provider.

Sources of authority
'We created man – We know what his soul whispers to him: We are closer to him than his jugular vein.' (Surah 50:16)

'Ask forgiveness from your Lord, and turn to him in repentance: my Lord is merciful and most loving.' (Surah 11:90)

'My mercy embraces all things.' (Surah 7:156)

Analyse and evaluate

Is describing Allah as 'omnipotent' the best way to understand him?	
Yes	No
Allah's power created everything in the first place.	There are multiple descriptions of Allah which all help in our understanding of him.
One meaning of Islam is 'submission' so describing Allah as all-powerful and to whom Muslims must submit accords with this belief.	The Qur'an teaches that Allah's mercy 'embraces all things', therefore this is the best way of making sense of Allah.
Many Muslims believe that just because Allah is omnipotent does not mean humans can fully grasp his nature. Language is limited, therefore all descriptions of Allah can be seen to be inadequate.	

Activities

Review
1. Identify any three attributes of Allah.
2. Why are images of Allah forbidden by many Muslims?

Develop
3. Read Surah 2:255, known as Ayat al-Kursi (the 'Throne verse'). Which divine attributes can you find?

Link
4. Why does the oneness of Allah come first in the list of core beliefs?

Debate
5. 'The most important divine attribute is merciful.' To what extent is this conclusion fair? Discuss and note down reasons for and against this view.

Stretch
6. Make a list of the attributes of Allah which 1) belong only to Allah and are separate from his creation, and 2) resemble or are shared in some way by other beings.

3.6 The nature of Allah: Tawhid and shirk

Aim
To explore the importance of Tawhid and the concept of shirk as understood by different Muslims

Starter
Does it matter if a person believes in one God or many gods? Share your thoughts with a partner.

Key words
Tawhid – oneness of Allah
Shirk – setting up equals to or worshipping anyone other than Allah

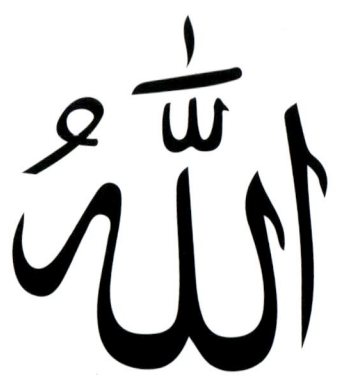

■ The name of Allah in Arabic

■ Muslims focus on one God – Allah – when they worship

The meaning of Tawhid

Tawhid means 'oneness' and is the belief that Allah is unique, indivisible and without any partner. The word 'Allah' is a combination of the Arabic words 'Al' (The) and 'Ilah' (God), therefore, it means 'The God'. People should worship Allah only. He is the originator of the universe, is self-sustaining and does not need to be supported by others. Whatever their needs, Muslims must turn to Allah and trust in him alone. This shows that Islam is a monotheistic faith.

The centrality of Tawhid in Muslim belief is captured in the first pillar of Islam, the Shahadah (Islamic declaration of faith, see spread 4.5), which requires Muslims to say: 'I bear witness that there is none worthy of worship except Allah alone and he has no partner.' Nothing and nobody can be more important than Allah, including family, friends, wealth and work.

Shi'a Muslims believe that there is a close relationship between Tawhid and imamate. This is because:

- Allah continued to choose people for guidance after the Prophet Muhammad
- Allah decides who is the Imam, so it is always the right person who is chosen
- the Imams speak on Allah's behalf so do not make any mistakes
- obedience to Allah and the Imams has equal importance because the Imams can never contradict Allah.

The meaning of shirk

Shirk is the opposite of Tawhid. Shirk includes worshipping statues or putting one's trust in anything or anyone except Allah. Belief in any other divine being, for example, idols, is shirk, which is the opposite of Tawhid and the greatest sin in Islam.

The implications of Tawhid and shirk for polytheism and Christianity

The Qur'an challenges polytheism (belief in multiple deities) and also the Christian concept of the Trinity as they are opposed to Tawhid. It also states that Allah will not forgive shirk. Many Muslims believe that this refers only to this life, because the Qur'an elsewhere states that all sins are forgiven by Allah and a person has a chance to repent of their sins before they leave this world.

Issues related to the nature of Allah

- **Allah's role as creator and judge demonstrate his omnipotence:** Muslims believe there is a close link between these attributes. Having all power ensures that Allah is able to create everything from nothing, including the universe and human life, and that he has ultimate authority in deciding the fate of every person in the afterlife. Some ask why Allah allows suffering if he is omnipotent. Muslims respond by saying that human beings need to go through tests in life to prove their worth, and some may deserve to be punished for their sins.

- **Allah's concern with humankind and intervention are evidence of his immanence:** Muslims believe that Allah's nearness to people is shown through his care for every individual and his 'stepping in' on Earth to help people, for example, through miracles, is a sign of his existence. Some criticise this belief as they question why Allah intervenes in some events and not others. Muslims respond by saying that Allah is omniscient, wise and knows when to exercise intervention.

- **Allah's guidance to humankind shows his merciful nature:** Muslims believe that Allah demonstrates his compassion for people by giving them teachings on how to live their lives in order for them to please him and earn a place in heaven. Others disagree with this belief and say that humans only need their ability to reason to guide them in life. Muslims would argue that this ability is limited and revelation is needed from Allah.

Sources of authority

'Say, "He is God the One, God the eternal. He begot no one nor was He begotten. No one is comparable to Him."' (Surah 112:1–4)

'We sent a messenger to every community, saying, "Worship God and shun false gods."' (Surah 16:36)

'My servants who have harmed yourselves by your own excess, do not despair of God's mercy. God forgives all sins: He is truly the Most Forgiving, the Most Merciful' (Surah 39:53)

Analyse and evaluate

Can Muslims make sense of Allah?

Yes	No
The 99 names of Allah help Muslims to understand something of his attributes.	The transcendent nature of Allah means that he is above and beyond understanding.
As Allah wants to have a relationship with humanity, he must make himself comprehendible to everyone.	Without pictorial representations of Allah, it is difficult to know enough about him.
Many Muslims believe that although some of Allah's attributes are relatable and can be demonstrated by humans to an extent (e.g. forgiving), it is impossible to fully grasp his nature.	

Activities

Review
1. Summarise Muslim understandings of Tawhid in 20–30 words.
2. What is shirk?

Develop
3. Explain the key points in Surah 112:1–4.

Link
4. What is the link between Tawhid and the other names of Allah?

Debate
5. 'There are more serious sins than shirk.' To what extent is this conclusion fair? Discuss and note down reasons for and against this view.

Stretch
6. Read Surah 1 of the Qur'an. It is called 'The Opening'. Select any two verses from it that show the importance of Tawhid.

3.7 Prophethood: the role and importance of the prophets

Aim
To examine Muslim beliefs about the role and importance of the prophets

Starter
How should Allah's messages be passed on to humans? Suggest up to three ways.

Key words
Risalah – 'message', referring to belief in prophets and messengers
Al-Nubuwwah – prophethood
Prophet – a person chosen by Allah to teach humans what is right and wrong

What is prophethood?
Muslims believe Allah has chosen special individuals to teach humanity about the right way to live. These people are called prophets and messengers. **Risalah** is the name given to how Allah communicates with humans.

Importance of prophethood and the prophets
Belief in prophethood is counted as one of the Six Articles of Faith (risalah) for Sunni Muslims and one of the five roots of 'Usul ad-Din (**al-Nubuwwah**) for Shi'a Muslims. It is important because:

- Allah has spoken to many prophets in the past and Muslims are required to follow their teachings
- the **prophets** bring knowledge from Allah to humanity
- societies need to be reformed according to the will and laws of Allah
- the prophets demonstrated great qualities and set an example of how to live.

Roles of the prophets
The roles of the prophets include the following:

Diagram showing Roles of the prophets: Be moral examples, Restore and strengthen belief in Tawhid, Purify people, Establish justice, Unite humanity

■ The roles of the prophets

■ Mirza Ghulam Ahmad, founder of the Ahmadiyya Muslim Community, who his followers believe was a prophet sent by Allah without a new law, and who came under the authority of the Qur'an and the Prophet Muhammad

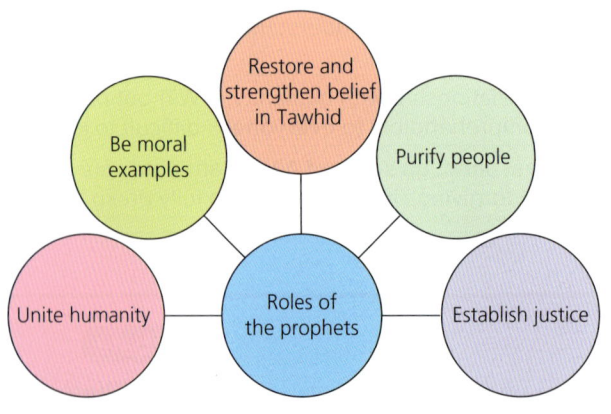

Muhammad said that Allah has sent 124,000 prophets to the world. Muslims must believe in all of them. Each prophet passes on messages from Allah to people living in their particular time and location. Many of these messages have been recorded in ancient scriptures (holy books or kutub).

Top tip

Whenever Muslims refer to Muhammad they say or write 'peace and blessings of Allah be upon him' (PBUH) as an expression of respect. They also say or write 'peace be upon him' after the name of any other prophet.

Key words

Rasul – messenger
Nabi – prophet

Sources of authority

'It is not granted to any mortal that God should speak to him except through revelation or from behind a veil, or by sending a messenger to reveal by His command what he will: He is exalted and wise.' (Surah 42:51)

The prophets also:
- have limited knowledge and therefore cannot know everything – only Allah is omniscient (all-knowing)
- can make mistakes but cannot commit sins
- are mortal and cannot return from the dead.

Shi'a Muslims, like the Twelver Shi'as, believe that their Imams are infallible – they are pure and do not have any faults. However, they are not considered prophets. Prophets bring revelation while the Imams protect it. This includes interpreting Allah's teachings.

Rasul and nabi

There is disagreement among Muslims about whether there is a difference between a **rasul** (messenger) and a **nabi** (prophet). According to some Muslims:

- a rasul is someone who is given a new message or law to replace an earlier one, when previous guidance has become unreliable or irrelevant because circumstances have changed
- a nabi is someone who passes on the same teachings given to a previous rasul to remind people of Allah's will.

Other Muslims believe that there is no difference between a rasul and a nabi as they are two roles given to all prophets. Every rasul is a nabi, and every nabi is a rasul.

Analyse and evaluate

Is a nabi different to a rasul?

Yes	No
A rasul is given a new religious law (shari'a) while a nabi continues a previous one.	Prophets can have multiple descriptions – nabi and rasul are two aspects of the same role of receiving a divine message and passing it on.
Rasuul and nabis are mentioned separately in the Qur'an.	Muslims must believe in all prophets whether they are called rasuul or nabis.
While some Muslims consider there to be a difference between the two, other Muslims believe that they are interchangeable terms – every nabi is also a rasul, and vice-versa.	

Activities

Review
1. Identify three roles of the prophets.
2. How are nabi and rasul defined?

Develop
3. Why might Allah choose people who do not commit sins to be prophets?

Link
4. Why is prophethood central to both Sunni and Shi'a core beliefs?

Debate
5. 'The world is in need of more prophets.' To what extent is this conclusion fair? Discuss and note down reasons for and against this view.

Stretch
6. Make a list of how the prophets and the 12 Imams (Shi'a) are similar and different.

3.8 Prophethood: prophets before Muhammad

Aim

To examine Muslim beliefs about some prophets before Muhammad's prophethood

Starter

Write the names of prophets who have been mentioned in the Hebrew Bible and New Testament.

Key word

Kaaba – cube-shaped building, first house of Allah in Makkah (Mecca)

The Qur'an mentions the names of at least 25 prophets. Examples include:

Adam

Adam is believed to be the first prophet and is called Allah's Khalifah. He was made of dust mixed with water to form clay that was shaped into a human being. Allah blew life into Adam and made him in his own image. This is often understood to mean that Adam, like other humans, was created with the ability to reflect some divine attributes, such as compassion.

Most Muslims believe Adam to be the first man but others say he was part of the first civilisation of human beings. Adam lived with his wife Hawwa (Eve) in a beautiful garden. Both were given reason (the ability to think about their actions) and free will (the freedom to make decisions). They were commanded to keep away from a 'tree' which represented evil but approached it after being deceived by Satan. Muslims believe Adam simply made a mistake, sought forgiveness and was honoured with Allah's mercy. This teaches Muslims that their faults can also be overlooked by Allah if they repent.

Ibrahim (Abraham)

Ibrahim is called the 'father of the prophets' and Allah's 'friend'. He was a hanif (inclined to God). One meaning of this is that he was a believer in Tawhid and for this reason he taught people to turn away from idolatry (worshipping idols). He saw a dream in which he was sacrificing his son Isma'il (Ishmael) and he asked for Isma'il's interpretation. Both agreed that this is what Allah wanted. Allah was testing Ibrahim's devotion and commanded that an animal be killed instead as a symbol of sacrifice. For this reason, Ibrahim is presented as an example of obedience. Ibrahim was given the Sahifah (Scrolls), one of the earliest known divine texts.

Isma'il (Ishmael)

Isma'il, Ibrahim's first son, like his father, demonstrated firm faith. Isma'il assisted Ibrahim with the rebuilding of the **Kaaba** after it had become disused. Muslims remember Ibrahim, Isma'il and their family and pray for them in their daily prayers.

Some Muslims emphasise that because Muhammad descended from the family of Ibrahim and Isma'il, special status should be given to Muhammad's family as leaders in Islam. For Shi'a Muslims, all Imams should be able to trace their lineage from this family. Others say that it is piety, not blood, that is the most important quality to have in any leader.

Do not worship any other gods
Do not make any idols
Do not misuse God's name
Keep the Sabbath holy

Honour your father and mother
Do not murder
Do not commit adultery
Do not steal
Do not lie
Do not covet

- The Ten Commandments given to Musa

Sources of authority

'We make no distinction between any of His messengers.' (Surah 2:285)

Musa (Moses)

Musa is the main prophet of Judaism. He freed the Israelites from slavery under the harsh rule of the Fir'awn (Pharaoh) in Egypt. Musa performed many miracles, like the parting of the seas to allow the Israelites to escape. Some Muslims understand some miracle accounts literally as breaking the laws of nature, as Allah can do as he wills. Others say that miracles only seem to go against them and actually occur within them. Musa was given the Tawrat (Torah) including the Ten Commandments.

Musa's life inspires Muslims to stand for justice and to oppose oppression.

Dawud (David)

Dawud is one of the Israelite prophets after Musa. He was born in 1040BCE at a time when there were conflicts between Jewish tribes and the Philistines. David was a great warrior and when he later became King of Israel, the Philistines, led by Jalut (Goliath), attacked the Israelites. Jalut's forces were much bigger but could not overcome Dawud's army because he was helped by Allah. The Tawrat mentions how Dawud struck Jalut down with a slingshot and then killed him with his sword. He was given the Zabur (Psalms) containing songs, prayers and poems inspired by Allah. Dawud's story provides strength to Muslims that they, too, can overcome powerful enemies if they are required to face them.

Isa (Jesus)

Isa is famous for many miracles, including creating birds out of clay and bringing the dead back to life, although many Muslims understand these acts to have a symbolic meaning (for example, bringing people out of darkness and into light). Sunni and Shi'a Muslims believe that Isa was not put on the cross, only a lookalike was, that Isa was taken up to heaven alive to return before the end of the world and that this will be one of the signs of the Day of Judgement.

Ahmadiyya Muslims believe that Isa survived the attempted crucifixion, left his country and reached as far as India, where he died naturally, and that the community's founder, Mirza Ghulam Ahmad, was the spiritual second coming of Isa appointed by Allah to restore the original teachings of Islam.

Isa was given the Injil (the Gospel). He is remembered by Muslims for his humility and trust in Allah.

Analyse and evaluate

| Will Isa return to Earth near the Day of Judgement? ||
Yes	No
The Qur'an speaks of Isa having been spared miraculously and taken to Allah.	According to the Qur'an, all prophets have passed away.
Hadiths speak of Isa coming back near the end of time to defeat evil.	Isa's return is a metaphorical expression and means that someone similar to Isa will be born in the ummah (worldwide community of Muslims).

Most Muslims, like Sunni and Shi'a, believe that Isa remains physically alive and will come to Earth again near the Day of Judgement with the Imam Mahdi (guided leader) to restore justice and to defeat the Antichrist. Others, like Ahmadiyya Muslims, believe that Isa has passed away and so cannot return. Instead, a messiah and also Mahdi named Mirza Ghulam Ahmad was chosen by Allah to lead a spiritual battle against evil.

Activities

Review

1. Name any three prophets before Muhammad.
2. Explain the need for prophets in Islam.

Develop

3. Many Muslim parents name their children after prophets. What might be the reasons for this?

Link

4. How can sending so many prophets be seen as part of the benevolence of Allah?

Debate

5. 'Muslims can learn more from some prophets than others.' To what extent is this conclusion fair? Discuss and note down reasons for and against this view.

Stretch

6. Find out about the lives and teachings of three other prophets: Nuh (Noah), Lut (Lot) and Yusuf (Joseph).

3.9 Prophethood: Prophet Muhammad

Aim

To examine Muslim beliefs about the Prophet Muhammad

Starter

Make a list of five qualities that makes someone a good leader.

Top tip

CE stands for the Common Era and is often used instead of AD.

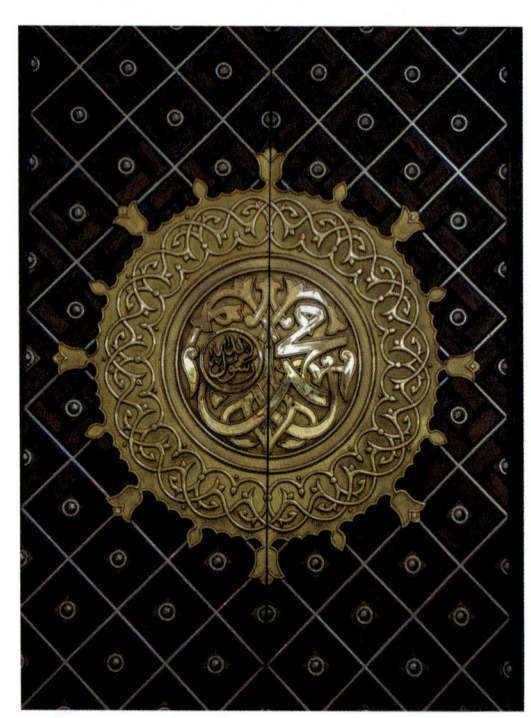

■ 'Muhammad the Messenger of God' inscribed on the gates of the Prophet's Mosque in Madinah (Medina), Saudi Arabia

Key word

Laylat al-Qadr – Night of Power

Muhammad's background

Muhammad was born in Makkah (Mecca), Arabia, in either 570 or 571CE. His name means 'most praiseworthy.' After having lost both his parents by the age of six, he was raised by his grandfather and then by his uncle, whom he accompanied on various trading trips to other countries for several years. Muhammad worked as a shepherd and then managed caravans – groups of merchants travelling together. He developed a reputation as an honest and successful trader. His integrity was well known by the people of Makkah, who gave him the titles 'al-Amin' (the Trustworthy) and 'al-Sadiq' (the Truthful).

He was employed by Khadija, a wealthy businesswoman who later sent him a marriage proposal. They married and had a loving and happy marriage. Together they had six children.

Laylat al-Qadr

There were many things happening in society that Muhammad disapproved of. This included gender inequality, poverty and the worship of idols in and around the Kaaba, the centre of pilgrimage. Being quiet and reflective, he often visited a nearby cave, Hira, to spend time in solitude and in the remembrance of Allah. During one of these retreats at night he had a powerful religious experience. He received a visit from the angel Jibril telling him that he had been chosen as a prophet for the purpose of conveying the message of Tawhid and teaching good morals. This was the moment that the Qur'an began to be revealed and is known as **Laylat al-Qadr** (Night of Power).

Muhammad's struggles and successes

Initially, very few people accepted him as a prophet. Muhammad and his community of followers (known as Muslims) were persecuted by the leaders of Makkah (Mecca), who disagreed with his teachings about God, peace and justice. This eventually led to him and the other Muslims to migrate to a city called Madinah (Medina), where they lived in relative safety. The number of Muslims increased dramatically. They were still targeted by those who wanted to end the new religion, and Muslims had to fight a number of battles in self-defence (see spread 4.16). Despite being outnumbered, they succeeded and were able to return to Makkah. By the time of Muhammad's death, almost the entire population of Makkah had become Muslim.

'Seal of the prophets'

The Qur'an refers to Muhammad as the 'seal of the prophets' (Surah 33:40). This is because he was given the final scripture and shari'a that was never to change or be replaced. Muhammad was the only prophet to have been given a universal message for all times. As 'seal of the prophets', the different qualities of all other prophets (for example, the justice of Musa and the patience of Isa) were found in Muhammad too.

A good prophet

Muhammad is unique among all prophets and messengers. The difficulties that he faced and the way he overcame them by relying on Allah provide Muslims with inspiration and make him the perfect example of how to live an ideal Muslim life. His Sunnah and the Hadith are the most important sources of authority after the Qur'an. These are some of the qualities that developed his influence and made him a good prophet.

Muslim worldviews

Many Sunni Muslims believe in the difference between a messenger (rasul) and a prophet (nabi) – only messengers brought a holy book. There can be no prophet or messenger after Muhammad.

Shi'a Muslims believe that Imams continue the work of prophets, are infallible and are the protectors of divine revelation, but they are not prophets.

Ahmadiyya Muslims believe that an ummati (follower) prophet can appear after Muhammad and would be under the authority of the Qur'an and Muhammad.

Sources of authority

'Say, "If you love God, follow me, and God will love you and forgive you your sins; God is most forgiving, most merciful."' (Surah 3:31)

'We sent to you [Muhammad] the Scripture with the truth, confirming the Scriptures that came before and protecting it, and with final authority over them.' (Surah 5:48)

Analyse and evaluate

Are all prophets equally important?

Yes	No
Risalah (Sunni) and al-Nubuwwah (Shi'a) require belief in all prophets as a fundamental aspect of belief.	Muhammad has been described in ways that no other prophet has (e.g. 'seal of the prophets').
The Qur'an teaches not to discriminate between prophets.	Some prophets were given a scripture while others were not.

Muslims have love for all prophets and will say and write 'peace be upon him' after their names, but this does not mean there is no difference of rank or status between them. Muslims will have greater reverence for the Prophet Muhammad due to his distinct qualities, as highlighted in the Qur'an.

Activities

Review
1. Identify three facts about the family life of Muhammad.
2. What did he become known as?

Develop
3. List some of the ways Muhammad has been described in Surah 68:4, Surah 5:15 and Surah 21:107.

Link
4. What personal qualities made Muhammad a good prophet?

Debate
5. 'The Night of Power was the most important event in the Prophet Muhammad's life.' To what extent is this conclusion fair? Discuss and note down reasons for and against this view.

Stretch
6. Research reasons why Ahmadiyya Muslims believe it is possible for an ummati prophet to come.

3.10 Books: books before the Qur'an

Aim

To explore the place of holy books in Islam before the Qur'an

Starter

What do you like to read? List up to three things that make a good book.

Key words

Kutub – holy books
Scrolls (Sahifah) – scriptures revealed to Ibrahim and Musa
Torah (Tawrat) – scripture revealed to Musa
Psalms (Zabur) – scripture revealed to Dawud

■ Texts and readings have played an important part in all religions

Top tip

The Muslim belief that Allah gave teachings gradually, over time, to different prophets can be compared to a parent teaching a child the alphabet, letter by letter. People who lived many thousands of years ago were given only a few commandments. These gradually increased over time as people's levels of intelligence and spirituality developed.

Islam started with Adam

Islam as the original religion dates back to Adam. This means Adam was the first prophet to receive messages from Allah. Each message given to any prophet was suited for their time, the people and the place. Many of these teachings were recorded in ancient scriptures (**kutub**), some of which have survived and continue to be a source of guidance for people today. Other beliefs that were given became distorted (changed) and this is the reason Allah had to send particular prophets to restore the true teachings as revealed by him.

Scrolls (Sahifah)

The **Scrolls** (**Sahifah**) of Ibrahim and Musa are one of the earliest known revealed texts. These are now believed to be lost and little is known about them. Some parts of the Sahifah have been preserved in the Qur'an. Muslims must still have respect for these as they were originally from Allah.

Torah (Tawrat)

Whenever the Qur'an refers to the Scrolls, the 'scriptures of Musa' are also mentioned. These are better known as the **Torah** (**Tawrat**). Muslims believe the Torah was meant for Jewish people and for a limited time. It became distorted while scribes were composing the books from memory 1000 years after Musa. The Torah is still an important record of some of the teachings of Musa and also contains a prophecy about the appearance of the Prophet Muhammad in the future.

■ An example of a Torah scroll

Psalms (Zabur)

The **Psalms** (**Zabur**) were given to the Jewish prophet Dawud. There are 150 Psalms, made up of songs, prayers and poems. Dawud did not write the Psalms but they were inspired by Allah. The Prophet Muhammad said that the most beloved prayer to Allah was the recitation of the Psalms of Dawud. Many Muslims recite the same prayer today too.

Top tip

Do not confuse the Injil with the four gospels in the Christian New Testament, which were written by followers of Isa and which Muslims don't regard as trustworthy.

Sources of authority

'Is he not acquainted with what is in the books of Moses and of Abraham ... that no bearer of burdens can bear the burden of another; that man can have nothing but what he strives for ... That to thy Lord is the final goal ... that it is he who granteth laughter and tears.' (Surah 53:36–44)

'We revealed the law [Torah] to Moses; therein was guidance and light. By its standard have been judged the Jews by the Prophet who bowed (as in Islam) to God's will by the rabbis and the doctors of law.' (Surah 5:44)

'We have sent thee inspiration as we sent it to Noah and the messengers after him; We sent inspiration to Abraham, Ismail, Isaac, Jacob and the tribes to Jesus, Job, Jonah, Aaron and Solomon, to David we gave the psalms ... apostles who gave good news as well as warning that mankind after (the coming) of the apostles should have no plea against God.' (Surah 4:163–65)

'We sent after them Jesus the son of Mary, and bestowed on him the gospel; and we ordained in the hearts of those who followed him compassion and mercy.' (Surah 57:27)

Gospel (Injil)

The **Gospel**, referred to as **Injil** in the Qur'an, is an account of Isa's life and teachings. Muslims believe that part of the Injil is included in the New Testament but some of it has been lost, forgotten or altered. What is preserved is considered a valuable collection of revelations which teach morals such as forgiveness and love.

Key word

Gospel (Injil) – scripture revealed to Isa

Analyse and evaluate

Are holy books more important than other types of books?	
Yes	No
Holy books are originally from Allah, which makes them more important than those written by people.	There are many important lessons that can be learned from all types of literature.
Moral teachings contained in holy books aim to make humans better people.	Some people consider religious teachings to be irrelevant and unhelpful today.
Religious believers look to holy books for inspiration and guidance on how to live their lives, while some argue that we can draw important messages from other types of reading too, including fiction.	

Activities

Review

1. Identify three holy books before the Qur'an.
2. Which prophets were these scriptures given to?

Develop

3. Look at the Torah, Deuteronomy 18:18 and explain how Muslims believe it refers to the Prophet Muhammad.

Link

4. Explain the relationship between the nature of Allah, prophethood and books in no more than 50 words.

Debate

5. 'Having so many holy books is confusing.' To what extent is this conclusion fair? Discuss and note down reasons for and against this view.

Stretch

6. What teachings might some holy books before the Qur'an contain that Muslims would say are no longer relevant and reliable?

3.11 Books: the Qur'an

Aim

To explore the place of the Qur'an in Islam

Starter

Why do Muslims believe there is a need for another holy book after the Tawrat and Injil? Share your thoughts with a partner.

■ Muslim leaders use teachings from the Qur'an during sermons and speeches

The revelation of the Qur'an

For Muslims, the Qur'an is supreme among all sacred texts and the highest source of wisdom and authority. It is the only scripture meant for all times, all people and all places. This is because Muhammad was chosen to be a universal messenger whose teachings are relevant until the end of time.

Muhammad received the Qur'an through regular revelations from Allah via the angel Jibril. These were recorded by scribes and great efforts were made by early Muslims to preserve them word for word. It was in the time of the third Khalifah, Uthman, that a standardised version of the Qur'an was printed and distributed throughout the ummah.

Muslims believe that the Qur'an is Allah's final and undistorted message. This means that no other revelation can replace it, and for 14 centuries the entire text of the Qur'an has remained free from error and unchanged, as promised by Allah.

■ The Qur'an is read from a young age

The message and treatment of the Qur'an

The Qur'an offers comprehensive information and guidance on all matters, from the creation of the universe and of human beings, to the right way to worship and how to treat others. It contains information that Muslims believe could only have come from Allah. There are references to things that would happen in the future that could not have been known in the time of Muhammad, for instance, human beings being able to travel in space and the development of nuclear weapons (Surah 104).

The Qur'an is treated with the utmost respect, with many Muslims performing wudu (ablution) before touching it, reciting

■ Many Muslims perform wudu before touching and reciting the Qur'an

it melodiously, covering it with a cloth and keeping it as high as possible, such as on the top shelf of a bookcase. This is to symbolise its authority in the lives of Muslims.

Common and divergent attitudes

Muslims are taught to believe in and respect all kutub and ancient texts as they were originally from Allah and are also mentioned in the Qur'an. This does not mean that they have equal status. As the Qur'an is Allah's last and perfect message to humanity, many Muslims do not consider the previous revelations to have the same value. Some Muslim homes have a copy of the Bible in addition to the Qur'an, while others consider only the Qur'an to be necessary.

Sources of authority

'This is the Scripture in which there is no doubt, containing guidance for those who are mindful of God.' (Surah 2:2)

'The Qur'an is nothing less than a revelation that is sent to him [Muhammad]. It was taught to him by [an angel] with mighty powers and great strength.' (Surah 53:4–5)

'Nor could this Qur'an have been devised by anyone other than God. It is a confirmation of what was revealed before it and an explanation of the Scripture. Let there be no doubt about it, it is from the Lord of all worlds.' (Surah 10:37)

Analyse and evaluate

Is the Qur'an the only guidance Muslims need?

Yes	No
Special care was taken by early Muslims to protect and preserve the text of the Qur'an so that Muslims would always be rightly guided.	The Sunnah and Hadith are also important sources of guidance to show how Muhammad followed the Qur'an. These form the basis of the shari'a.
It is the perfect word of Allah and does not contain any faults and so is reliable, unlike previous scriptures which were changed or whose original teachings are now lost.	The Qur'an confirms the truth of many teachings and guidance in earlier revelations, so Muslims should make use of these too.

While there are other sources available to Muslims for guidance, the Qur'an remains superior and incomparable.

Activities

Review
1. Which angel revealed the Qur'an to the Prophet Muhammad?
2. What teachings does the Qur'an contain?

Develop
3. Why do Muslims believe that the Qur'an must be from Allah?

Link
4. Why was the Qur'an revealed to the Prophet Muhammad?

Debate
5. 'Too much attention is given to how a holy book is treated, not how it is followed.' To what extent is this conclusion fair? Discuss and note down reasons for and against this view.

Stretch
6. If Islam as a religion has been followed since Adam, is it essential to believe in the Qur'an?

3.12 Angels: the nature of angels

Aim

To explore the nature of angels in Islam

Starter

How are angels shown in books and films? Do these depictions reflect how religious believers perceive them?

■ Angels are described in the Qur'an as having wings, which many Muslims understand as being a metaphor for having certain responsibilities

Characteristics of angels

According to Islam, angels are supernatural beings that are created from light.

- They are Allah's creation.
- They govern the physical and spiritual laws in the universe.
- They cannot be seen by the naked eye, unless they appear in a physical form.
- They have no gender.
- They are countless in number.
- Angels live for as long as Allah wills. Most Muslims believe that one day everything except Allah will perish, and then angels will be resurrected to carry out their roles as long as Allah wills.
- They fulfil Allah's commands.
- They cannot be manipulated by external forces.
- They are free of sin and therefore unable turn away from Allah.
- They have no free will – they can only obey Allah's commands and cannot go against this, for instance, by making their own decisions. When Allah instructed the angels to serve Adam, they all did so.

Top tip

Although angels are heavenly beings, they are not worshipped by Muslims – only Allah is worshipped.

Sources of authority

'Praise be to God, Creator of the heavens and earth, who made angels messengers with two, three, four [pairs of] wings.' (Surah 35:1)

'They do not speak before He speaks and they act by His command.' (Surah 21:27)

'When We said to the angels, "Bow down before Adam", and they did.' (Surah 20:116)

Apart from also being created by Allah, these characteristics make angels different from human beings. The Qur'an speaks of a figure at the time of Adam known as Iblis, who was disobedient to Allah. When Allah told the angels to bow down to Adam out of respect, Iblis refused and was consequently thrown out of heaven. For many Muslims, Iblis is often identified with al-Shaytan (the devil) and is the reason why he could not have been an angel.

Nature of angels

Many Muslims believe that angels are part of the unseen world and do not possess any fixed material form but that they can still be identified by people when they appear to them (such as in a vision). For instance, it is believed the angel Jibril (Gabriel) appeared to Isa (Jesus) in the form of a dove and to Muhammad as an ordinary human being.

The Qur'an refers to angels having wings. While some Muslim would read this literally, others would understand this to be a metaphor for having certain powers and responsibilities given to them by Allah.

Muslims have great respect for angels and say 'peace be upon them' when their names are mentioned.

Analyse and evaluate

| Should belief in angels be added to the five roots of 'Usul ad-Din in Shi'a Islam? ||
Yes	No
The Qur'an and Hadith mention them clearly.	Shi'a scholars have worked hard to establish the five roots of 'Usul ad-Din as the most important aspects of belief.
Their importance cannot be underestimated and needs to be reflected in the roots of 'Usul ad-Din.	It is impossible to capture all beliefs in just a few core beliefs.
Just because the five roots of 'Usul ad-Din does not include angels does not mean they are not important. Muslims believe many things which are not included in the Six Articles of Faith and five roots of 'Usul ad-Din.	

Activities

Review

1. How might some Muslims understand the use of the word 'wings' in Surah 35:1?
2. Give two characteristics of angels.

Develop

3. Read the Qur'an's account of Adam (Surah 20:116–123) and explain what it says about the nature of angels.

Link

4. Start a mind map linking all the core beliefs of Islam. Build on this as you cover the next two spreads.

Debate

5. 'If Allah is omnipotent, there should be no need for angels.' To what extent is this conclusion fair? Discuss and note down reasons for and against this view.

Stretch

6. Find further examples of references where Muslims may understand teachings metaphorically.

3.13 Angels: the roles and importance of angels

Aim

To explore the roles and importance of angels in Islam

Starter

Would you live life differently if someone was recording all of your actions?

Key word

Archangels – higher-ranking angels

■ All the actions of human beings are recorded by angels

Top tip

The role of angels conveying God's messages to humanity can be compared to that of a postal worker delivering a letter from the writer to the addressee.

■ The angel Mika'il's role includes being the guardian of heaven and bringer of thunder

The role of angels

Muslims believe that while Allah is omnipotent, angels have an important place in the universe. This is one of the reasons belief in angels is the second article of faith for Sunni Muslims.

Angels are a primary source of communication between Allah and his humanity. Other important roles include:

- giving people strength in times of need and assuring them of heavenly support, as happened in the early struggles in Islam (e.g. battles that Muslims had to fight to defend freedom of belief)
- protecting individuals against danger
- accompanying the souls of people to the next life.

There are numerous angels in Islam. The highest-ranking ones are called '**archangels**'. These include Jibril, Mika'il, Izra'il and Israfil.

Jibril

Jibril is described in the Qur'an as 'the Holy Spirit' and 'the Trustworthy Spirit'. He is the chief angel responsible for communicating messages between Allah and the messengers (rasul), including the Prophet Muhammad, to whom he revealed the entire Qur'an. This began during the experience known as Laylat al-Qadr and was completed in the last year of Muhammad's life. Jibril helped to comfort Muhammad in difficult situations and guided him throughout his prophethood, including showing him how to perform prayer.

Mika'il

Mika'il's role is to take care of the provision and maintenance of life. He is the guardian of heaven and bringer of thunder. He is believed to be in charge of plants and the rain, which many Muslims have interpreted more generally to mean that he provides food for the body and soul. He also rewards the righteous.

Izra'il

Izra'il is referred to as the angel of death in the Qur'an and is responsible for taking the final breath from people before they return to Allah. The time and place of every individual's death is still known only to Allah.

Israfil

Israfil is known as the angel of the Day of Judgement. He blows a trumpet, first to announce the end of time when everything will be destroyed, and second to announce the Day of Judgement when everyone is brought back to life.

Recording angels

There are also recording angels who note every individual's deeds. These will be presented in the form of a book and read out on the Day of Judgement.

This affects the behaviour of Muslims in daily life and reminds them to ensure they strive to live in accordance with the teachings of Islam. Muslims try their best to live moral lives and to please Allah as they are conscious that they will be judged for their actions in the next life.

Common and divergent attitudes

All Muslims believe in angels. It is one of the Sunni Six Articles of Faith. While belief in angels is not one of the Shi'a five roots of 'Usul ad-Din, it is essential for Shi'a Muslims to believe in them too.

Shi'a Muslims believe that Jibril visited much of the Ahl al-Bayt, including Ali and Fatimah (Muhammad's daughter and wife of Ali). They also believe that a special group of angels are present at the graves of the Imams. This indicates that for Allah's chosen people, there are blessings in the places where they are buried due to the legacy they left on the Earth and the love Allah has for them. This is another reason why Shi'a Muslims also make pilgrimages to such sites.

Sources of authority

'If anyone is an enemy of God, His angels and His messengers, of Gabriel [Jibril] and Michael [Mika'il], then God is certainly the enemy of such disbelievers.' (Surah 2:98)

'Since the day Imam Hussain was martyred, Allah has appointed seventy thousand angels who are dishevelled and covered with dust; to invoke blessings on Imam Hussain and pray for mercy on him.' (Hadith, Kamil al-Ziyarat)

Analyse and evaluate

Is belief in angels still relevant?	
Yes	No
Belief in angels is essential to be a Muslim.	If Jibril has revealed Allah's final message to humanity, what is the need for him today?
Recording angels note down the actions of every person.	Angels generally cannot be seen and so don't seem to make a difference to people's lives.
Belief in angels is one of the Six Articles of Faith for Sunni Muslims but is not included in the five roots of 'Usul ad-Din for Shi'a Muslims, suggesting they do not have the same importance for all Muslims even though they all believe in them.	

Activities

Review
1. What important roles do angels have in Islam?
2. Why might having recording angels make a difference to how a Muslim lives their life?

Develop
3. Write down arguments for and against Jibril being the most important angel in Islam.

Link
4. How are Christian and Muslim beliefs about angels similar and different?

Debate
5. 'Allah should not need to go through angels to communicate with humanity.' To what extent is this conclusion fair? Discuss and note down reasons for and against this view.

Stretch
6. Find out more about the role Jibril played in Laylat al-Qadr and the impact this had on the Prophet Muhammad.

3.14 Eschatological beliefs and teachings: predestination and Allah's plan

Aim
To examine Muslim beliefs and teachings about predestination and Allah's plan

Starter
How much of your life is based on your own choices? How much of it is beyond your control?

Key words
Al-Qadr – predestination; belief that Allah is in control of the outcome of good and evil actions
Sifat – characteristics of Allah, for example foreknowledge

■ Allah has predestined many things, such as the fixed positions of planets in space

Eschatology and predestination

Eschatology is concerned with death, judgement and the final destiny of all human beings. In Islam, al-Qadr khayrihi washarrihi (**al-Qadr** for short), or predestination, is the belief that Allah is in control of the outcome of good and evil actions. Allah is omnipotent and has foreknowledge (one of his many '**sifat**', or characteristics). Everything is part of Allah's masterplan, therefore, he already knows everything that will happen and what everyone's fate will be. This is written in the preserved tablet in the heavens.

Every individual has a book of life that records all knowledge of a person's faith and action. Nothing is excluded from it and Allah knows everything it contains. This is the book that will be read out on the Day of Judgement and which will confirm the deeds of each person, which will or will not be accepted to Allah.

Allah has put in place certain laws in the universe. Many of these laws are predetermined and unchangeable. This applies to human beings too. There are many things that are outside of a person's control, such as the genes that are passed down

■ The preserved tablet contains Allah's masterplan for everything

Sources of authority

'He has subjected the sun and the moon each to pursue its course for an appointed time.' (Surah 13:2)

'No soul may die except with God's permission at a predestined time.' (Surah 3:145)

'"Death will overtake you no matter where you may be, even inside high towers." When good fortune comes their way, they say, "This is from God," but when harm befalls them, they say, "This is from you [Prophet]." Say to them, "Both came from God."' (Surah 4:78)

from parents, a family's social and economic status, and the fact everyone will eventually die.

Common and divergent attitudes

Sunni and Shi'a Muslims agree that nothing happens unless it is the will of Allah. But there are minor differences between these groups:

- Sunni Muslims believe that everything that is to happen is already predetermined, known and unalterable by Allah. Allah knows the choices people will make before they have made them.
- Shi'a Muslims believe in the concept of **Bada'** which states that Allah can change a person's destiny according to their actions. Therefore, not every event is fixed.

These beliefs remind a Muslim that wherever they will end up in the afterlife will be the correct decision as Allah is all-knowing and just. Therefore, they must accept all things as part of Allah's masterplan.

Key word

Bada' – Shi'a belief that Allah can change a person's destiny

Analyse and evaluate

Is it possible to know Allah's masterplan?	
Yes	No
The Qur'an and Hadith teach many things about Allah's masterplan, such as his decree that truth will win over falsehood.	It is impossible to know Allah's masterplan fully.
Allah uses human beings to fulfil his will, such as sending prophets to teach humanity the difference between right and wrong.	Allah is omniscient, whereas the minds of human beings are limited.
While some aspects of Allah's masterplan have been revealed to the Prophet Muhammad and whatever has happened has been predestined, much of this is beyond human understanding.	

Activities

Review
1. What is meant by the preserved tablet?
2. Identify three things that human beings cannot change.

Develop
3. Explain the relevance of Surah 9:51 to predestination and Allah's masterplan.

Link
4. What is the relationship between belief in predestination and Akhirah?

Debate
5. 'If Allah has predestined everything, this must mean our lives are already mapped out.' To what extent is this conclusion fair? Discuss and note down reasons for and against this view.

Stretch
6. Research the Shi'a concept of Bada'.

3.15 Eschatological beliefs and teachings: the free will debate

Aim
To examine Muslim beliefs and teachings about free will and the debate between Mu'tazilite and Ash'arites

Starter
Is it possible to believe in both a divine master plan and free will?

- How free are we to make decisions?

Key terms
Mu'tazilite – a group that believed everyone has free will and is responsible for their actions
Al-Ashari – founder of the Ash'arites, a group that believe Allah is the cause and controller of everything

Free will

As well as believing in predestination, Muslims also believe that humans are given the ability to make many choices about their actions. For instance, if a person is hungry and has food in front of them, they have the choice to eat straight away or to wait until later. Freedom applies in religion too. Muslims believe that Islam is Allah's chosen religion but no one can be forced to believe in it. There is also a difference between what Allah wills and what he allows. He may want all humans to treat each other with respect but he gives people freedom to do the opposite.

Compatibility with predestination

Muslims believe that people's choices are sometimes in harmony with Allah's will, which forms part of al-Qadr. These choices can lead to Allah's plan being fulfilled. For example, if Allah wants more done to reduce poverty and people freely choose to give money to charity, this shows al-Qadr and free will working together.

Allah's will, known as divine decree, can also be affected by human needs and behaviour. For example, a person facing problems may turn to prayer, which leads to Allah accepting the prayer.

Divine decrees can fall into two types:

- **Mu'allaq** – God's will can change as a result of people praying, repenting and giving to charity.
- **Mubram** – God's will cannot be changed by anything, as these are part of a predetermined plan, like the law of gravity.

So a prayer asking Allah for the recovery of a sick relative may be granted but asking to be transported back in time would not.

Mu'tazilite and Ash'arites

Despite Allah being transcendent and therefore not completely knowable, both Sunni and Shi'a Muslims consider divine control and human freedom to be perfectly compatible. Many Muslims, such as Sunni, take the position that Allah knows the outcome of a person's choice but does not force or create it – divine foreknowledge does not mean an exercise in control. Some Shi'a Muslims agree with this but offer the possibility that Allah can change his pre-written plan as an act of mercy if someone who has done wrong can change their ways.

These beliefs have been influenced by two groups from the early period of Islam, **Mu'tazilite** and Ash'arites (followers of the scholar **Al-Ashari**), between the eighth and tenth centuries CE.

Mu'tazilite	Ash'arites
• Humans must have free will and be genuine sources of their own actions, and therefore be responsible for them. There is no divine masterplan. • There must be a clear separation between Allah, who is unseen, and human beings. Allah cannot determine what people think or do. • Evil is a product of human freedom. • Allah allows human suffering as a moral test and does not burden people more than they can bear. • Actions are either good or evil and Allah must honour his promise to reward virtue and punish sin. • Reward and punishment are fair if humans have genuine freedom. • Mu'tazilites influenced Shi'a beliefs and the views of some Muslims.	• Humans have some freedom of action but do not have the power to create actions. They are themselves created while only Allah is the creator and cause of everything. • A person is only able to raise a finger because Allah enabled them to. • Humans cannot truly understand ideas about freedom and justice – these are known to Allah alone. • Allah's judgement is right and fair as he has ultimate power and authority over everything.

Sources of authority

'God does not burden any soul with more than it can bear: each gains whatever good it has done, and suffers its bad.' (Surah 2:286)

'God does not change the condition of a people [for the worse] unless they change what is themselves, but if He wills harm on a people, no one can ward it off – apart from Him, they have no protector.' (Surah 13:11)

'Do the believers not realize that if God had so willed, He could have guided all mankind?' (Surah 13:31)

Analyse and evaluate

Can humans be free if Allah has control over everything?

Yes	No
Allah has authority in the whole universe but allows people to make many choices.	There are many things humans cannot make decisions about, such as where and when they were born.
If humans were not free, why would Allah reward some with heaven and punish others with hell?	Allah's foreknowledge of all things suggests there is a divine masterplan and therefore no free will.
While Allah knows everything that will happen and has established predestined laws, people will be held accountable for decisions that are within their control.	

Activities

Review
1. Give an example of something human beings have freedom over.
2. What is the difference between Mu'tazilite and Ash'arite beliefs about free will?

Develop
3. What is the link between Surah 13:31, a divine masterplan and free will? Explain your answer.

Link
4. Explain the relationship between predestination, human freedom and risalah – in particular the story of Adam.

Debate
5. 'We either have free will or we don't.' To what extent is this conclusion fair? Discuss and note down reasons for and against this view.

Stretch
6. How relevant is the Mu'talizite and Ash'arite debate about free will today?

3.16 Life after death: Akhirah and the Day of Judgement

Aim

To examine Muslim beliefs and teachings about life after death

Starter

Do we only have one life? What reasons do some people give for believing in an afterlife?

■ Is death really the end?

Key words

Akhirah – belief in the afterlife and the Day of Judgement
Stewardship – the role of human beings as trustees of the Earth

Top tip

Do not confuse stewards and trustees of the Earth (khalifahs) with the leaders chosen after the Prophet Muhammad (Khalifahs).

Life after death

Muslims believe that our physical life will one day come to an end and that everyone will be raised again in the next life, known as **Akhirah**. Belief in life after death is one of the Six Articles of Faith for Sunni Muslims and one of the five roots of 'Usul al-Din for Shi'a Muslims (al-Ma'ad).

Human responsibility and accountability

Muslims are conscious that everyone's time on Earth is limited and so they must live according to the will of Allah. The Qur'an refers to the concept of **stewardship**, where people have been made khalifahs (trustees) with the responsibility to care for fellow human beings, animals and the environment. Only humans have been appointed stewards because they have been given the gifts of reason and free will and the power to make important decisions, unlike other parts of creation. Muslims believe that the way they live their life affects what will happen in the next life. The recording angels record each person's deeds which are then taken into account at the time of judgement. This life is seen as a preparation for the life to come and so Muslims know they will be held to account for how they have lived their lives on Earth.

> **Key word**
>
> **Barzakh** – 'barrier'; the intermediate state between death and judgement, when the soul has left the body

Barzakh and judgement

At the point of death, many Muslims believe that the soul leaves the body and goes to the intermediate or waiting state between death and judgement. This is called **barzakh**. At this point the soul is provided with a new body that is either bright or dark depending on the goodness of its deeds. Pure souls will be bright, indicating they will go to heaven, and the impure will be dark, indicating they will go to hell. At this stage, the soul already knows its fate. This is followed by resurrection which is when Israfil blows a trumpet and all graves will be opened and each person will be given another body that will see and know Allah.

Some consider this resurrection to be physical and believe this is why bodies need to be buried and remain in their graves until judgement. Many Muslims say that dead bodies are buried out of respect and it is just the soul that is taken away and provided with a new form in the afterlife.

Judgement

The Day of Judgement is believed to be Allah's final assessment of humanity. People will gather on a plain of judgement awaiting their fate. Muslims believe that Allah is omniscient and therefore his judgement will always be right and fair. For Shi'a Muslims, this links to divine justice. Allah's mercy can be requested by special individuals (intercession). For Sunni Muslims this can only be Muhammad, while for Shi'a Muslims it can be anyone in the Ahl al-Bayt (Prophet's family).

> **Sources of authority**
>
> 'They [non-believers] also say, "What? When we are turned to bones and dust, shall we really be raised up in a new act of creation?" Say, "[Yes] even if you were [as hard as] stone, or iron, or any other substance you think hard to bring to life." Then they will say, "Who will bring us back?" Say, "The One who created you the first time."'
> (Surah 17: 49–52)
>
> 'It is God who gives you life, then causes you to die, and then He gathers you all to the Day of Resurrection of which there is no doubt, though most people do not comprehend.'
> (Surah 45:26)

Analyse and evaluate

Is belief in life after death the most important belief?

Yes	No
Everything that happens in the world is a preparation for the next life.	All core beliefs have equal importance.
Actions seem meaningless if they are not done for reward in the Akhirah.	Without belief in Allah, there would be no purpose to the afterlife.
Belief in the afterlife is central in Sunni and Shi'a traditions and influences the way that Muslims live their life, as do the other core beliefs.	

Activities

Review
1. What is the meaning of stewardship?
2. Explain barzakh in no more than 30 words.

Develop
3. What argument is being made in Surah 17:49–52?

Link
4. Explain the relationship between divine justice and the Day of Judgement.

Debate
5. 'It doesn't make a difference if resurrection is physical or spiritual.' To what extent is this conclusion fair? Discuss and note down reasons for and against this view.

Stretch
6. Create a table of arguments and evidence for and against the concept of life after death.

3.17 Life after death: heaven and hell

Aim
To examine Muslim beliefs and teachings about heaven and hell

Starter
Write three words each to describe your ideas about a) heaven and b) hell

Key words
Al-Jannah – heaven
Martyrdom – dying or being killed for religious beliefs
Jahannam – hell

■ Some consider heaven to be like a perfect beach

■ Hell is often understood to be a place full of fire

Heaven

In the Qur'an, **Al-Jannah**, or heaven, is described as a beautiful place where people who have pleased Allah will enjoy various comforts and rewards. Many passages appear to refer to material things being provided in the afterlife, such as rivers of water and milk. These are understood by some Muslims to be literal while others apply metaphorical interpretations, saying that water and milk represent purity and wealth respectively. The meaning of a word depends on the context in which it is used.

Comparisons are also made between this life and the next to show that life after death is based on what we experience on Earth. Believers who obey Allah's will are promised 'two gardens' (Qur'an 55:46) – one in this life and one in the next.

Martyrdom

Death is certain and can happen in a number of ways, including by being martyred. For centuries, there have been Muslims who have lost their lives defending their faith, including in conflicts. This started in the time of the Prophet Muhammad when Muslims were required to fight many battles under strict conditions to protect religious freedom (see spread 4.16). Many Muslims believe that a person killed because of their beliefs is a martyr (shaheed) and will be rewarded straight away with a place in heaven. A shaheed can also be someone who lives their life striving to be the best Muslim possible and sacrifices much of their time and wealth in the service of Islam. **Martyrdom** is one of the four highest ranks in Islam, the others being prophets, truthful and righteous (Surah 4:69).

Many Muslims believe that the idea of martyrdom has been exploited by terrorist groups who have called for Muslims to be ready to die for an extreme cause and that such beliefs are misguided.

Hell

Unlike al-Jannah, **Jahannam** is described as a place of pain and suffering for people who did not live moral lives. Some Muslims believe that the graphic descriptions of hell as a fiery place of torture, where sinners are chained, made to drink boiling water, eat scalding food and choke columns of fire, are literally true. Other Muslims say much of the Qur'an's language is symbolic and believe that the ways in which hell is portrayed are intended to highlight the danger of not believing in Allah and to put people off from committing sins.

Many Muslims believe that Jahannam, like al-Jannah, is the final destination for those Allah decides to place there. Other Muslims argue that hell is only temporary, as Allah is al-Ghaffar (forgiving) and will pardon all sins, meaning everyone will eventually enter al-Jannah.

Sources of authority

'When the Hour arrives, on that Day people will be separated: those who believed and did good deeds will delight in a Garden, while those who disbelieved and denied Our messages and the meeting of the Hereafter will be brought into torment.' (Surah 30:14–16)

'Here is a picture of the Garden promised to the pious: rivers of water forever pure, rivers of milk forever fresh, rivers of wine, a delight for those who drink, rivers of honey clarified and pure, [all] flow in it; there they will find fruit of every kind; and they will find forgiveness from their Lord. How can this be compared to the fate of those stuck in the Fire, given boiling water to drink that tears their bowels?' (Surah 47:15)

'A time will come in Jahannam when not a single man would be left in it. Its doors and windows will rattle to the blowing wind.' (Hadith)

Analyse and evaluate

Should everyone enter al-Jannah?

Yes	No
The Qur'an says that Allah forgives all sins.	Many sins are so serious that they should not be forgiven, for example, shirk.
People should not be permanently made to suffer because of poor choices in life, often due to negative influences in their lives.	Some people, such as hardened criminals, do not deserve to enter al-Jannah.

While some Muslims consider shirk to be unforgiveable, others say that after experiencing punishment for sins, souls have no need to spend eternity in Jahannam and will be pure enough to enter al-Jannah.

Activities

Review

1. What is martyrdom?
2. Give examples of literal and metaphorical interpretations of heaven and hell.

Develop

3. What impact would teachings like Surah 30:14–16 have on the way Muslims live their lives?

Link

4. Can Allah be merciful and send someone to hell?

Debate

5. 'Every believer should be willing to become a martyr.' To what extent is this conclusion fair? Discuss and note down reasons for and against this view.

Stretch

6. If al-Jannah and Jahannam didn't exist, would Muslims still strive to live morally?

Summary activities

CHECK YOUR NOTES

STAGE 1

Check that you have detailed notes that cover the following:

- [ ] The core beliefs in Sunni Islam: Allah, angels, holy books, prophets, Day of Judgement, Predestination and issues relating to these core beliefs
- [ ] The core beliefs in Shi'a Islam: 'Usul-ad-Din: oneness of God, divine justice, prophethood, Imams and the Day of Resurrection
- [ ] The importance of the 99 names of Allah including the ideas of Allah as one (Tawhid), Merciful, Omnipotent, Benevolent, Fair and Just, Transcendent and immanent
- [ ] Different beliefs around the ideas of Tawhid and shirk
- [ ] The idea of Prophethood (Risalah) and the importance and role of prophets before Muhammad: Adam, Ibrahim, Isma'il, Musa, Dawud and Isa
- [ ] The role of Muhammad as the seal of the prophets
- [ ] The belief in the 12 Imams in Shi'a Islam
- [ ] Books (kutub) before the Qur'an: the Scrolls (Sahifah) Torah (Tawrat), Psalms (Zabur), and Gospel (Injil) and how they became distorted
- [ ] The Qur'an as the final message
- [ ] The role and importance of angels (Malaikah), specifically Jibril, Izra'il, Mika'il, Israfil and recording angels
- [ ] Eschatological beliefs and teachings including discussion of predestination (al-Qadr) and human freedom
- [ ] Life as preparation for the life to come after the Day of Judgement; idea of stewardship
- [ ] Life after death (Akhirah): how different Muslims understand heaven (al-Jannah) and hell (Jahannam)

GETTING READY

STAGE 2

Quick quiz

1. How do Sunni and Shi'a Islam differ on the leadership of the Muslim community?
2. What does Shi'a Islam teach about Imams?
3. Give an example of something that a Muslim may consider to be Shirk.
4. Which of the prophets were connected with the rebuilding of the Kaaba?
5. What do Muslims believe about the role of Isa on the Day of Judgement?
6. What do Muslims believe has happened to books (kutub) written before the Qur'an?
7. Complete this statement. Angels were Allah's first _____: they are i_____, free from _____. They do not have ____ _____.
8. What is al-Qadr?
9. What is barzakh?
10. How is hell (Jahannam) described in the Qur'an?

Quick quiz answers can be found online at
www.hoddereducation.co.uk/ocr-gcse-rs-answers

ACTIVITIES

STAGE 2

1. Create a mind map showing what Muslims believe about the nature of Allah. For each key term below, aim to add a definition and a source of wisdom or authority to illustrate the point.

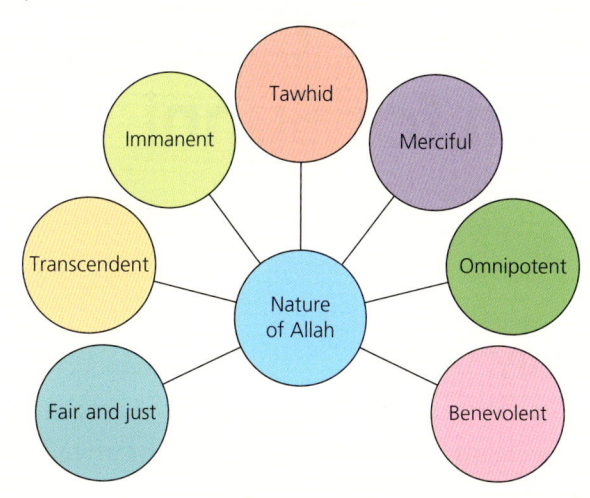

Mind map – Nature of Allah:
- Tawhid
- Immanent
- Merciful
- Transcendent
- Omnipotent
- Fair and just
- Benevolent

2. **AO1 focus:** key terms Make a set of flashcards for the key terms used in this chapter. You should aim to have a definition and a development point on each card. Where appropriate you could add a source of wisdom or authority.

GET PRACTISING

STAGE 3

Use this section to help you develop your understanding of how to answer exam-style questions.

Ask the expert

Jack writes:

I have really enjoyed studying Islam but find I struggle to write clearly on the 6-mark questions because I get muddled between ideas and confuse some of the technical terms. Is there anything I can do to get better at this?

Expert answer:

Examiner's reports often suggest that knowledge of key terms is something that people struggle with, so you are not alone. Unfortunately, if a term is listed in the specification then you do need to know it. One of the best strategies is to use flashcards. Go through your specification and make a card for each key term. On the reverse, provide a definition, a development point, and maybe a link to a source of wisdom if relevant. Then perhaps get quizzing with a friend!

Retrieval boxes

A further technique that can help revision is the use of retrieval boxes. Use the main sub-headings in the topic to make your grid. Then, to check your understanding of a topic you have revised, attempt to fill in three to four bullet points in each box.

CHAPTER 4

Practices

4.1 Importance of the Five Pillars of Islam for Sunni Muslims

Aim
To explore the importance of the Five Pillars of Islam for Sunni Muslims

Starter
What are pillars and why are they important parts of a building?

Pillars are essential to ensure a building remains strong, safe and secure

Key word
Five Pillars of Islam – the most important duties for Sunni Muslims

Top tip
Shi'a Muslims have a set of fundamental practices known as the Ten Obligatory Acts. These incorporate some of the Five Pillars of Islam, but not all. You will learn about these in spread 4.2.

Islam as a way of life

Muslims believe that Islam is a complete way of life. It covers all aspects of day-to-day living, whether that be public or private, from the spiritual (prayer, fasting and pilgrimage) to the secular (politics, banking and business). These all link to shari'a. Shari'a sets out the behaviour and actions expected of Muslims at all levels – personal, social, national and global.

The two main purposes of a Muslim's life are to serve and fulfil the:
- rights of Allah (Huquq Allah)
- rights of Allah's creation (Huquq al-'Ibad).

Muslims must live in total submission to Allah. This is, in fact, the meaning of the word 'Muslim', which comes from the same root as 'Islam' (meaning peace and submission to Allah). Submission involves surrendering oneself and putting something or someone else first and living in obedience to them. For Muslims, this can only be Allah. It is this submission that enables Muslims to carry out both Huquq Allah and Huquq al-'Ibad, and therefore fulfil their responsibilities.

Five Pillars of Islam

All religions have a firm foundation that sets out the key duties of followers. In Sunni Islam, this foundation is known as the **Five Pillars of Islam**. They are called pillars because just as columns support a building, they support the main principles and practices of the faith. Each pillar is essential, offering strength, security and safety to Muslims in order for them to follow their religion properly. Without these pillars, the foundations would be weak and Islam could not remain standing firmly.

The Five Pillars of Islam are intended to demonstrate faith and obedience to Allah:

1. **Shahadah** is sincerely reciting the Muslim declaration of faith: 'There is no god but God; Muhammad is the messenger of God.'
2. **Salah (Salat)** is performing ritual prayers in the proper way at five set times each day.

3. **Zakah (Zakat)** is paying an alms (or charity) tax that is 2.5 per cent of one's wealth to benefit the poor and needy.
4. **Sawm** is fasting, mainly in the month of Ramadan.
5. **Hajj** is pilgrimage to Makkah (Mecca) in Saudi Arabia, to be completed at least once in a Muslim's life, as long as certain conditions are met.

The Five Pillars of Islam are based on the Qur'an and Hadith (see spread 3.1), which are the two main sources of Muslim belief, and the details of how to follow each pillar are found in the Sunnah. There is a close relationship between the outward actions and the intention behind them.

Importance of the Five Pillars of Islam

The Five Pillars of Islam are important to Sunni Muslims because:

- they are mentioned in the Qur'an
- they are commanded by Allah and must be performed at specific times and places
- they enable Muslims to fulfil their two main purposes – serving Allah and serving his creation
- they bring believers together and thereby strengthen the ummah
- believers will be accountable for practising these pillars in the afterlife.

Sources of authority

'Guide us to the straight path: the path of those You have blessed.' (Surah 1:6–7)

'True Religion, in God's eyes, is *islam*: [devotion to Him alone].' (Surah 3:19)

'Islam is based on five pillars.' (Hadith)

Analyse and evaluate

Is serving Allah more important than serving his creation?

Yes	No
Serving Allah is essential before serving his creation, as without Allah there would be no creation.	Serving Allah's creation is more important because it involves serving others and making a positive difference in their lives, while Allah does not need help.
If there is a clash between serving Allah and serving his creation, serving Allah will always come first as he is the creator of all.	It is only through serving Allah's creation that one can serve Allah directly.
For many Muslims, serving Allah and serving his creation are two sides of the same coin, and therefore they need to perform both.	

Activities

Review
1. What is shari'a?
2. What are the names of the Five Pillars of Islam?

Develop
3. 'The reward of deeds depends upon the intentions and every person will get the reward according to what he has intended' (Hadith, Bukhari). Explain the relevance of this to the Five Pillars of Islam.

Link
4. Explain the connection between any of the Five Pillars of Islam and the Sunni Six Articles of Faith.

Debate
5. 'It should be up to each person what beliefs are most important to them.' To what extent is this conclusion fair? Discuss and note down reasons for and against this view.

Stretch
6. What might be the benefits and challenges of living in submission to the will of Allah?

4.2 Importance of the Ten Obligatory Acts for Shi'a Muslims

Aim
To explore the importance of the Ten Obligatory Acts for Shi'a Muslims

Starter
Should any rules on how to live your life be compulsory? Are there others that should be optional?

Key word
Ten Obligatory Acts – the most important duties for Shi'a Muslims
Salah/Salat – Muslim prayer

Ten Obligatory Acts for Shi'a Muslims

Similar to Sunni Muslims, Shi'a Muslims also have a list of key practices which form the building blocks of their tradition. These are known as the **Ten Obligatory Acts** and are as follows:

1 **Salah** (also spelt **Salat**) is the offering of five daily prayers. This is the primary way of worshipping Allah and can be performed privately at home or in congregation, such as at a mosque. While there are five separate prayers, Shi'a Muslims combine and offer some of them at three different times during the day. This is based on their interpretation of the Qur'an and the practice of the Prophet Muhammad (see spread 3.9).

2 **Sawm** is fasting, including in the month of Ramadan. According to Shi'a legal experts, a person must avoid a number of things from just before sunrise to just after sunset, including eating, drinking, acts of a sexual nature and deliberately lying about Allah, the Prophet Muhammad and the Imams (see spread 4.11).

3 **Hajj** is pilgrimage to Makkah (Mecca) in Saudi Arabia, which every adult Muslim should perform once in their lifetime, as long as they are in good health and can afford the costs. While on pilgrimage, Shi'a Muslims also visit the graves of their Imams. This is known as Ziyara (visitation) (see spread 4.8).

4 **Zakah** (also spelt Zakat) is an act of purification of one's wealth through giving money to charity. It is paid yearly on one of three categories: coins (gold and silver), cattle (cows, sheep, goats and camels) and crops (wheat, barley, dates and raisins). The Zakah percentage can be 2.5, 5 or 10 per cent, depending on the quantity and item (see spread 4.9).

5 **Khums** is annual taxation of one-fifth of gains (surplus income or profits) in a year. This is compulsory for all Shi'a Muslims and is seen as wealth that the Prophet Muhammad's family and the needy is entitled to. It is paid to Shi'a leaders, collected in a mosque or could be taxed in Shi'a majority countries (see spread 4.10).

6 **Jihad** is struggle or striving in the path of Allah. This can range from trying one's best to be a better person (Greater Jihad) to defending Muslims from an attack (Lesser Jihad) (see spreads 4.15 and 4.16).

Sources of authority

'Know that one-fifth of your battle gains belongs to God and the Messenger, to close relatives and orphans, to the needy and travellers.' (Surah 8:41)

'I did not revolt for the cause of evil tyranny or corruption, but to reform my grandfather's (Prophet Muhammad) nation. I want to enjoin the good and forbid the evil, and take the course of my father (Imam Ali) and grandfather.' (Imam Hussain, Hadith in Bihar al-Anwar)

7 **Amr bil-Maroof** is commanding what is good. This can be through words and actions, such as speaking the truth, promoting equality and standing up for justice.

8 **Nahi Anil Munkar** is forbidding what is evil. This includes challenging and working to correct anything that causes suffering, such as corruption and oppression. Like Amr bil-Maroof, Nahi Anil Munkar should be carried out with the right manners and etiquette.

9 **Tawalla** is expressing love towards God. This specifically refers to love and devotion towards Allah, the Prophet Muhammad and the Ahl al-Bayt (see spread 3.1), as commanded in the Qur'an. The Ahl al-Bayt are seen as the best models of morality, whom Allah loves the most. Their births are celebrated and their deaths are mourned.

10 **Tabarra** is expressing disassociation from evil. This refers to the opponents of Allah, the Prophet Muhammad and the Ahl al-Bayt. Shi'a Muslims are forbidden from seeking guidance from those seen to be morally corrupt and religiously misguided. This includes some companions of the Prophet Muhammad, whom Sunni Muslims hold in the highest regard (for example the first three Rightly Guided Khalifahs – see spread 3.4). Any use of foul or disrespectful language for such figures must be avoided.

As you can see, Shi'a Muslims share many of the same duties as Sunni Muslims. For instance, four of the Five Pillars are included in the Ten Obligatory Acts. The other acts, while seen as good, are not considered obligatory by Sunni Muslims.

Just because Shahadah is not included in the Ten Obligatory Acts does not mean it is not important to Shi'a Muslims. Shi'a Muslims see Shahadah more as a belief than a practice.

Importance of the Ten Obligatory Acts

The Ten Obligatory Acts are important to Shi'a Muslims because they:

- are taught in the Qur'an, by the Prophet Muhammad and the Imams
- are crucial in guiding the practices of Shi'a Muslims
- show how to be committed to Islam through action, not just words
- enable Shi'a Muslims to connect with Allah, purify their hearts, ease the suffering of the poor and promote a better society
- are a means for Shi'a Muslims to be blessed with a good afterlife.

Sources of authority

'Be a community that calls for what is good, urges what is right, and forbids what is wrong.' (Surah 3: 104)

Five Pillars (Sunni) — **Ten Obligatory Acts (Shi'a)**

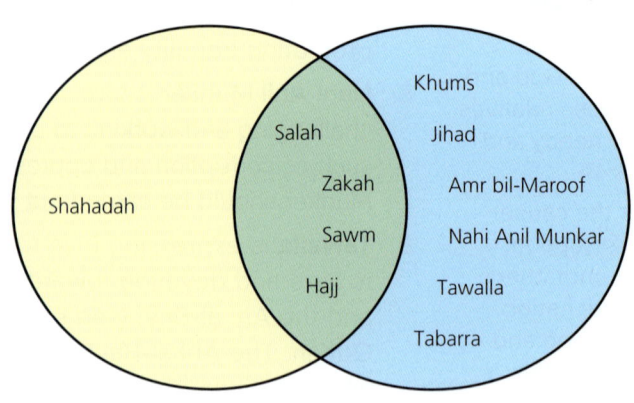

- Shahadah
- (Shared): Salah, Zakah, Sawm, Hajj
- Khums, Jihad, Amr bil-Maroof, Nahi Anil Munkar, Tawalla, Tabarra

■ Sunni and Shi'a Muslims share many of the same practices, while differing in others

Analyse and evaluate

Are some of the Ten Obligatory Acts more difficult than others?

Yes	No
Jihad, particularly Greater Jihad, is considered to be extremely challenging – the word 'jihad' itself means something that involves a struggle.	All are equally challenging, especially in non-Muslim countries where there are many temptations (for example becoming materialistic) that go against so many religious rules.
Nahi Anil Munkar is especially difficult, as it often requires speaking out and standing up to something evil which may be popular in society.	The Qur'an teaches that 'God does not burden any soul with more than it can bear' (Surah 2:286) and so it is not beyond any person to follow each of the acts.
While many Shi'a Muslims would accept that there will always be obstacles that stand in the way of following the Ten Obligatory Acts, the main thing is to persist and that Allah rewards efforts made for his sake.	

Activities

Review

1. Spend five minutes looking at the list of Ten Obligatory Acts. On your own or with a partner, close your books and write down as many as you can remember. Check and correct your work.
2. Which practices are shared by Sunni and Shi'a Muslims?

Develop

3. Identify which of the Ten Obligatory Acts are about individual actions and which relate to society.

Link

4. How do some of the Ten Obligatory Acts link to the five roots of 'Usul ad-Din?

Debate

5. 'The more rules there are to follow, the more difficult it is to live by them.' To what extent is this conclusion fair? Discuss and note down reasons for and against this view.

Stretch

6. What is the need for Khums in addition to Zakah?

4.3 Public acts of worship: Salah

Aim

To explore some key requirements in Salah

Starter

If Allah is perfect, do human beings need to worship him?

Key words

Wudu – ablution ritual before prayer
Niyyah – intention, made before prayer
Qibla – direction of prayer, towards Makkah (Mecca) in Saudi Arabia
Rak'ats – cycles or sequences of actions during prayer

■ Salah is a worshipper's direct communication with Allah

Top tip

Some Muslims put shirk into two categories:
- Major shirk involves worshipping idols or statues and putting someone else on the same level as Allah.
- Minor shirk involves putting trust in another person, for example to provide money.

Salah as direct communication with Allah

Muslims believe that the purpose of life is to worship Allah, and the most effective way of achieving this is through Salah (also spelt Salat). Salah is one of the Sunni Five Pillars and Shi'a Ten Obligatory Acts and enables Muslims to establish a direct communication, or personal relationship, with Allah. This is a reminder of the need for belief in Tawhid – Allah is the one and only God who is to be worshipped. All prophets came to restore and strengthen Tawhid. To pray to anyone or anything apart from Allah is shirk – the worst sin in Islam.

Salah helps with attaining taqwa (God-consciousness) and keeping away from sin. The Prophet Muhammad said that the first question a Muslim will be asked on the Day of Judgement is about Salah. This makes Muslims very conscious of fulfilling this duty, particularly those for whom it is compulsory: men, women (except under some conditions, including those who are menstruating or have just given birth) and children from around the age of ten.

Wudu

Physical and spiritual cleanliness are an important part of Salah. This is why all prayers must begin with a washing ritual known as **wudu**. This consists of a sequence of washing or wiping various parts of the body with water, including the head and the feet. Not only does this ensure physical cleanliness, but it also reminds a worshipper to approach prayer with a pure mind and heart. Salah without wudu is not valid.

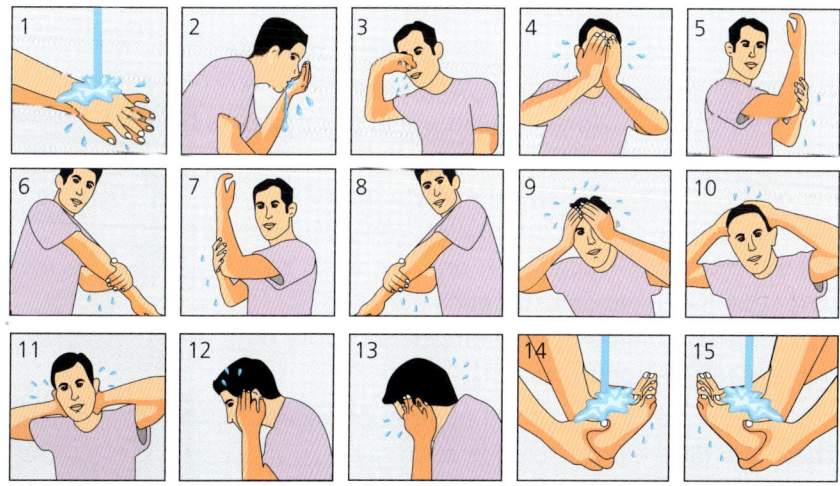

■ Wudu is performed through a number of actions involving water

Another form of ablution, known as ghusl, is required when the entire body needs to be clean, such as after sex or menstruation. If water is not available, an alternative method known as tayammum (symbolic wudu using clean earth or soil) is used.

Niyyah

Salah must start with **niyyah**, or intention, in order to focus the mind on the prayer and to try to avoid any distractions, such as materialistic things. Muslims believe Salah should be offered with complete attentiveness and a desire to have direct communication with Allah. Any lapses in concentration could make Salah void.

Qibla

The direction of prayer during Salah is known as the **qibla**. Muslims must face Makkah (Mecca), which is where the Kaaba is located. This is for the sake of unity – not because the Kaaba is being worshipped. A compass or a mobile phone app can be used to determine the qibla.

Some Muslims may be exempt from this rule, for example those travelling in a vehicle or immobile due to health reasons, in which case they can offer prayers facing any direction.

Times and rak'ats

The Qur'an instructs Muslims to offer Salah at five set times each day:

- Salah al-Fajr – before sunrise
- Salah al-Zuhr – noon
- Salah al-Asr – mid-afternoon
- Salah al-Maghrib – just after sunset
- Salah al-Isha – later in the evening.

Prayers are spread out over the course of the day in order to bring the minds of Muslims back to their purpose – to worship Allah – and to put this duty above all others. Each Salah is preceded by the adhan (call to prayer), called by a muezzin, announcing the time of the prayer. While Muslims will try to observe each Salah on time, work and other commitments can sometimes make this challenging. In some circumstances, a couple of prayers can be combined.

Each prayer has a prescribed number of **rak'ats**. There are different postures in each rak'at, mainly:

- qiyam (standing)
- ruku' (bowing)
- sajdah (prostrating)
- qa'dah (kneeling).

These actions combine the physical aspects of prayer with mindful and spiritual focus.

The number of rak'ats may differ among Sunni and Shi'a Muslims. The cycles in some of the prayers are halved if a person is travelling a distance.

Shi'a Islam

During wudu, Shi'a Muslims wipe rather than wash the feet.

It is common for Shi'a Muslims to combine Salah al-Zuhr and Salah al-Asr, and to combine Salah al-Maghrib and Salah al-Isha. This is because according to their interpretation, the Qur'an refers to three times for prayers, rather than five. They also say that the Prophet Muhammad sometimes combined these prayers. However, it is allowed to separate these prayers.

Shi'a Muslims put a clay or earthen tablet called a turba on the ground where they will place their head in prostration. This is because the Prophet Muhammad and early Muslims used to prostrate directly on the earth or something natural, rather than on carpets. This is a reminder that everyone has come from the earth and will return to it. The turba is commonly from Karbala, Iraq, due to its sacred status for Shi'a Muslims.

■ Turbas are small pieces of clay used by Shi'a Muslims during prayer to symbolise earth

> **Sources of authority**
>
> 'I created jinn and mankind only to worship Me.' (Surah 51:56)
>
> 'Turn your face in the direction of the Sacred Mosque: wherever you [believers] may be, turn your faces to it.' (Surah 2:144)
>
> 'Keep up the prayer: prayer restrains outrageous and unacceptable behaviour.' (Surah 29:45)
>
> 'The earth has been made a place of prostration for me.' (Hadith)

Recitations

Salah must be offered in Arabic and from memory using set prayers taken from the Qur'an and Hadith. One example recitation is Allahu Akbar, which means 'God is the greatest'.

The opening chapter of the Qur'an (Surah al-Fatihah) and other chapters are recited in the qiyam position. In sajdah, Muslims can offer prayers for a specific purpose in their own language and words in the additional optional prayers. Salah ends with offering salam (peace) to others.

Analyse and evaluate

Should worship include set prayers?

Yes	No
This is the way the Prophet Muhammad mostly offered his prayers and it is his example that Muslims strive to follow.	Some Muslims prefer to pray spontaneously and focus on specific things they wish to ask of Allah.
When imams lead Salah, there are specific words they need to recite and responses required from the congregation.	Some Sufi groups allow for musical instrumentals, incense, singing and dancing in order to connect with Allah.

Although Islam allows worshippers to pray in their own words during some parts of worship, this must come after the set prayers which have come from the Qur'an, Sunnah and Hadith. Praying in this way also carries more blessings, as it unites the Muslim community, rather than prayers offered individually.

Activities

Review

1. What is niyyah?
2. How many daily prayers are there?

Develop

3. How does a common qibla for all Muslims support the idea of the ummah?

Link

4. How is Salah a helpful way for a Muslim to stay away from shirk?

Debate

5. 'The niyyah matters more than wudu.' To what extent is this conclusion fair? Discuss and note down reasons for and against this view.

Stretch

6. Explain the symbolism in the actions and movements before and during prayer. How and why might these enhance the experience of communicating with Allah?

4.4 Public acts of worship: Salah at home and mosque

Aim
To explore how Salah (Salat) is performed in the home and mosque

Starter
Is it better to pray on your own or with other people?

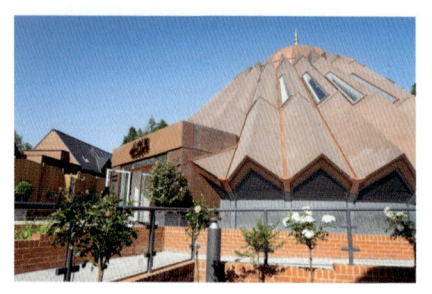

■ The Mubarak Mosque in Tilford, Surrey

■ The Prophet Muhammad taught that prayers offered in congregation are 27 times more blessed than worship performed by oneself

Key word
Khutba – sermon given on Friday and other major Islamic festivals such as on Eid days

Salah in the mosque and elsewhere

The mosque is the beating heart and spiritual home of the Muslim community. The Prophet Muhammad's first action on arrival in Madinah (Medina) was to build a mosque, which became the religious, political, educational and social headquarters for the city.

This purpose of a mosque continues to this day. Offering prayers in congregation became a way for the ummah to gather, to become stronger in their spirituality, to learn more about their faith to serve the needs of the community. The mosque is the hub of the ummah, playing a pivotal role in making Muslims feel like they belong to a global family made up of brothers and sisters in faith and promoting a spirit of unity.

The Arabic word for mosque is 'masjid', literally 'a place of prostration', which signifies its most important primary function: prayer. All of the five daily prayers are offered in mosques, led by an imam. Worshippers must keep straight rows and stand shoulder to shoulder. This symbolises unity, equality and brotherhood/sisterhood. Men and women traditionally pray in separate areas to ensure they remain focused on Allah.

If a mosque is not available, an alternative place such as a community hall can be used. Wherever prayers are offered, the ground should be clean, or a prayer mat should be used. This is to ensure cleanliness at every stage of worship.

A mosque is used for other religious purposes, including:

- celebrating key festivals, such as Eid-ul-Fitr and Eid-ul-Adha (see spread 4.13)
- marking important rites of passage and providing support to families for occasions such as an aqiqah (ceremony marking the birth of a baby), nikah (marriage contract) and funerals
- offering counselling to individuals and families, such as those requiring resolutions to disputes.

Salah at home

Men should, as far as possible, offer Salah in a mosque. Women are excused from Salah during menstruation. Where going to a mosque may be difficult, Salah can be offered at home, work or other suitable places. The Prophet Muhammad taught Muslims not to leave their homes empty of spirituality.

In some extreme circumstances, prayer is advised only in homes such as during the COVID-19 pandemic.

Families ensure that a clean area of the house, with as few distractions as possible, is designated for Salah. Salah at home is usually led by the head of the household.

Jummah prayer

The most important part of the week is the offering of the Jummah prayer on Friday afternoon, which replaces the Salah al-Zuhr. Muslims congregate in mosques to listen to a **khutba** (sermon) by the imam and worship together. They are told in the Qur'an to 'leave off your trading' and 'hurry towards the reminder of God' on this day (Surah 62:9–10). This highlights Jummah as an important prayer for the purposes of unity and harmony in the ummah. There is no day of rest in Islam, so Muslims are free to return to work after the Jummah prayer.

The khutba must be listened to in silence. It contains a moral message and often refers to teachings from the Qur'an, stories from the life of the Prophet Muhammad and other sources of belief. The purpose is to remind Muslims about the key requirements of their faith and to guide, encourage and inspire them to become better people. It is often the only formal opportunity for the community to learn important lessons from an imam, and therefore crucial in its educational and spiritual value.

There are many blessings linked to Jummah, as it is an opportunity for sins to be forgiven. As a congregational prayer, it promotes community and provides opportunities for believers to reconnect and ensure each other's well-being. Many Muslims consider attendance at the Jummah prayer to be compulsory, particularly for men. The Prophet Muhammad said that a person who misses three consecutive Jummah prayers, without a proper excuse, suffers a loss of faith. This indicates the great significance of Jummah as a prayer for the ummah.

For Shi'a Muslims, Jummah is currently optional in the absence of the final Imam. They have the option of choosing between Salah al-Zuhr and Jummah prayer. However, it is strongly encouraged to perform Jummah prayer.

Sources of authority

'The only ones who should tend to God's places of worship are those who believe in God and the Last Day, who keep up the prayer, who pay the prescribed alms, and who fear no one but God: such people may hope to be among the rightly guided.' (Surah 9:18)

'Prayer is obligatory for the believers at prescribed times.' (Surah 4:103)

'The most beloved of places to Allah are the mosques.' (Hadith)

Analyse and evaluate

Is Salah better at the mosque than at home?

Yes	No
The Prophet Muhammad taught that 'prayer with the congregation is 27 times better than prayer performed by oneself' (Hadith, Bukhari).	It is not always possible to attend the mosque for prayers, especially when people are busy or may live at some distance.
Mosques are built for the purpose of communal worship.	The Prophet Muhammad taught Muslims to also pray in their homes and not to make them 'like graveyards' (Hadith, Bukhari) – that is, empty of spirituality.

Many Muslims would agree about the need to strike a balance between personal, family and community life. Mosques are houses of Allah and prayers offered in them are more blessed, so they should be availed of as much as possible.

Activities

Review

1. What is the meaning of 'masjid'?
2. Give one purpose of the khutba.

Develop

3. Read Surah 62:9. What does it say about the Jummah prayer?

Link

4. How is praying at the mosque seen as a way of strengthening the ummah?

Debate

5. 'The Jummah prayers are just as important as the daily prayers.' To what extent is this conclusion fair? Discuss and note down reasons for and against this view.

Stretch

6. Look at the teachings given in the Analyse and evaluate box. Do they appear to be contradictory? How would Muslims explain that they are not?

4.5 Public acts of worship: Shahadah

Aim

To explore the place of Shahadah in Muslim practice

Starter

If you could sum up your personal beliefs in a single sentence, how would it read?

Key word

Shahadah – the Muslim declaration of faith

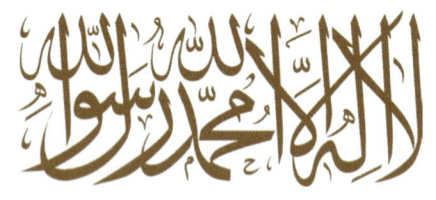

The Shahadah in Arabic

The Shahadah

The **Shahadah** is the Muslim declaration of faith. It is the first pillar for Sunni Muslims and forms the core of Islamic belief. In Arabic, it reads:

lā ʾilāha ʾillā-llāh, muḥammadur-rasūlu-llāh

which translates as:

'There is no god but God; Muhammad is the messenger of God.'

Many Shi'a Muslims add 'Ali is the Friend/Divinely appointed authority of God.' This is because of their belief in Ali as the rightful leader after Muhammad.

The first part of the Shahadah relates to al-Tawhid and the second to Risalah and al-Nubuwwah (two of the Six Articles of Faith and 'Usul ad-Din respectively). For Shi'a Muslims, the third statement also links to al-Imamah (one of the 'Usul ad-Din).

Muslims believe that Allah commanded all prophets, including the Prophet Muhammad, to preach strict monotheism, which is the opposite of shirk, the worst sin. Therefore, the Shahadah, as an expression of al-Tawhid, is an important cornerstone of Muslim faith.

It is also an important Muslim belief that Muhammad, while being a prophet, was just a man. As a messenger, he was unique, delivering the final and universal message to the world. He is 'the seal of the prophets' (Surah 33:40) and the greatest inspiration for Muslims, who look up to him as the exemplary Muslim leader.

The Shahadah is the basis for all actions of a Muslim, including the Five Pillars and Six Articles of Faith.

Place of the Shahadah in Muslim practice

There are a number of ways that the Shahadah features in the lives of Muslims:

- It is the first thing uttered to a newborn baby. This is to ensure that the first words it hears are about Allah and to act as a reminder to the parents to bring the child up in the teachings of Islam so that it lives a life of submission to the will of Allah.

- When someone wishes to convert to Islam, they are required to recite the Shahadah. Most Muslims believe this must be done in the presence of a witness, such as an imam. Without belief in the Shahadah, a person cannot be a Muslim. Making the declaration is the starting point of a convert's journey to following Islam as best as they can.

- It is important for the Shahadah to be recited by or to a dying person. This is so that they or their loved ones bear witness

The Shahadah is the first thing uttered to a newborn baby

to them living their life according to Islam and that just as they entered the world hearing the words of Allah, they leave it with the same experience. This is another reminder of every Muslim life being lived in submission to Allah.

The Shahadah is seen as an expression of personal belief, confirming a Muslim's recognition and acceptance of the oneness of Allah and prophethood of Muhammad. It is also a public declaration of faith, helping to unite and strengthen the ummah, as well as to spread the message of Islam.

'Non-action' pillar

For Sunni Muslims, the Shahadah is the only 'non-action' pillar of the Five Pillars. This is because it is a statement of belief that it is essential to have faith in, without which Salah, Sawm, Zakah and Hajj would not be possible. The Shahadah has been described as the backbone to all the actions of a Muslim.

For Shi'a Muslims, Shahadah is a belief rather than a practice and therefore not included in the Ten Obligatory Acts. However, it is represented in three of the five roots of 'Usul ad-Din, namely al-Tawhid, al-Nubuwwah and al-Imamah, and so is still part of their beliefs.

Sources of authority

'God bears witness that there is no god but Him, as do the angels and those who have knowledge.' (Surah 3:18)

'God suffices as a witness: Muhammad is the Messenger of God.' (Surah 48:28–29)

Analyse and evaluate

Is Shahadah the most important of the Five Pillars of Islam for Sunni Muslims?	
Yes	No
Belief in Salah, Zakah, Sawm and Hajj is not possible without belief in the Shahadah.	All pillars are equally important, as each one is needed to keep Islam upright.
The Shahadah has to be recited both at the beginning and end of a Muslim's life, whether or not they have practised the other pillars.	Shahadah is the only 'non-action' pillar and so has less value than the other pillars.
Without declaring the Shahadah, a person cannot be a Muslim, yet belief in all the pillars is required just as columns are required in a building.	

Activities

Review

1. What are the two parts of the Sunni Shahadah?
2. What is the additional part of the Shahadah recited by Shi'a Muslims?

Develop

3. Why is it important for a Muslim convert to recite the Shahadah?

Link

4. Explain the relationship between the Shahadah and al-Tawhid.

Debate

5. 'A non-action pillar should not be a pillar at all.' To what extent is this conclusion fair? Discuss and note down reasons for and against this view.

Stretch

6. 'Too much focus is on words rather than actions.' How true is this of different Muslims in relation to the Shahadah?

4.6 Private acts of worship

Aim
To explore the importance of private acts of worship for Muslims

Starter
List possible reasons why some people prefer to pray using their own words.

Key word
Du'a – personal prayer or supplication

Du'a

Apart from Salah, there are other ways Muslims are able to worship. This includes **du'a**.

Du'a is a personal prayer or supplication, calling upon Allah. It literally means 'cry (of the heart)' or to summon. It is usually performed with the raising of hands.

First, set prayers are recited, such as from the Qur'an and Hadith, and then a person prays for anything they wish. This can include an improvement to their own or someone else's health, family problems, work stress and financial difficulties. The du'a ends with the words 'Amin' (so be it) and wiping one's hands over one's face, just as the Prophet Muhammad did.

Du'a can be offered individually or collectively, at any time and in any place. It is not necessary to perform wudu beforehand, nor to face Makkah (Mecca), though some Muslims still prefer to do these actions.

■ A Muslim offering private prayer

■ A Muslim offering a late-night prayer – Tahajjud

There are other optional forms of private worship that Muslims are encouraged to offer:

- Extra prayers throughout the day outside of Salah. These are rewarded by Allah, as a believer has gone out of their way to offer extra prayers. These are performed in rak'at like in Salah.

- A pre-dawn prayer specifically offered late at night, before Salah al-Fajr. It carries particular blessings, as the worshipper has given up sleep for the sake of Allah. The Prophet Muhammad used to offer night prayers until his feet became swollen. When his wife Aishah asked him, 'Why do you do this when Allah has forgiven your previous and future faults?' he replied, 'Shouldn't I be a thankful servant (of Allah)?' (Hadith, Bukhari).

- Tasbih means 'glorifying' (Allah) and, like du'a, is not a formal prayer. Many Muslims use tasbih beads to remind them of the names of Allah. Du'a and tasbih can be offered at any time, including instinctively.

The manner and frequency of these and other forms of private worship may differ according to the group that Muslims belong to. For instance, chanting about Allah's attributes is common in certain Sufi orders.

Importance of private worship

Private worship is important to Muslims because it:

- follows the practice of the Prophet Muhammad, who used to retreat to Cave Hira for private worship before the Night of Power and continued with du'a and other forms of prayer after this
- enables a Muslim to develop a personal relationship with Allah, as they are able to communicate with Allah in their own way; this is particularly important in areas where there are not many Muslims or mosques.

Sources of authority

'If My servants ask you about Me, I am near. I respond to those who call Me, so let them respond to Me, and believe in Me, so that they may be guided.' (Surah 2:186)

'After performing the ritual prayer, continue to remember God – standing, sitting, and lying on your sides.' (Surah 4:103)

'Indeed your Lord – blessed and almighty is he – is shy and most generous. He is shy when his servant raises his hands to him (in du'a) to turn them away empty.' (Hadith)

Analyse and evaluate

Are private acts of worship more meaningful than public acts of worship?

Yes	No
Private acts of worship help a Muslim develop a more personal and deeper connection with Allah.	Public acts of worship strengthen community spirit and the unity of the ummah. This is seen in congregational prayer, when Muslims stand shoulder to shoulder.
A Muslim can use their own words during worship and therefore speak and pray from the heart.	There are more blessings and rewards in praying together with others than by oneself.
Islam offers a balance between the two and recognises the meaningful place of both private and public acts of worship. At times, du'a might be more significant in a person's life. Muslims are also conscious of the Prophet Muhammad teaching that prayers in congregation are rewarded 27 times more than those offered on one's own.	

Activities

Review

1. What does du'a mean?
2. Why are extra prayers rewarded?

Develop

3. Make a list of things someone might pray for individually.

Link

4. Can prayer change anything? Refer back to Allah's characteristics on spread 3.5.

Debate

5. 'There isn't much difference between du'a and Salah.' To what extent is this conclusion fair? Discuss and note down reasons for and against this view.

Stretch

6. Research the attitudes of different groups towards private and public acts of worship.

Practices 4.6 Private acts of worship

4.7 Hajj: origins and importance of Hajj

Aim

To explore the origins and importance of Hajj

Starter

What is the most special place in the world to you? Why?

The holy Kaaba in Makkah (Mecca), which is at the centre of the Hajj pilgrimage

Hajj and the origins of the pilgrimage

Hajj is a pilgrimage to Makkah (Mecca) in Saudi Arabia. Makkah is the holiest city on Earth for Muslims, as it is where prophets like Ibrahim, Isma'il and Muhammad lived and taught about al-Tawhid.

The origins of pilgrimage can be traced back around four thousand years to the time of Ibrahim. According to the Qur'an (2:125), Ibrahim and his son Isma'il were commanded by Allah to rebuild the Kaaba, and this restored the city as a place of pilgrimage.

The Kaaba is believed to be more than five thousand years old, and the first masjid (mosque) in the world dedicated to the worship of one God. This makes it the holiest site in Islam and the focus of Hajj. The Kaaba has also been called other names in the Qur'an, such as Bayt al-Atiq (ancient house) and Bayt al-Haram (sacred house).

Muslims have been travelling to Makkah to complete Hajj ever since the time of the Prophet Muhammad, who performed similar rituals in the last year of his life. For hundreds of years, the Kaaba housed many idols, but the Prophet Muhammad cleansed it to ensure it became a centre of al-Tawhid once more.

Rules about Hajj

Making a pilgrimage to Makkah is obligatory for all Muslims who are healthy and can afford it (Surah 3:97). Those who are not physically or mentally fit enough or struggling financially are

> **Top tip**
>
> Muslims make many sacrifices to perform Hajj. These can be financial due to the expenses involved, and also personal, especially for a parent whose young children would need to be left with other relatives during the days of Hajj.

excused from Hajj. Similarly, Muslims should not attempt Hajj if there is no safe route to Makkah. This is a mercy from Allah. Hajj must be completed at least once in a Muslim's life, and someone who has completed Hajj is given the honorific title 'Hajji' (for men) or 'Hajjah' (for women).

The timing of Hajj is based on the lunar calendar, culminating with the festival of Eid-ul-Adha. This is two months and ten days after Eid-ul-Fitr. The pilgrimage starts on the eighth day of the last month of the Islamic calendar, Dhu al-Hijjah, and lasts about five days.

■ Muslims in Makkah (Mecca) completing Hajj

Importance of Hajj

Performing Hajj enables Muslims to commemorate some of the trials Ibrahim and his family faced in Makkah and to learn from their great example.

Hajj is a symbol of unity between Muslims regardless of gender, age, race or status, all submitting themselves completely to Allah. In recent years, the nature of the pilgrimage has changed with the worldwide spread of Islam and the introduction of fast direct travel by plane, car and train, which has made access to Makkah much easier. As a result, Hajj has become one of the largest annual gatherings of people anywhere in the world, with approximately three million pilgrims making the journey every year. Hajj is seen to be a powerful demonstration of the unity of the ummah, with Muslims from different denominations, countries and races converging in one place for the purpose of worshipping Allah and fulfilling a requirement of their faith.

Hajj also offers an opportunity for sins to be forgiven, and a person who has completed the pilgrimage is considered to be like an innocent newborn baby.

Sources of authority

'Proclaim the Pilgrimage to all people. They will come to you on foot and on every kind of lean camel, emerging from every deep mountain pass to attain benefits and mention God's name, on specified days, over the livestock He has provided for them. Feed yourselves and the desperately poor from them. Then let the pilgrims perform their acts of cleansing, fulfil their vows, and circle around the Ancient House.' (Surah 22:27–29)

'We made the House a resort and a sanctuary for people, saying, "Take the spot where Abraham stood as your place of prayer." We commanded Abraham and Ishmael: "Purify My House for those who walk round it, those who stay there, and those who bow and prostrate themselves in worship."… As Abraham and Ishmael built up the foundations of the House [they prayed], "Our Lord, accept [this] from us. You are the All Hearing, the All Knowing."' (Surah 2: 125–27)

Analyse and evaluate

Should there be restrictions on performing Hajj?

Yes	No
Hajj is compulsory for all Muslims to complete at least once in their lives and so only they should be allowed to enter Makkah.	Restrictions can prevent many people from undertaking a journey to a sacred place.
Hajj is a physically demanding experience and so it is only right that healthy and able people go.	Many Muslims lost out on the chance to go to Makkah for two years due to the Covid-19 pandemic and wish to fulfil a requirement of their faith.
Sometimes, too many pilgrims coming to Makkah has created problems like stampedes, therefore it is right that limits are placed on numbers of Muslims who travel to Hajj.	

Activities

Review
1. How many years can the origins of Hajj be traced back?
2. In which city is the Kaaba located?

Develop
3. Summarise Surah 2:125–127 in four bullet points.

Link
4. How does the Kaaba symbolise belief in al-Tawhid?

Debate
5. 'There is no need to go to pilgrimage to show your devotion to your faith.' To what extent is this conclusion fair? Discuss and note down reasons for and against this view.

Stretch
6. Research the difficulties faced by Ibrahim and his family, including his wife Hajar.

4.8 Hajj: rituals of Hajj

Aim
To explore the rituals of Hajj

Starter
Does going on a pilgrimage show greater devotion to your beliefs?

Key word
Ihram – state of purity and dedication that Muslims must enter before performing Hajj; also, two pieces of white clothing worn by male pilgrims

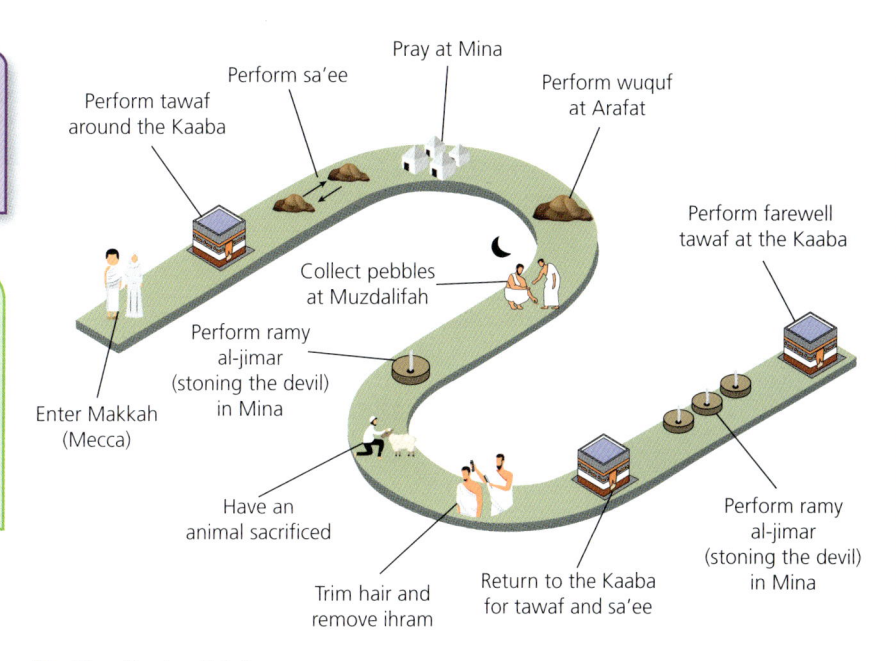

The rituals of Hajj

Hajj is made up of different rituals, many of which originate with Ibrahim.

The rituals of Hajj, shown in order:
- Enter Makkah (Mecca)
- Perform tawaf around the Kaaba
- Perform sa'ee
- Pray at Mina
- Perform wuquf at Arafat
- Collect pebbles at Muzdalifah
- Perform ramy al-jimar (stoning the devil) in Mina
- Have an animal sacrificed
- Trim hair and remove ihram
- Return to the Kaaba for tawaf and sa'ee
- Perform ramy al-jimar (stoning the devil) in Mina
- Perform farewell tawaf at the Kaaba

■ The rituals of Hajj

Top tip
Muslims who are unable to perform Hajj are encouraged to do as many good deeds during this period, including fasting on the day of Arafat and spending more time in worship. This is because of a Hadith that states the most blessed 10 days of the year are during the month of Dhu al-Hijjah.

The rituals of Hajj	
Prepare to enter Makkah (Mecca) and ihram regulations	Pilgrims make niyyah (intention) to perform Hajj and enter a state of *ihram*, where they think about the importance of what they are about to undertake. They must keep their minds pure of any grudges, worries and desires. Ihram symbolises that all believers are united and equal before Allah. Ihram is also the name for two unsewn pieces of white cloth that male pilgrims must wear, one wrapped around the lower body and one wrapped around the upper body. In addition, Shi'a Muslims cover their shoulders. Women must observe modest dress (covering of their hair and body) of any colour. They must be accompanied by a mahram (a male relative with whom marriage is not permissible, or their husband). Ihram clothes are used by some people as shrouds when they die, reinforcing that this life is a preparation for the next.
Perform tawaf around the Kaaba	Tawaf is making seven anti-clockwise circuits of the Kaaba, starting from the hajri aswad (a black stone or meteorite that Muslims believe was sent by Allah). If possible, pilgrims kiss the hajri aswad.

129

Perform sa'ee	The sa'ee is a brisk walk or run between two hills, Safa and Marwa, completed seven times. It re-enacts Hajar's (Ibrahim's wife) search for water when she and Isma'il were thirsty in the desert and she ran between the two hills. When Isma'il's heels struck the ground, a fountain miraculously sprouted in the shape of a blessed well. This well is known as Zamzam and pilgrims drink water from it.
Perform wuquf at Arafat	Wuquf is the act of standing before God. Pilgrims pray for forgiveness on the plain of Arafat, nine miles from Makkah. This can last any number of hours between sunrise and sunset. The pilgrims stay in tents or now also in hotels during wuquf, due to the large numbers making the pilgrimage. This stage is often described as the climax of Hajj, as the practice of wuquf symbolises what will happen on the Day of Judgement when everyone must stand in front of Allah. 
Stone the devil at Mina	Pilgrims collect pebbles at Muzdalifah for the ramy al-jimar (stoning of walls representing evil). They sleep under the sky at night. This is to re-enact Ibrahim driving away the Devil when it tried to tempt him and Isma'il to disobey Allah. 
Have an animal sacrificed	At the end of Hajj, pilgrims who can afford it arrange to have an animal (for example a sheep, goat or camel) sacrificed. The meat is distributed to people who need it.
Trim hair and remove ihram	Men shave their heads, symbolising new life and forgiveness of past sins. Women cut only a lock of their hair. All pilgrims return to normal dress.
Return to the Kaaba for tawaf and sa'ee	Pilgrims perform a farewell tawaf and repeat the run between Safa and Marwa. Shi'a Muslims perform an additional tawaf, in order to resume sexual relations with their spouses. They visit the tombs of members of the Ahl al-Bayt – part of the wider Shi'a practice of Ziyara (visitation) that includes pilgrimage to the graves of their Imams, including Imam Ali, whose grave they believe to be in Najaf, Iraq (considered by Shi'as to be the holiest site after Makkah and Madinah) and Imam Hussain in Karbala, Iraq.

■ Mount Arafat, where the Prophet Muhammad delivered his final sermon and Muslims pray for forgiveness

■ Pilgrims throw stones at walls representing the devil

■ The shaving of heads symbolises the completion of Hajj and the start of a new spiritual journey

■ Pilgrims performing tawaf

Significance of Hajj rituals for Muslims

Throughout the rituals of Hajj, pilgrims are expected to maintain a state of continuous worship and repentance. The primary purpose of Hajj is to fulfil an individual duty to obey Allah's will.

The lessons learned during Hajj are to be kept for life. Many Muslims who perform the pilgrimage are seen to have become more spiritual. A famous example is Malcolm X, who was moved by the spectacle of unity and warmth he experienced during Hajj.

The opportunity to visit the graves of the Prophet Muhammad, his companions and his family members also allows Muslims to pay respect and earn blessings.

While Hajj must take place in a specific month, Muslims can make a smaller and voluntary pilgrimage at other times of the year. This is known as umrah and involves less time and fewer rituals.

For many Sunni and Shi'a Muslims, performing Hajj completes their obligation of following all the Five Pillars and Ten Obligatory Acts, as well as providing a once-in-a-lifetime opportunity to pray with a large section of the ummah.

Source of authority

'Those who go to Makkah for obligatory and voluntary pilgrimage are the envoys of Allah and his gift to them is forgiveness.' (Imam Ali)

Analyse and evaluate

Are there more benefits than challenges of Hajj?

Yes	No
Hajj is a chance for individual Muslims to leave the affairs of the world for a short time and to focus on their own spirituality and relationship with Allah.	Not all pilgrims are physically capable of completing all the rituals of Hajj.
The Qur'an allows Muslims to engage in trade during Hajj (Qur'an 2:198) and does not deny believers to discuss or do business when so many people are gathered together. This shows that Islam is a practical faith.	While at Makkah, pilgrims are able to focus on Allah, but this often becomes difficult once they return home and some of the lessons learned can be forgotten.

Despite the challenges faced by pilgrims, most return from Makkah inspired, refreshed and reformed.

Activities

Review
1. What is the hajri aswad?
2. Identify any three rituals during Hajj.

Develop
3. Create a memorable image for each stage of Hajj, then practise rewriting the information from memory.

Link
4. Why are some Muslims buried in the same clothes as worn at Hajj?

Debate
5. 'There should be limits on how many people can perform Hajj each year.' To what extent is this conclusion fair? Discuss and note down reasons for and against this view.

Stretch
6. Find out more about Malcolm X and the impact his Hajj experience had on him.

4.9 Zakah: the role and importance of giving alms

Aim

To explore the role and importance of giving alms

Starter

Should it be compulsory to give to the poor?

Key word

Zakah/Zakat – 'purification' of wealth

Wealth given by Allah

Muslims believe that all wealth comes from Allah and is therefore a God-given gift. This will be used to provide for oneself and one's family, such as to pay for a house, bills and other costs relating to everyday living.

However, support for the poor is also a key teaching of Islam. Giving and spending in the way of Allah, and the difference this makes to others, strengthens the ummah. Therefore, wealth is also seen as a trust to be used wisely and for the benefit of those who are less fortunate. This ensures that no member of the community is neglected and is one of the ways that society can be at peace, which is one of the meanings and aims of Islam.

Zakah (which can also be spelt as **Zakat**), also called almsgiving, is the third of the Sunni Five Pillars. Making any financial sacrifice is a way for believers to attain nearness to Allah. The word Zakah comes from the Arabic word for purification; it is seen as a way of purifying not only one's wealth but also one's soul.

■ Zakah is one of the Five Pillars of Sunni Islam

Zakah is usually given to and distributed by a central mosque and can be used for a number of things, including:

- relieving poverty
- helping those in debt
- providing assistance for travellers
- paying ransom for prisoners of war
- improving the welfare of society in any other way.

The Qur'an states that those in need of Zakah can often be identified by characteristics such as their appearance, and that just because they do not ask for help does not mean they do not need it: 'you will recognise them by their characteristic of not begging persistently' (Surah 2:273).

All acts of financial giving, including Zakah, are compared to a loan which will be repaid by Allah. Those who pay Zakah and make personal financial sacrifices are also counted among the successful believers (Surah 23:4).

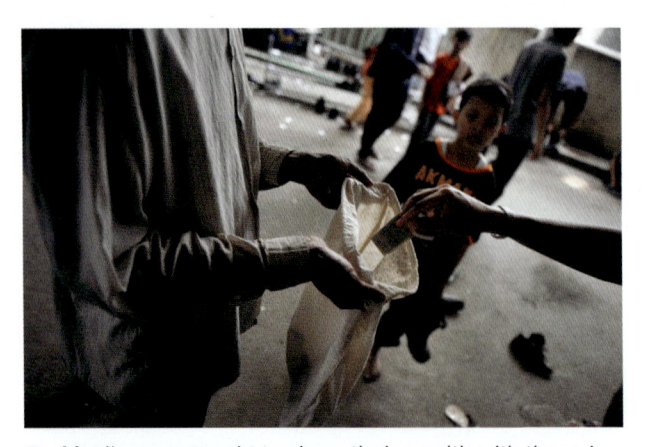

■ Muslims are taught to share their wealth with those in need

Sources of authority

'[Give] to those needy who are wholly occupied in God's way and cannot travel in the land [for trade]. The unknowing might think them rich because of their self-restraint, but you will recognize them by their characteristic of not begging persistently. God is well aware of any good you give.' (Surah 2: 273)

'None of you [believers] will attain true piety unless you give out of what you cherish: whatever you give, God knows about it very well.' (Surah 3:92)

'The faithful have succeeded: those who pray humbly, who shun frivolity, who pay the prescribed alms...' (Surah 23:1–4)

'Keep up the prayer, pay the prescribed alms, and lend God a good loan' (Surah 73:20)

Analyse and evaluate

Does giving wealth to a divine cause make you a better person?

Yes	No
The Qur'an frequently mentions Zakah along with Salah, which shows a close relationship between them as bringing about a moral change in a person.	Money cannot buy purity – giving their wealth is not a guarantee that a person is or will become more righteous.
Spending in the way of Allah leads to Allah blessing one's wealth even more, and granting many more rewards including a purer life.	Just because a person can afford to give in the way of Allah does not mean that they will change into a better Muslim.
Allah rewards people according to their intentions and knows the state of a person's heart – those who are sincere will see their wealth and souls become purer.	

Activities

Review
1. What is Zakah also known as?
2. List three things Zakah can be used for.

Develop
3. Why has the Qur'an described giving in the way of Allah as a 'good loan'?

Link
4. Is Zakah an example of serving Allah, serving his creation or both (see spread 4.10)? Explain your answer.

Debate
5. 'Giving to charity should be a personal choice.' To what extent is this conclusion fair? Discuss and note down reasons for and against this view.

Stretch
6. What else does the Qur'an teach about wealth? An example is Surah 2:215.

4.10 Zakah: comparing Sunni and Shi'a Muslims

Aim
To compare and contrast Zakah and Khums

Starter
What does the government spend income tax on? Think of services that benefit the public.

Key words
Khums – 20 per cent tax paid by Shi'a Muslims
Nisab – the minimum amount that a Muslim must have before being required to give Zakah

Top tip
The rule of 2.5 per cent for Zakah comes from the Hadith of the Prophet Muhammad.

■ Ali Khamanei in Iran is one of the Grand Ayatollahs who decides what causes Khums will be utilised for

Zakah and Khums

Zakah is the fourth of the Shi'a Ten Obligatory Acts. While many beliefs and practices are shared between Sunni and Shi'a Muslims in terms of Zakah, there are also differences. One of these is the practice of **Khums**, which applies only to Shi'a Muslims.

In the time of the Prophet Muhammad, Khums primarily concerned the spoils of war (Surah 8:41). Following his death, Shi'a Muslims interpreted this verse to apply to their Imams. Since then, Twelver Shi'a Muslims have given 20 per cent of their annual savings to the Imam of the time to spend on whatever he thinks is necessary for the community. Khums is compulsory on seven items, including the spoils of war, precious items, land and business profit.

In the absence of the 12th and final Imam, Khums is paid to one of his representatives called the Grand Ayatollah, who decides how the money should be used. This usually goes towards the building of mosques, schools, orphanages and other religious causes. Some Shi'a Muslims choose to distribute Khums themselves to good causes as it is seen as a personal responsibility. Like Zakah, Khums must be paid annually. Shi'a Muslims believe that failure to do so is a violation of the Prophet Muhammad or the Imams' right to the funds.

Nizari Shi'a Muslims give approximately 10 per cent of their monthly income as both Zakah and Khums.

Sunni	Shi'a
All Muslims consider Zakah, the giving of a proportion of one's wealth to help the poor, as an essential obligation for all who own '**nisab**' (a minimum threshold of wealth based on the price of a specific amount of gold).	
Sunni Muslims use qiyas (reasoning) to decide how much to donate – about 2.5% of their total wealth in all forms. This is to prevent wealth becoming 'idle' and not being used for any social responsibilities.	Shi'a Muslims calculate Zakah based on how much of specific commodities they own: coinage, cattle and crops. Nowadays, many Shi'a Muslims don't own these things and are not strictly obliged to donate Zakah at all. It is instead 'mustahab' (recommended).
In Muslim countries, Zakah is collected directly by the state. In the UK, it is made as a confidential donation to the local mosque/masjid.	
Muslims are also encouraged to provide voluntary aid to their communities in the form of money or good deeds, called sadaqah, and, in the UK, to registered charities.	
	Though Shi'a Muslims may not pay Zakah, they do pay Khums which is one-fifth (khums) of their savings, after they have deducted their living expenses, for the benefit of other causes too.

■ Comparison between Sunni and Shi'a Muslims in terms of Zakah

Key word

Sadaqah – voluntary alms

Sadaqah

There are other types of charity in Islam which are optional and can be of any amount. One of these is **sadaqah**, which was recommended by the Prophet Muhammad.

Sadaqah is not just financial and can also extend to deeds, such as kindness to animals, planting a tree, offering a smile, or any other humanitarian cause. There is also sadaqah jariyah (ongoing charity), which is an act that continues to benefit others after a person's death, for example building a hospital.

Both Sunni and Shi'a Muslims believe that by giving sadaqah, a person increases their good deeds which will be rewarded both in this life and the next. The commitment of Muslims to give Zakah, Khums and sadaqah means that they are one of the groups who donate most to charities in the UK. This spirit of giving has an enormous impact on the ummah too, ensuring that people's needs are met and the community is united.

Sources of authority

'Know that one-fifth of your battle gains belongs to God and the Messenger, to close relatives and orphans, to the needy and travellers.' (Surah 8:41)

'Every kindly act is considered charity.' (Hadith)

Analyse and evaluate

Should it be up to individual Muslims how much they give to the poor?

Yes	No
The Qur'an says 'there is no compulsion in religion' (Surah 2:256), so giving to the poor should be a personal choice.	If no minimum rate is set, it may mean that very few will give any wealth away. This will leave the rich richer and the poor poorer.
People may have other financial priorities and possibly be unable to afford to give to the less fortunate.	Islam requires submission to Allah, who is wise and all-knowing. Whatever Allah commands should be obeyed.

Zakah is taught in order for wealth not to be stored and left idle but to keep it circulating and to benefit those who need it the most, particularly society's most disadvantaged.

Activities

Review

1. What percentage of wealth do Shi'a Muslims give in Khums?
2. What is sadaqah?

Develop

3. 'When a man dies, his deeds come to an end except for three: an ongoing charity, beneficial knowledge and a child who prays for him' (Hadith). Explain the meaning of this Hadith.

Link

4. Salah and Zakah are often mentioned together in the Qur'an. Why might this be?

Debate

5. 'Alms should only be given to those who deserve them.' To what extent is this conclusion fair? Discuss and note down reasons for and against this view.

Stretch

6. Research the reasons why Zakah is set at 2.5 per cent.

4.11 Sawm: the origins of fasting

> **Aim**
>
> To explore the origins of fasting and the Night of Power

> **Starter**
>
> Do you ever take food and drink for granted?

> **Key words**
>
> **Sawm** – fasting
> **Ramadan** – the month of fasting for Muslims
> **Tarawih** – voluntary night prayer during Ramadan
> **I'tikaf** – retreat

Origins of fasting

Sawm is the Arabic word for fasting. It is one of the Five Pillars in Sunni Islam and one of the Ten Obligatory Acts for Shi'a Muslims.

The practice of fasting goes back many centuries and can be found in religions before Islam. For example, in Judaism fasting takes place on Yom Kippur (the Day of Atonement), the holiest day for Jews. Muslims believe that many prophets throughout history have fasted in some form, and that with the appearance of the Prophet Muhammad the practice of fasting was further developed.

There are two types of fasting in Islam:

- optional – weekly, following the practice of the Prophet Muhammad
- compulsory – during the month of **Ramadan**.

Fasting as devotion to Allah

While fasting, Muslims spend their time reflecting on Allah's blessings and attributes as a way of avoiding inappropriate thoughts and actions. There is a greater focus on reading the Qur'an and praying with more devotion. The Prophet Muhammad made it clear that the purpose of observing Ramadan was self-improvement and condemned people who neglect this while observing the fast. He said that Allah would rather people mended their behaviour than perform the fast.

There are some differences in the way that Shi'a Muslims observe Ramadan:

- The fast is broken a little later than sunset, when darkness has set in: 'until the white thread of dawn becomes distinct from the black' (Surah 2:187).
- The martyrdom of the first Imam, Ali, is also commemorated during the month, on the days he was attacked (19th) and died (21st).

Ramadan and the Qur'an

There is a special link between the Qur'an and the month of Ramadan. It was in Ramadan that the angel Jibril visited the Prophet Muhammad in Cave Hira to reveal the first of many Qur'anic revelations, an event known as the Night of Power (Laylat al-Qadr).

Muslims spend the month reciting the Qur'an more frequently than they would at other times of the year. They try to recite the whole Qur'an within Ramadan, as the angel Jibril did with the Prophet Muhammad. One way many Sunni Muslims achieve this is through a voluntary night prayer known as **tarawih**, offered after Salat al-Isha, a tradition that started in the time of the second Khalifah, Umar. Shi'a Muslims do not offer the tarawih prayer, as it was not the Prophet Muhammad's practice.

■ The Cave Hira, where the Prophet Muhammad experienced the Night of Power

■ There is a close relationship between the month of Ramadan and the revelation of the Qur'an, which is why many Muslims read it more frequently during the days of fasting

Night of Power

Muslims also strive to experience their own Night of Power. This is a night when a person has all their prayers accepted, or a moment when angels come to support them. When this happens, it is 'better than a thousand months' (Surah 97:3), which means that no one can measure the extent of its impact and rewards. It can lead to a person becoming spiritually purer and closer to Allah.

For Sunni Muslims, this is done in the last ten days of Ramadan, particularly during the odd-numbered nights. Shi'a Muslims seek the Night of Power on the 19th, 21st and 23rd nights of Ramadan. For this reason, mosques are very busy during this period. Some Muslims spend this time in **i'tikaf** (retreat), during which they have a private space in the mosque to study, worship and rest. They withdraw from the world and focus purely on the remembrance and worship of Allah. Muslims believe that the Night of Power can remove past sins.

Sources of authority

'O ye who believe! Fasting is prescribed to you as it was prescribed to those before you that ye may (learn) self-restraint … Ramadan is the (month) in which was sent down the Qur'an as a guide to mankind also clear (signs) for guidance and judgement (between right and wrong).' (Surah 2:183–85)

'The Night of Power is better than a thousand months; therein come down the angels and the spirit by God's permission, on every errand; peace! … This until the rise of morn!' (Surah 97:3–5)

'Whoever spends this night in prayer out of faith and in the hope of reward will be forgiven their previous sins.' (Hadith)

Analyse and evaluate

Should all Muslims perform i'tikaf?

Yes	No
I'tikaf takes place in the last ten days of Ramadan, when the Prophet Muhammad said it is more likely to experience the Night of Power, and many Muslims claim to have experienced it during i'tikaf.	Spending ten days away from one's family and other commitments, such as work, is not practical.
I'tikaf is a highly spiritually transforming experience during which Muslims cut themselves off from the world and can focus on becoming closer to Allah more than ever.	I'tikaf is purely optional and just one of many ways of achieving nearness to Allah.

There is no requirement for Muslims to perform i'tikaf as it is a demanding spiritual discipline that not everyone is ready to undertake. Those who do feel that they are far more likely to experience the Night of Power.

Activities

Review
1. What is the Arabic for fasting?
2. Identify two types of fasting.

Develop
3. How might the Night of Power for the Prophet Muhammad and for Muslims be similar and different?

Link
4. What qualities did the Prophet Muhammad have that made him worthy of experiencing the Night of Power? (see spread 3.9)

Debate
5. 'You cannot rely on one night to have all your sins forgiven.' To what extent is this conclusion fair? Discuss and note down reasons for and against this view.

Stretch
6. Research how fasting is practised in other religions before Islam. What is similar and different?

4.12 Sawm: the duties during fasting and its benefits

Aim
To explore the main duties during fasting and its benefits

Starter
What might be the different motivations for someone to experience hunger and thirst?

■ Breaking the fast in the month of Ramadan with dates and water

Source of authority
'Whoever does not give up lying and evil deeds and saying bad words to others then God is not in need of their leaving food and drink.' (Hadith, Bukhari)

■ Big Iftar events, inviting people of all faiths and none, are hosted in many parts of the UK, including Bristol

Duties during fasting

Fasting involves giving up food and drink, sex, and close intimacy such as kissing. Additionally, there is fasting of the eyes, ears, tongue, hands and feet, meaning they are not to be used for anything that will disobey Allah's commands.

Ramadan lasts either 29 or 30 days, starting with the sighting of the crescent moon and ending with the festival of Eid-ul-Fitr. The lunar calendar is not fixed, so the length of each daily fast depends on the time of year Ramadan falls in and where in the world it is being observed.

Fasting starts at the first light of dawn and ends at sunset. The Prophet Muhammad would eat something at the start of the fast (suhur) and break the fast at the end (iftar) with dates and water, and Muslims follow his example. The quantity of food consumed at suhur and iftar should be moderate – people are discouraged from eating and drinking too much.

Benefits of fasting

Muslims believe that there are many religious and moral benefits to fasting, both to individual Muslims and the ummah as a whole:

- It helps them to get close to Allah and develop spirituality and God-consciousness.
- The extra prayers offered, especially at night, receive special acceptance from Allah.
- Hunger and thirst help them to appreciate the suffering of the less fortunate.
- Fasting instils self-restraint, giving Muslims an opportunity to reflect on what they say how they treat others.
- There are health benefits as well as spiritual ones.

Exemptions from fasting

Only Muslims who are in good health are required to fast. People who are exempt from fasting include:

- the sick
- travellers on long journeys (for example flying abroad)
- elderly people whose health would be affected
- menstruating, pregnant and breastfeeding women
- young children (the age of fasting varies in different Muslim communities).

According to the Qur'an, the reason for excusing these people from fasting is because Allah recognises their situation and 'wants ease for you, not hardship' (Qur'an 2:185). Muslims who cannot keep the fast in Ramadan, apart from children and the elderly, must either make up the missed days at another time or pay fidya, a monetary donation that supports the poor.

Fasting in Muslim and non-Muslim countries

In Muslim countries, most of the population keep fasts in Ramadan. In some cases, government offices and private businesses slow down during the month and reduce working hours, in consideration for people's tiredness, especially in hot climates such as in the Middle East. Some countries observe Ramadan more strictly, such as Saudi Arabia where the majority of eateries are closed during daylight hours. The call to prayer may be heard in public, announcing the start and end of the fast.

The experience of Muslims living in non-Muslim countries like the UK is considered more challenging as the majority of people are not fasting. This can make those observing Sawm at school or in the workplace feel isolated. However, many Muslims also experience a lot of support from schools and businesses who recognise the importance Ramadan has for Muslims and make different arrangements accordingly.

For instance, prayer space is often provided to Muslim students at school, and superstores run special offers on various products during Ramadan. It is also common to see political leaders and representatives of other religions wishing Muslims 'Ramadan Mubarak' in order to make Muslims feel a valued part of society. Some non-Muslims also choose to experience the fast in solidarity with their Muslim friends, neighbours and colleagues, helping to foster good relations in the community. 'Big Iftar' events are also held in many cities.

During the winter months, when fasts are shorter due to daylight hours, Muslims who work may arrange to have their break when it is time to eat the iftar meal.

Analyse and evaluate

Is Sawm the most important of the Five Pillars of Islam?

Yes	No
The month of Ramadan provides an opportunity for Muslims to experience the Night of Power, which is 'better than a thousand months'.	There are some who are exempt from fasting, such as children, pregnant women and the sick.
During Ramadan, Muslims recite the Qur'an more frequently and mosques are full of worshippers.	The spiritual benefits of fasting can also be achieved through Salah and Hajj.
Many Muslims look forward to Ramadan every year because fasting with fellow Muslims is a source of great support, strength and solidarity. Other pillars can also help achieve this, showing that all the pillars are equally important.	

Activities

Review

1. Give two benefits of fasting.
2. Identify one way that fasting for Sunni and Shi'a Muslims is different.

Develop

3. Explain the Hadith 'Whoever does not give up lying and evil deeds and saying bad words to others then God is not in need of their leaving food and drink.'

Link

4. Compare the spiritual and moral benefits of Sawm and Salah.

Debate

5. 'Fasting has no relevance and value in the twenty-first century.' To what extent is this conclusion fair? Discuss and note down reasons for and against this view.

Stretch

6. Is it more difficult to fast in a non-Muslim country than a Muslim country? Give reasons to justify your view.

Practices 4.12 Sawm: the duties during fasting and its benefits

4.13 Festivals and special days: Eid-ul-Adha and Eid-ul-Fitr

Aim
To explore the origins and meaning of Eid-ul-Adha and Eid-ul-Fitr

Starter
What days are important to you? How do you celebrate?

Key words
Eid-ul-Adha – festival of sacrifice
Eid-ul-Fitr – festival marking the end of Ramadan

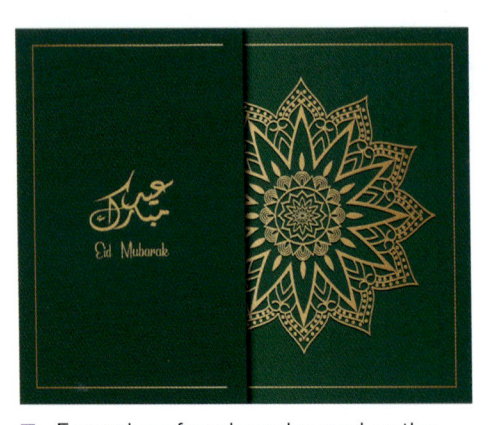

Celebrations and commemorations play an important part in the lives of all Muslims. Two of these are **Eid-ul-Adha** and **Eid-ul-Fitr**.

Eid-ul-Adha

Eid-ul-Adha means the festival of sacrifice. It takes place on the tenth day of the Islamic month of Dhu al-Hijjah, at the end of the Hajj pilgrimage, and commemorates the story of Ibrahim and Isma'il's obedience to Allah.

Ibrahim had a dream that he was sacrificing Isma'il. He interpreted it to mean that Allah wanted him to sacrifice Isma'il (child sacrifice was a common cultural practice at this time). Isma'il was willing to be sacrificed, as he believed Allah commanded it. When Ibrahim was about to sacrifice Isma'il at an altar, Allah called out to him to stop. Even though the dream had been intended to symbolise something else, Allah praised both of them for their spirit of devotion. A ram was sacrificed instead.

During Hajj, in the desert of Mina, animals are sacrificed and their meat is shared out among people in need. This is called qurbani, or udiyah in Arabic, meaning sacrifice. Many Muslims in the UK arrange for this to be done in countries where halal (permissible) methods are used. Some also give meat to food banks and homeless shelters. Qurbani is a reminder to Muslims that just as animals may be sacrificed for a higher purpose, so should they be prepared to give up their own lives for the sake of Allah.

People buy new clothes and families go to the mosque to offer a special Eid Salah prayer and listen to a sermon. For Shi'a Muslims, the Eid Salah is not obligatory but optional and highly recommended. Everyone says 'Eid Mubarak' ('Have a blessed Eid') to each other.

■ Examples of cards exchanged on the occasion of Eid-ul-Fitr

Importance of Eid-ul-Adha

Eid-ul-Adha is not merely a celebration of a story but a reminder to all Muslims to be ready to follow the example of Ibrahim and his family and offer themselves in Allah's service as taught in the Qur'an. It is this sacrifice that gave Ibrahim and his family the reward of being the ancestors of the Prophet Muhammad. Muslims are grateful for this and therefore offer prayers for them.

■ Muslims embrace each other and say 'Eid Mubarak' ('Have a blessed Eid')

Source of authority

'The Day of al-Fitr became an Eid so that Muslims congregate to glorify God and thank him for his blessings. The Eid al-Fitr is a day of congregation, a day of celebration, a day of breaking the fast, and a day of giving charity.' (Imam Ali bin Musa al-Rida, eighth Twelver Shi'a Imam)

Eid-ul-Fitr

Eid-ul-Fitr originated in the time of the Prophet Muhammad and takes place on the first day of Shawwal, the month following Ramadan. It is a joyous occasion when Muslims express their gratitude to Allah for the blessings of Ramadan.

Just as on Eid-ul-Adha, people wear new clothes, families go to the mosque to offer a special Eid Salah and listen to a sermon, and everyone says 'Eid Mubarak' to each other. People including children exchange gifts and cards and celebrate with food at home, in a community hall or in a restaurant. No fasting is allowed. The head of each family gives money known as zakat al-fitr, which goes towards less fortunate members of society.

Importance of Eid-ul-Fitr

Muslims emphasise that Eid-ul-Fitr, while a social celebration, is first and foremost a religious occasion, as it is supposed to remind Muslims to maintain the self-discipline and other benefits gained during Ramadan all year round. For example, if during Ramadan a Muslim has become more regular in offering prayers and attending the mosque, they should continue doing this afterwards too.

Analyse and evaluate

Do Eid-ul-Adha and Eid-ul-Fitr have the same importance?	
Yes	**No**
Both occasions enable Muslims to come together to celebrate important times of the year with each other.	Eid-ul-Adha is often called the 'great Eid' owing to its importance in teaching Muslims to be willing to make the ultimate sacrifice of giving their lives for the sake of Allah if required.
Both festivals require Muslims to give to the poor and needy, therefore this benefits society's most disadvantaged people.	Eid-ul-Fitr involves fasting every day for an entire month, which is a demanding physical, mental and spiritual discipline.
The Prophet Muhammad spoke about the need to celebrate both Eids and did not distinguish between their importance, therefore neither do most Muslims.	

Activities

Review
1. Whom did Ibrahim believe he had to sacrifice?
2. Give two ways that Eid-ul-Fitr is celebrated.

Develop
3. Read the account of Ibrahim and Isma'il in the Qur'an (Surah 37:102–11) and explain it in your own words.

Link
4. What qualities did Ibrahim and his family have that make their memory during Eid-ul-Adha important?

Debate
5. 'Celebrating festivals is a waste of time and money.' To what extent is this conclusion fair? Discuss and note down reasons for and against this view.

Stretch
6. Research the symbolism and significance of an animal being sacrificed on the occasion of Eid-ul-Adha.

4.14 Festivals and special days: Eid-ul-Ghadeer and Ashura

Aim
To explore the importance of Eid-ul-Ghadeer and Ashura for Shi'a Muslims

Starter
How do people express grief?

Key words
Eid-ul-Ghadeer – Shi'a festival commemorating the choice of Ali as the Prophet Muhammad's successor
Ashura – Shi'a commemoration of Imam Hussain's martyrdom

Eid-ul-Ghadeer

For Shi'a Muslims, **Eid-ul-Ghadeer** is the most important of all Islamic festivals, as it celebrates the day that they believe Ali was named as the Prophet Muhammad's successor (see spread 3.4).

The Prophet Muhammad received a revelation at a pond called Ghadir Khumm, instructing him to convey an important message. He gathered the Muslims who were with him and announced: 'Whoever took me as his mawla (authority), Ali is his mawla' (Hadith). Immediately afterwards, he received the last Qur'anic revelation, that Islam had been perfected for Muslims. Shi'a Muslims believe that this means that Ali had been designated as the Prophet Muhammad's successor.

Eid-ul-Ghadeer is:

- celebrated on the 18th of Dhul Hijjah (shortly after Hajj)
- observed by Shi'a Muslims to mark the occasion when, they believe, the Prophet Muhammad appointed Ali as the leader of Muslims after him
- the most important of all Eids for Shi'a Muslims which is celebrated in many ways, including eulogies of the Ahl al-Bayt, talks and entertainment.

Sunni Muslims do not celebrate Eid-ul-Ghadeer because they do not believe Ali was chosen to be the immediate successor to the Prophet Muhammad.

Ashura

Ashura takes place on the tenth of Muharram and commemorates the anniversary of the martyrdom of Imam Hussain, the grandson of the Prophet Muhammad and third Imam for Shi'a Muslims.

■ Millions of Shi'a Muslims visit the shrine of Imam Hussain in Karbala, Iraq, to mark Ashura

Imam Hussain was martyred along with his family and companions in 680CE in Karbala, Iraq. This happened during the rule of Yazid, who became leader of the Muslims following the end of the Rightly Guided Caliphate. Yazid demanded allegiance from Hussain but he refused because Yazid was acting against the teachings of Islam and was ruling like a tyrant.

While Hussain and 72 of his relatives and companions were heading towards Kufa in Iraq, Yazid sent an army to surround them in the desert of Karbala. Hussain refused to give Yazid their loyalty and they were subsequently deprived of water and food. Yazid's army was under strict orders not to let Hussain and his people leave. Yazid's army martyred most of Hussain's party, including Hussain and his six-month-old son, and took the remaining women and children captive. Hussain's decapitated head was sent to the governor of Kufa.

How Ashura is commemorated today

- Gatherings are held at the mosque every night from the first day of Muharram to Ashura. Mosques are usually draped in black and attendants also wear black to symbolise mourning.
- Mourning processions are held in the streets, for example those in central London organised by British Shi'a Muslims. The processions include rallies against injustice and speaking up for minority groups who are discriminated against anywhere in the world. For this reason, they are also seen as protests for peace.
- Every year, millions of Shi'a Muslims go on a pilgrimage to the shrine of Hussain in Karbala.
- The period of mourning stops 40 days after Ashura. This is because 40 days after the massacre, Hussain's family returned to Karbala to grieve over their loved ones. Some Shi'a Muslims express their grief through poetry and ta'ziyah, a play to re-enact the death of Imam Hussain.
- There is no fasting during Ashura.

■ Mourning processions are organised by Shi'a Muslims every year in London to mark Ashura

Some Shi'a Muslims carry out acts of self-flagellation (striking their own chests) as a symbol of their reverence and willingness to give their blood for the Ahl al-Bayt. By scratching and cutting themselves, they feel closer to Ali and Hussain, who suffered greatly at the hands of their enemies. This is seen as an important expression of their devotion to the Imams.

Many Shi'a scholars reject such acts of self-harm which they see as excessive, arguing that they misrepresent Shi'a tradition, but consider more gentle methods, such as tapping oneself, acceptable. Some young Shi'a Muslims in the UK also choose to donate blood through the NHS to honour Hussain's sacrifice.

Importance of Ashura

Imam Hussain is seen as one of the greatest martyrs in Islam. Martyrs are praised highly in the Qur'an and are described as 'living' in terms of their spirit and example. The massacre at Karbala and martyrdom of Hussain and other members of the Ahl al-Bayt are remembered by all Muslims, even though the rest of the ummah does not mark Ashura in the same way as Shi'a Muslims.

Other Muslims still express love for the Prophet Muhammad and his family and offer special prayers for them known as salawat ala al-Nabi. Ashura coincides with the anniversary of the time when Musa (Moses) and the Israelites were liberated from the Pharaoh in Egypt. On this day (and the day before and after), many Sunni Muslims fast, as this was the practice of the Prophet Muhammad.

Shi'a Muslims have been committed to maintaining the tradition of Ashura, seen largely through the pilgrimage of millions of people to Karbala, so that the sacrifices of past Imams and the Ahl al-Bayt are not forgotten and so that Shi'a Muslims can also show similar courage in standing up to injustice.

Issues relating to celebrating festivals and special days in Muslim and non-Muslim countries

Both Eid-ul-Adha and Eid-ul-Fitr are public holidays in Muslim countries. Eid-ul-Ghadeer is a public holiday in Iran and Iraq, as there are more Shi'a Muslims there. Government offices, banks and schools are closed on these occasions.

Sources of authority

'Today I have perfected your religion for you, completed My blessing upon you, and chosen as your religion *islam* [total devotion to God].' (Surah 5:3)

'Messenger, proclaim everything that has been sent down to you from your Lord – if you do not, then you will not have communicated His message' (Surah 5:67)

Commemorating these special days is not so easy in non-Muslim countries and requires Muslims to take time off school and work, which may be unpaid. There can be difficulties when Muslim students have important study commitments, such as examinations.

Ashura processions, such as in central London, can cause inconvenience to the public and businesses. However, festivals like Eid-ul-Adha and Eid-ul-Fitr are also celebrated by different sections of the community. For instance, assemblies and activities are held in schools for non-Muslim students to learn more about the significance of these special days. Members of the royal family and leaders of different political groups also broadcast messages wishing Muslims 'Happy Eid'. This helps Muslims feel confident about their faith and like valued members of society.

Analyse and evaluate

Is the grief shown during Ashura excessive?

Yes	No
No one should feel as though they must hurt themselves – self-harm is against the teachings of Islam.	The love for members of the Prophet Muhammad's family, including Imam Hussain, runs very deep, especially for Shi'a Muslims.
There were many martyrs in Islam before Imam Hussain but processions have never been held for them.	The manner of Imam Hussain's martyrdom is particularly painful, which is the reason events at Karbala are re-enacted in Shi'a communities.
The Qur'an tells Muslims to be steadfast in their faith, including at times of tragedy, and to ensure any expression of grief is in line with shari'a.	

Activities

Review
1. Give a reason why Eid-ul-Ghadeer is the most important festival for Shi'a Muslims.
2. When does Ashura take place?

Develop
3. Why do Shi'a Muslims believe that Surah 5:3 refers to the Prophet Muhammad's choice of Ali as his successor?

Link
4. In no more than 50 words, explain the link between Ashura and al-Imamah.

Debate
5. 'All commemorations are equally important.' To what extent is this conclusion fair? Discuss and note down reasons for and against this view.

Stretch
6. Research Arbaeen and its link to Ashura.

4.15 Jihad: Greater Jihad

Aim

To explore Muslim beliefs about Greater Jihad

Starter

What things in life do you struggle with? How do you try to overcome them?

Key words

Jihad – struggle
Greater Jihad – spiritual or inner struggle
Munkar – doing what is wrong
Ma'ruf – doing what is right

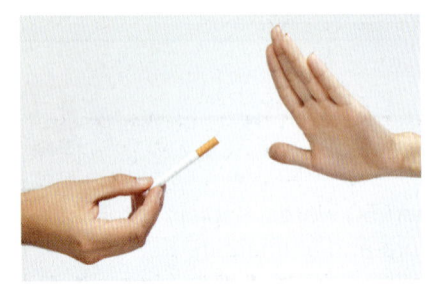

■ Resisting temptation is an example of Greater Jihad

Sources of authority

'Guide us to the straight path: the path of those You have blessed.' (Surah 1:6–7)

'You who believe, be mindful of God, seek ways to come closer to Him and strive for His cause, so that you may prosper.' (Surah 5:35)

'The believers, both men and women, support each other; they order what is right and forbid what is wrong' (Surah 9:71)

Importance of Jihad

Jihad is one of the main duties of a Muslim, and both Sunni and Shi'a Muslims believe in its importance. For Shi'a Muslims, it is one of the Ten Obligatory Acts.

The Prophet Muhammad said that Jihad is the pinnacle of faith (Hadith, Ibn Majah). Based on the Hadith, there are two types of Jihad in Islam:

- **Greater Jihad**
- Lesser Jihad.

A person who engages in Jihad is called a mujahid.

Greater Jihad

The Qur'an says that the purpose of human creation is to worship Allah. This goes deeper than just the performance of Salah and requires a Muslim to reflect Allah's attributes, such as love, mercy and kindness. This is not always easy, particularly as humans have been created weak and may easily give in to temptation, which makes it difficult to live life in submission to Allah.

The role of Greater Jihad is to struggle against evil and perform good deeds to become a better person — it is the struggle to live according to the straight path. It is sometimes called 'inner Jihad' and is a spiritual battle against a person's own desires. The main way of succeeding in this is by following the teachings of the Qur'an, the Five Pillars (Sunni) and Ten Obligatory Acts (Shi'a), and working for the good of society.

Munkar and ma'ruf

Muslims are required to avoid what is wrong (**munkar**) and do what is right (**ma'ruf**) in order to stay on 'the straight path'. The Qur'an, Sunnah and Hadith make clear which actions are forbidden and which are acceptable:

- Examples of munkar include lying, adultery, stealing and terrorism.
- Examples of ma'ruf include honesty, acts of charity, respecting the law and promoting peace.

A like for ma'ruf naturally leads to a dislike for munkar, therefore Muslims will strive to perform as many good deeds in their lives as possible. This is part of Greater Jihad.

It is believed that through Greater Jihad, a person can rise from the lowest state of human existence (the self that is inclined to evil, Surah 12:53) to the highest level (the self at peace, Surah 89:27) where the soul is purified and enjoys a lasting relationship with Allah. The Prophet Muhammad said that the remembrance of

One type of Greater Jihad for Muslims is sharing information about Islam with others in society

Allah is better than gold, silver and fighting in the cause of Allah. Worship, suppressing anger and helping the poor are all examples of Greater Jihad and were also exemplified by the Prophet Muhammad.

Muslim scholars have identified some categories for Greater Jihad, including:

- striving with the soul – aiming to improve one's character, for example through prayer or fasting
- striving with the tongue – speaking the truth or telling others about Islam
- striving with the pen – writing about, or in defence of, one's beliefs.

Analyse and evaluate

Is Greater Jihad the most difficult aspect of being a Muslim?

Yes	No
Life has been made a test; who succeeds will earn Allah's blessings. The trials that people face are part of Greater Jihad.	Observing all the Salah on time, fasting in Ramadan and completing Hajj can be considered more difficult.
It is called 'Greater' Jihad for the clear reason that the difficulty of succeeding is greater – therefore, the reward is greater too.	Greater Jihad is just one of many demanding aspects of being a Muslim.
All challenging actions required of Muslims can be seen as part of Greater Jihad. This is the best way for them to become stronger spiritually, morally and intellectually.	

Activities

Review
1. What does Jihad mean?
2. Name two types of Jihad.

Develop
3. What other examples can be added to the three categories of Greater Jihad?

Link
4. Why might Amr bil-Maroof and Nahi Anil Munkar be linked to Jihad for Shi'a Muslims?

Debate
5. 'Greater Jihad is more difficult in today's world.' To what extent is this conclusion fair? Discuss and note down reasons for and against this view.

Stretch
6. 'The strongest among you is not the one can defeat another in fighting, but the one who can control his anger' (Hadith). Explain what you think this teaching means.

4.16 Jihad: Lesser Jihad

Aim

To explore Muslim beliefs about Lesser Jihad

An army at war

Lesser Jihad

One of the aims of Islam is to ensure that the world is an abode of peace, in accordance with the will of Allah. People should have freedom and security, and be able to live their lives feeling safe. Sometimes various things can get in the way of this, including physical or military attacks on people because of their beliefs.

Islam gives permission for Muslims to stop such evil in the world and to fight to protect freedom of faith, even if this means going to war. This is known as **Lesser Jihad** (also referred to as 'holy war', although this term is not accepted by most Muslims). Based on the Qur'an, Sunnah and Hadith, this can be declared when:

- persecution threatens the life of believers
- religious freedoms (such as the right to worship) are denied
- Islamic countries have been attacked and need to be defended
- a recognised Muslim leader (Prophet, Khalifah or Imam) authorises it.

Starter

Is war ever justified? What rules should apply?

Key word

Lesser Jihad – removing evil from society with the aim of making the world an abode of peace

There are strict conditions for how Lesser Jihad should be conducted, which include the following:

- It must be a last resort after attempts to avoid conflict.
- It is forbidden to target innocent civilians, including women, children and elderly people. Taking one innocent life is like killing all of humanity (Surah 5:32).
- The leaders of other faiths, trees and buildings cannot be attacked.
- Violence must cease if there is an offer of peace (Surah 8:61).
- War must not be waged to gain converts, as the Prophet Muhammad's task was only to deliver the message of Islam.

- Responses to attacks must be proportionate.
- Prisoners should be treated with compassion.

Muslims must fight not only for Islam but for people of all faiths, and are specifically commanded to protect buildings like synagogues and churches where 'God's name is much invoked' as well as the rights of people of other religions (Surah 22:39–40).

Lesser Jihad in the time of the Prophet Muhammad

The Prophet Muhammad engaged in Lesser Jihad during the persecution of early Muslims. When he started preaching, he began to attract followers, including influential converts. The leaders of Makkah (Mecca) felt threatened by this and began to persecute Muslims.

During 13 continuous years of persecution in Makkah, Muslims were taught never to retaliate or use violence. As Muslims lived in constant danger, the first set of migrants went to Abyssinia and the later ones to Yathrib (renamed Madinah) to live in freedom and safety. The Makkan oppressors came after the Muslims in Madinah and the Prophet Muhammad received revelations from Allah instructing Muslims to defend themselves.

Despite being outnumbered and poorly equipped, the Prophet Muhammad, along with 313 Muslims, won the first battle at Badr against a thousand non-believers. This success was repeated in further battles.

Lesser Jihad today

Many Muslims argue that the context of the fighting in the Prophet Muhammad's time was different from the modern world: there were no national laws and institutions like the United Nations which uphold human rights, including religious freedoms. They argue that while Muslims have basic rights where they live, such as freedom of conscience, there is no need for Lesser Jihad – this is why some Muslims are pacifists.

On the other hand, some Muslims consider wars which are sanctioned by governments to be a modern example of Lesser Jihad and consistent with the Prophet Muhammad's reasons for engaging in war. In addition to obedience to Allah and the Prophet Muhammad, Muslims are also commanded to obey people in authority, whether Muslim or not. Almost six million Muslims fought in the First and Second World Wars.

Misunderstandings about Jihad

In recent years, terrorist groups like ISIS have claimed to fight in the name of Islam. Their methods include kidnapping, torture and suicide bombings, with promises that martyrs in their cause will go to heaven. The large majority of Muslims respond that such acts have no justification in Islam.

Prominent Islamic scholars and organisations, from different sects and schools of thought around the world, have worked together to condemn all forms of extremism, radicalism and terrorism in the name of Islam. Many Muslim organisations have attempted to address misconceptions about Jihad by organising regular peace symposiums and interfaith forums, actively encouraging fellow Muslims to donate blood and organising litter-picking and tree-planting initiatives. This is to highlight their commitment to peace, the environment and the well-being of everyone, whether Muslim or not.

Muslims groups condemn terrorist organisations for misrepresenting Islam

Precedence of Greater Jihad over Lesser Jihad

Many Muslims believe that Greater Jihad is more important than Lesser Jihad because:

- the Qur'an and Hadith teach mainly about the spiritual struggle of overcoming evil within oneself
- in a period of 22 years, the Prophet Muhammad and early Muslims spent only a few months at war
- Lesser Jihad can only be declared under very strict conditions, many of which are not often met – for instance, all Muslims do not follow one recognised leader.

Sources of authority

'There is no compulsion in religion.' (Surah 2:256)

'Fight in God's cause against those who fight you, but do not overstep the limits.' (Surah 2:190)

'Those who have been attacked are permitted to take up arms because they have been wronged.' (Surah 22:39)

Analyse and evaluate

Is Lesser Jihad still relevant today?

Yes	No
Lesser Jihad is permitted in the Qur'an and it was the Sunnah of the Prophet Muhammad.	Islam is firmly established as a religion and no longer under threat as it was in the time of the Prophet Muhammad.
Muslims have gone to war when conditions of Lesser Jihad have been met (for example in nineteenth-century India or Bosnia in the 1990s).	Lesser Jihad is not possible without a Khalifah (Sunni) or Imam (Shi'a).
Sunni and Shi'a Muslims believe that in the time of Isa and the Mahdi, war will be waged against non-believers, whereas Ahmadiyya Muslims refer to the Hadith that there would be an end to religious wars in that period.	

Activities

Review

1. What is meant by Lesser Jihad?
2. Give two conditions for the declaration of Lesser Jihad.

Develop

3. Look at Surah 9:13–14:

   'Will ye not fight people who have violated their oaths, plotted to expel the apostle, and took out the aggressive by being the first to assault you? Do ye not fear them? Nay, it is God whom ye should more justly fear, if ye believe! Fight them, and God will punish them by your hands, cover them with shame, help you (to victory) over them, heal the breasts of believers.'

   a. Highlight up to three parts and explain their importance.
   b. Summarise the passage in your own words.
   c. Match parts of the passage with the conditions for Lesser Jihad.

Link

4. Why do some Muslims consider Jihad to be the sixth Pillar of Islam?

Debate

5. 'No war can be holy.' To what extent is this conclusion fair? Discuss and note down reasons for and against this view.

Stretch

6. Following one of the battles, the Prophet Muhammad said to his followers that they were returning from the Lesser Jihad to the Greater Jihad. What might he have meant by this?

Practices 4.16 Jihad: Lesser Jihad

Summary activities

CHECK YOUR NOTES

STAGE 1

Check that you have detailed notes that cover the following:

- [ ] The importance of the Five Pillars: Shahadah, Salah (Salat), Zakah (Zakat), Sawm and Hajj in Sunni Islam
- [ ] The importance of the Ten Obligatory Acts to Shi'a Muslims: Salah (Salat), Sawm, Zakah (Zakat), Khums, Hajj, Jihad (struggle), Amr-bil-Maroof, Nahi Anil, Tawalla, Tabarra
- [ ] Public acts of worship such as prayer: how and why Muslims pray including Jummah prayers
- [ ] The place of the Shahadah in Muslim practice at birth, conversion and in death
- [ ] The importance of private acts of worship such as du'a
- [ ] The Hajj: reasons why Muslims go on pilgrimage, the rituals of Hajj and who is exempt
- [ ] The importance of Zakat and Khums; Muslim attitudes to wealth
- [ ] How alms are collected and distributed in Muslim communities
- [ ] The role and importance of Sawm (fasting): how and why Muslims fast, different experiences of Sawm in Muslim and non-Muslim countries
- [ ] Ramadan as the month the Qur'an was sent down; the Night of Power
- [ ] The origin and meaning of key festivals such as Eid-ul-Fitr, Eid-ul-Adha, Eid-ul-Ghadeer and Ashura for different groups of Muslims
- [ ] Different understandings of Greater and Lesser Jihad

GETTING READY

STAGE 2

Quick quiz

1. What two beliefs are asserted in the Muslim profession of faith, the Shahadah?
2. What is meant by the term rak'at?
3. What name is given to personal prayer that is made in addition to Salat?
4. Give two reasons why a Muslim might be exempt from going on Hajj.
5. What event do Shi'a Muslims commemorate during Ashura?
6. In which festival might Muslims remember Ibrahim's sacrifice of an animal rather than his son Isma'il?
7. How might a Muslim observe the Night of Power?
8. How does Khums differ from Zakat?
9. What is meant by the term sadaqah?
10. Give two conditions that must be observed in declaring Lesser Jihad.

Quick quiz answers can be found online at www.hoddereducation.co.uk/ocr-gcse-rs-answers

ACTIVITIES

STAGE 2

① **Practices match up:** below are a list of the most important practices to Sunni and Shi'a Muslims. Match up the key term with its explanation. You could also note whether this is a practice for Sunni, Shi'a or both.

Shahadah	Almsgiving, typically 2.5% of money
Salat	Express disassociation from evil
Zakat	Forbidding what is evil
Khums	The profession of faith
Sawm	Expressing love for what is good
Hajj	Performing the ritual prayers
Jihad	Pilgrimage to Mecca
Amr-bil-Maroof	Fasting during the month of Ramadan
Nahi Anil Munkar	A tax of $\frac{1}{5}$ of gains earned during the year
Tawalla	Commanding what is good
Tabarra	Struggle, can be greater or lesser

② **Say why:** to access higher marks on practices questions it is often helpful to say why the practice is important to followers of Islam. Choose three of the practices listed in the previous question and write a sentence or two explaining their significance to Muslims.

GET PRACTISING

STAGE 3

Use this section to help you develop your understanding of how to answer exam-style questions.

Ask the expert – 6-mark questions

Shanika was asked about Salat. Here is part of her answer:

Muslims think that prayer is important. Prayer is where you speak to God and ask him to help with the things you are struggling with. Muslims pray five times a day. They have to wash before they pray. They make various movements during prayer such as bowing and kneeling whilst they say their prayers.

Expert comment:

This is a rather vague attempt at the question which doesn't show any depth of understanding. There are very general statements which are not going to get many marks. The second sentence is also incorrect and Shanika is either thinking of du'a or a Christian idea of prayer. It is worth looking at what the mark scheme requires and moving beyond the 'what' to the 'which' and the 'why'.

Level (mark)	AO1
3 (5–6)	A **good** demonstration of knowledge and understanding in response to the question: • Good understanding of the question shown by appropriate selection of religious knowledge • Selection of appropriate sources of wisdom and authority with detail and/or developed description. • Good knowledge and understanding of different viewpoints within Islam • Good knowledge and understanding of the influence on individuals, communities and societies • Good knowledge and understanding of the breadth and/or depth of the issues
2 (3–4)	A **satisfactory** demonstration of knowledge and/or understanding in response to the question: • Satisfactory understanding of the question shown by some use of religious knowledge • Selection of appropriate sources of wisdom and authority with superficial description • Satisfactory knowledge and understanding of different viewpoints within Islam • Satisfactory knowledge and understanding of the influence on individuals, communities and societies • Satisfactory knowledge and understanding of the breadth and/or depth of issues

Notice the phrase 'appropriate selection' – you need to focus on the question

Notice the phrase 'sources of wisdom and authority' – you need to say WHY something is believed

Notice the phrase 'different viewpoints' – you need to think about WHICH Muslims believe this

Notice the word 'influence' – think about IMPORTANCE. How does the belief affect a Muslim's practice?

The 'which', the 'why' and the 'importance'

As we can see from the Levels of Response table above, there are a number of things that you need to do to get top marks on the medium-length questions. Whilst you may start with 'what' a Muslim believes or does, it is important that answers go beyond this.

- **Which** – you may be able to show that there are differences in what different groups of Muslims believe.
- **Why** – you could bring in a source of authority to show why something is believed or done.
- **Importance** – you may show a link between a belief and a practice showing why this matters to Muslims and how it affects their life.

Look again at Shanika's answer to the question above. How might you improve her answer using these tips?

Religion, philosophy and ethics

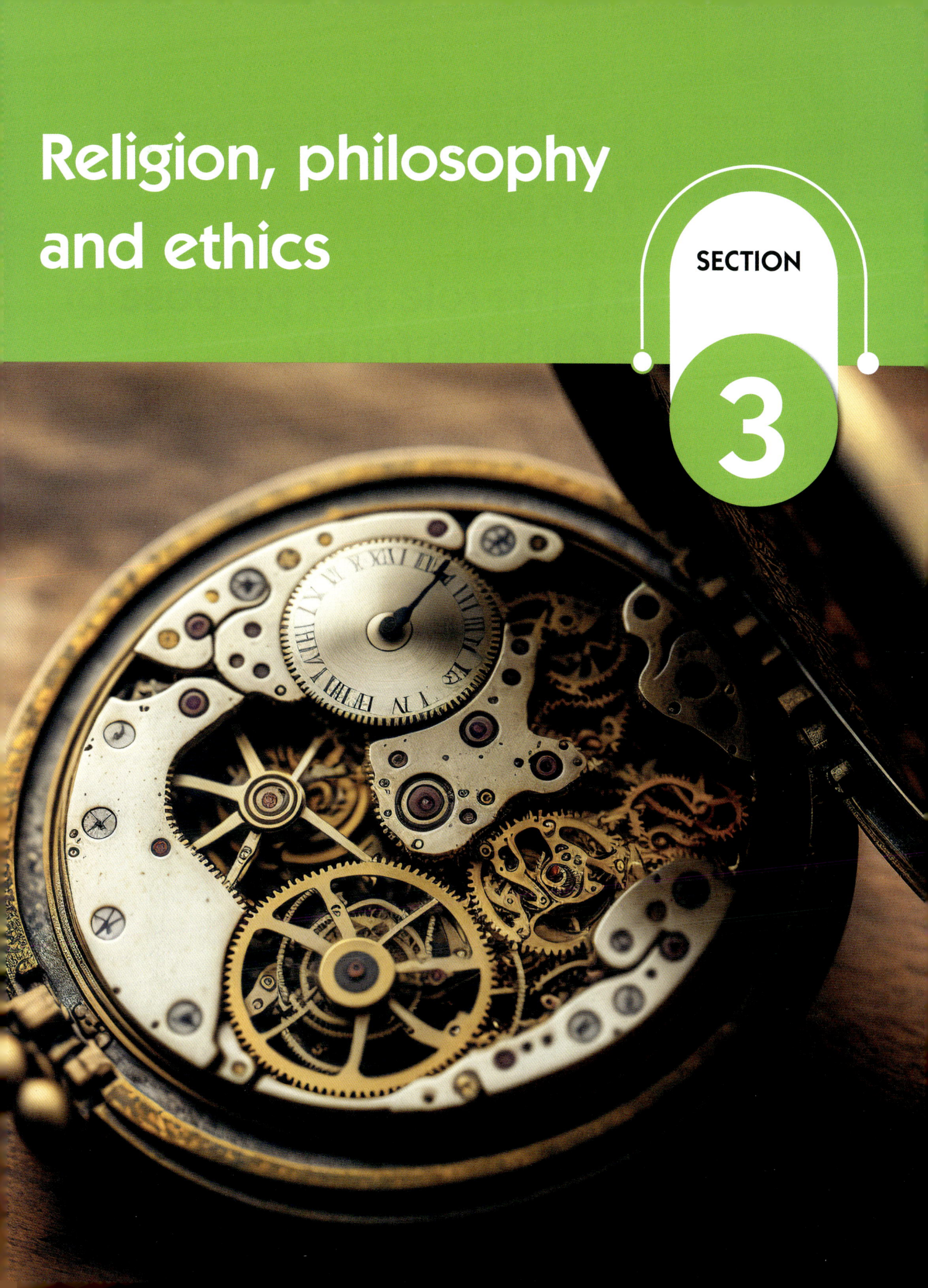

SECTION 3

CHAPTER 5

Relationships and families

5.1 The role and purpose of a Christian family

Aim

To explore how different Christians understand the importance of the family

Starter

For many Christians, the nuclear family would typically be a married man and woman and their biological children. This is not the only type of family. What other types of families can you think of?

What are the purposes of a Christian family?

The idea of family is very important to Christians for a number of reasons:

- It provides stable and loving relationships.
- It allows the procreation of children and a place for them to be nurtured.
- It is where children can be raised and educated in the faith – raised with Christian values.

The Bible describes the Church as a family of believers; Christians are described as children of God and fellow brothers and sisters with each other. God himself in the Trinity is revealed as both Father and Son. Christians believe that this shows the importance of the family unit in God's plan for the universe.

Roman Catholics and the family

Roman Catholic Christians see the family as very significant. It is 'the original cell of social life' (Catechism of the Catholic Church 2207). It is an institution that is part of God's created order; the members of it benefit each other and the existence of families benefits society. The family also has a religious purpose. It is a 'domestic church' (Catechism of the Catholic Church 2204) and part of the family's role is to raise children in the faith through the example of parents and the practice of the faith such as prayer at home. Raising the children in the faith is also likely to include infant baptism and worshipping as a family in church. It may also involve sending the children to a faith school.

■ Families are important in Catholicism as they help to educate children in the faith

Evangelical Christians and the family

Evangelical Christians such as members of Pentecostal churches also believe the family to be important for stability and the raising of children. There may be prayer or Bible reading at home which will include children. However, the idea of faith as a personal choice is important and for young people in these families, baptism would only occur when they are old enough to come to faith in their own right (see spread 2.7).

Christian responses to non-nuclear families

Some Christians can find the emphasis on families in churches a challenge. Many churches set up support networks so that single people and single-parent families are included in church activities or invited for meals with other church members. Christians also recognise that family life can be challenging and groups such as CARE (Christian Action Research and Education), an evangelical group, organise parenting courses and marriage courses to support Christian families. Christians also recognise the importance of fostering and adoption. Christian organisations such as Home for Good help to raise awareness of such issues in churches and encourage Christian families who feel that this may be their calling.

Sources of authority

'Honour your father and your mother, so that you may live long in the land the Lord your God is giving you.' (Exodus 20:12

'Start children off on the way they should go, and even when they are old they will not turn from it. (Proverbs 22:6)

Analyse and evaluate

Is a Christian family the best place to raise children?

Yes	No
A Christian family is a stable family as parents are more likely to be committed to staying together.	Biblical ideas of family are unhelpful. There is polygamy (a man having more than one wife) in the Old Testament and husbands and wives are not always viewed as equals.
Christian families are vital in terms of passing on the faith to the next generation.	Society is now too complex and there is a wide variety of family types of various faiths and of no faith. It is arrogant to suggest that Christian families are superior.
A Christian family provides a good model for children to understand love, respect and moral behaviour.	The Biblical references to discipline and raising in the faith can be overemphasised. There may be a risk of brainwashing children.

Some Christians might agree that Christian families are the best place to raise children but may feel that some Christian definitions of what a family is are no longer suitable for the twenty-first century.

Activities

Review

1. Suggest three purposes of Christian families.
2. What do the Ten Commandments teach about Christian family life?

Develop

3. How do Catholic Christians understand family life?

Link

4. God is described as Father, Son and Spirit. Review spread 1.4 on the Trinity and explain how this helps Christians understand the importance of family.

Debate

5. 'Christians seem to think that all children should be raised by two married heterosexual parents'. To what extent is this statement fair? Discuss and note down reasons for and against this conclusion.

Stretch

6. Find out more about the work of CARE. How does it support Christian families?

5.2 What do Christians believe about the purpose and importance of marriage?

Aim

To consider different Christian views about the importance of marriage

Starter

Look at the photo below. Is it possible to love someone so much that you choose to spend the rest of your life with them? How can you be sure that you will both remain committed and faithful to each other despite the changing circumstances of life?

- This couple are still in love many years into their marriage

Why is marriage important for Christians?

A Christian **marriage** in the UK legally recognises a relationship, in the same way that a civil ceremony might. However, this is not the only important thing about a Christian marriage; there is also a theological aspect as a Christian couple understands marriage as a covenant or agreement made before God. They regard themselves as being married 'in the sight of God', having made promises both to each other and before God. For most Christians, the creation story in Genesis 2 suggests marriage is something that takes place between a male and a female, although some Christian churches are open to the idea of same-sex marriage (see spread 5.6).

In the Bible (Ephesians 5), the relationship between husband and wife is compared to the relationship between Christ and the Church. This imagery is also shown in the book of Revelation where the writer describes the Church as a bride being presented to Christ at the end of time. Marriage should ideally be a lifelong relationship. Jesus' words in Mark 10:9 about humans not separating what God has joined are often read at Christian wedding ceremonies.

The importance of marriage for Christians is linked to its purposes.

Key word

Marriage – a legally recognised union between two people in a relationship (historically between a man and a woman)

Purposes of Christian marriage:
- Unites the couple
- Faithfulness
- Fidelity
- Raising of children
- Place for sexual activity
- Sacrament

Sources of authority

'But for Adam no suitable helper was found. So the Lord God caused the man to fall into a deep sleep; and while he was sleeping, he took one of the man's ribs and then closed up the place with flesh. Then the Lord God made a woman from the rib he had taken out of the man, and he brought her to the man. The man said: "This is now bone of my bones and flesh of my flesh; she shall be called 'woman,' for she was taken out of man." That is why a man leaves his father and mother and is united to his wife, and they become one flesh' (Genesis 2:20–24)

'Therefore, what God has joined together, let no one separate.' (Mark 10:9)

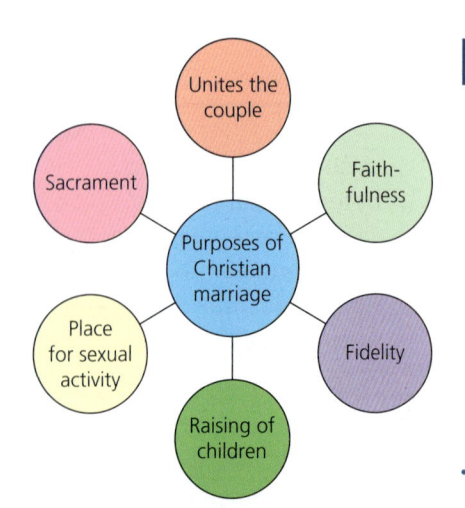

Roman Catholic Church

The Roman Catholic Church believes that marriage is a sacrament (see spread 2.6). The Catechism of the Catholic Church 1603 refers to marriage as a vocation or calling. God has made a desire for marriage a feature of human nature. In his 1968 letter, *Humanae Vitae*, Pope Paul VI states that the sexual relationship between a couple in marriage gives love that is total, is faithful and exclusive until death. It is this loving relationship of marriage that is the best place for the raising of children. Children are a gift and the importance of producing children is a key aspect of Catholic teaching on marriage.

Source of authority

'Marriage invests the dignity of a sacramental sign of grace, inasmuch as it represents the union of Christ and of the Church.' (*Humanae Vitae*, Pope Paul VI, 1968)

Liberal Protestant attitudes

Other Christians, while agreeing that marriage is important, do not regard marriage as a sacrament. Some liberal Christians are also sympathetic to the idea that marriage does not have to be between a male and a female. In 2021, the Methodist Church voted to allow its ministers to conduct same-sex marriages.

Analyse and evaluate

Are Christians right to value the idea of a Christian marriage?

Yes	No
Marriage brings stability and happiness: research suggests that married people are happier and children of married couples statistically do better at school.	The Christian ideas of marriage are outdated. Many Christian groups exclude the possibility of same-sex marriage and in a world of overpopulation it is irresponsible to focus on procreation.
Marriage is an institution created and blessed by God. It is important to Christians to live the way he commands.	Some feminists see marriage as oppressive, particularly where Christians see different roles for men and women.

It is possible for Christians to value the idea of Christian marriage as it is significant and helpful, yet this doesn't mean that other views of marriage are inferior as these provide meaning for those with different worldviews.

Activities

Review
1. Why do Christians believe that marriage is important?
2. Which group of Christians believes that marriage is a sacrament?

Develop
3. How do Catholic and Protestant Christians' views of marriage differ? Are there also some similarities?

Link
4. What does the creation story (see spreads 1.5 and 1.6) teach about the purpose of human beings? How does this relate to marriage?

Debate
5. Is the Christian idea of marriage realistic in the twenty-first century? Discuss this question and make a note of the arguments (both religious and non-religious) that you raise.

Stretch
6. In the twentieth century, feminists such as Simone de Beauvoir (1908–1986) objected to the idea of marriage for reinforcing patriarchal views. Find out a little more about the reasons behind this view.

5.3 What is the significance of the beliefs and teachings reflected in a Christian marriage ceremony?

Aim
To explore different Christian marriage ceremonies and consider how these reflect Christian beliefs and teachings

Starter
Suppose a friend asks you whether there is any significant difference between a civil ceremony in a registry office and a religious wedding. How might you answer? Are there key differences?

Preparing to marry

In addition to the practical arrangements for weddings, a Christian marriage is likely to involve some form of spiritual preparation. This can be done on an informal basis with a couple meeting with their priest or pastor for conversations about marriage, or there may be a course that couples are encouraged to attend such as the marriage preparation courses run by the Church of England. These activities show that Christians regard getting married as a significant and serious undertaking.

Features of a Christian marriage ceremony

There are no specific guidelines in the Bible as to what a wedding ceremony should involve but most Christian weddings involve making vows, the giving and receiving of rings, and acts of worship such as prayers or hymns. It is central to Christian weddings that all that happens occurs in the presence of God.

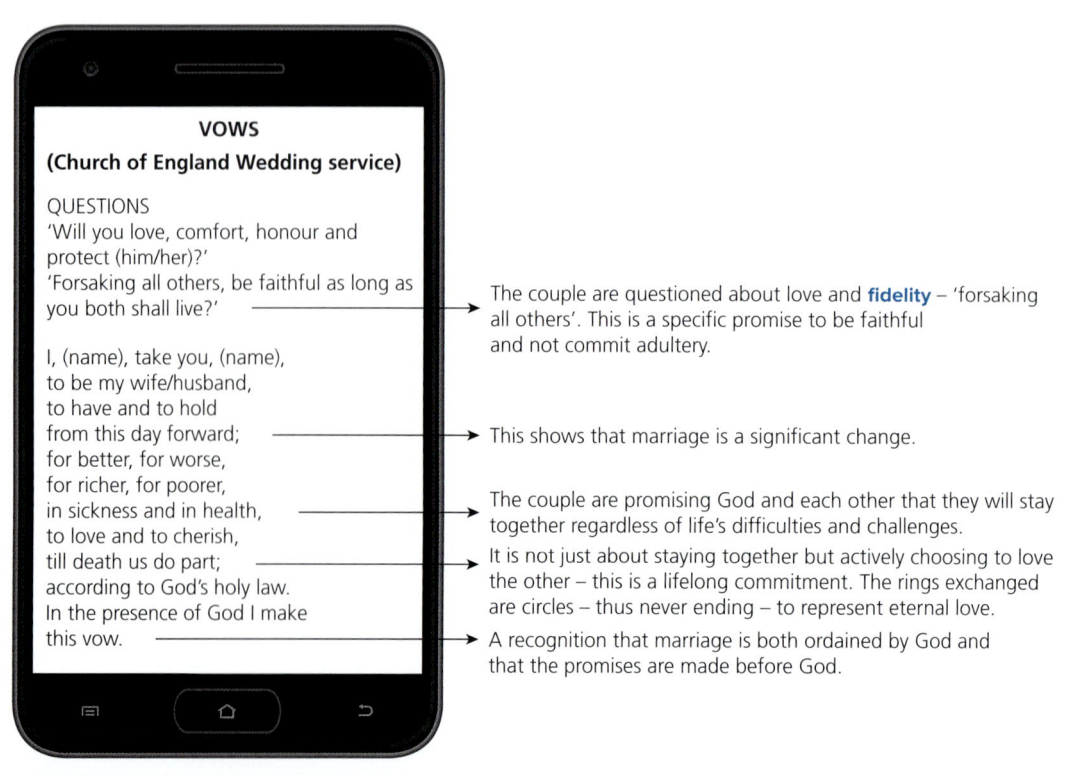

VOWS
(Church of England Wedding service)

QUESTIONS
'Will you love, comfort, honour and protect (him/her)?'
'Forsaking all others, be faithful as long as you both shall live?' —— The couple are questioned about love and **fidelity** – 'forsaking all others'. This is a specific promise to be faithful and not commit adultery.

I, (name), take you, (name),
to be my wife/husband,
to have and to hold
from this day forward; —— This shows that marriage is a significant change.
for better, for worse,
for richer, for poorer,
in sickness and in health, —— The couple are promising God and each other that they will stay together regardless of life's difficulties and challenges.
to love and to cherish, —— It is not just about staying together but actively choosing to love the other – this is a lifelong commitment. The rings exchanged are circles – thus never ending – to represent eternal love.
till death us do part;
according to God's holy law.
In the presence of God I make —— A recognition that marriage is both ordained by God and this vow. that the promises are made before God.

■ These vows show a number of key beliefs that Christians have about marriage

Key word

Fidelity – faithfulness to a cause or person

Top tip

If a question asks about the purpose or importance of marriage, you are being asked to explain the significance – why it matters – to different Christians. If you merely describe different things that happen in a marriage ceremony, you are in danger of missing the point.

Marriage ceremonies in the Roman Catholic Church

For Catholics, marriage is considered to be one of the seven sacraments (see spread 2.6). A Catholic couple may opt to have a full nuptial Mass to celebrate their marriage. This involves readings from the Bible, hymns and the taking of communion together. This shows that faith is at the heart of the couple's marriage. The congregation may stand as the couple marries. This represents the importance of the whole church community supporting and helping those who are getting married.

A marriage between a Catholic and a non-Catholic requires special permission from a bishop and is known as a mixed marriage. Similarly, permission is required for a Catholic person to marry someone of a different faith. This shows the importance of a couple having shared spiritual values and beliefs. A Catholic church will not carry out weddings for non-members whereas many Protestant groups do allow weddings for those who do not regularly attend church.

Analyse and evaluate

Should a Christian marriage ceremony only be available to Christians?	
Yes	**No**
There are distinctly theological ideas in the marriage ceremony, such as the promises being made before God. These have no meaning for those without faith.	Christians believe God's love is universal. Offering a Christian ceremony is a way of showing love to those who do not yet have faith.
The Catholic Church only allows a nuptial Mass when a marriage is taking place between two practising Catholics.	It is part of the Church's role of being 'salt and light' in the community to bless those who choose to marry.
While it seems that a Christian marriage will only really have meaning for those of faith, every couple's situation is different and it is difficult to make hard and fast rules.	

Activities

Review

1. What makes a Christian marriage ceremony different from a civil ceremony?
2. What do couples promise each other in a Christian marriage?

Develop

3. How are different Christian beliefs about marriage shown in the marriage ceremony?

Link

4. For Catholics, marriage is a sacrament. Review spread 2.6 and explain what is meant by this term.

Debate

5. Is it hypocritical to expect to have a church wedding if you are not a practising Christian? Discuss this issue and note down arguments for and against this view.

Stretch

6. Research marriage ceremonies. How many people get married in the UK each year? What percentage of these are church weddings? What conclusions might this data show?

Relationships and families 5.3 What is the significance of the beliefs and teachings reflected in a Christian marriage ceremony?

5.4 Is sex something that should only take place within marriage?

Aim
To explore Christian attitudes to premarital sex and cohabitation

Starter
Alex and Kelisha are committed Christians who are engaged and will be married in three months' time. Kelisha rents her own house. Does Alex really have to wait until they are married to move in? Would it be wrong if they started to sleep together? What do you think different Christians might advise?

Key word
Premarital sex – sex that takes place before marriage

Sources of authority
'[Jesus] … said, "For this reason a man will leave his father and mother and be united to his wife, and the two will become one flesh."' (Matthew 19:5)

'Marriage should be honoured by all, and the marriage bed kept pure, for God will judge the adulterer and all the sexually immoral.' (Hebrews 13:4)

■ Is it wrong for a Christian couple in a committed relationship to sleep together if they are not married?

Different Christian attitudes to premarital sex

The term **premarital sex** covers a range of different circumstances. It is possible to apply the term to sexual acts between a couple in a stable relationship who are not yet married as well as to casual sexual encounters. For some more liberal Christians this distinction matters. If moral decision making is about doing whatever is the most loving thing, as explained by Joseph Fletcher in his theory of Situation Ethics, then it would be possible to accept that there is nothing wrong if the couple in question are in a stable and exclusive relationship – particularly if there is an intention to marry.

Catholic Christians and evangelical Christians are less likely to support premarital sex. They would argue that the Bible suggests that sex and marriage are linked in the creation story which is referenced by Jesus in Matthew 19. It is only after the man has left his family and been united with his wife that they become 'one flesh'. For Catholic Christians, this is particularly important as the main purpose of both marriage and sexual relationships is to be open to the possibility of procreation.

Different Christian attitudes to cohabitation

There are almost 4 million households in the UK where couples are cohabiting. This is over 18 per cent of the total number of households and is the fastest-growing type of family (Office for National Statistics, 2019). Cohabiting couples vary from those who

Key word

Cohabitation – when a couple in a relationship live together without being married

Source of authority

'"I have no husband," she replied. Jesus said to her, "You are right when you say you have no husband. The fact is, you have had five husbands, and the man you now have is not your husband. What you have just said is quite true."' (John 4:17–18).

have cohabited faithfully for years with no intention of marrying, to those who may be cohabiting as a trial marriage before getting married. For some liberal Christians, this latter idea of a trial marriage can be seen as a good thing. The Church of England has accepted that in some cases, **cohabitation** can be a useful first step towards the ideal, which is marriage.

Roman Catholic and evangelical Christians generally oppose cohabitation. They argue that a relationship can only be truly committed once promises have been exchanged in the presence of God in a marriage ceremony. For Catholics, marriage involves being wholly committed so the idea of a trial marriage where you may or may not decide to proceed makes no sense. Although Jesus does not specifically refer to cohabitation, his remarks to the woman at the well in John Chapter 4 might suggest a distinction between marriage and cohabitation.

Analyse and evaluate

Does Christianity teach that sex should only take place within marriage?

Yes	No
The creation story and the teachings of Jesus suggest that a couple are united in marriage and only then do they become one flesh.	The Bible does not explicitly say that sex should only take place within marriage; this is not the only interpretation of the text.
Sex should take place within a relationship that is blessed by God. Even stable cohabiting relationships lack this.	It is difficult to take the Bible as a guide to sexual ethics. Some Old Testament characters had many wives.
Many Christians point to the stable family units that are possible within a Christian marriage.	Christianity is based on love; it is difficult to see what the difference is between a marriage and a loving committed relationship.

Some Christians argue that although sex should be generally reserved for within marriage, it is important to exercise love, particularly if the couple have an intention to marry.

Activities

Review

1. Why do some Christians believe that sex should not take place before marriage?
2. Why do some Christians believe that cohabitation could be permitted in some cases?

Develop

3. What different attitudes do Christians have regarding premarital sex? Why do their views differ?

Link

4. Review the spreads 2.12, 5.2 and 5.3 on Christian marriage and the marriage ceremony. How do these views affect Christian beliefs on premarital sex and cohabitation?

Debate

5. 'Over 75 per cent of people in Britain see no issue with premarital sex' (British Social Attitudes Survey 2019). Surely Christians are out of step in their views and need to move with the times.' Discuss this claim and note down the arguments presented.

Stretch

6. A 2018 study by Rosenfeld and Roesler suggests that couples who cohabit before marriage are statistically more likely to divorce if they do marry. What reasons might there be for this?

163

5.5 Should all Christians marry and have children?

Aim
To examine Christian attitudes to celibacy and contraception

Starter
Look at the cartoon below. Overpopulation is a key aspect of the environmental challenges humans face. Is there really a duty for a married couple to have children?

Key word
Celibacy – abstaining from sex, particularly for religious reasons

You can stop being fruitful and multiplying now!

Key word
Contraception – use of various methods to avoid a woman becoming pregnant, particularly by artificial means

Family life is important in Christianity, as the previous pages have shown, but what about Christians who choose not to fit in to the perceived norm of Christian family life: those who remain single and celibate by choice and those who opt not to have children?

Christian beliefs about celibacy and marriage

In his letter to the Church in Corinth, the Apostle Paul seems to encourage an unmarried life of **celibacy**. He states that he wishes everyone to be as he is so that they can be fully focused on living for God's Kingdom. One reason for Paul's argument may be that he expects the Parousia (the Second Coming of Jesus) to be in his lifetime and, if believers settle down and get married, this may distract from the core task of spreading the gospel. This argument, that those who remain single can be more focused on God, is part of the reason why Roman Catholic priests are not allowed to marry.

While celibacy may be seen as an ideal for some Christians, Paul recognises that this is not possible for everyone. He states that if someone is struggling with celibacy then it is better for them to marry than to 'burn with passion'. Protestant denominations have traditionally allowed their clergy to marry; this was one of the key dividing lines in the Reformation.

Christian beliefs about contraception

In his 1968 letter, *Humanae Vitae*, Pope Paul VI expresses a key truth of Catholic teaching on sex and marriage when he states that the sexual act 'whilst uniting husband and wife' should 'also render them capable of generating new life'. So although Catholics accept natural means of **contraception** such as monitoring the menstrual cycle, they do not accept unnatural means such as condoms, pills or implants. The Catholic Church bases much of its moral teaching on an idea called natural law ethics. This states that people should carry out actions that help them fulfil their purpose. Natural law states that reproduction is one of the key purposes of human life. One of the unintended consequences of this view has been the spread of diseases such as AIDS, particularly in the continent of Africa. Recently, some senior Catholics have suggested that the use of condoms to prevent the spread of AIDS may be permissible.

> **Top tip**
>
> It is important to know the 'why' behind the different beliefs that Christians have on various topics. An in-depth answer does not just know that Catholics tend to believe it is important to have children, it is able to explain 'why' using a source of authority.

The Bible teaches that children are a gift from God and one of the first commands that God gives is that human beings are to be fruitful and to fill the Earth. Elsewhere in the Bible there is the sense that to have children (and many of them) is a sign of God's blessing. This leads some evangelical Christians to oppose contraception, although generally this is considered a matter of the couple's choice. Some Christians also believe that contraception enables the enjoyment of sex and of physical love which binds a couple together, without the consequence of pregnancy.

Liberal Christians, particularly in modern times, may be concerned about overpopulation and feel that it is irresponsible to have lots of children.

Sources of authority

'God blessed them and said to them: "Be fruitful and increase in number; fill the earth and subdue it."' (Genesis 1:28)

'Now to the unmarried and the widows I say: it is good for them to stay unmarried, as I do. But if they cannot control themselves, they should marry, for it is better to marry than to burn with passion.' (1 Corinthians 7:8–9)

Analyse and evaluate

Are Christian teachings about contraception helpful?

Yes	No
The Bible doesn't directly address contraception, so this is a matter for the individual consciences of Christians.	Catholic teaching against condoms has caused much suffering, particularly in terms of the spread of AIDS.
Availability of contraception may lead to more casual sex which may cause harm to some of those involved.	There are already close to 8 billion people in the world. The human race needs to make more responsible decisions about having children.

Activities

Review

1. What are the differences between Catholics and Protestants over the issue of whether clergy should be allowed to marry?
2. Why do Roman Catholics oppose artificial contraception?

Develop

3. What do different Christians believe about the importance of having children? Why do they have these views?

Link

4. Paul's views about celibacy might be affected by his eschatological views. Review spread 1.16 on early Church beliefs about the Parousia.

Debate

5. 'It is irresponsible to have large families in this day and age.' Discuss how Christians might feel about this statement. Note down the arguments that are made.

Stretch

6. The debate over whether priests should be allowed to marry was one of the key disputes that led to Protestants breaking away from the Catholic Church. What other issues were debated during the Reformation?

165

5.6 Christian views on same-sex marriage

> **Aim**
>
> To explore different Christian perspectives on civil partnerships and same-sex marriage

> **Starter**
>
> Lily and Rhian are members of a Christian youth group in an evangelical church. Their church does not support same-sex marriage and most of the leaders in the church do not approve of homosexuality. Lily and Rhian have been dating secretly for a year. As committed Christians, they hope that one day they might get married but this is unlikely to happen in their church. What advice might you give them?

Homosexuality and same-sex marriage

Historically, most Christians have opposed homosexuality and have argued that marriage is an institution given by God that unites a man and a woman. **Homosexual** acts have been viewed as sinful based on commands taken from the Bible. While many Christians would argue that it is important to 'love the sinner even if you hate the sin', the reality is that gay people have felt excluded and in some cases have actually been persecuted by churches. Same-sex marriage was legalised in the UK in 2014 but the modern Church is still quite divided on this. Churches have a legal right to opt out of conducting same-sex marriages.

Catholic attitudes to same-sex marriage

The Roman Catholic Church opposes same-sex marriage. For Catholics, marriage is ordained by God and is a sacrament. It is not possible for human beings to redefine marriage in this way. Catholic moral thinking follows natural law ethics, which state that one of our purposes as human beings is reproduction. This should occur within a **heterosexual** marriage. The Catechism of the Catholic Church 2357–2359 states that while homosexual acts are sinful, and thus gay people are required to be celibate, they should be treated with 'respect, compassion and sensitivity'.

> **Key words**
>
> **Homosexual** – being sexually attracted to members of the same sex; in some contexts, the word can be intended as a slur
> **Heterosexual** – being sexually attracted to members of the opposite sex

Sources of authority

'"Do not have sexual relations with a man as one does with a woman; that is detestable."' (Leviticus 18:22)

Jesus replied, "that at the beginning the Creator made them male and female, and said, 'For this reason a man will leave his father and mother and be united to his wife, and the two will become one flesh.'"' (Matthew 19:4–5)

Protestant attitudes to same-sex marriage

Liberal Christians accept same-sex marriage. They argue that the Bible needs to be understood as a document of its time and statements about homosexuality are no longer applicable as moral commands. It was argued by the Anglican Archbishop Desmond Tutu that accepting same-sex marriage and equality for gay people is as important as accepting racial equality and rejecting discrimination against people of colour. In 2021, the Methodist Church voted to permit same-sex marriages in its churches, albeit with an opt-out clause for ministers who do not approve.

Most evangelical Christians would reject this and would argue that the Biblical references to marriage being between a male and a female should still apply today.

Civil partnerships

Civil partnerships were legalised in the UK in 2005 with the primary aim of allowing same-sex couples to have their relationship legally recognised. To some extent, the legalisation of same-sex marriage in 2014 has meant that civil partnerships have less significance. For Christians, marriage is ordained by God and those Christians who support same-sex marriage tend to see less value in civil partnerships. For some Christians, who feel that marriage should be between a male and a female, a civil partnership may be a way of recognising and celebrating a relationship without extended full marriage rights.

Key word

Civil partnership – a legal relationship which can be registered by two people who aren't related to each other. Civil partnerships are now available to both same-sex couples and opposite-sex couples

Source of authority

'I would refuse to go to a homophobic heaven. No, I would say sorry, I mean I would much rather go to the other place. I would not worship a God who is homophobic and that is how deeply I feel about this.' (Archbishop Desmond Tutu, speaking in 2013)

Top tip

It is important to remember that the issues in this spread are complex and it is dangerous to oversimplify Christian views. All Catholics or evangelicals (or even all Baptists and Anglicans) will not necessarily have the same view. Rephrasing to say 'most Catholics' or 'some evangelicals' helps to convey nuance.

Analyse and evaluate

Should modern Christians support same-sex marriage?

Yes	No
Jesus taught that Christians should love their neighbours, especially those who are marginalised. It is right to extend marriage rights to gay people.	Marriage is not something that the law or culture can define. It is a God-given institution which is between a male and a female.
There are many things in the Bible that Christians don't believe should apply today, such as forbidding the eating of shellfish. It is wrong to continue to apply outdated texts to homosexuality.	The Bible contains clear guidance on marriage and homosexuality; the Old Testament states that it is wrong for a 'man to lie with a man'.

Some Christians are unsure on this issue as they understand the Bible seems to support only heterosexual marriage yet they are aware that the time in which it was written needs to be understood when interpreting.

Activities

Review

1. Why do Catholic Christians oppose same-sex marriage?
2. What does the Methodist Church believe about same-sex marriage?

Develop

3. Why do Christians come to different conclusions on the issue of same-sex marriage?

Link

4. Review the creation stories of Genesis 1–2 (see spreads 1.5 and 1.6). How do Christians use these to justify the view that marriage can only be heterosexual?

Debate

5. 'Discrimination is always wrong. All churches should be forced to carry out same-sex marriages even if the vicar/pastor does not approve.' Discuss this statement, noting arguments for and against it.

Stretch

6. Research natural law ethics and find out how this theory applies to issues of homosexuality including same-sex marriage.

5.7 When relationships end: the ethics of divorce and remarriage

Aim
To explore different Christian attitudes to divorce and remarriage

Starter
Jack and Emma approach their minister to arrange a date for their wedding. Jack explains that he divorced from his first wife some years before joining the church. He wonders if this will be a problem in terms of a church wedding. The minister says that it depends on the reason for the divorce. Look at the diagram below. Which of the reasons (if any) should prevent them getting married in church?

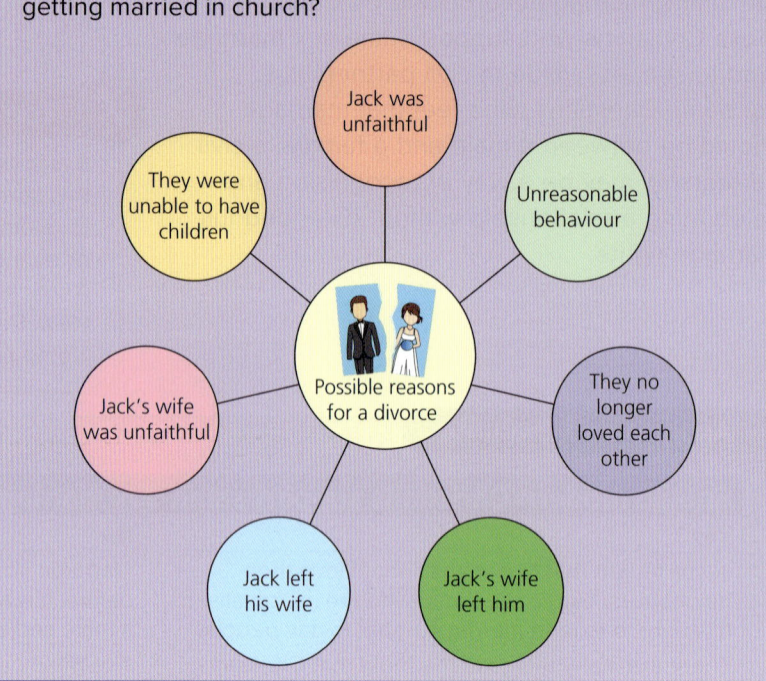

Possible reasons for a divorce:
- Jack was unfaithful
- Unreasonable behaviour
- They no longer loved each other
- Jack's wife left him
- Jack left his wife
- Jack's wife was unfaithful
- They were unable to have children

Sources of authority

'Anyone who divorces his wife and marries another woman commits adultery against her. And if she divorces her husband and marries another man, she commits adultery.' (Mark 10:11–12)

'Divorce is a grave offence against the natural law… Contracting a new union, even if it is recognised by civil law, adds to the gravity of the rupture: the remarried spouse is then in a situation of public and permanent adultery.' (Catechism of the Catholic Church 2384)

Key words

Divorce – the legal dissolution or ending of a marriage

Remarriage – where someone marries again after divorce or the death of their first husband/wife

Annulment – a declaration that a marriage was invalid, so that legally it never properly existed

Catholic attitudes to divorce

The Catholic Church opposes **divorce**. Marriage is a sacrament and couples promise to stay together until one of them dies. Where a couple does divorce, the Catholic Church does not allow **remarriage** to take place within church as the text from Mark's Gospel seems to indicate that to remarry is the equivalent of committing adultery. The Catechism of the Catholic Church 2384 states that remarrying makes the original sin of divorce worse. Divorcees should remain single and celibate if a divorce occurs.

The Catholic Church does recognise that **annulment** of marriage can take place. This is a process where the Church decrees that the marriage was not valid in the first place. There are a number of reasons why this might be the case, including that one of the parties did not freely consent to the marriage, perhaps as a result of some external pressure.

Key word

Adultery – sex between a married person and someone else that they are not married to

Source of authority

'But I tell you that anyone who divorces his wife, except for sexual immorality, makes her the victim of adultery, and anyone who marries a divorced woman commits adultery.' (Matthew 5:31)

Source of authority

'But if the unbeliever leaves, let it be so. The brother or the sister is not bound in such circumstances; God has called us to live in peace.' (1 Corinthians 7:15)

Divorce is permitted where adultery has occurred

Evangelical Christians also oppose divorce in most circumstances but will often make an exception where **adultery** has occurred. This exception seems to be allowed in Matthew's version of Jesus' teaching. If a partner has been unfaithful, they have broken the 'one flesh' covenant. The other partner in the marriage may choose to forgive and try to work things out but if they do not or cannot, they are permitted to seek a divorce.

Divorce is allowed for various reasons

Many Christians, particularly more liberal Christians, accept that married life is challenging and there are a range of reasons why marriages do not work out. For instance, some relationships are abusive and it does not seem very loving to insist that the marriage must continue, even though this situation is not mentioned in scripture. Some Christians note that Paul's advice in 1 Corinthians about one partner who is not a Christian leaving the marital home might suggest that there are other valid reasons for divorce.

Analyse and evaluate

Should Christians who divorce be allowed to remarry?	
Yes	**No**
It is important to approach these difficult issues with love and grace. It is an imperfect world and it is not right to judge those whose relationships break down.	In Catholicism, marriage is a sacrament and it is not possible for humans to reverse that which God has ordained.
There are a number of other circumstances, such as abusive relationships or desertion, where it would seem wrong to suggest that the victim cannot remarry.	In Mark's Gospel, Jesus does not offer any exceptions that permit divorce. He states that the law of Moses permitted divorce because of sin.

While divorce is not ideal, there are situations where it is permitted, including where it follows adultery. Jesus permits this exception in Matthew's Gospel.

Activities

Review

1. What is an annulment?
2. What is the difference between Catholic views on divorce and those held by more liberal Christians?

Develop

3. How do different Christians use the Bible to justify their views on divorce and remarriage?

Link

4. Review spread 5.3 on the marriage ceremony. How do the ideas of marriage conveyed in the different ceremonies affect attitudes to divorce?

Debate

5. Is annulment really the same thing as divorce? Discuss this issue, noting down reasons for and against this view.

Stretch

6. Read 1 Corinthians 7 and note down anything else that it might show a Christian about marriage and relationships.

169

5.8 Men and women within Christian families

Aim
To explore different Christian attitudes to gender roles within the family

Starter
Alex is a 'house husband'. He chose to stay at home when he and Suzanne had children. Alex cannot earn as much as Suzanne, who is a lawyer. What do you think the members of their church will think about Alex's role in the family?

■ Is the idea that there are typical male and female roles old fashioned?

Gender roles

If you were to read books or watch programmes set in the period before the late twentieth century, these would make Alex and Suzanne's family roles seen unusual. A traditional family would usually have one income, from the husband, and the wife's role would often be to stay at home and fulfil the bulk of the childcare and housework. Things have changed considerably. Now, over two-thirds of women in the UK are in work compared to less than half in 1970 (Office for National Statistics). During this time, the employment rate for men has declined from 92 per cent to 76 per cent. Yet this hasn't led to a rebalancing of domestic roles. Women are still doing more childcare than men and a 2020 YouGov survey suggested that over 25 per cent of men in the UK leave all cleaning to their female partners.

Roman Catholic views on gender roles

Roman Catholic Christian attitudes may differ widely and these differences may to some extent depend on culture and society (see spread 5.12). However, the woman's role as a mother is seen to be significant in Catholicism. This is illustrated in a letter written by Pope John Paul II in 1988, *Mulieris Dignitatem*, where he seeks to explain the Church's view on the dignity and importance of women, partly in response to twentieth-century feminism. Drawing on the example of Mary, he argues that women are created with the skills needed for motherhood and that it is the woman who has the primary role as parent.

Sources of authority

'Scientific analysis fully confirms that the very physical constitution of women is naturally disposed to motherhood – conception, pregnancy and giving birth – which is a consequence of the marriage union with the man.' (*Mulieris Dignitatem*, Pope John Paul II, 1988)

'But women will be saved through childbearing – if they continue in faith, love and holiness with propriety.' (1 Timothy 2:15)

Protestant views on gender roles

As with Catholic views, there can often be differences which are as much cultural as they are religious. More conservative Christians such as members of some Pentecostal churches may agree that one of the key roles of the women in a family is motherhood and that they may well be the primary carer for the children. They may also, in some cases, argue that the husband is the 'head of the household' and that the wife should submit to him. Yet this does not mean that the husband can abuse this leadership role. The Bible says that he must love his wife and be prepared to lay down his life for her if necessary. These Protestants may also take the Biblical references to women dressing and behaving modestly a little more literally than more liberal Christians

Liberal Christians are more likely to have moved away from these traditional attitudes, viewing the Biblical references to female submission and modesty as a reflection of the time period in which the Bible was written rather than anything that has to be adopted today.

> **Top tip**
>
> It is worth remembering that Christians don't just disagree because of religious reasons such as their denomination or way of interpreting the Bible. Culture, upbringing and personal experiences will also affect beliefs and attitudes.

Sources of authority

'I also want the women to dress modestly, with decency and propriety, adorning themselves, not with elaborate hairstyles or gold or pearls or expensive clothes but with good deeds, appropriate for women who profess to worship God.' (1 Timothy 2:9–10)

'Wives, submit yourselves to your husbands, as is fitting in the Lord. Husbands, love your wives and do not be harsh with them.' (Colossians 3:18–19)

Analyse and evaluate

Should men and women have different roles in a Christian family?

Yes	No
The Bible suggests that the husband has authority in the household and that childbearing is part of a woman's purpose.	Christianity teaches love and that all are equal in the eyes of God so it is wrong to enforce strict views about different roles.
The importance of motherhood to the wife's role is taught by Pope John Paul II in the *Mulieris Dignitatem*. It is argued that this is something that women are both biologically and psychologically suited to.	Modern feminism challenges the outdated views on gender roles. Theologian Mary Daly argues that suggesting the Virgin Mary is an ideal gives Christian women an impossible ideal to live up to – either virginity or motherhood.
Difference does not mean that women are any less than men. It is possible to be equal yet play different roles.	The ideas of different roles is largely a matter of culture or the expectations of society. Christians don't need to follow them.

Activities

Review

1. What does the Bible say about the role of the husband in a Christian family?
2. What does the Bible say about the role of the wife in a Christian family?

Develop

3. Why is motherhood so important to Roman Catholic Christians?

Link

4. Look at Christian attitudes to contraception in spread 5.5. How do these link to the issues discussed here?

Debate

5. Are there things that men or women are generally better at? Does this mean that different roles within a relationship are a good idea? Note down the arguments presented as you discuss this.

Stretch

6. Research the ideas of Mary Daly on how Christianity has historically oppressed women. To what extent are her criticisms fair?

5.9 Men and women within Christian communities

Aim
To explore different Christian attitudes to gender roles within Christian communities

Starter
It is now commonplace to see female clergy, yet it is only relatively recently (1992) that the Church of England voted to ordain women. Why do you think this took so long? Why do other Christian churches still not accept female priests?

■ Rev. Kate Bottley is a famous female vicar who also works in TV and media

Key words
Ordination/ordain – a ceremony where someone is authorised to become a priest or vicar
Lay people – church members who are not ordained
Clergy – a religious leader such as a priest or vicar who is ordained/authorised to carry out religious duties

Roman Catholic approaches to gender roles in Christian communities

The Roman Catholic Church believes that the role of a priest is a male role. The justification for this is partly Biblical. One of the roles of Jesus is to act as a priest or mediator between humans and God. Both Jesus and the disciples he appoints are male. The other justification for opposing the **ordination** of women is that this has never been part of the tradition and teaching of the Church. Hence women are not allowed to carry out baptisms or lead the Mass.

Women are able to carry out duties as **lay people** of the church, including giving out bread and wine at Mass or visiting the sick. This type of role received formal recognition by Pope Francis in 2020. His *Spiritus Domini* decree changed the wording of the canon law from 'lay men' to 'lay people', which meant that more traditional priests who were reluctant to permit women to assist at Mass or to give readings were now required to do so. Catholicism allows both monks (male) and nuns (female) to undertake religious orders. They are not ordained but do have a slightly higher status than lay people.

Sources of authority

'Women should remain silent in the churches. They are not allowed to speak, but must be in submission, as the law says. If they want to inquire about something, they should ask their own husbands at home; for it is disgraceful for a woman to speak in the church.' (1 Corinthians 14:34–35)

'A woman should learn in quietness and full submission. I do not permit a woman to teach or to assume authority over a man; she must be quiet.' (1 Timothy 2:11–12)

Protestant approaches to gender roles in Christian communities

Most Protestant denominations ordain both men and women. The words 'vicar', 'minister' or 'pastor' tend to be preferred to 'priest' as the idea of a priest is one that acts as a mediator between humans and God. Protestants tend not to see **clergy** as a continuation of the role of Jesus; humans have direct access to God and there is a 'priesthood' of all believers. The church is like a human body (see 1 Corinthians 12) made up of many parts and roles: leadership, administration, preaching, prophecy, prayer and hospitality. Each of these roles are available to both men and women and there is no distinction for most Christians.

Sources of authority

'When Priscilla and Aquila heard him [Apollos], they invited him to their home and explained to him the way of God more adequately.' (Acts 18:26)

'Greet Andronicus and Junia, my fellow Jews who have been in prison with me. They are outstanding among the apostles.' (Romans 16:7)

Some evangelical Christians can be cautious about appointing women to leadership roles but this is sometimes due to culture and tradition rather than for religious reasons. Where religious reasons are given, it is often a literal reading of 1 Corinthians 14 or 1 Timothy 2, where Paul seems to reject female leadership or preaching. Yet other evangelical churches such as the Hillsong Church, a Pentecostal group, are more progressive and often a married couple will share the role of 'senior pastor'. The Bible describes the role of Priscilla and Aquila, a married couple, in Christian leadership and also arguably refers to Junia as an Apostle along with her husband.

Analyse and evaluate

Should both men and women be able to carry out all duties within religious communities?

Yes	No
It is important to recognise that the Bible is influenced by the culture of the time it was written so the limited role for women in Christian communities is not something that must continue today.	The Biblical model of leadership comes from the example of Jesus as a priest and mediator. It is not for Christians today to change the role of women in response to changing culture.
There is some Biblical evidence for a wider role for women in the church community: unusually for religious teachers, Jesus gave his teaching to both men and women and women such as Priscilla had key roles in the church.	There are many roles to be played in the life of the Christian community, each of which is important. The vast majority of these roles can be undertaken by women so it should not matter if there are some roles that women cannot undertake.

Activities

Review

1. What are the two main reasons that Catholics do not ordain women?
2. What do Protestants believe about the role of men and women in church?

Develop

3. How do different Christians understand Bible passages such as 1 Corinthians 14 and 1 Timothy 2?

Link

4. Some Christians use the role of Eve in the Fall as grounds for treating men and women differently. Review spread 1.5 and consider whether this can be justified.

Debate

5. Gender is a protected characteristic but so is religion, which means churches are permitted to express religious beliefs about the gender of employees. Do you think this is right or should governments be able to make churches ordain women?

Stretch

6. Make a list of the different roles and activities that the Bible speaks about as occurring in Christian communities (see Romans 12:7–8; 1 Corinthians 12:8–10 and 28, and Ephesians 4:11). Which ones might not be open to both genders for some Christians?

5.10 Gender roles in the religious upbringing of children

Aim

To explore different Christian attitudes to raising children within the Christian faith

Starter

'There is no such thing as a Christian child: only a child of Christian parents. ... Do not indoctrinate your children. Teach them how to think for themselves, how to evaluate evidence, and how to disagree with you.' (*The God Delusion*, Richard Dawkins, 2006)

Is Richard Dawkins right that religious upbringing is a form of indoctrination?

■ The evolutionary biologist and author Richard Dawkins (1941–) has argued that religion is dangerous and should not be imposed upon children

Raising children

For all Christians, children are seen as a blessing and it is one of life's most important responsibilities to bring them up well. The Bible commands that children 'honour their parents' – it is one of the Ten Commandments. Children are also encouraged to obey and respect their parents (Proverbs 6:20–22).

The role of bringing up children in the faith, and the extent to which this is important, is generally something shared by both parents.

Evangelical views

Being a good parent who trains and educates their children well is important to evangelical Christians. In the New Testament, Paul writes that one of the key marks of a potential Christian leader is that he is able to manage his own family well. Parents are likely to pray with their children, read Bible stories at bedtime and take children to Sunday school. Although many Christians do not see much difference between the father's and mother's roles, some see the Biblical references to the father's training as a suggestion that he is responsible for discipline and Christian education while the mother is seen as more nurturing and loving.

Some evangelical families may be quite strict in their parenting and may not allow certain TV programmes or media for fear of bad influences. For example, one group expressed concern about children reading the *Harry Potter* series of books as it was felt to encourage an interest in witchcraft and the occult. In a minority of cases, this might lead parents to consider sending children to small Christian independent schools or home schooling their children. Although the Bible speaks of the role of fathers in teaching children, the reality is that this role often falls to the woman as the husband is more likely to work full time.

The aim of Christian education is for the child to be able to make their own decision to follow Christ when they are old enough. This is likely to be marked with a believer's baptism or a confirmation service (see spreads 2.7 and 2.13).

Sources of authority

'An elder must be blameless, faithful to his wife, a man whose children believe and are not open to the charge of being wild and disobedient.' (Titus 1:6)

'Fathers, do not exasperate your children; instead, bring them up in the training and instruction of the Lord.' (Ephesians 6:4)

'Do not withhold discipline from a child; if you punish them with the rod, they will not die.' (Proverbs 23:13)

Catholic views

The Catholic Church teaches that parents have the main responsibility in terms of the moral and spiritual education of their children. The Catechism of the Catholic Church 2225 states that it is almost impossible to find a substitute if parents do not fulfil this role. The family should teach children to pray and, in conjunction with the parish, help them to understand their faith. This begins with ensuring that children are baptised as infants.

Parents also have a duty to choose a school that will help them with the task of Christian education. For most Catholics, it is very important that their children are able to receive education in a Catholic school.

The Church does not specify gender roles in the upbringing of children; the sections in the Catechism of the Catholic Church 2225 are addressed to both parents. However, the apostolic letter, *Mulieris Dignitatem*, does suggest that the mother is the primary parent and may be biologically more suited to the raising of children than the father.

Sources of authority

'My son, keep your father's command, and do not forsake your mother's teaching.' (Proverbs 6:20)

'Parents receive the responsibility and privilege of evangelising their children.' (Catechism of the Catholic Church 2225)

Analyse and evaluate

Are women more suited to the role of raising children in the faith than men?

Yes	No
In practical terms, in most families, women still provide the bulk of the childcare so rightly or wrongly do have more time to develop the required skills.	Modern families are complex. Not every family is able to make choices about which parent focuses more on the children. There are families where this is the man's role and other families where there is only one parent.
In the *Mulieris Dignitatem*, it is argued that women are biologically and psychologically more suited to parenthood than men.	The Bible suggests that the role of discipline and Christian education is part of the father's role.
Even assuming some biological differences in the skills and traits of men and women – which is arguable – both roles are useful and it is wrong to favour one over the other.	

Activities

Review

1. Why do some evangelical Christians believe the role of educating children in the faith is mainly the father's role?
2. How do Catholics help to ensure their children follow the faith of their parents?

Develop

3. What are the main similarities and differences in how Catholic Christians and evangelical Christians raise their children?

Link

4. Review spread 2.7 on believer's baptism and spread 2.13 on confirmation.

Debate

5. Is the idea of raising children in the faith a reasonable one or does it sound like indoctrination? Discuss this issue and note down the arguments raised.

Stretch

6. Do some research into Richard Dawkins' and Sigmund Freud's views that religion can harm children and find out about their ideas.

5.11 Christian teachings and beliefs about equality

Aim
To explore Christian beliefs and attitudes on the importance of equality for individuals, communities and society

Top tip
As is often the case with key terms, the word 'equality' means different things to different people. Sometimes when using a key term, it is a good idea to state what you understand the term to mean or why others may understand it differently.

Sources of authority
'There is neither Jew nor Gentile, neither slave nor free, nor is there male and female, for you are all one in Christ Jesus.' (Galatians 3:28)

'So God created mankind in his own image, in the image of God he created them; male and female he created them.' (Genesis 1:27)

'Then Peter began to speak: "I now realise how true it is that God does not show favouritism but accepts from every nation the one who fears him and does what is right."' (Acts 10:34–35)

Key word
Embedded inequalities – the idea that inequality or unfairness is built into the structure and working of society

Starter
Look at the image. Discuss the two different ideas of equality that are presented. Which is fairer?

The importance of equality for individuals

The Bible teaches that all human beings are equal; the creation story in Genesis refers to humans being created in the image of God regardless of gender. The New Testament also reinforces the idea of equality: Paul, in the book of Galatians, suggests that there are to be no distinctions in terms of race, gender or social status. Christians widen this to include persons with disabilities who are also seen as equal in the sight of God. In Acts 10, Peter has a vision in which God shows him that what he had previously thought to be unclean was now to be understood as clean; the Old Testament and the message of Jesus had been thought to be for the Jewish people but this was to be widened to include all of humanity. One modern evangelical Christian writer, Vicky Beeching, has argued that the idea of equality should also extend to sexual orientation: in the past, some Christians may have thought of gay people as in some way 'unclean' but this should no longer be the case.

The importance of equality for communities

Equality is also important in Christian communities, both in the Church and the wider community. In his letter, the Apostle James, the brother of Jesus, argues that a church should not discriminate on the grounds of wealth or social status. The church must not copy the unjust structures that may be found in the outside world. The Communion service models this as all members, regardless of race, gender or status, break bread and drink wine to show that they are part of Christ's body. Some Methodist and Baptist churches have attempted to reflect equality in the design of their buildings and in the clothing of clergy by moving away from high altars and robes in favour of a simpler design.

The importance of equality for society

The importance of equality does not end at the doors of the church building. Many Christians believe that there is a Christian duty to work towards making society more equal. This may involve working more with those who are disadvantaged, as some members of society need more of the church's help due to **embedded inequalities**. These Christians argue that, in his earthly life, Jesus is very much on the side of the disadvantaged: he interacts with those marginalised (or looked down upon) in his society such as women, foreigners such as the Samaritans and even the tax collectors who were outcasts due to their links with the Romans.

Sources of authority

'My brothers and sisters, believers in our glorious Lord Jesus Christ must not show favouritism. Suppose a man comes into your meeting wearing a gold ring and fine clothes, and a poor man in filthy old clothes also comes in. If you show special attention to the man wearing fine clothes and say, "Here's a good seat for you," but say to the poor man, "You stand there" or "Sit on the floor by my feet," have you not discriminated among yourselves and become judges with evil thoughts?' (James 2:1–4)

'Just then his disciples returned and were surprised to find him talking with a woman. But no one asked, "What do you want?" or "Why are you talking with her?"' (John 4:27)

Analyse and evaluate

Does equality have to mean that everyone gets the same?

Yes	No
Even if we accept people's differences, everyone ought to get the basic rights such as food, water and shelter. Christians should work towards this and they have a duty to love everyone.	Equality should not mean all get the same because this is not fair. If someone is privileged and wealthy, it is wrong to give them the same attention as someone who is in poverty or struggling with difficult issues.
All humans are made in the image of God and the New Testament talks of there being no difference between male and female, so there is no justification for different treatment.	Jesus did not give his time and resources equally. He went where the need was and seemed particularly concerned for those who were marginalised.

Activities

Review
1. How did Peter's vision change his understanding of who should receive God's message?
2. How does the story of the Good Samaritan (Luke 10:25–37) show Jesus' attitude to outsiders?

Develop
3. How does the Bible show the importance of treating people equally in both the church and wider society?

Link
4. Can the Church treat people of differing sexual orientations equally? Review spread 5.6 on same-sex marriage.

Debate
5. Is equality – treating everyone the same – or is equality of opportunity more important? Discuss the issue and note down some of the arguments given.

Stretch
6. Research the case of Vicky Beeching, who came out in 2014. How was she treated by the church community?

5.12 Christian views on equality, prejudice and discrimination on the basis of gender

Aim
To examine different Christian attitudes to prejudice and discrimination on the grounds of gender

Starter
In the United States, the Supreme Court, which comprises five male Justices and four female Justices, voted in 2022 to reduce women's rights to seek an abortion. Those opposed to abortion often cite religious reasons against it. Is this an example of discrimination on the grounds of gender?

The issue of abortion gives rise to strong opinions on both sides of the debate

Key words
Complementarian – the belief that men and women, although equal in status, have different but complementary roles and responsibilities

Egalitarian – the principle that all people are equal and deserve equal rights and opportunities

Equality issues and Christianity

Almost all Christians would say that they believe in gender equality yet they may understand 'equality' differently. These differences are seen in various areas including the three below:

- **Attitudes to female clergy:** should both men and women be ordained to Christian ministry?
- **Attitudes to abortion rights:** should women be allowed to control their own fertility or does this contravene God's laws?
- **Attitudes to women in the workplace**: is the fact that men dominate senior positions in many industries a justice issue that Christians should campaign to address?

Equality as complementarianism

For many Christians, equality between genders does not mean that men and women perform the same roles. Just as the members of a sports team may play different positions or the members of a band may play different instruments, so too men and women are equally important yet this does not mean that they have identical responsibilities. This view is known as **complementarianism**.

The creation story gives Eve the role of helper to Adam. Some Christians might feel that this also implies inferiority but this is not the only possible reading of the text. Roman Catholic Christians argue that women are better suited to parental responsibilities; they see Mary, the mother of Jesus, as an ideal role model.

Some evangelicals may also support a different role for men and women based on their understanding of texts such as Ephesians 5. Even churches that take a more **egalitarian** view of the status of men and women recognise that the two groups may have different needs and, just as there may be children's or youth group meetings in church, so too churches may hold meetings that are specifically for the men or women of the church.

Sources of authority

'The Lord God said, "It is not good for the man to be alone. I will make a helper suitable for him." (Genesis 2: 18)

'Wives, submit yourselves to your own husbands as you do to the Lord. For the husband is the head of the wife as Christ is the head of the church, his body, of which he is the Saviour.' (Ephesians 5:22–23)

Source of authority

'But Martha was distracted by all the preparations that had to be made. She came to him and asked, "Lord, don't you care that my sister has left me to do the work by myself? Tell her to help me!" "Martha, Martha," the Lord answered, "you are worried and upset about many things, but few things are needed – or indeed only one. Mary has chosen what is better, and it will not be taken away from her."' (Luke 10:40–42)

Equality as egalitarianism

Other Christians see the equality of gender in terms of egalitarianism. They see no distinction between the roles of men and women. The passage in Genesis 2 in which Eve is created from Adam's rib may not be the most accurate translation. The Hebrew word for 'rib' could equally be translated as 'side' – which would make Eve more significant to Adam than merely being a body part that he wouldn't miss!

Christians might argue that the gender inequalities seen in society are not part of God's design but are the effects of the Fall and are reinforced by culture. These inequalities are something for Christians to fight against rather than just accept. They may point to the story of Mary and Martha, where Jesus challenges the stereotypes of his day by allowing Mary to sit at his feet as he taught rather than fulfilling the expected domestic role.

Analyse and evaluate

Does Christianity support discrimination on the basis of gender?

Yes	No
Whether it is intended or not, the strict pro-life stance of many Christians enables an embedded inequality which puts women at a disadvantage.	To say that men and women are different does not logically mean that one gender has lower status.
The refusal of Roman Catholics and some evangelicals to ordain women is a form of discrimination, regardless of whether they believe they can justify it with scripture.	Much of the gender discrimination we see around us is not to do with Christianity but is more to do with culture and society – possibly as an effect of the Fall. Christians can often be found actively campaigning to reverse this.

There are a wide range of views within Christianity and the issues surrounding gender equality are complex so the best answer that can be given is not a simple yes or no; as it depends on which issue and the form of Christianity.

Activities

Review

1. What evidence might a Christian who believes that men and women have different roles give to support their view?
2. What evidence might a Christian who believes that men and women are equal in role and status give to support their view?

Develop

3. How might different Christians see the issues of abortion, gender roles at work and female clergy?

Link

4. Look back at the discussion of the *Mulieris Dignitatem* in spread 5.8. How do Pope John Paul II's views affect this topic?

Debate

5. Is the right to life more important than gender equality? Discuss the gender issues relating to the abortion debate and note down the arguments that are given.

Stretch

6. Compare and contrast Genesis 1 and Genesis 2. How do these texts contribute to the debate on gender equality? How do God's punishments to Adam and Eve in Genesis 3 affect the debate?

5.13 How does culture influence Christian attitudes to equality?

Aim
To explore how different Christian attitudes to equality are influenced by culture

Starter
Most of the countries in the table below are majority Christian. What other factors might explain the difference between average male and female pay in these countries?

Key word
Culture – the ideas, customs and social behaviour of a particular people or society

Sources of authority
'Women should remain silent in the churches. They are not allowed to speak, but must be in submission, as the law says.' (1 Corinthians 14:34)

'Does not the very nature of things teach you that if a man has long hair, it is a disgrace to him, but that if a woman has long hair, it is her glory? For long hair is given to her as a covering. if anyone wants to be contentious about this, we have no other practice —nor do the churches of God.' (1 Corinthians 11:14–16)

Understanding culture

The beliefs and attitudes of different Christians can often be affected by **culture** as much as by religious faith. Culture is quite a broad term, referring to the ideas, customs and behaviour of a society or sub-group in society. Culture may be a product of our background, our ethnicity, our history and even our political outlook. We may have a culture that is more conservative – keen to preserve the traditions of the past – or more progressive – open to change.

Christianity, culture and gender

Culture is often a significant factor when it comes to issues of gender roles and equality. In 1 Corinthians, Paul argues that women should remain silent in church and that they ought to modestly cover their heads. He suggests that women should have longer hair and cover their hair in church. Some Christians do feel that women ought to dress conservatively and in some black Pentecostal churches it is still common, particularly for older women, to wear a hat in church, whereas in some evangelical churches with a similar theological view, this custom is not necessarily enforced.

Liberal Christians may point out that Paul's attitudes are in themselves an expression of the culture of his day and that Christians in the twenty-first century are not bound by those views on the role of women in church and in the family.

Country	% Difference between average male and female pay
South Korea	36.7
Japan	25.7
USA	18.1
United Kingdom	16.8
Germany	15.5
Spain	11.5
France	9.9
Italy	5.6

■ There is a noticeable gap between the average pay of men and women in most countries (OECD 2016)

Christianity, culture and wealth

Different branches of the Christian Church are also affected by culture when it comes to one of the biggest inequalities in the world: the imbalance between the rich and the poor. In Latin America, many Christians have been influenced by a movement called liberation theology, which argues that a key aspect of Jesus' teaching is about reversing the injustices caused by poverty. The movement is actively involved in politics and argues for a 'preference for the poor'. Although the movement is largely Catholic, it has been criticised by the established Catholic Church because 'preference for the poor' seems to suggest that God does not love all equally.

Some evangelical Christians in the United States have been influenced by prosperity teaching – the idea that God favours believers and blesses their faithfulness by granting wealth. However, this view is not shared by evangelical Christians in the developing world, which again shows that views can be shaped by culture rather than theology. Both liberal and evangelical Christians might feel that Bible passages used to support prosperity teaching, such as Jeremiah 29, are being taken out of context.

Source of authority

'"For I know the plans I have for you," declares the Lord, "plans to prosper you and not to harm you, plans to give you hope and a future."' (Jeremiah 29:11)

Analyse and evaluate

Are attitudes to equality influenced more by culture than by religion?

Yes	No
It is often possible for Christians with similar theological outlooks to take different views on a topic due to their background.	Christians' attitudes to equality issues do have roots in theological ideas – either from Biblical texts or from Church teaching.
One aspect of culture that influences Christians is politics. Christians in the United States take very different views on issues depending on whether they support the Republican Party or the Democratic Party.	For a Christian, beliefs and attitudes should come from their faith. They should put God first and shouldn't be swayed by cultural attitudes.

Religion and culture are not necessarily opposites. They are connected in quite complex ways and often a Christian's views are a combination of both religion and culture.

Activities

Review

1. What different things might be part of someone's culture?
2. How might different Christians understand Paul's writing on women covering their heads?

Develop

3. How does culture affect Christian attitudes to the inequality caused by poverty?

Link

4. Look at spreads 5.8 and 5.9 which consider areas where Christians disagree about the roles of women in families and churches. Which of these disagreements might also be affected by culture?

Debate

5. Think about prosperity teaching. Does it make sense that God will financially reward those who follow him or might this encourage Christians to follow Jesus for the wrong motives?

Stretch

6. Find out a little more about liberation theology. What are its key concerns? Why has the Roman Catholic Church criticised its views?

Summary activities

CHECK YOUR NOTES
STAGE 1

Check that you have detailed notes that cover the following:

- [ ] Different Christian ideas about the role and purpose of a Christian family
- [ ] Different Christian ideas about marriage including the beliefs reflected in the marriage service
- [ ] Different Christian ideas about premarital sex, celibacy and contraception
- [ ] Different Christian ideas about civil partnerships, cohabitation and same-sex marriage
- [ ] Different Christian views about the ethics of divorce, annulment and remarriage
- [ ] Differing Christian views on the roles of men and women within the family including the raising of children
- [ ] Different Christian views about the roles of men and women in Christian communities
- [ ] How different Christians understand the idea of equality including the extent to which this might be affected by culture
- [ ] Christian attitudes on the importance of equality for individuals and society
- [ ] What Christians teach about equality and discrimination on the basis of gender
- [ ] Different Christian attitudes to prejudice and discrimination on the basis of gender

GETTING READY
STAGE 2

Quick quiz

1. In Ephesians 5, what is the relationship between husband and wife compared to?
2. In Matthew's Gospel, what is the one circumstance where Jesus appears to permit divorce?
3. What institution is called the 'domestic church' by Roman Catholics?
4. What does the word 'fidelity' mean?
5. Why do Roman Catholics oppose same-sex marriage?
6. How might a Christian use the creation story in Genesis 1 to argue for gender equality?
7. Which Christian groups allow both men and women to serve as priests/ministers?
8. What word can be used to describe the view that men and women are equal but have differing roles?
9. What might a Christian family do to help ensure their children grow up in the faith?
10. What is an annulment?

Quick quiz answers can be found online at **www.hoddereducation.co.uk/ocr-gcse-rs-answers**

ACTIVITIES
STAGE 3

1. Create a set of flashcards for the key technical terms you have come across in this topic. Use them to test yourself on the definitions.
2. **AO2 focus:** Can Christians support the idea of …? Fill in the gap with one of the issues you've studied in this topic. Come up with reasons for and against the statement making sure you use at least some evidence from Christianity.

STAGE 3

GET PRACTISING

Use this section to help you develop your understanding of how to answer questions on this topic.

Ask the expert

Mark writes:

I can never seem to get more than 6 or 7 marks on the 15-mark questions. I often write more than some of my classmates. The teacher explained that it was to do with something called assessment objectives. What do they mean?

Expert comment:

Longer 15-mark questions are marked by levels of response. There are 3 marks for AO1 – knowledge and understanding – and 12 marks for AO2 - analysis and evaluation. My suspicion is that you are focusing on explaining different views (AO1) rather than writing an argument. Compare your essay plan with Nazreen's. Notice the 'because' in most of her paragraphs. This plan enables her to write an argument focused on AO2.

4 (10–12)	A **good** attempt to respond to the stimulus, demonstrating some or all of the following: • A variety of viewpoints explored with good use of reasoned argument and discussion • Good analysis and evaluation of the significance and/or influence of the issue on different Christian groups • Evidence of critical evaluation including comment on, and comparison of, arguments from different Christian groups • Evidence of judgement on the issue in the stimulus and some conclusion to the evidence
3 (7–9)	A **satisfactory** attempt to respond to the stimulus, demonstrating some or all of the following: • Different viewpoints offered with some evidence of reasoned argument and/or discussion • Satisfactory analysis and evaluation of the significance and/or influence of the issue on some Christian groups • Evidence of comment on, and comparison of, arguments • Evidence of judgement on the issue in the stimulus and some conclusion to the discussion

- You will need to make the case for your conclusion
- You need to weigh up the arguments you present
- You need to reflect on answers given by different Christians
- You need to reach a conclusion

TASK

Choose a 15-mark question on this topic and have a go at writing a plan that focuses on the argument (AO2) as opposed to information (AO1).

Mark's plan	Nazreen's plan
Intro: Historical background	**Intro:** Christians allow divorce but never the best option
P1: Explain Catholic views on divorce	**P1:** Because Jesus opposes divorce (except for adultery – 2 views)
P2: Explain Church of England views on divorce	**P2:** Because marriage is a sacrament (Catholics) BUT other Christians do not see marriage as sacrament
P3: What Jesus said in Matthew and Mark on divorce	**P3:** Counterargument – Because of importance of love – sometimes ending marriage is most loving thing
P4: Atheists allow divorce – UK law allows divorce too	**P4 and conclusion:** But Bible stresses importance of marriage (Gen 1) so divorce not best option
My view:	

The existence of God

CHAPTER 6

6.1 Christian beliefs about God and his goodness

> **Aim**
>
> To review key Christian ideas about God and consider what it means for Christians to refer to God as good

> **Starter**
>
> In Section 1 (Beliefs and teachings: Christianity), you examined the Christian idea of God. Attempt to write a brief definition or (one phrase or sentence) of each of the terms in the spider diagram:
> - Benevolent
> - Omniscient
> - Omnipotent
> - Monotheistic
> - Judge
> - Eternal
> - Transcendent
> - Immanent
> - Personal
> - Forgiving

> **Key word**
>
> **Atheist** – someone who believes that God does not exist

Christian beliefs about what God is like

Christianity, like the other Abrahamic faiths (Judaism and Islam), is a monotheistic religion. Christians believe in one all-powerful, all-knowing God who is responsible for the creation of the world. Christians believe that God is actively involved with his creation. This active involvement is not an essential aspect of monotheism. It is possible to believe that there is a God who made the world but is no longer involved or even is unaware of how the world is progressing. This idea is called Deism.

The belief that God is all powerful yet is still involved in the world creates a tension between the idea of transcendence and immanence. God is both the all-powerful judge high above the universe and the loving, forgiving God who is close at hand. Christians may differ in terms of which of these two aspects they consider more important but this may be more to do with temperament and upbringing rather than their denomination.

Most Christians are also Trinitarian, believing that God is revealed in three persons – Father, Son and Holy Spirit – as stated in the Church creeds. Some newer groups who would identify as Christian, such as Jehovah's Witnesses, do not believe in the Trinity. They reject the idea that Jesus is divine.

Understanding God's goodness

The idea that one of God's attributes is goodness causes a problem for **atheists** who may point to the evil in the world as evidence that this cannot be the case (spread 6.3). However, it is not only the existence of evil in the world that may cause people to question God's goodness. The atheist Richard Dawkins argues that it is hard to conclude that God is good if we examine God's actions in the Old Testament. He states that:

'the God of the Old Testament is arguably the most unpleasant character in all fiction: jealous and proud of it; ... an unforgiving control-freak ... [a] malevolent bully.' (*The God Delusion*, Richard Dawkins, 2006)

Dawkins' view is based on incidents such as the destruction of entire cities (like Sodom and Gomorrah), the plagues that are

Lot's wife is turned into a pillar of salt by God as she disobeyed his command not to look back towards Sodom

visited upon the Egyptians and the punishment of nations who turn to other gods. While Christians find some of these Biblical accounts difficult to explain, they suggest that it is important to understand what is meant by God's goodness. Christian philosopher Richard Swinburne (1934–) has argued that one way to think of God's goodness is like the goodness of a parent. The actions of an adult parent may often be difficult to understand from the perspective of a child. A parent may not always give a child everything they ask for and may discipline a child in order to help them to develop in the right way. This idea is seen in some of the Old Testament books of the prophets, such as Jeremiah, where God's people are seen to be suffering as a consequence of abandoning God.

Sources of authority

'Do not worship any other god, for the Lord, whose name is Jealous, is a jealous God.' (Exodus 34:14)

'And when the people ask, "Why has the Lord our God done all this to us?" you will tell them, "As you have forsaken me and served foreign gods in your own land, so now you will serve foreigners in a land not your own."' (Jeremiah 5:19)

Analyse and evaluate

Does the Bible really show that God is a good God?

Yes	No
Taken as a whole, the Bible shows that God is good. He makes covenants or agreements with his people and continues to seek relationships with humans, even when the covenants are broken.	It is difficult to suggest that God is good. He is a being that demands worship and becomes jealous when this does not happen.
Goodness does not mean that everything God does should be what we want. Like a parent, God disciplines and gives boundaries for our benefit.	While goodness may involve justice and punishment, it is difficult to justify some passages which show the destruction of whole peoples.

Isaiah 55:8-9 suggests that God's ways are higher than our ways. Christians may accept that the Bible's evidence could be seen as mixed but still believe by faith in the goodness of God.

Activities

Review

1. State four things that Christians believe about God.
2. Why might someone reading the Bible find it difficult to believe in the goodness of God?

Develop

3. How does the idea of God being like a parent help some Christians to understand his character?

Link

4. Look at the definitions you gave in the starter activity. Which of them help Christians to understand aspects of God's goodness?

Debate

5. Can a good God punish people as he does in the Old Testament? Discuss whether this seems fair and note down the arguments that are given.

Stretch

6. Find out more about Deism. One example of a deistic belief is Aristotle's idea of a prime mover, which you will explore if you go on to study A-level Religious Studies.

185

The existence of God 6.1 Christian beliefs about God and his goodness

6.2 How does a good God relate to the world and to human beings?

Aim
To explore how God's goodness is shown in his actions in the world and his relationship to human beings

Starter
One image that helps Christians understand the goodness of God is the idea of God as Father. How helpful is this image? What other images or pictures of God might help a Christian understand God's goodness?

■ Christians believe that God is similar to a parent. How helpful is this analogy?

Key words
Anthropic principle – the belief that the universe was created/allowed to evolve by God to bring about intelligent human life

Divine providence – the protective care and provision of God

Goodness in relationship with the world

One of the main ways that God's goodness is revealed for Christians is in the act of creation. At the end of each of the six days of creation he declared that the creation was good. The **anthropic principle** (see spread 6.7) suggests that the world is well-suited as an environment for human beings. Roman Catholic Christians refer to creation as being part of **divine providence**; although the creation is good, it is not yet perfect but God continues to guide it towards its goal. Catholics, along with other Christians, believe that part of the role of human beings is to help work towards this goal. This may include taking actions to protect and save the environment.

All Christians see the created order as evidence of the goodness of God. However, some evangelical Christians do not feel as strongly about the need to save the environment. They argue that this world will pass away and that God will create a 'new heaven and new earth' (Revelation 21). This also shows God's goodness in providing an ideal future state for his people.

Sources of authority

'God saw all that he had made, and it was very good. And there was evening, and there was morning – the sixth day.' (Genesis 1:31)

'The universe was created "in a state of journeying" toward an ultimate perfection yet to be attained, to which God has destined it. We call "divine providence" the dispositions by which God guides his creation toward this perfection.' (Catechism of the Catholic Church 302)

God's goodness in relationship with humanity

The Bible shows God as a being who desires to relate to his creation. This is particularly true of human beings, who are given a special place in creation (see spread 1.3). In addition to the act of creation, the goodness of God is revealed in a number of ways and via a number of images:

- **God is seen as a law-giver:** in the Ten Commandments and in the moral teachings of Jesus, God provides clear boundaries for human beings which show them the right way to live.
- **God is also revealed to be a Father:** Jesus refers to God as 'Abba' – an intimate word which can be translated as 'daddy' – and Christians are also encouraged to share this intimate understanding of God in several of Paul's letters. There are also some passages, such as Isaiah 49, which compare God to a mother.

- **God is revealed to be similar to a shepherd:** Psalm 23 describes God as providing for the needs of his people, providing rest and comfort, and giving guidance through his 'rod and staff' – instruments that ancient shepherds would use to keep their sheep moving in the right direction.
- **God is also seen as a mediator:** in the Old Testament, he makes agreements or covenants with his people – and then new covenants once these are broken. For Christians, the supreme act of God's love comes in the Incarnation of Jesus, who takes human form to die for people's sin.

The goodness of God does not end with the events described in the Bible. Christians believe that God continues to work in believers today through his Holy Spirit and through answered prayer. Some of the ways in which this happens are discussed in spread 1.4. Different Christians may emphasise different aspects of this work.

Different Christian views

- For liberal Christians, the role of Jesus as a moral example may be more significant. In particular, the role of love in the Christian life as suggested in 1 John 4. For some Christians, who are influenced by the perspectives of feminism, some of the male images of God's goodness are unhelpful and may be rejected in favour of more feminine aspects of God's nature.
- For evangelical Christians, personal religious experience and answered prayer shows God's continual goodness towards individuals. Some evangelical Christians in the USA have been influenced by prosperity theology, which teaches that part of God's goodness involves financial provision.

Sources of authority

'"Can a mother forget the baby at her breast and have no compassion on the child she has borne? Though she may forget, I will not forget you! See, I have engraved you on the palms of my hands."' (Isaiah 49:15–16)

'Whoever does not love does not know God, because God is love. This is how God showed his love among us: He sent his one and only Son into the world that we might live through him.' (1 John 4:8–9)

Analyse and evaluate

Is God good to all his creation?

Yes	No
The world is a gift to all creatures, regardless of whether they choose to worship God or not.	There is considerable inequality in the world and some people suffer greatly compared to others. Is this something that a good God could allow?
God's goodness, as revealed through the life of Jesus, offers all people the gift of salvation.	The images used by Christians to convey the idea of God's goodness are often male images which may not help women to connect to God's goodness.

Activities

Review

1. How is God's goodness shown in the story of creation?
2. How does the idea of God as a parent show God's goodness?

Develop

3. How does the Bible show that God is good in his relationship with humanity?

Link

4. Review the creation stories of Genesis 1 and 2. How do these stories show God's relationship with human beings?

Debate

5. Should a good God answer every prayer that Christians pray? Discuss this and note down the arguments that are raised.

Stretch

6. Research some of the Biblical examples suggested in this spread on God's goodness. To what extent do they present God as male?

6.3 What do Christians teach about the relationship between God and human suffering?

Aim

To explore the problem of evil and consider different ways in which Christians attempt to solve the problem

Starter

If God created the world, then surely all the suffering and evil in it is his fault. What other explanations could there be that might defend God against the problems raised by evil and suffering?

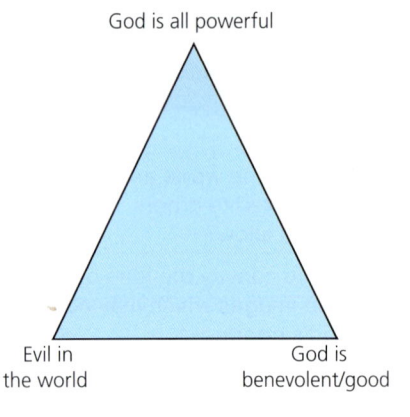

God is all powerful

Evil in the world — God is benevolent/good

■ The inconsistent triad

Key word

Inconsistent triad – the idea that the goodness of God, the power of God and the existence of evil are incompatible

Understanding the problem of evil

When conversations take place about whether God exists, it is not unusual for the issue of human suffering and evil in the world to be raised. This is a problem both in terms of moral evil – things caused by human beings – and natural evil – such as earthquakes or volcanoes. The margin diagram shows the **inconsistent triad** which is one way that a number of atheists express the problem of evil.

They argue that:

- If God is all powerful then he is able to prevent evil and suffering.
- If God is all good then he would desire to prevent evil and suffering.
- Given that evil and suffering exist, it does not seem possible that a God who is all good and all powerful can also exist.

As well as the fact that evil exists in the world at all, human suffering is often unfair. There are wicked people who live a long and happy life while young children are tragically killed. There are also parts of the world where suffering is greater and, as a result of climate or war, the chances of a person living a long and happy life are far less than someone living in a wealthier country.

The Bible is aware of the problem of suffering. The writer of Psalm 22 cries out that he feels that God has abandoned him. Jesus also understood what it was to suffer in life; he quotes Psalm 22 when dying on the cross.

Suffering as a consequence of the Fall and free will

One way that some Christians attempt to answer the problem of evil and suffering is to look back at what went wrong with creation. In Genesis 1, the Bible states that the original creation was good but this is damaged by human sin. This event, in which the first human beings disobeyed God, is known as the Fall and it leads to Original Sin; the idea that all humans are born with a sinful nature and as a result tend to do the wrong thing (see spread 1.7).

This explanation of evil has been popular among many Christians. It emphasises human free will as the cause of suffering in the world rather than the actions of God. Roman Catholic Christians, influenced by St Augustine, have tended to use Original Sin as an argument for infant baptism. For evangelical Christians, this explanation uses

Top tip

When discussing a viewpoint or statement, it is important to remember that you are evaluating – weighing arguments. Assess the viewpoint rather than just describing it.

Sources of authority

'"My God, my God, why have you forsaken me? Why are you so far from saving me, so far from my cries of anguish?"' (Psalm 22:1)

'Therefore, just as sin entered the world through one man, and death through sin, and in this way death came to all people, because all sinned.' (Romans 5:12)

'We can rejoice too, when we run into problems and trials, for we know that they help us to develop endurance.' (Romans 5:3 (NLT))

---

the creation story and is supported by other parts of the Bible, such as Romans 5, where the Apostle Paul explains that it is through the actions of Adam that sin and death enter the world.

Suffering as a way of developing character for heaven

A second way that some Christians answer the problem is to look forward and ask what God hopes to achieve by allowing suffering and evil in the world. It is argued that suffering and evil are able to help develop character. The Christian philosopher John Hick (1922–2012) argued that certain aspects of our character cannot be ready-made; they can only be acquired through difficulties. For example, it is not possible to become forgiving unless there are wrongs to forgive, nor is it possible to develop courage unless there are actual dangers to respond to.

There is some support for this idea in the Bible, again in Romans 5, where Paul talks about character development and also the future hope of heaven. Some liberal Christians argue that the only way that suffering can ultimately be justified is if everyone is saved and goes to heaven. This idea is known as universalism. Evangelical Christians and Catholics mostly reject this as they argue that for God to save all would be unjust and that this is contrary to what is revealed in the Bible.

Analyse and evaluate

Can the problem of human suffering be answered by Christians?

Yes	No
Focusing on the idea of free will and the Fall is helpful. Most of the suffering in the world is the direct result of human action and not the actions of God.	The problem of evil can't be fully answered because of the unfairness of suffering. Some people suffer far more than others and at times it seems there is little purpose or anything to be gained from their suffering.
The idea of character development is helpful. We recognise that overcoming difficulties makes us better people so it makes sense for God to allow some difficulties in the world.	Most of the answers to the problem of evil focus on moral evil and the role of human beings. This does not explain why there is natural evil such as earthquakes.
The arguments used to defend God may provide some philosophical justification of evil in the world but they do not bring comfort to those who suffer.	

Activities

Review

1. What are moral evil and natural evil?
2. Why does the existence of evil cause a problem for belief in God?

Develop

3. Which of the two answers to the problem of evil is better? Explain your answer.

Link

4. Review spread 1.7 about the Fall and Original Sin. Add in any extra material from there to the notes you have made on this spread.

Debate

5. An atheist might claim that it is easier to reject God than to believe that God allows evil to develop our character. What do you think? Discuss this issue and note down any arguments made.

Stretch

6. Two famous responses to the problem of evil come from Augustine (the Fall and free will) and John Hick (character building). Find out a little more about their ideas.

6.4 Does it matter whether God's existence can be proved?

Aim
To consider how important the arguments for and against God are to Christians

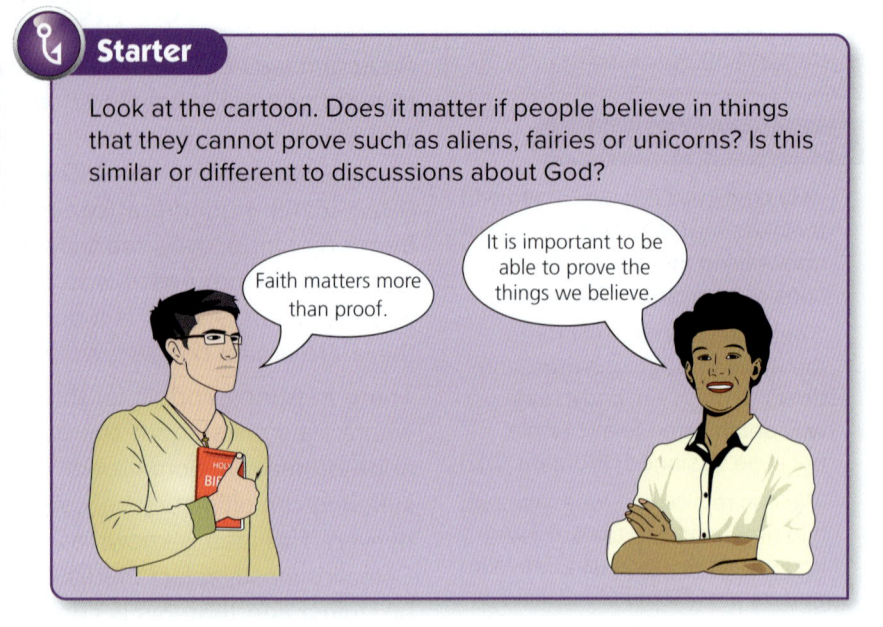

Starter
Look at the cartoon. Does it matter if people believe in things that they cannot prove such as aliens, fairies or unicorns? Is this similar or different to discussions about God?

Faith matters more than proof.

It is important to be able to prove the things we believe.

Key words
Reason – the use of intelligence, philosophy and argument to reach a conclusion

Revelation – the idea that God shows truths about himself to human beings, for example, through the Bible or religious experience

Sources of authority
'The fool says in his heart, "There is no God."' (Psalm 14:1)

'The heavens declare the glory of God; the skies proclaim the work of his hands.' (Psalm 19:1)

'the Church teaches that God ... can be known with certainty from the created world by the natural light of human reason.' (Catechism of the Catholic Church 36)

God's existence can be proved

The Bible supports the idea of there being evidence for God, such as the design of the universe (see spread 6.5), and suggests that only a fool could think that there was not a God. Some Christians throughout history have believed that it is possible to prove God's existence. The thirteenth-century philosopher St Thomas Aquinas (1224–1274) (see spread 6.6) famously had five ways to prove the existence of God. However, it is not clear whether he thought that these arguments would convert atheists or whether they were intended to support the faith of those who already believed. Generally speaking, arguments and proof of God have tended to be more important to Catholic Christians than to Protestants. The Catechism states that God can be known through human **reasoning** even if people also need God's **revelation** to help them come to understanding.

There is evidence that helps to show God's existence

Most Christians (and atheists) do not think that it is possible to completely prove the existence or non-existence of God. In his book *The God Delusion*, the atheist thinker Richard Dawkins entitles a chapter 'Why there is almost certainly no God'. Christian philosopher Richard Swinburne (1934–) suggests that, when taken together, the arguments for God show that God probably exists. The arguments that are commonly used by Christians, such as the design argument and the first cause argument, and our experience of morality are considered in the next four spreads.

It is pointless trying to prove God's existence

A number of Christians, particularly some Protestants, see little value in attempting to discuss the existence of God. The Bible encourages faith and suggests that this is the route to knowledge of God. Martin Luther (1483–1546) famously taught 'justification through faith' – the idea that it was simple trust and faith that brought him to God, not the arguments of philosophers. In his book *Fear and Trembling*, Søren Kierkegaard (1813–1855) shows that Abraham is rewarded for his faith – a faith that takes the illogical step of being willing to sacrifice his son Isaac. Some modern evangelical Christians are cautious about arguments for and against God. Faith and belief in the Bible are seen as more important.

Source of authority

'Without faith it is impossible to please God, because anyone who comes to him must believe that he exists and that he rewards those who earnestly seek him.' (Hebrews 11:6)

Analyse and evaluate

Are human beings able to use reason to prove God?

Yes	No
St Thomas Aquinas and other philosophers believe that there are good arguments for the existence of God.	If human beings do use their reasoning to think about God's existence, the amount of evil and suffering in the world (see spread 6.3) suggests that there is no such thing as God.
Human observation of the world shows order and beauty which enables human beings to understand that there must be a creator.	Human beings' abilities to reason are limited. It is not possible for humans to understand or figure out an issue such as this.
All cultures and societies have a sense of divine beings. Some philosophers have argued that this idea of God is something that God has given to give us a clue to his existence.	The lack of agreement on the issue suggests that proof is not possible. Typically, when we are able to prove things, for example, that the world is round, there is widespread agreement.
Thinkers such as Swinburne accept that God cannot be proved but they do think that there is a value in discussing the evidence and that it may be possible to show God as probable.	

Activities

Review

1. What does the Catechism of the Catholic Church suggest about the role of reason and revelation?
2. What did Martin Luther believe about the role of philosophy and faith?

Develop

3. What does the Bible say about evidence for God and the role of faith? Show that you have considered different points of view.

Link

4. Review spread 6.3 on the problem of evil. How does this make it harder to believe in God? How might a Christian answer the problem?

Debate

5. 'The fool says in his heart, "There is no God."' (Psalm 14:1) Discuss whether it is foolish not to believe in God. Are people who do believe in him more foolish? Note down reasons for and against each view.

Stretch

6. The idea of Kierkegaard that faith is the most important thing is called fideism. Find out more about Kierkegaard and fideism.

6.5 Does the design argument prove God's existence?

Aim

To consider whether there is evidence of design and purpose in the world and whether this leads to God

Starter

Imagine someone said to you that the watch in the picture had been produced by accident and that no human beings had been involved in its production. How sensible does this seem? Could there be other explanations of how it came to be?

Key words

Teleological argument – the argument that the apparent design of the world is proof or evidence of God's existence

Agnostic – someone who believes that we cannot know whether God exists

William Paley and the design argument

The most famous design argument (or **teleological argument**) was put forward by William Paley (1743–1805) using the example of a watch. Paley suggests that if we were walking across a field and we came across a watch on the ground, we would know just by studying it that it had to have an intelligent designer. Even if we had never seen such an object before and didn't know what it was, the way in which the cogs and dials were placed together would show us that an intelligent mind had been involved due to both the complexity – many parts moving together – and the fact that the parts fulfil a purpose.

Paley suggests that we should have similar views when we look at the world. The world has many different parts that work together and fulfil their purposes. Paley has a second example to illustrate this and asks us to consider the human eye. It is made up of many parts and when these parts are combined, they fulfil the purpose of seeing. When we consider this, it should be obvious to us that the eye and other features of our world are designed by an intelligent being, God.

A number of thinkers have produced similar arguments including St Thomas Aquinas and Richard Swinburne. Their arguments have tended to focus on the fact that the universe has fixed laws of nature that work and allow things to achieve their aim: the water cycle, the seasonal pattern of plants and trees, and the habits of birds are all things that require an intelligent mind behind the universe to make it work. There is some support from the Bible for these types of arguments. In his letter to the Romans, Paul suggests that people are without excuse if they can't see the existence of God from looking at the heavens.

Charles Darwin and evolution

One of the difficulties that leads both Christians and atheists to reject the design argument comes from Charles Darwin's theory of evolution. In *The Origin of Species*, Darwin explains that the process of evolution causes changes in species which lead to them adapting to fit their surroundings. This explains minor differences between species but, more importantly, it suggests that all creatures have a common origin. This seems to provide an alternative and better explanation of the complexity of the world than the explanation provided by the design argument. Darwin himself was an **agnostic** rather than an atheist but accepted that his theory posed a problem for the design argument.

Sources of authority

'The heavens declare the glory of God; the skies proclaim the work of his hands.' (Psalm 19:1)

'For since the creation of the world God's invisible qualities – his eternal power and divine nature – have been clearly seen, being understood from what has been made, so that people are without excuse.' (Romans 1:20)

'The old argument of design in nature, as given by Paley, which formerly seemed to me so conclusive, fails, now that the law of natural selection has been discovered.' (*The Autobiography of Charles Darwin*, Charles Darwin, 1958 edition; originally published 1876)

Christians have differed in their responses to Darwin. Roman Catholics and liberal Christians accept the theory of evolution but still support the design argument. They argue that the fact that evolution works and produces intelligent life is remarkable. The chances of evolution on its own producing intelligent life is so that that it seems more logical to believe that there is an intelligence, God, who plans and directs evolution. The idea that God is the guiding hand behind evolution is known as the anthropic principle (see spread 6.7).

Some evangelical Christians, particularly those who take the Bible more literally, reject Darwin's theory of evolution. The creation stories in Genesis 1 and 2 (see spreads 1.5 and 1.6) are seen as literal truths and show that God designed the world.

Top tip

The different arguments for God are key terms that appear in the course. Use flashcards to help you learn and remember them.

Analyse and evaluate

Is the design of the world good evidence that God exists?

Yes	No
Paley's analogy makes sense. Things that are ordered and complex do require intelligence. It makes no sense to believe that the universe is the product of chance.	The philosopher David Hume (1711–1776) rejects the design argument. He suggests that our understanding of the world is too limited to draw the conclusion that an intelligent designer is needed.
Even if evolution is accepted, the anthropic principle suggests that the involvement of God is needed to bring about human life.	There are a number of things in the world, such as the suffering of humans and animals, that suggest poor design. See spread 1.8 or 6.3 on the problem of evil.
It could be argued that while design does not prove God's existence, the complexity of the world and the beauty within it suggests that the idea of a designer is a reasonable theory.	

Activities

Review

1. How does Paley use the example of a watch to prove the existence of God?
2. Why does Darwin's theory of evolution cause a problem for the design argument?

Develop

3. How have different Christians responded to Darwin's theory of evolution?

Link

4. Review the accounts of creation in spreads 1.5 and 1.6. What do these show about God as designer? How do different Christians read them?

Debate

5. 'Scientists like Darwin have disproved God.' Is there a role for religious views in a scientific age? Discuss the quotation and make a note of the different arguments used.

Stretch

6. Richard Dawkins has developed the work of Darwin and has been highly critical of religious views. Find out a little more about his ideas of 'selfish genes' and 'blind watchmakers'.

The existence of God 6.5 Does the design argument prove God's existence?

6.6 Does the world need a first cause?

Starter

The person in the picture claims that there is no real explanation for the broken window. Is it possible that something can just happen without explanation or do things that happen always have a cause/explanation?

It just broke!

Aim

To consider different views on whether the first cause argument provides good evidence for God's existence

Key word

Cosmological argument – an argument for the existence of God that claims that God has to be the cause or explanation of the world

Sources of authority

'In the beginning God created the heavens and the earth.' (Genesis 1:1)

'For in him all things were created: things in heaven and on earth, visible and invisible … all things have been created through him and for him. He is before all things, and in him all things hold together.' (Colossians 1:16-17)

St Thomas Aquinas and the first cause argument

Many Christians use the **cosmological argument** (or first cause argument) to provide evidence for the existence of God. Perhaps the most famous example comes from St Thomas Aquinas.

Aquinas argues that it is only God that can ultimately give an explanation for the existence of the universe. The Bible also suggests this in its very first verse in Genesis 1: God is the maker of heaven and Earth.

Christians don't just believe that God created the universe and then stopped being involved (like someone striking a match). They believe that he also sustains the world moment by moment. He continues to cause its existence. This is reflected in one of Aquinas' other arguments, which uses the idea of contingency – that everything is dependent on something else. Ultimately, all things, including scientific laws, depend upon God. This idea is shown in Colossians 1:16–17: God is not just creator, he also continues to hold things together.

Christian responses to the idea of the Big Bang

The scientific theory of the Big Bang was developed by Georges Lemaître (1894–1966) (a Catholic priest) and Edwin Hubble (1889–1953) in the early twentieth century. Around 14–15 billion years ago, all matter and energy was compressed into a small, dense ball known as a singularity. There was a rapid explosive expansion known as the Big Bang whereby, upon cooling, particles began to form and then, due to gravity, stars and galaxies formed.

Christians differ in their responses to this idea:

- Most Roman Catholic and liberal Christians accept the idea of the Big Bang. They understand the creation narratives in the Bible to be symbolic rather than literal and believe that faith and science are compatible. They suggest that science explains how the world came to be but that Christianity is able to explain the 'why'. They note that the first cause argument actually still works regardless of the Big Bang theory; after all, it may be possible to ask 'What caused the Big Bang?'

All things and objects have a cause – something that brings them into existence or keeps them existing.

↓

These things in turn also have causes, which also have causes and so on.

↓

However, this cannot go on forever and ever or we would have a never-ending chain and we would never get an explanation.

↓

So there must be a first cause – something that doesn't need a cause. This is God.

■ St Thomas Aquinas' cosmological argument

○ Some evangelical Christians, particularly those who read the Bible more literally, reject the idea of the Big Bang. They believe that the creation happened largely as the Bible claims and that the Earth is thousands rather than millions of years old. While they may believe that the first cause argument provides good evidence of God, this often matters less to evangelical Christians as their belief in God tends to be based on faith and the Bible rather than intellectual argument.

Do we need an explanation?

The first cause argument relies on the principle of sufficient reason, developed by Gottfried Leibniz (1646–1716). The principle states that there has to be an explanation for everything that happens – we might not know what the explanation is but an explanation does exist.

Some modern atheists have challenged this argument. In a debate on the existence of God, the philosopher Bertrand Russell (1872–1970) rejected the principle of sufficient reason, famously stating 'I should say that the universe is just there, and that's all.'

Analyse and evaluate

Does the first cause argument prove that God exists?

Yes	No
The first cause argument supports human intuition that things need an explanation. It makes no sense to say that things just happen.	Even if the argument manages to prove that there is a first cause, it hasn't proved that God is the cause. It could be an absent God, a group of gods or something more scientific.
The first cause argument fits well with the ideas of modern science. It agrees with the Big Bang theory that the universe must have a beginning.	Although everything needs a cause, does there have to be just one overall cause of the universe?

Activities

Review
1. What is St Thomas Aquinas' first cause argument?
2. What does the Big Bang theory state about the beginning of the universe?

Develop
3. How do different Christians respond to scientific views of the origin of the universe?

Link
4. Review spread 6.5 on the teleological (design) argument. What are the similarities and differences to the first cause argument?

Debate
5. Does the universe have a beginning or could it have always existed? Discuss this issue and make a note of the arguments that are raised.

Stretch
6. These pages have considered Aquinas's first cause argument. He has two other similar arguments based on Motion and Contingency. Research these arguments.

6.7 What do Christians believe is the purpose of the world?

Aim
To consider the idea that the world was made by God for human beings

Starter
Why did God create the world? Which of the reasons in the diagram make the most sense? Are there other reasons you can think of that are not in the diagram?

- To show his glory and power
- He was lonely
- For human beings to enjoy
- To enjoy relationships/share his life
- For all life to flourish

Why did God create the world?

Key word
Dominion – the idea that Christians are to rule and take control, in this case over animals and the natural world

Christian understanding of the purpose of creation

Christians believe that God is perfect and is self-sufficient. He does not get bored or lonely so did not need to create the world. The Roman Catholic Church teaches that one of the purposes of creation is to bring glory to God. The Catechism states that 'both scripture and tradition teach that the world was made to show the glory of God' (Catechism of the Catholic Church 293). However, many Christians also believe that the world was created for human beings. The creation story shows that humans have a role as rulers over the Earth and some Christians see this as showing the importance of human beings to God's plans.

How do different Christians understand the role of human beings?

Some Christians tend to be more likely to see the world as created for the purpose of human beings. This means that the role of human beings is to have **dominion** over the Earth; the Earth is for human beings. This has led, to some extent, to a lack of concern over environmental ethics. One study conducted by the Pew Research Center suggested that only 28 per cent of evangelical Christians in the USA think humans cause global warming. Some evangelical Christians see climate events as evidence that the world is coming to an end and that Jesus will soon return.

Liberal Christians reject these views. They see the leadership role of human beings more in terms of stewardship. Christians have been given the gift of creation and have a responsibility to look after it. (The role is similar to being placed in charge of a young child or a pet.)

The anthropic principle as an argument for God

Some Christians have developed anthropic ideas to present an argument for the existence of God. While everyone agrees that the conditions on this planet are especially suited to human life, the anthropic principle goes one step further to claim that the world was designed this way.

The principle states that the chance of evolution randomly producing intelligent human life is so remote that the most probable explanation is that the universe was designed with the purpose of producing human life. The Christian philosopher Richard Swinburne illustrates the principle with the following example.

- Suppose a kidnapper locks you in a cell with a card-shuffling machine and says 'Unless the machine randomly draws the ace of hearts out of each of the ten packs, the explosives will go off.' The machine then draws the cards and, amazingly, you survive. You would probably conclude that the machine was rigged. So, too, we should be amazed that evolution has produced intelligent human life and consider that God has 'rigged' the process.

Sources of authority

'Then God said, "Let us make mankind in our image, in our likeness, so that they may rule over the fish in the sea and the birds in the sky, over the livestock and all the wild animals, and over all the creatures that move along the ground."' (Genesis 1:26)

'Then God said, "I give you every seed-bearing plant on the face of the whole earth and every tree that has fruit with seed in it. They will be yours for food. And to all the beasts of the earth and all the birds in the sky and all the creatures that move along the ground – everything that has the breath of life in it – I give every green plant for food."' (Genesis 1:29–30)

'Both scripture and tradition teach that the world was made to show the glory of God.' (Catechism of the Catholic Church 293).

Analyse and evaluate

Is it arrogant to believe that the Earth is just for the benefit of human beings?

Yes	No
The theory of evolution shows that we have a common origin. We are just a species that is a little more evolved.	It is suggested in Genesis 1 that the Earth is made to enjoy for our benefit.
The idea that humans are more important is dangerous and leads to mistreatment of animals and a lack of care for the environment.	Humans are fundamentally different to all other species on the planet. In particular, we have moral ideas; we are able to reflect on right and wrong.

It is possible to believe that the Earth is for human beings without this leading to arrogance. The belief ought to lead to stewardship and the type of servant leadership that Jesus modelled.

Activities

Review
1. What are some of the reasons that God created the world according to Christians?
2. What do different Christians believe about stewardship?

Develop
3. Explain how some Christians use the anthropic principle to prove the existence of God.

Link
4. Re-read the stories of creation in both Genesis 1 and 2. What does God say to the first human beings about their purpose and the purpose of creation?

Debate
5. Is it just too much of a coincidence that intelligent life has evolved? Discuss the anthropic principle and note down any points raised.

Stretch
6. Research the idea of 'rapture theology'. Why does this lead some evangelical Christians to be less interested in this world?

6.8 What does morality show about God and the purpose of human life?

Aim
To consider what our experience of morality suggests about God and human existence

Starter
You may disagree with a friend about whether a wall should be painted blue or green, or whether Instagram or TikTok is a better platform. Is it possible to disagree about whether torture should be permitted? Is it possible to disagree about whether cannibalism is good?

Key words
Moral argument – the idea that the existence of right and wrong provides evidence or proof of the existence of God
Soul-making – the idea that one of God's purposes in allowing humans to experience good and evil is to allow the development of character

■ The author C.S. Lewis (1898–1963) was a committed Christian and believed that the existence of morality could be used to prove the existence of God

Morality and God

If we think that there is such a thing as right and wrong, and that this is not just a matter of human opinion, then there are three possible implications:

- It may be possible to use morality to prove the existence of God (the **moral argument**).
- Our choices about right and wrong matter and develop our character (**soul-making**).
- There may be consequences for the choices we make regarding right and wrong (judgement).

The moral argument

A number of Christian thinkers, including the author C.S. Lewis, have put forward moral arguments for the existence of God. These arguments often start with our feeling or sense of right and wrong; for example, our conscience (see spread 6.11). They ask where these feelings come from and argue that God must be the source.

A simple moral argument might consist of the following three steps:

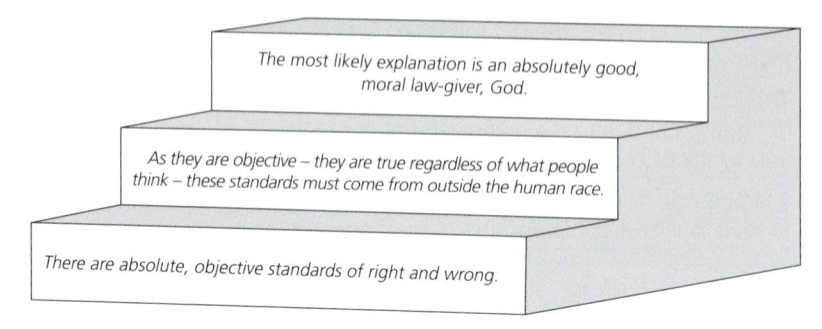

- The most likely explanation is an absolutely good, moral law-giver, God.
- As they are objective – they are true regardless of what people think – these standards must come from outside the human race.
- There are absolute, objective standards of right and wrong.

These arguments can be seen in the Bible. When Paul writes to the Romans, he notes that the Gentiles (non-Jews) – who did not have access to the Old Testament – still knew what was right and wrong as they had their God-given conscience.

Soul-making

A second consequence of our experience of morality is that we are able to make choices about what we do and, depending on the choices we make, we are able to become better (or worse) people. This is known as soul-making or character development (see spread 6.3). The Christian philosopher John Hick has suggested that the possibility of soul-making is the main reason that God has allowed a world where there is evil and suffering, and that in order to achieve it, God has to give humans free will, even if this risks some people carrying out wicked actions.

Judgement

A final aspect of human experience of moral choice is that there are consequences to the choices that are made. Christians believe that God judges human deeds in the afterlife (see the Parable of the Sheep and the Goats in spread 1.3).

Christians differ as to how this judgement takes place and the consequences of such a judgement:

- Catholic Christians believe that for most Christians, a period in purgatory is required to purify the soul ready for heaven.
- Evangelical Christians are more likely to believe in a literal hell for those who make the wrong choices; God is holy and requires that his people are holy too.
- More liberal Christians are less likely to believe that judgement leads to hell. They believe that God is a God of love and that references to a fiery hell in the Bible are symbolic. Some liberal Christians believe that all people will ultimately be saved.

Source of authority

'Indeed, when Gentiles, who do not have the law, do by nature things required by the law … They show that the requirements of the law are written on their hearts, their consciences also bearing witness, and their thoughts sometimes accusing them and at other times even defending them.' (Romans 2:14–15)

Analyse and evaluate

Does morality provide evidence of the existence of God?

Yes	No
Despite many different cultures and periods in history, there is widespread agreement on what is right and wrong, which suggests these standards are not just a matter of opinion.	The first point on the left is overstated. There is in fact a lot of disagreement when it comes to morality between different groups and in different periods of history.
People experience morality as a series of commands – things they ought to do or not do. H.P. Owen (1926–1996) suggests we can only have commands if there is a commander.	There are a number of psychological explanations about how we get our moral standards. Freud and others suggest they are acquired from our parents and society.

The idea that there is no such thing as right and wrong could lead to chaos. However, even if we were to accept that right and wrong do actually exist, this does not mean that the moral rules are given by God, as Christians believe.

Activities

Review
1. What is the moral argument for the existence of God?
2. What is meant by soul-making?

Review
3. How do different Christians view the link between moral behaviour and judgement?

Link
4. Review the topic of the problem of evil in spread 1.8. How does John Hick's idea of soul-making compare to other solutions, such as those of Augustine?

Debate
5. Are right and wrong just opinions passed down in society or does our sense of morality mean that God exists? Discuss this issue and make a note of any arguments presented.

Stretch
6. Research the moral argument for the existence of God. In addition to C.S. Lewis, there are famous versions produced by Immanuel Kant (1724–1804) and J.H. Newman (1801–1890).

6.9 Christian beliefs about revelation and experiencing God

Aim

To explore how different Christians understand the role of revelation in experiencing God

Key words

General revelation – refers to knowledge of God that is acquired through natural means that are available to all humans

Special revelation – the communication of truths about God that come to certain people at certain times, often through supernatural means

Starter

How important, do you think, are each of the elements, in helping Christians understand God? Rewrite the list in what you consider to be their rank order with 1 being the most important.
- Reasoning
- The Bible
- Church teaching
- Religious experience
- Miracles
- Conscience
- Other people
- Worship
- Sacraments

Understanding revelation

Christians believe that God desires to communicate with human beings. Some Christians believe that God has made it possible for humans to understand his existence and his plans. They may point to the experience of design or morality as evidence for God's existence (see spread 6.5). They also point to things such as reasoning and intelligence or the conscience (see spread 6.8) as ways in which God can communicate to all people. What these types of revelation have in common is that they are available to all people. This type of communication is known as **general revelation**.

However, this is not the only type of revelation and is probably not the main way that Christians understand revelation. **Special revelation** refers to specific events or means by which God communicates to individuals. This might include the Bible, miracles and direct religious experiences. In each of these, God has to take the initiative.

Revelation and perception of the divine

Another way of thinking about the different types of ways that God might be revealed might be to separate them into direct and indirect forms.

- **Direct forms:** many Christians believe that it is possible for God to directly reveal himself to human beings through religious experiences; these are direct perceptions of the divine. Religious experiences are particularly important to evangelical Christians such as the Pentecostal Church, which emphasises conversion and charismatic experiences such as speaking in tongues. Spreads 6.12–6.14 look at a variety of religious experiences.

- **Indirect forms:** see spread 6.10. God is revealed through something such as scripture or other people. For Roman Catholic Christians, this may include God's revelation through the teaching of the Church.

Different perspectives on revelation and experience

The issue of the roles of reasoning, revelation and experience is one where it is difficult to make generalisations.

- Broadly speaking, liberal Christians, such as some members of the Church of England, may place more weight on reasoning than on revelation or experience.
- For some evangelical Christians, such as members of the Pentecostal Church, the revelation of God through scripture is more important than reasoning and there is a strong emphasis on personal religious experience.
- For Catholic Christians, both the revelation through Christian history and the Bible are important but this is also balanced with an understanding that human reasoning is an important part of that tradition. Some Catholics are also drawn to direct experiences of God such as mystical experiences and experiencing God in the sacraments.

Top tip

Better answers to 6-mark questions tend to show awareness of different Christian views and why those Christians take those views. You should aim to identify different views on topics and a source of wisdom or authority for each Christian group.

Source of authority

'I want you to know, brothers and sisters, that the gospel I preached is not of human origin. I did not receive it from any man, nor was I taught it; rather, I received it by revelation from Jesus Christ.' (Galatians 1:11–12)

Analyse and evaluate

Do Christians need revelation in order to understand God?

Yes	No
Human reasoning is naturally flawed. Christians believe this may be partly due to the Fall, so knowledge of God without revelation may be limited.	Human beings are made in the image of God and this is partly about our God-given intellect. There is a rational case that can be made for the existence of God.
It is a key aspect of the Christian message that God takes the initiative and reveals himself to human beings through scripture and through the Incarnation of Jesus.	Reason is needed because some claims of revelation and religious experience can be harmful; it is important to logically assess ideas.

Many Christians think that a balance of reason and revelation is needed. There may be some truths about God that we can gain from the world around us but the more detailed points of Christian theology can only be known through revelation.

Activities

Review

1. What different types of revelation might be available to all people at all times?
2. What different types of revelation might be available only to specific people at particular times?

Develop

3. Explain what different Christian groups might believe about the ways in which God reveals himself.

Link

4. Review spreads 6.5 and 6.6 on the case for God's existence. In what ways might this be seen as general revelation?

Debate

5. 'God has shown me that the world will end on Thursday.' Is focusing too much on revelation potentially harmful? Discuss the issue and make a note of the arguments.

Stretch

6. Choose one of the methods of understanding God. What arguments are there to suggest whether this is a good approach to understanding God?

6.10 How might God be revealed through scripture and tradition?

Aim
To explore how different Christians understand God's revelation through the Bible, through Jesus and from history

Starter
'Honest Harry is the most truthful student in school, he told me so himself.'

What is the problem with the statement above? Is it also a problem if the Bible claims to be the Word of God?

Understanding how God is revealed in the Bible

The Bible is not really one book but is a collection of 66 books or documents written by various people over a period of hundreds of years. The Old Testament was written before Jesus and contains historical records, poetry and works of prophecy. The New Testament gives accounts of the life of Jesus, has letters to early Christian churches and includes a book of prophecy, the book of Revelation.

Christians believe that the Bible is inspired and that its contents are a revelation from God as suggested in the Bible itself (2 Timothy 3:16). However, the Bible is not an easy document to understand and, in order to do so, a Christian may look at a number of things:

- the context of the passages, for example, what the surrounding verses are about
- the genre or type of literature of the section
- the current situation the writer is addressing
- how the verse has been translated from the original Hebrew or Greek.

■ The word 'Bible' comes from the Greek *biblia* which means books or library

Different Christian views

- Roman Catholic Christians believe that there is an important role for the Church in interpreting the Bible; the tradition of the Church – the agreed teaching passed down through history – carries equal weight.
- Among Protestant Christians, there is less emphasis on tradition and Christians are encouraged to read the Bible for themselves.
- Evangelical Christians see the Bible as being a direct revelation from God. Some believe that God inspired the writers precisely, even down to their exact choice of words.
- More liberal Christians reject this idea of direct inspiration; writers were moved by God to write but we see human ideas and personalities in their work, hence the Bible contains the message of God but is not the Word of God in a literal sense.

Jesus Christ as God's ultimate revelation

Christians often refer to both the Bible and Jesus as the 'Word of God'. The Bible is the written Word of God but Christians believe that Jesus is the living Word of God. In John Chapter 1, the writer develops this idea and refers to Jesus as God's Word made flesh – come in human form. Christians believe that the Bible as a whole points towards Jesus; the Old Testament contains prophecies of Jesus which foretell details of his life. Jesus is seen as the fulfilment of the Old Testament law, the awaited Messiah. The Roman Catholic Church states in the Catechism that he is the ultimate and final revelation.

Most Christians believe that Jesus is God in human form, a mediator between human beings and God, an example of how to live and the saviour of the world. A more liberal Christian may not believe in the more divine aspects of Jesus' identity but may emphasise the moral teachings of Jesus and the role of Jesus in providing an example.

Sources of authority

'All Scripture is God-breathed and is useful for teaching, rebuking, correcting and training in righteousness.'
(2 Timothy 3:16)

'Sacred Tradition and Sacred Scripture make up a single deposit of the Word of God.' (Catechism of the Catholic Church 97)

'The task of interpreting the Word of God authentically has been entrusted solely to the Magisterium of the Church, that is, to the Pope and to the bishops in communion with him.' (Catechism of the Catholic Church 100)

Sources of authority

'The Word became flesh and made his dwelling among us. We have seen his glory, the glory of the one and only Son, who came from the Father, full of grace and truth.' (John 1:14)

'God has revealed himself fully by sending his own Son ... The Son is his Father's definitive Word; so there will be no further revelation after him.' (Catechism of the Catholic Church 73)

God's revelation in history and tradition

For Roman Catholic Christians, God is revealed through Christian history in the decisions made by the Church. It is believed that God's will is revealed through the magisterium; the official teaching of the Church. God is believed to guide these processes of reflection. This includes a belief in papal infallibility – that the Pope, when speaking officially from the papal throne, cannot make a mistake.

Although most protestants reject the Catholic view on tradition as the Church and individual churches can make mistakes, they recognise that God can act through the events of history guiding the course of events. Liberal Christians may not see God as directly involved in history but may instead be drawn to inspirational figures such as Dietrich Bonhoeffer (1906–1945) or Mother Teresa (1910–1997).

Analyse and evaluate

Is scripture the most important means of revelation?

Yes	No
The fact that the Bible is the Word of God is declared in the Bible.	The Bible is difficult to interpret and this might mean that the tradition of the Church may be more significant for some Christians.
Ultimately, both Jesus and church tradition are based on the Bible. The Bible gives accounts of Jesus' life. Church tradition is based on reflection upon the Bible.	The Bible is not always helpful. It has material which can be seen as unscientific and there are modern issues that the Bible says nothing about.

It can be argued that the Bible is important to Christians but this importance has to be balanced against other forms of revelation. Some parts of the Bible – such as the stories of Jesus – may be more important than others.

Activities

Review

1. What different types of books would you find in the Bible?
2. What difficulties do Christians have when trying to decide what a section of the Bible means?

Develop

3. What different views do Christians have about how the Bible is inspired?

Link

4. Review spreads 1.9 and 1.14 on the Incarnation and salvation. How is Jesus shown to be a revelation from God?

Debate

5. Is it a good idea to let people read and interpret the Bible for themselves or do they need guidance from the Church? Discuss this issue and make a note of the arguments raised.

Stretch

6. Catholic Christians also have the Apocrypha as part of the Bible. Find out more about these books.

6.11 How might God be revealed today?

Aim

To examine beliefs about how God may be revealed today through miracles and through the conscience

Starter

In May 1940, Allied forces in the Second World War were trapped near Dunkirk as the Nazis advanced. It was feared that over 300,000 troops would be lost. King George VI declared a National Day of Prayer for Sunday, 26 May. Crowds flocked into churches and cathedrals. In the days that followed, a combination of events led to almost all of the troops being safely evacuated: storms grounded the German air force; the waters in the English Channel were calm, which helped the civilian boats used for the rescue; and there was a strange order from Hitler to pause the attack. **(based on the account in *How to Pray* by Pete Greig)**

Does God act in the world in response to prayer as described above? What do you think?

Evacuation from Dunkirk (1940) by Charles Cundall (1890–1971)

The previous pages looked at ways in which Christians believe that God has been revealed during the course of history, such as through scripture and Jesus. These pages explore ways in which some Christians believe that God might still be revealed today.

God acting in the world through miracles

Christians believe that God has performed **miracles** during the course of history and is capable of performing miracles today. There are numerous miracle stories in the Bible, such as the ten plagues experienced by the Egyptians and the rescue of the Israelites by the parting of the Red Sea. The Gospel accounts of Jesus also record a number of miracles. These can be divided into healings, such as restoring sight to the blind, and nature miracles, when extraordinary events take place, such as the feeding of the 5000 or Jesus walking on water. There are even some accounts of Jesus raising the dead, including the raising of his friend Lazarus in John 11.

Key word

Miracle – an extraordinary event that is not explained by natural or scientific laws and is therefore attributed to a divine agency

Many Christians believe that, although rare, God still performs miracles today. One place particularly associated with miracles for Roman Catholics is Lourdes in France. In one famous case, a 51-year-old multiple sclerosis patient, Jean-Pierre Bély, who was paralysed regained the ability to walk and made a full recovery within days of his visit.

Different Christian views

- Many evangelical Christians also believe in the possibility or miracles. Services in the Pentecostal Church in particular often feature prayer for the sick. Some believe that there are evangelists to whom God has given a special gift of being able to perform miraculous healings.

- Not all Christians believe that God still performs miracles today. These Christians may believe that the miracles in the Bible did not actually happen and that they should be read symbolically; for example, the feeding of the 5000 teaches that Jesus provides for his people. Other Christians may believe the miracles in the Bible but believe that these miracles were for the apostolic age – the generation that was present at the start of the Church. They no longer happen now that the Apostles' generation has passed.

Sources of authority

'When I pray, coincidences happen, and when I don't, they don't.' (attributed to William Temple (1881–1944), Archbishop of Canterbury)

'The decision is announced by messengers, the holy ones declare the verdict, so that the living may know that the Most High is sovereign over all kingdoms on earth and gives them to anyone he wishes and sets over them the lowliest of people.' (Daniel 4:17)

God acting in the world through history

Belief in miracles is a belief that God dramatically intervenes and changes the laws of nature at certain points in time. Many Christians believe that God may act within history in more subtle ways by guiding human events. The rescue of troops from Dunkirk (see starter box) may be due to good fortune or may indicate some divine help. This idea of God acting in the world is seen in the Bible, where God refers to Cyrus, the King of Persia, as his anointed servant who does his bidding by releasing the exiled Jewish people to return to their homeland.

God acting in individuals through conscience

A less dramatic but more personal way in which God might be revealed to individuals is through the conscience. Christians believe that the moral instincts showing us what we ought to do or not to do come from God.

Cardinal John Henry Newman (1801–1890) suggested that conscience is almost like a voice within us. This 'voice' gives us feelings of guilt and shame – a sense that we are responsible for our actions. Newman argues that this sense of being responsible can only be explained by God: conscience is a very powerful means by which God reveals himself.

Some evangelical Christians would broadly agree with Newman. They may argue that the experience of conscience is a result of the Holy Spirit working within Christians.

Source of authority

'Deep within his conscience man discovers a law which he has not laid upon himself but which he must obey ... conscience is man's most secret core and his sanctuary. There he is alone with God whose voice echoes in his depths.' (Catechism of the Catholic Church 1776)

Analyse and evaluate

Does God still reveal himself to Christians today?

Yes	No
In his letter to the church in Corinth, Paul refers to the gift of healing and miracles. Miracles should be part of a Christian experience today.	The age of miracles has passed. These were signs purely for the age of the Apostles while the early Church was established.
People are aware of a moral impulse that we call conscience. The best explanation of this is that it is a revelation from God.	The conscience can be explained by social factors and upbringing. Moral views differ and this suggests that God is not the best explanation.

While God may reveal himself today, most Christians would argue that it is important to test these revelations against the Bible, which is God's ultimate revelation.

Activities

Review

1. How does the Bible show God as a miracle worker?
2. How does the conscience act as a revelation of God?

Develop

3. What do different Christians believe about God performing miracles today?

Link

4. Look at spread 6.8. What are the similarities between the moral argument and the claim that God is revealed through conscience?

Debate

5. Is it harder to believe in miracles in our modern scientific age? Discuss this view and note down the arguments that are raised.

Stretch

6. Research some of the cases of alleged healings and miracles at Lourdes. What do you think of the evidence presented?

6.12 Christian beliefs about experiencing God: conversion and charismatic experiences

Aim

To examine different Christian beliefs about how God might be experienced through conversions and charismatic experiences

Starter

Davey Falcus' life involved drugs, gang membership and violence. He was regularly in trouble with the police and served various prison sentences. He describes a powerful conversion experience:

'On 16 August 1995, I picked up a Bible … I opened it and read a sentence: "He who seeks finds." It was something Jesus said. Desperately, I shouted, "Fine! Jesus, if you are really there and you are God, and if you come now and help me, then I'm yours!"

To my amazement the room seemed to grow brighter. Waves of joy rolled over me. I felt I could see Jesus standing over me and I heard him say, "Son, your sins are forgiven, go now and sin no more."'

Davey is now a church pastor and regularly shares his story in prisons.

Do stories such as Davey's persuade you that God exists or are there other explanations for the change in his life?

Key word

Conversion – a change of heart or priorities which leads to faith; can be sudden or gradual

In spread 6.11, we explored the idea that God may reveal himself in history and to individuals in various ways. Related to this, some Christians argue that there can be direct perceptions of God, such as religious experiences. Conversion and charismatic experiences are particularly important in evangelical churches.

Conversion experiences

A religious **conversion** was described by William James, in *The Varieties of Religious Experience*, as a change in the centre of a person's energies – their sense of what life is about and what matters to them. The most famous example of such an experience in the Bible is the conversion of Saul (who becomes known as the Apostle Paul) in Acts 9. Saul was an active member of a group that persecuted the early Christians before he experienced a powerful vision. He went on to be one of the greatest of the Apostles, responsible for spreading the Christian message throughout the Roman Empire.

Conversion experiences are particularly emphasised within evangelical denominations such as the Baptist Church and the Pentecostal Church. These Christians may refer to the conversion as being 'born again'. Not all conversions are as sudden and dramatic as the experiences of Saul or Davey Falcus; some conversions are more gradual. The Christian writer C.S. Lewis describes how, after a series of discussions

■ The conversion of Paul

and debates with friends who were Christians, he finally 'admitted that God was God, knelt and prayed, perhaps the most dejected, reluctant convert in all England' (*Surprised by Joy*, C.S. Lewis (1955)).

Not all Christians have conversion experiences. Many Christians, particularly those who have been raised within a Christian family, may struggle to identify a particular point where they came to faith. Generally speaking, conversion experiences are less significant in the Catholic Church and the Church of England, but confirmation or first communion services may be held to mark the fact that someone has come to faith for themselves (see spread 2.13).

Source of authority

'Meanwhile, Saul was still breathing out murderous threats against the Lord's disciples. He went to the high priest and asked him for letters to the synagogues in Damascus, so that if he found any there who belonged to the Way, whether men or women, he might take them as prisoners to Jerusalem. As he neared Damascus on his journey, suddenly a light from heaven flashed around him. He fell to the ground and heard a voice say to him, "Saul, Saul, why do you persecute me?"

"Who are you, Lord?" Saul asked.

"I am Jesus, whom you are persecuting," he replied. "Now get up and go into the city, and you will be told what you must do."' (Acts 9:1–6)

Charismatic and ecstatic experiences

Charismatic experiences are described in the New Testament accounts of the early Church. In Acts 2, the Holy Spirit descends on the early Church and one of the consequences of the people 'being filled with the spirit' is that they begin to 'speak in tongues' unknown languages that they have not learned. This ability, known as glossolalia, is one of a number of 'gifts of the spirit' referred to in the New Testament letter that Paul (formerly Saul) wrote to the church in Corinth.

Pentecostal Christians, who take their name from the feast of Pentecost where the events of Acts 2 happened, believe that it is possible for modern Christians to experience speaking in tongues and the other gifts of the spirit during communal worship and in everyday life. Some Christians in other denominations also believe in these spiritual gifts and would identify themselves as 'charismatic' – from the Greek word *charisma* meaning 'a gift of grace'.

Many Christians in the Catholic Church and more traditional Protestant churches reject the idea that spiritual gifts and speaking in tongues continue today. They argue that these gifts ceased with the Apostles and that these experiences are more about people's psychological state than an actual experience of God.

Key word

Charismatic – in Christianity, the idea that the Holy Spirit's gifts are in operation today

Sources of authority

'All of them were filled with the Holy Spirit and began to speak in other tongues [languages] as the Spirit enabled them.' (Acts 2:4)

'Now to each one the manifestation of the Spirit is given for the common good. To one there is given through the Spirit a message of wisdom, to another a message of knowledge by means of the same Spirit, to another faith by the same Spirit, to another gifts of healing by that one Spirit, to another miraculous powers, to another prophecy, to another distinguishing between spirits, to another speaking in different kinds of tongues, and to still another the interpretation of tongues.' (1 Corinthians 12:7–10)

Analyse and evaluate

Are conversion experiences evidence for God's existence?

Yes	No
One of the most powerful arguments in support of conversion experiences is their dramatic effects. It is hard to explain such powerful changes in behaviour without reference to God.	There are psychological explanations for religious experiences such as conversions; they are based on our need for comfort and our fear of death.
Conversion experiences are not just isolated examples. They occur in quite large numbers so cannot be dismissed.	Research has suggested that most conversions occur between the ages of 15 and 25 which might suggest this is a natural part of growing up.
Some Christians recognise that people differ and that while conversion experiences are persuasive for those who have them, most people do not have such dramatic experiences so they only provide evidence in some cases.	

Activities

Review
1. What are the two different types of conversion experience?
2. Describe some of the gifts of the spirit that charismatic Christians believe in.

Develop
3. What different attitudes do Christians have to charismatic and ecstatic experiences?

Link
4. Review spreads 6.5 and 6.6 on the arguments for the existence of God. What is different about the attempts to use religious experience to prove God?

Debate
5. Most people who have conversion experiences are younger than 25. Does this make them more or less credible as evidence? Discuss this issue and make a note of any arguments raised.

Stretch
6. Research the life of C.S. Lewis. Find out more about his journey to faith.

6.13 Christian beliefs about experiencing God: mystical experiences and visions

Aim
To explore different Christian perspectives about mystical experiences and visions

Starter
'There is no difference between someone who eats too little and sees Heaven and someone who drinks too much and sees snakes' (attributed to Bertrand Russell).

Do all religious experiences have a physical explanation as Russell suggests?

Key word
Vision – an experience of seeing something significant or supernatural

Key word
Mystical experience – a direct experience of God, or ultimate reality; a sense of the oneness of all things

One famous vision in the Bible is where Moses meets God at the burning bush

Understanding visions

Visions are typically religious experiences where a Christian sees or has a sense of something supernatural. Although visions are generally described in terms of what is 'seen', it is usually the case that, unlike the experiences of everyday life, the vision or objects that are seen are only seen by the person having the experience.

Some visions are of objects or persons; these are known as corporeal visions. One famous example from the Bible is the experience of Moses who saw the burning bush. The fire seen did not cause the bush to be burned up. Other visions can be described as intellectual visions; they are seen as a mental picture rather than through open eyes. In the book of Isaiah, the prophet has such a vision where he sees God, angels known as seraphim and the throne of heaven. Some Christian thinkers also believe that visions from God may come in dreams.

Understanding mystical experiences

The term '**mystical experience**' can be defined in different ways. In religion, it is used to describe direct intimate experiences of either connection to God or a sense of the oneness of all things. Those who have mystical experiences often seem to enter an altered state of consciousness. According to William James (1842–1910), in *Varieties of Religious Experience* (1902), mystical experiences provide deep and powerful knowledge of God but due to their nature are almost impossible to put into words.

The mystical tradition in Christianity was a key part of the experience of monks and nuns in monasteries and captured the idea that God could not be fully described in words but could be experienced intimately. Probably the most famous example of Christian mysticism comes from the Catholic nun St Teresa of Ávila, whose writings carry accounts of a number of mystical experiences. This includes one occasion (which might also be described as a vision) where she had a strong sense of a golden spear piercing her side which left her with an overwhelming sense of peace. St Teresa recognised that experiences needed to be tested to see whether they were genuine experiences of God. She argued that a genuine experience had to produce positive change in a person, leave the person with a sense of peace, and be in line with the teaching of the Church.

> **Top tip**
>
> Mystical experiences, visions, conversion and charismatic experiences can often overlap and there are times when more than one description can apply to an experience.

Different Christian perspectives on visions and mystical experiences

Christians differ on the significance of religious experiences such as visions and mystical experiences.

- Evangelical Christians tend to emphasise religious experience and believe that visions can be experienced by Christians who are filled with the Holy Spirit (see spread 1.4). These visions tend to be more intellectual or to be mental visions or 'pictures' where the believer senses that these are from God and not just their imagination. Although many evangelical Christians may have experiences that are mystical in nature, the term 'mystical experience' is not one that is common for evangelical Christians; some may even be suspicious of the term and feel that it implies non-Christian experiences similar to Buddhism or New Age thinking.

- In Roman Catholic thought, visions and mystical experiences tend to be associated with Christians of special status rather than ordinary believers. The mystical tradition is generally linked to monasteries rather than the lives of lay members.

Both Roman Catholic and evangelical Christians would be keen to test any visions or experiences to check that they are in line with the teachings of the Bible.

■ St Teresa of Ávila was well known for her mystical visions

Sources of authority

'There the angel of the Lord appeared to him in flames of fire from within a bush. Moses saw that though the bush was on fire it did not burn up.' (Exodus 3:2)

'In the year that King Uzziah died, I saw the Lord, high and exalted, seated on a throne; and the train of his robe filled the temple. Above him were seraphim, each with six wings: With two wings they covered their faces, with two they covered their feet, and with two they were flying.' (Isaiah 6:1–2)

'I saw Christ at my side – or, to put it better, I was conscious of Him, for neither with the eyes of the body or of the soul did I see anything.' (St Teresa of Ávila in *Life of the Mother Teresa of Jesus* (1611))

Analyse and evaluate

Are visions and mystical experiences genuine?

Yes	No
There are a lot of similarities between the experiences which suggest that they have a common source and are genuine.	The human brain is incredibly complex and it is likely that there is some explanation based on the human subconscious.
Experiences generally have positive effects. They produce a change in people's lives and give a sense of peace.	Mystical experiences are found in all faiths and the believers interpret them according to their own faith.

It could be argued that some mystical experiences may be genuine and some may not. This reinforces the idea that there needs to be tests and checks on each experience.

Activities

Review

1. What are the different types and categories of visions that Christians may experience?
2. What is meant by the term 'mystical experience'?

Develop

3. How do Christians differ in their views on visions and mystical experiences?

Link

4. Descriptions of religious experiences often overlap. Look back at spread 6.12. Could some of these experiences also be visions or mystical experiences?

Debate

5. Religious experiences are found in all faiths. Does this make you think they are more or less likely to be genuine? Discuss this issue and note down any arguments raised.

Stretch

6. The Bible contains a number of accounts of visions. Look at some examples in Ezekiel 1, Revelation 1, Exodus 3 and Amos 7 and note down some key features.

6.14 Christian beliefs about experiencing God: worship and sacraments

Aim
To explore how different Christians believe that worship and sacraments may provide a means of experiencing God

Starter
What does public and private worship involve for Christians? Make a list of some of the similarities and differences between worship in a Roman Catholic, Methodist and Pentecostal church.

■ There is a wide variety of different styles and expressions of Christian worship

For many Christians, God is experienced through private and public worship as well as the sacraments. While this may involve moments that can be described as religious experiences in the sense of those explored in spread 6.13, the experience of God in worship may not be sensed or felt but nonetheless Christians believe that God is really present in these moments.

How Catholics experience God through worship and sacraments

Catholic Christians stress the importance of both public and private worship. When Christians are gathered for public worship, the Bible states that God, through Jesus, gathers with them. Catholic churches are often designed to convey a sense of God's majesty and worshippers may experience a sense of awe and wonder in that environment. Catholics believe that this presence of God within worship is a reality whether it is experienced or not – a little like when we are travelling and we cross a border into a different country without being aware of the change. For some Catholics, public worship in certain places, such as cathedrals or sites associated with saints, may also hold a special significance.

For Catholics, the experience of God through the sacraments is particularly significant. The Catechism states that Christ is especially present in liturgical celebrations. This particularly applies to the Mass where Catholics believe that the elements of bread and wine are transformed into the body and blood of Christ, a belief known as transubstantiation. In participating in this act of worship, Catholic Christians encounter Christ in a real sense.

How Protestants experience God through worship and sacraments

Protestants also believe that God can be experienced through public and private worship. Many evangelical Christians in Baptist or Pentecostal churches may stress the importance of a 'quiet time' each time – a time for personal prayer and Bible reading. They believe that they can, in a sense, meet with God on these occasions.

Similar to Catholics, Protestant Christians also believe that God is present where 'two or more are gathered' in public worship. Again,

Sources of authority

'"For where two or three gather in my name, there am I with them."' (Matthew 18:20)

'Christ is always present in his Church, especially in her liturgical celebrations. He is present in the Sacrifice of the Mass … especially in the Eucharistic species. By his power he is present in the sacraments so that when anyone baptises it is really Christ himself who baptises.' (Catechism of the Catholic Church 1088)

it does not matter whether God's presence is sensed or not – this does not change their belief that he is present as the Bible claims. There is a variety of styles of public worship (see spread 2.5) and some Christians may believe they have a sense of God's presence with them, whether that is in the stillness of a more traditional service or in the joyful and lively singing of a more modern setting. Although sacred places may be less important to Protestant Christians, many evangelical Christians recognise the importance of larger gatherings where God is felt to be especially present. For UK Christians, this might include gatherings such as Spring Harvest or the Hillsong Conference.

Although Protestants believe in fewer sacraments than Roman Catholics, these are still important and are opportunities to experience God. This is particularly true for members of the Church of England where there is a liturgy for such services. In the case of the Eucharist or Communion, the bread and wine are seen as symbolic by most Protestants, rather than the actual body and blood of Christ.

Analyse and evaluate

Is public worship the most important way of experiencing God?

Yes	No
Of all the different ways of experiencing God, the gathering of Christians together is the only one that the Bible states guarantees God's presence.	Some Christians may argue that public acts of worship can be dull and off-putting and that private worship is the best way of experiencing God.
Gathering together for Christians is an important way to test revelations and experiences in order for the community to establish which are genuine.	Individual Christians are responsible for their own faith and commitment. Christians should not rely on public worship as the only means of their relationship with God.

Some Christians suggest that both public and private worship are important. The way in which different people experience God may also depend on temperament, with extroverts favouring lively public worship and introverts benefiting from a quiet time.

Activities

Review
1. What do some Christians do during their 'quiet time?'
2. What do Catholic Christians believe happens during the Mass?

Develop
3. What do different types of Christians believe about how they experience God in public worship? What are the similarities and differences?

Link
4. Review spread 2.6 on the sacraments. What are the key differences between Protestant and Catholic Christians with regard to the sacraments?

Debate
5. Does it make sense to say that God can be experienced even if believers are not aware of his presence? Discuss this statement and note down the arguments raised.

Stretch
6. Find out more about what happens at events such as Spring Harvest, where large groups of Christians from different denominations gather together.

Summary activities

CHECK YOUR NOTES

STAGE 1

Check that you have detailed notes that cover the following:

- [ ] The Christian understanding of God and how God relates to the world and to human beings
- [ ] Christian beliefs about the goodness of God and the relationship between God's goodness and human suffering
- [ ] The design argument for the existence of God and the anthropic principle, the idea that the world was formed for humanity
- [ ] The argument from first cause
- [ ] How morality may provide evidence for God; soul-making and judgement
- [ ] The extent to which it matters to different Christians whether God can be proved
- [ ] How God might be revealed through scripture and Christian history
- [ ] How God might be revealed through his actions in the world including miracles
- [ ] How God might be revealed through conscience
- [ ] Different types of religious experience such as conversion, mystical experiences, charismatic/ecstatic experiences, visions, worship and sacraments

GETTING READY

STAGE 2

Quick quiz

1. What does the word providence mean?
2. What are the three elements of the inconsistent triad?
3. What is the difference between natural evil and moral evil?
4. What word is used to describe truths that God shows to human beings through the Bible or through religious experience?
5. Which thinker used the analogy of the watch to provide an argument for God?
6. How does the Bible show support for the first cause argument?
7. Which theory was first put forward by the Catholic priest George Lemaître?
8. Which type of Christians are more likely to be in favour of charismatic experiences?
9. How is the idea of miracle generally defined?
10. How does Cardinal Newman define the idea of conscience?

Quick quiz answers can be found online at www.hoddereducation.co.uk/ocr-gcse-rs-answers

ACTIVITIES

STAGE 2

1. Fill in the retrieval boxes below without looking at your notes. Can you add three to four points in each of the boxes?

Christian idea of God	God's goodness	Problem of suffering	Design argument
First cause	Anthropic argument	Morality	Revelation through scripture
God's actions and miracles	Conscience	Conversion	Mystical and visions

2. **AO2 focus:** Choose one of the arguments for God or one of the types of religious experience. List some for and against points. Which are the most persuasive? Arrange the points into an essay plan.

GET PRACTISING

STAGE 3

Use this section to help you develop your understanding of how to answer questions on this topic.

Jamal writes:

I found the section on experiencing God quite difficult as there were a number of different types of experience and Christians often differ as to which ones are important. This is part of a recent essay where I thought I'd done this quite well. How can I get more marks?

Essay extract

One important type of religious experience is conversion experiences which is a sudden or gradual change of priorities leading to religious faith. This type of experience, particularly the sudden type of experience, is often important to evangelical Christians such as Baptists. Conversion is less important to Roman Catholic Christians who may have been baptised as infants and grown up within the church, so they may not really have a process of coming to faith in the same way as a Baptist.

Expert comment:

Jamal's answer is clear on what conversion is and shows he has awareness of different Christian perspectives. He has got the 'what' and the 'which'. In order to provide an even better answer, he needs to think about the 'why' – perhaps by including a source of authority such as Saul's conversion as shown in Acts 9.

The 'which', the 'why' and the 'importance'

Remember there are a number of things that you need to do to get top marks on medium-length questions. While you may start with 'what' a Christian believes or does, it is important that answers go beyond this.

- **Which** — you may be able to show that there are differences in what is believed by different groups of Christians.
- **Why** — you could bring in a source of authority to show why something is believed or done.
- **Importance** — you may show a link between a belief and a practice showing why this matters to Christians and how it affects their life.

CHAPTER 7: Religion, peace and conflict

7.1 Christian teaching about violence in society

Aim
To examine how individual Christians and Christian communities respond to violence in society

Starter
When is violence acceptable, if ever? How might a Christian answer that question? How should they respond to those who are violent?

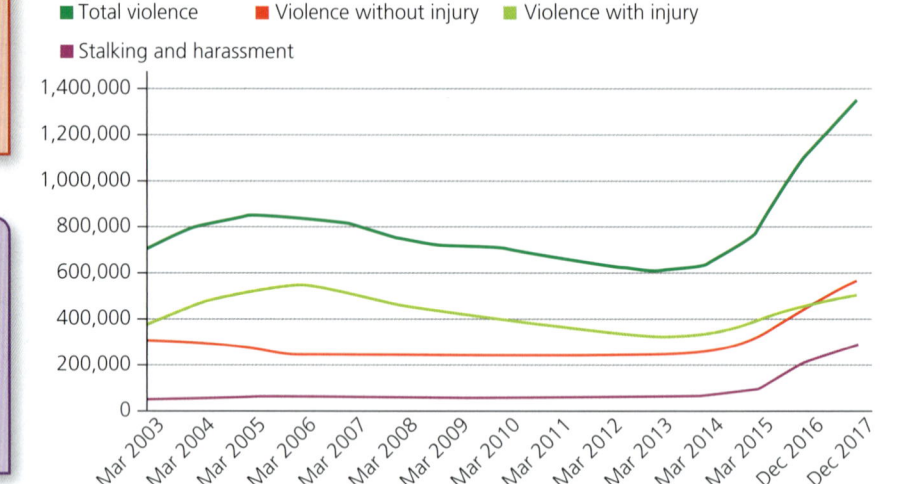

Sources of authority

'You have heard that it was said, "Love your neighbour and hate your enemy." But I tell you, love your enemies and pray for those who persecute you.' (Matthew 5:43–44)

'…and forgive us our sins, as we have forgiven those who sin against us.' (Matthew 6:12 NLT)

'…the act of self-defence may have two effects, one is the saving of one's life, the other is the slaying of the aggressor. Therefore this act, since one's intention is to save one's own life, is not unlawful.' (*Summa Theologica* (1265–73), St Thomas Aquinas)

Violent crime in England and Wales recorded by the police, 2003–2017

The following pages focus on violence and conflict. They examine how Christians might respond to violence experienced as individuals or in society, including terrorism (see spread 7.2) and violence on a wider scale in war (see 7.3).

The graph above may suggest that violence in society is increasing but it has been suggested that the police have changed the way that they classify crime and that levels of violence may have been higher in the 1980s or 1990s.

Violence and individuals

Christians understand that the root cause of violence is anger. Anger in itself is not viewed as wrong but it has to be expressed appropriately. Jesus himself was angry enough to clear out the temple traders with a whip, and he was angry at how the Pharisees treated people. Yet in his teachings, he consistently urges people not to respond to violence and hostility with violence. Jesus, in commenting upon the Old Testament teaching of 'an eye for an eye', urges his followers to turn the other cheek instead. They are to love and forgive those who sin against them.

While some Christians understand this to be an absolute command that prevents any form of violence, even in self-defence, other Christians believe that force is permitted in self-defence. Roman Catholic moral teaching uses the idea of double effect – that actions may have more than one consequence. In this case, St Thomas Aquinas argues that defending yourself against an attacker is permitted, even if this results in the attacker being killed. Their death was not intended.

Some evangelical Christians in the USA feel strongly about the right to bear arms – to carry a gun with them. Their arguments generally revolve around self-defence. However, this tends to be more of a political viewpoint rather than anything specifically linked to Christian teaching.

Violence and the Christian community

While it may be possible for individual Christians to forgive and to avoid responding to violence aggressively, it is argued that society cannot run in this way: crime has to be punished in order to protect society and deter people from committing crime, particularly violent crime. However, for Christians, a key aim in dealing with those who commit violence is to restore and rehabilitate. Although human beings are fallen and prone to sin, there is the possibility of repentance and change. This is seen in the New Testament, where Paul urges the Corinthian Church to readmit a member who had been excluded for sinful behaviour.

A number of Christians belong to organisations that work to rehabilitate offenders. Christians recognise that it is important to deal with the root causes of offending, such as addiction or unemployment, and to provide stability. One group that works across different Christian denominations is the Langley House trust. This group provides housing and employment support for ex-offenders as well as running education programmes in prisons to reduce the risk of re-offending.

Source of authority

'The punishment inflicted on him by the majority is sufficient. Now instead, you ought to forgive and comfort him, so that he will not be overwhelmed by excessive sorrow.' (2 Corinthians 2:6–7)

Analyse and evaluate

Is it always wrong to respond with violence?

Yes	No
Meeting violence with violence almost always makes things worse. It is better not to respond as this escalates the situation.	The Christian Church permits self-defence in the teaching of double effect.
Avoiding retaliation is the right way for Christians as it follows the essence of Jesus' teachings.	A key aspect of Christianity is standing up for others who are persecuted; if they are being violently attacked, defending them cannot be wrong.
Although anger is not necessarily wrong, violence usually is. It is important that Christians are careful in how they express their anger.	

Activities

Review

1. Which teachings of Jesus might help a Christian understand how to respond to violence?
2. In the New Testament, how does the Apostle Paul suggest that the Corinthian Church deal with a member who has sinned?

Develop

3. What do different Christians believe about whether violence is allowed in self-defence?

Link

4. Review Jesus' teachings in the Sermon on the Mount (see spread 1.11). Which teachings may help a Christian faced with violence?

Debate

5. Are Christians too soft on those who commit violent crime? Discuss this issue and note down any arguments raised.

Stretch

6. Research an organisation such as Langley House Trust and find out more about how they work with offenders.

7.2 Christian responses to terrorism

Aim
To consider how Christians respond to terrorism in the twenty-first century

Starter
'If I sit next to a madman as he drives a car into a group of innocent bystanders, I can't, as a Christian, simply wait for the catastrophe, then comfort the wounded and bury the dead. I must try to wrestle the steering wheel out of the hands of the driver' (Dietrich Bonhoeffer (1940s)).

What does the quotation suggest about how Christians should act towards terrorism?

It could be argued that the storming of the US Capitol in January 2021 was an act of terrorism

Key words
Terrorism – the unlawful use of violence and intimidation, especially against civilians, in the pursuit of ideological (political or religious) aims
Radicalisation – the process by which an individual or group comes to support extreme views

Understanding terrorism and its causes

Acts of **terrorism** are carried out in order to advance a religious, ideological or political cause. They tend to involve acts of serious violence against another person, people or property – acts that endanger another person's life or that are carried out with the intent of causing significant interference or serious disruption to systems. In the twenty-first century, there are terrorist threats from Islamist groups, far-right racist groups and 'incel' groups that are driven by hatred of women.

In some situations it can be difficult for people to agree on what is and what is not terrorism. A person may be considered a terrorist by some people but a freedom fighter, trying to advance their cause, by others.

The main cause of terrorism is the **radicalisation** of individuals and groups. Radicalisation can occur because of a range of connected reasons:

- experience of traumatic events
- bullying or discrimination
- anger at government or authorities
- becoming increasingly withdrawn
- spending more time online
- interacting with like-minded individuals on social media.

Christian responses to terrorism

A key strategy of terrorism is to create fear but the New Testament teaches that 'perfect love casts out all fear'. Christians believe that part of the loving response is to pray for victims and to care for those who have suffered. Christians are also called to forgive the attackers.

Christian responses to acts of terrorism are not limited to the aftermath. The quotation from Dietrich Bonhoeffer (1906–1945) at the start of the spread suggests a duty to try to prevent acts of terrorism in the first place. This sense of duty leads some Christians to work with those who are at risk of being radicalised as part of re-education and support programmes.

Christianity, politics and terrorism

The vast majority of Christians oppose all forms of terrorism. They believe that it is important to respect and obey governments. However, as mentioned above, it can sometimes be difficult to draw the line between what is and what is not terrorism. Dietrich Bonhoeffer was part of a group of Christians in Nazi Germany who actively opposed Hitler. Although their actions were not acts of

Sources of authority

'Let everyone be subject to the governing authorities, for there is no authority except that which God has established. The authorities that exist have been established by God.' (Romans 13:1)

'But Peter and John replied, "Which is right in God's eyes: to listen to you, or to him? You be the judges!"' (Acts 4:19)

Top tip

In terms of their responses to the issues raised in this spread, individual Christians may have different views and they will not necessarily think the same as others in their denomination.

---

terrorism, they did involve breaking the law. Just as in the New Testament, when Peter and John were forbidden from preaching about Jesus, it could be argued that there are occasions when obeying God's laws becomes more important than obeying the government's laws.

In Latin America in the twentieth century, a group of mainly Catholic theologians put forward a view known as liberation theology, which argued that one of the duties of the Christian Church was to stand up for the poor, even if this meant disobeying the government. A small minority of liberation theologians supported violent acts of sabotage to further their aims. The Catholic Church condemned the behaviour and argued that the view owed more to politics than religion.

In the USA, some evangelical Christians who supported former President Donald Trump's re-election campaign, including the idea that the 2020 election had been 'stolen', were supportive of the storming of the Capitol building in January 2021, despite the fact that this led to the injury of over 100 police officers and caused $1.5 million's worth of damage to the Capitol building.

In the case of both liberation theologians and the Capitol riots, those Christians who supported the use of violence were motivated by politics as much as by religion, though many would dispute whether their actions came under the definition of terrorism.

Analyse and evaluate

Should Christians always stay within the law?

Yes	No
The New Testament in Romans 13 is quite clear that authority comes from God and that Christians should be obedient to government.	A Christian has a duty to respond to injustice and take the side of the oppressed. Governments are sometimes unjust and have to be opposed.
Jesus tells his disciples that they should render to Caesar what is Caesar's. A Christian must fulfil their duty in society.	Peter and John continued to preach about Jesus despite the command not to do so. A Christian's first duty is to God, not human beings.
Christians should obey the law at all times unless there is a situation that is so extreme that breaking the law is the only possible response.	

Activities

Review

1. What are the main causes of terrorism today?
2. How might a Christian respond to terrorists and to acts of terrorism?

Develop

3. What do different Christians believe about whether it is ever possible for a Christian to support acts of terrorism?

Link

4. In the New Testament, Peter and John chose to break religious law by continuing to preach about Jesus. Look back at spread 2.14 on the Church's mission. Is there anything that would require the modern Church to break the law?

Debate

5. 'It is hard to define exactly what is or isn't terrorism'. Discuss this statement and note any arguments raised.

Stretch

6. Research the life and teaching of Dietrich Bonhoeffer.

7.3 The just war theory

Aim
To explore the Christian belief that there are just and fair ways of engaging in warfare

Starter
There are many different reasons why nations go to war: a desire to claim land or resources, hatred of a certain race or people, religion, opposing an evil regime, defending your country against an attack, supporting an ally.

Which of these is the most acceptable reason for going to war? Which is the least acceptable? Is there ever an acceptable reason? Compare your answers to others in the group.

■ For many Ukrainian Christians, opposing the Russian invasion would count as a just war

Key word
Just war theory – the belief that some wars are morally justifiable and that there are criteria for deciding whether to go to war and how that war should be fought

Introducing the just war theory

Jesus' message was one of peace and in Matthew 5 he urges his followers to 'turn the other cheek'. He does not resist when arrested and does not allow his disciples to defend him. However, there are also passages which are more difficult to interpret, such as Luke 22:36 where he urges his followers to take up a sword. Most early Christians were pacifists (see spread 7.6) but, as Christianity spread and became the dominant faith of the Roman world, Christians started to hold positions of political power and faced decisions about whether and how to engage in war. The **just war theory** was developed in response to this. It is part of the teaching of the Roman Catholic Church.

There are two main parts to the theory: the decision to go to war and the manner in which the war should be fought.

The decision to go to war

The decision to go to war is not one that should be taken lightly. The just war theory identifies the following six conditions that must be met for a war to be declared a 'just war'.

1. **Legitimate authority:** the war must be declared by the legitimate authority in that country. In the past this would have meant a king but now might refer to a president or prime minister. It can be argued that in the modern world such a decision should be approved by the United Nations (UN).

2. **Just cause:** there must be a just and fair cause or reason to go to war. St Augustine suggested that defending against attack, recapturing things taken wrongly or punishing a nation's wrongdoing might be just causes. In the Second World War, opposing the Nazi regime was considered a just cause.

3. **Right intention:** while the cause may appear just, there should also be a right intention. This should be to bring about peace and safety so that the final situation is improved.

4. **Proportionality:** war should not be an excessive response to the wrong that has taken place. The Catechism of the Catholic Church 2309 refers to ensuring that war 'must not produce evils and disorders greater than the evil to be eliminated'.

5. **Likely success:** there should be a reasonable probability of success otherwise, even if the cause is just, the loss of life will be ultimately pointless.

6. **Last resort:** all other means of solving the conflict, such as peace talks and negotiation, should have been explored.

How to fight the war

The just war theory also covers how those who are fighting should conduct themselves during the war. The Catechism of the Catholic

Church (2213–2214) states that the mere fact that war has broken out does not mean that all methods of fighting are permitted.

The two main criteria that should be considered, according to the Catholic Church, are proportionality and discrimination.

1. **Proportionality:** the amount of force that is used should be enough to win the war with as few casualties as possible and no more. This is particularly important now there are weapons of mass destruction (see spread 7.5).
2. **Discrimination:** it is important to discriminate between combatants, who are legitimate targets, and civilians, who are not to be seen as legitimate targets.

This second condition can be difficult to uphold. As well as some weapons such as bombs inevitably causing unintended casualties, it is also difficult to draw a line between combatants and civilians. It could be argued that civilians working in a factory producing weapons are part of the war effort.

Some Protestant thinkers, such as Reinhold Niebuhr (1892–1971), would argue that the just war theory is too optimistic about human nature. Niebuhr's theory of Christian realism teaches that political leaders sometimes have to operate by different ethical standards when dealing with sinful actions.

Source of authority

'He said to them, "But now if you have a purse, take it, and also a bag; and if you don't have a sword, sell your cloak and buy one."' (Luke 22:36)

'It is lawful for Christian men, at the commandment of the Magistrate, to wear weapons, and serve in the wars.' (Church of England Thirty-nine Articles, article 37)

'Non-combatants, wounded soldiers and prisoners must be respected and treated humanely.' (Catechism of the Catholic Church 2313)

'Every act of war directed to the indiscriminate destruction of whole cities or vast areas with their inhabitants is a crime against God and man.' (Catechism of the Catholic Church 2314)

Analyse and evaluate

Is the just war theory the best approach to the issues of war?

Yes	No
Unlike pacifism, the theory provides a way for Christians to stand up for the rights of the innocent.	The theory is not easy to apply. Who is guilty or innocent, or who has the right intentions, is often a matter of opinion and perspective.
The theory provides some rules that, if followed, would help prevent some of the worst atrocities of warfare.	Wars almost always do more harm than good. It is highly unlikely that greater justice will result in the end.
The just war theory has some limitations but is better than pacifism, which fails to stand up to evil, and is also better than the idea that war should have no rules or limits.	

Activities

Review

1. What different examples might there be of a just cause?
2. According to the just war theory, what other things should be considered before going to war?

Develop

3. How do different Christians understand proportionality and discrimination in fighting a war?

Link

4. Look back at the ethical teaching of Jesus (see spread 7.1). How likely is it that Jesus would have supported the just war theory?

Debate

5. The just war theory might seem like a reasonable idea but it doesn't work in practice. Discuss this view and note down any arguments raised.

Stretch

6. Choose a war from history that you are aware of such as the First or Second World War, the invasion of Iraq in 2003 or the Russian invasion of Ukraine in 2022. Try to apply the just war criteria to the case you have chosen.

7.4 Can a Christian ever support holy war?

Aim
To consider the extent to which the idea of holy war has been important within Christianity

Starter
Look at the two definitions of holy war suggested in the Key word box. What are the main differences? Which do you think is the best definition?

Key word
Holy war – a war where the main cause or purpose of the war is religious OR a war that God has commanded

Holy war in the Bible and early Christianity

The Bible does not use the phrase **holy war** and nor do any of the established churches teach that there is such a thing. However, in the Old Testament of the Bible, God often commands his people of Israel to go to war. The history of Israel in this period involves escape from Egypt, being led by Joshua to conquer the promised land by dispossessing other nations and then a series of battles with neighbouring nations who believe in other gods.

Christians recognise that these passages need interpreting carefully. God's focus in the New Testament is not the nation of Israel but rather the Church – a group made up of both Jewish and non-Jewish people. The Church does not initially have political power; Christians are encouraged to put on their armour for a spiritual fight against sin and the Devil rather than going to war in a literal sense. Most early Christians were pacifists but this changed when the Roman Emperor Constantine converted to Christianity in the fourth century. As we saw in spread 7.3, things become more complicated when religion and politics come together.

Holy war: the Crusades and Catholic perspectives

Although the Roman Empire declined, the power of the Church through its popes continued. It was not unusual during the Middle Ages for the Pope to be more powerful than the leaders of some countries. In 1095, Pope Urban II declared it to be a duty for Christian soldiers to travel to the Holy Land to fight to conquer Jerusalem from Muslim rulers, in the name of Christ. He declared that those who died en route or in battle would have their sins forgiven. Whether Pope Urban actually used the words 'holy war' is a matter of debate, but this was certainly how it was understood by thousands of knights who travelled in what became known as the Crusades.

Modern Catholics, along with other Christians, would wish to distance themselves from the Crusades as they represent some of the cruellest and most unpleasant periods in Church history. The Catholic Church today teaches that war is never an ideal and that while there may be occasions where war is justified (see spread 7.3), it is never something that is commanded by God.

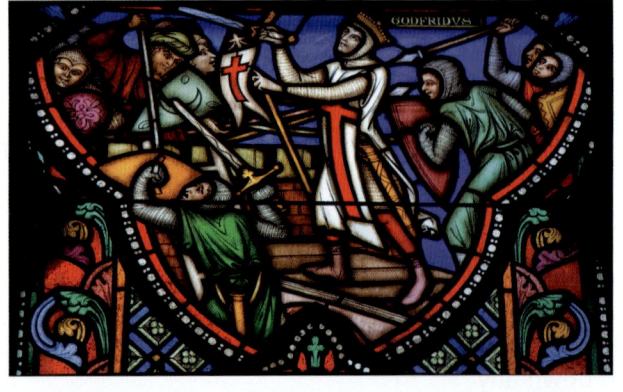

■ This stained glass window depicts Christian knights fighting for God

Sources of authority

'Then the Lord said to Joshua, "Do not be afraid; do not be discouraged. Take the whole army with you, and go up and attack Ai. For I have delivered into your hands the king of Ai, his people, his city and his land."' (Joshua 8:1)

'Put your sword away, for all who live by the sword will die by the sword.' (Matthew 26:52)

'All who die by the way, whether by land or by sea, or in battle against the pagans, shall have immediate remission of sins.' (Pope Urban II, 1095)

Top tip

Sometimes presenting different perspectives within Christianity might involve showing where there is agreement as well as where there is disagreement.

Holy war: Protestant perspectives

The idea of holy war is also absent from the official teachings of the main Protestant churches. However, because of the complicated relationship between religion and politics there have been occasions where some Christians may have understood certain events as a holy war.

- The birth of the Protestant Church resulted in wars in some countries as Catholics and Protestants tried to gain control. This often led to one side persecuting the other.
- In Northern Ireland in the twentieth century, Catholics, who were mostly nationalists (wanting a united Ireland), and Protestants, who were mostly unionists (wanting Northern Ireland to be part of the UK), were engaged in a conflict known as the Troubles. Some Christian leaders, such as Reverend Ian Paisley, a political and religious leader, were prominent in the conflict.
- In 2003, the evangelical Christian President of the USA, George W. Bush, led an invasion of Iraq, claiming that he felt that God had told him to do it.

For some of the people involved, each of these examples might have elements of a holy war, but this view was not supported by the official churches. The conflicts in the examples often owed more to politics than to religion.

Analyse and evaluate

Can a Christian fight in a holy war?

Yes	No
The Old Testament shows that holy war is not an un-Christian idea. God may command action against ungodly nations.	None of the main Christian churches support the idea of a holy war. This idea was not even present in the eleventh- and twelfth-century Crusades.
Even if conflicts are not described as holy wars, the idea has affected some Christians' views of certain conflicts.	The idea of a holy war makes no sense in the modern world as the Church does not hold a position of power where it can declare war.
The idea of holy war is unclear. While very few people believe that God commands war, it may be that a conflict that defends the rights of oppressed Christians could be seen as a holy war.	

Activities

Review
1. What does the Old Testament teach about war?
2. Why does the New Testament have a different approach?

Develop
3. What do different Christians believe about the idea of holy war?

Link
4. Review spread 7.3 on just war. Does the idea of holy war satisfy the just war criteria?

Debate
5. Are holy wars more about politics than religion? Discuss this question and note down the arguments raised.

Stretch
6. Find out more about divine command theory. This is the idea that whatever God commands (even if it is killing in a war) is good.

7.5 Christian responses to modern warfare

Aim

To examine Christian responses to issues raised by modern warfare such as technological and apocalyptic warfare

Starter

A drone operator's story:

'I fired a missile at the house as directed. A man rushed out carrying an injured little girl in his arms, they got into a car. The commander told me, "OK, your new target is that car." I replied, "Absolutely not. I'm not going to strike that car knowing there's a wounded girl in there." I was reprimanded by the general the next day' (adapted from *On Killing Remotely: The Psychology of Killing with Drones*, Wayne Phelps, 2021).

The man in the car was part of a terrorist group. Was his car a legitimate target for a drone strike?

■ Modern warfare increasingly uses drones to gather information and to carry out targeted strikes

Apocalyptic warfare

Advances in technology led to the possibility of **apocalyptic warfare** with the creation of weapons that could cause widespread destruction. In August 1945, the USA launched two nuclear weapons on Japanese cities. Thousands of people were killed instantly and many thousands more died from radiation-related illnesses. In the decades that followed, a number of other countries developed nuclear weapons. One justification for having nuclear weapons is that they act as a deterrent – this is the idea that one country will not deploy nuclear weapons if they know that another country may do the same in response.

Key word

Apocalyptic warfare – any form of warfare that can result in widespread and utter destruction of huge areas

In Micah, the Bible refers to an age of peace at the end of time where weapons are turned into farming tools. It is this aim of peace that has led some Christians to campaign actively against nuclear weapons. For example, Bruce Kent (1929–2022) was a former Catholic priest who was a key figure in the Campaign for Nuclear Disarmament (CND). As part of this group, he led protests against missiles being stored at Greenham Common in Berkshire in the 1980s.

The official position of the Catholic Church is not quite as radical as that of Bruce Kent. The Catechism (2314) criticises the use of weapons that are able to destroy whole cities but does not absolutely condemn the possession of nuclear weapons as a deterrent. The Church does, however, express reservations about whether this is an effective strategy due to the huge costs involved. In addition to the loss of life, the huge financial cost of the weapons could have been spent on more important things such as supporting those in poverty.

Protestants are also divided about the possession of nuclear weapons. The theory of Christian realism (see spread 7.3) teaches that there is a difference between the personal moral standards of Christians, and the moral decisions that nations and their leaders have to take. This may mean accepting things that are not ideal, such as holding nuclear weapons.

- As a result of President Truman's decision, atomic bombs were dropped on the Japanese cities of Hiroshima and Nagasaki in 1945

Technological warfare

Recent advances in technology, particularly in computing, have meant that the **technological warfare** in the twenty-first century may be very different to conventional warfare. This may involve **surgical strikes**, where missiles can be programmed to hit key targets and minimise civilian deaths. Surgical strikes were used by the US and British in Iraq in 2003, where government and military targets were destroyed ahead of the invasion. This meant that the actual war on the ground in Iraq was very short.

Remote drones that do not require pilots have also been developed. These can be operated thousands of miles away – almost like playing a computer game. In his book, *On Killing Remotely: The Psychology of Killing with Drones*, retired American Lieutenant Colonel Wayne Phelps states that the average drone operator will, in their career, kill more than 50 enemy combatants. On leaving the service, they are given an envelope with details of what their missions have achieved. Some drone operators choose not to open their envelopes.

Key words

Technological warfare – any form of warfare that uses advanced technology, for example, drones and AI (artificial intelligence)

Surgical strike – a military attack intended to damage only a legitimate military target, with no or minimal collateral damage

Sources of authority

'They will beat their swords into plowshares and their spears into pruning hooks. Nation will not take up sword against nation, nor will they train for war anymore.' (Micah 4:3)

'Every act of war directed to the indiscriminate destruction of whole cities or vast areas with their inhabitants is a crime against God and man.' (Catechism of the Catholic Church 2314)

The ability to carry out precise targeted attacks without endangering your own troops raises interesting ethical debates. The ability to target the attacks means that the risk of killing civilians is greatly reduced, which may fit better with the just war theory. At the same time, there is concern that the ability to kill in real life in the same way that you would in a video game may devalue human life. However, as the technology improves – particularly video quality – it has been suggested that drone operators may find it harder to kill because as they closely monitor their targets over a period of time they can see them not only in their roles as combatants but also in their roles as husbands and fathers.

Analyse and evaluate

Can a Christian ever support apocalyptic warfare?

Yes	No
While use of nuclear weapons is horrific, Christian realism argues that it can never be completely ruled out if it is needed for the greater good.	The just war theory absolutely rules this out as nuclear weapons inevitably cause many civilian deaths. |//
It could be argued that possessing nuclear weapons may help to keep the peace but that it would be wrong to use such weapons.	

Activities

Review
1. What is meant by technological warfare? Give some examples.
2. Why do some countries think it is a good idea to possess nuclear weapons?

Develop
3. What do different Christians think about the possession of and use of nuclear weapons?

Link
4. Review the just war theory (see spread 7.3). Does this theory support or oppose technological and apocalyptic warfare?

Debate
5. Is it worse if killing in warfare is done remotely using drones rather than by conventional means? Discuss this issue and note down any arguments raised.

Stretch
6. Find out more about the idea of Christian realism which was put forward by Reinhold Niebuhr (1892–1971).

7.6 What are the different Christian attitudes to pacifism?

Aim
To explore different Christian attitudes to ideas of pacifism

Starter
You may be familiar with the idea of conscientious objectors – those who refuse, on religious or ethical grounds, to fight in a war. Do you think that people should be allowed to refuse the orders of their government in this way? Is it only right that everyone should have freedom of conscience?

Key words
Absolute pacifists/pacifism – the belief that it is never right to take part in war, even in self-defence

Absolute pacifism

At the risk of generalising, **absolute pacifism** is more common in the history of Protestant Christianity than in Catholicism.

The 1660 'Declaration from the harmless and innocent people of God, called Quakers' is a good example of the absolute pacifist approach. It argues that 'Christ's kingdom is not of this world, therefore do not his servants fight.' Primarily, the Quakers understood themselves to be part of God's kingdom rather than citizens of any country. Rather than becoming involved in this world's conflicts, they are waiting for God's kingdom to come.

This teaching is seen as a continuation of the true teachings of Jesus, who encouraged his followers to be peacemakers and commanded that they turn the other cheek rather than respond with violence. The early Church, whose members were generally not serving members of the Roman army, tended to follow this teaching. This has led many individual Christians to declare themselves as conscientious objectors over the years, particularly in the two World Wars.

One example of an absolute pacifist approach is the Quaker Stephen Hobhouse (1881–1961). Hobhouse was called up to fight in the First World War but objected on religious grounds. He was offered a non-combat role in the ambulance service but he refused this role and as a result was sent to jail.

■ During the First World War, women were encouraged to give white feathers to those who refused to join the army. It was intended to shame them as cowards

> **Sources of authority**
>
> 'Blessed are the peacemakers, for they will be called children of God.' (Matthew 5:9)
>
> 'You have heard that it was said, "Eye for eye, and tooth for tooth." But I tell you, do not resist an evil person. If anyone slaps you on the right cheek, turn to them the other cheek also.' (Matthew 5:38–39)

Catholic views on pacifism

Applying the just war theory, the Roman Catholic Church recognises that war is, to some extent, a necessary evil. The Catechism of the Catholic Church (2310) goes so far as to state that authorities can impose on citizens a duty to defend the country. Those who fight in such conflicts will ultimately contribute to peace. This may occur at the end of the war, or it may apply to the work of soldiers in peacekeeping or defensive roles.

There is a general sense in Catholicism that it is not wrong, and it may even be a duty, to fight in a just war. However, on an individual level, the Church also recognises that for some individuals, their conscience may prevent them from a role in active combat. The Catechism of the Catholic Church (2311) suggests that these individuals should support the war effort or the community in some other way.

Conditional pacifism

There are some Christians who would identify themselves as pacifists. They do not accept the just war theory and argue that all war is wrong. For some, however, this is not a clearcut issue. **Conditional pacifists** recognise that there may be extreme circumstances where war is the lesser of two evils.

> **Key word**
>
> **Conditional pacifists/pacifism** – the belief that war and violence are wrong in principle, but there may be occasional circumstances when war may lead to less suffering than not going to war

One example of a conditional pacifist approach comes from the Austrian Catholic Christian, Franz Jägerstätter (1907–1943). Jägerstätter was called up to fight by Nazi Germany in the Second World War. He was a vocal critic of the Nazis and was initially exempt from military service as a farmer. As a devout Catholic, he saw all that the Nazis stood for as being in complete opposition to God. When a second call-up came in 1943, his experience of military training and his understanding of what the Nazis were engaged in led him to declare himself a conscientious objector. He offered to serve as a medic but this was refused and he was executed in July 1943. The Catholic Church beatified Jägerstätter in 2007.

> **Top tip**
>
> In this topic, it is important to show what different Christians believe and why they believe it. It is often helpful to illustrate your 'why' with a reference to a source of authority such as the Bible.

Sources of authority

'Public authorities, in this case [just war] have the right and duty to impose on citizens the obligations necessary for self-defence ... If they [combatants] carry out their duty honourably, they truly contribute to the common good of the nation and the maintenance of peace.' (Catechism of the Catholic Church 2310)

'Public authorities should make equitable provision for those who for reasons of conscience refuse to bear arms; these are nonetheless obliged to serve the human community in some other way.' (Catechism of the Catholic Church 2311)

Analyse and evaluate

Is pacifism a duty for Christians?

Yes	No
War wastes lives and the cost in terms of resources is also enormous. These resources would be better served in the fight against poverty.	Pacifism is too idealistic. Evil succeeds when good people do nothing. Sometimes war is just and necessary.
Christians are followers of Jesus. The teachings of Jesus, together with his example when arrested, are non-violent.	The Bible does not condemn war. In the Old Testament, God's people are at times commanded to go to war.
Pacifism can be effective in standing up to violence. See Martin Luther King's campaign of non-violent direct action (spread 7.8).	Christians have a duty to obey leaders and governments because authority is placed there by God (Romans 13).

Although there may not be a general duty for Christians to always be pacifists, for some people their conscience forbids them from fighting.

Activities

Review

1. What is meant by absolute pacifism?
2. What is meant by conditional pacifism?

Develop

3. What views do different Christians have about absolute pacifism?

Link

4. Review spread 7.3 on the early Church and the just war theory. Why was it easier for the first Christians to be pacifists?

Debate

5. Is pacifism too idealistic? Discuss this idea and note down any arguments raised.

Stretch

6. Look up some of the following Bible references: Matthew 5:39, Matthew 10:34, Luke 22:36, Matthew 26:52, John 2:13–22. Do they establish whether Jesus was or was not a pacifist?

7.7 How do Christians show their commitment to peace?

Aim
To explore different Christian teachings on working for peace as individuals, in the community and in society

Starter
Is peace more than just the absence of war? Can there be peace in a society if racism, poverty or homelessness exist? How would you define peace?

Many Christians believe that the struggle for racial equality is part of working for peace in society

Sources of authority
'Blessed are the peacemakers, for they will be called children of God.' (Matthew 5:9)

'If it is possible, as far as it depends on you, live at peace with everyone.' (Romans 12:18)

Top tip
Terms such as 'peace' and 'justice' are hard to define. When writing about them it can be useful to explain the implications of different ways of defining the terms.

Understanding peace

Many dictionary definitions would describe peace as the absence of war or conflict. Yet Christians would generally argue that peace is more than this – while a country may be free from war, there are often conflicts within society caused by injustice and unfairness. Hence the task of working for peace often includes working for justice. St Augustine argued that a society without justice cannot really call itself a society. He asks, **'What are kingdoms without justice? They're just gangs of bandits'** *(St Augustine, The City of God, around 413).*

How individuals work for peace

The mission of bringing about peace begins at an individual level – Jesus commands his followers to be peacemakers. It is worth noting that this is more than peacekeeping. Being a peacemaker is an active duty that involves a Christian seeking to bring about an end to conflict in their personal relationships. This may involve mediating between work colleagues who are in disagreement or supporting a couple from their church who are having difficulties in their marriage. Bringing about peace is not an easy task and sometimes is not possible. In his letter to the Roman Church, the Apostle Paul recognises this and states that where possible, believers should be at peace with everyone.

Christian communities and peace

Christians also believe that part of the role of the church and Christian groups within society is to work for peace. Most Christian denominations have organisations within them that are committed to peace such as the Anglican Pacifist Fellowship and the Baptist Peace Fellowship.

Within the Catholic Church, Pax Christi (Latin for 'Peace of Christ') works to promote: a peace based on justice, a world where human rights are respected and basic needs are met, reconcilliation and non-violence.

Other organisations work across different strands or denominations of the Church, such as the 'Church and Peace' group.

Some of these organisations work on wider issues regarding justice within society such as racism, poverty and homelessness.

The evangelical group Christians Against Poverty works with people who are in debt, providing counselling and financial support regardless of the faith background of the client.

Members of Pax Christi on a peaceful demonstration

Sources of authority

'Also, seek the peace and prosperity of the city to which I have carried you into exile. Pray to the Lord for it, because if it prospers, you too will prosper.' (Jeremiah 29:7)

'Therefore go and make disciples of all nations, baptizing them in the name of the Father and of the Son and of the Holy Spirit.' (Matthew 28:19)

Christians and society

In addition to working within Christian communities, many Christians are active within secular organisations working to bring about peace and justice. In his fifth-century book, *The City of God*, St Augustine states that the Church (God's kingdom) and the secular society are like two different cities: they exist together at this time and the Christian may work to bring about a better society, but ultimately human kingdoms will end and only God's kingdom will remain.

For some Christians, the work they do in society is very important. In the Old Testament, when the Jewish people are exiled and made to live in a foreign country, they are encouraged by the prophet Jeremiah to pray and work for the peace of their new country. In St Thomas Aquinas' natural law theory, the task of bringing about order and stability to society is seen as one of the primary rules or precepts. This idea has been influential in Roman Catholic teaching. Many Christians, both Catholic and Protestant, see political action as part of their Christian duty to work for peace. They may write to their MPs, join campaign groups such as CND (see spread 7.5) or become members of political parties.

Other Christians see working to change society as a lesser priority. Some evangelical Christians may argue that God's kingdom is more important than society and that the great commission (the final instruction of Jesus to his disciples) was to spread the Christian message, to produce converts or disciples. These Christians may be concerned that social action misses the main point of Jesus' message.

Analyse and evaluate

Is working for peace the most important activity for Christians?	
Yes	**No**
Jesus urges his followers to work for peace. He states that those who do are blessed.	The great commission shows that Jesus' last instruction was about making disciples. The Gospel is spiritual, not social.
Peace also involves the idea of justice so working for peace is the most important activity.	The Bible suggests that true peace will only be achieved when the kingdom of God comes in full.
Working for peace is part of a wider understanding of the kingdom of God; the Gospel is about the whole person which includes both the spiritual and the social.	

Activities

Review

1. In what ways might an individual Christian work for peace?
2. What are the aims of Christian groups that work for peace?

Develop

3. Why do Christians differ about getting involved in secular groups that aim to bring about peace in society?

Link

4. Review spread 7.6 on pacifism. How might Christians who join CND work for peace?

Debate

5. Should Christians work mainly within their own organisations rather than getting involved in political action? Discuss this statement and note any arguments raised.

Stretch

6. Research the Network of Christian Peace Organisations (https://ncpo.org.uk). What do the different groups that are linked with this organisation do?

7.8 Understanding non-violent action

Aim

To explore Christian approaches to the use of violence to achieve peace, including non-violent action

Starter

The ethical system of utilitarianism argues that anything can be allowed if it results in the greater good. Would this justify violence in exceptional circumstances? Is this something that a Christian could support?

Non-violent action – Martin Luther King

Non-violent action, sometimes called **non-violent direct action**, is a term used to describe protests that go beyond the normal legal routes, such as using the courts, or political routes. This may involve protests, sit-ins, strikes and other things that may not be legal and may cause great disruption. Whatever the means chosen, the crucial aspect is that the protesters do not resort to violence.

The civil rights campaigns led by Martin Luther King (1929–1968) in the USA in the 1950s and 1960s made skilful use of this method. King was a Baptist minister and a doctor of theology who studied widely. He was impressed by the work of Mahatma Gandhi, whose use of these tactics had proved particularly effective in helping India achieve independence from British rule.

Key word

Non-violent direct action – protest techniques that go beyond normal lawful means but are peaceful in nature

■ Martin Luther King's approach of non-violent action was inspired by his study of Mahatma Gandhi

King's strategy included organising a bus boycott when a black woman, Rosa Parks, was arrested for refusing to give up her seat to a white woman as the law required. The black community in Montgomery, Alabama, stopped using the buses altogether. The law was changed within a year partly due to the bus company complaining over lost money. King's civil rights campaigners also protested by staging sit-ins at the segregated lunch counters. His March on Washington in 1963 saw 200,000 people of all races gather for a rally and to hear him speak.

King and his supporters often faced violence, including having his house firebombed. He was imprisoned on occasions for his activism. Key to King's strategy was to cause difficulty but without resorting to violence. On one occasion, when marchers had been beaten by police, King's next march changed tactic. Marchers dropped to their knees in prayer and turned around rather than face police. In 1965, equal voting rights for black Americans was achieved and King received the Nobel Peace prize. He was assassinated while giving a speech in 1968.

In one letter, King challenges those who criticise him for taking direct action rather than negotiating. He argues that direct action is only happening because those in power have refused to negotiate, and it is only by direct action that negotiation will begin to happen.

Source of authority

'In the temple courts he found people selling cattle, sheep and doves, and others sitting at tables exchanging money. So he made a whip out of cords, and drove all from the temple courts, both sheep and cattle; he scattered the coins of the money changers and overturned their tables. To those who sold doves he said, "Get these out of here! Stop turning my Father's house into a market!"' (John 2:14–16)

How far can Christians go to achieve peace and justice?

There was disagreement about King's tactics among both the Christian community and the wider African-American community. Some felt his tactics were too disruptive whereas other activists felt that King was not going far enough.

Some Christians support non-violent action on important issues. Some members of the Green Christian movement have faced arrest while being involved in sit-ins and protests over climate change. Other Christians would reject this type of action even if the cause is important. They would argue that it is a key Christian duty to obey the law, as Romans 13:1 urges Christians to submit to rulers and authorities.

Analyse and evaluate

Is non-violent action the most effective way for Christians to achieve peace?	
Yes	**No**
The experience of Martin Luther King suggests that this can be effective in bringing about change in society.	The Bible commands Christians to submit to authority. Christians should not be involved in breaking the law regardless of the cause.
This type of action has the ability to draw attention and publicity to a cause in a way that legal protests do not.	Sometimes even non-violent action is not enough and even Christians must enter into conflict to bring about justice.
The example of Jesus driving the traders out of the temple is difficult to interpret. Although, as far as we know, he did not injure anyone, his actions would have been highly disruptive and would not be permitted by the authorities.	

Activities

Review
1. What is non-violent (direct) action?
2. What types of non-violent action did Martin Luther King engage in?

Develop
3. What do Christians believe about whether they should be involved in non-violent action?

Link
4. Review the pages on pacifism (see spread 7.6). How is non-violent action similar to pacifism? How does it differ?

Debate
5. Were Jesus' actions in the temple (John 2) an example of non-violent action? Discuss this issue and note any arguments given.

Stretch
6. Camillo Torres (1929–1966) was a Roman Catholic priest who left the priesthood to join a resistance group protesting against the corrupt Colombian government. He was killed in battle. Find out more about his life and beliefs.

7.9 Understanding reconciliation

Aim
To explore how individual Christians and Christian communities understand the idea of reconciliation

Starter
Think of a time when you have experienced a conflict or the breakdown of a friendship. How easy was it to repair the relationship? What needed to happen?

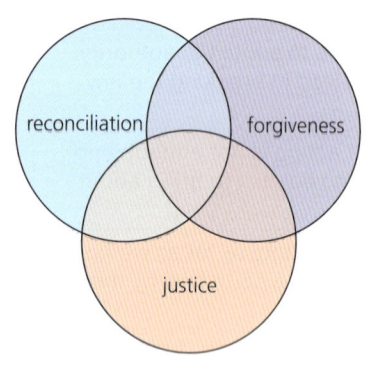

- Reconciliation, forgiveness and justice cannot be easily separated from each other

- The sacrament of reconciliation involves confession to a priest who has the power to forgive sins

Justice, forgiveness and reconciliation

The concepts of **reconciliation**, forgiveness and justice are very much linked. Reconciliation focuses on attempting to put right a relationship that has gone wrong due to conflict, wrongdoing or disagreement. This may require forgiveness of things that one person or group has done to the other. This is explored in spread 7.10.

Key word
Reconciliation – the restoring of a good relationship after a conflict or disagreement

The concept of justice is a little broader than this – it is more forward-looking and considers how we can make society fairer. This is explored in spread 7.11.

The impact of reconciliation on individuals

The Bible has much to say on reconciliation and forgiveness. In the Sermon on the Mount, Jesus urges his followers to make reconciliation a priority. If they are aware that their relationship with a fellow believer is not right, they are told to leave their act of worship and sort out their relationship before returning.

The theme of reconciliation is also shown in the Parable of the Lost Son. In this parable (Luke 15:11–32), a son gains his inheritance early from his father. He wastes the money and decides to return to his home to beg for forgiveness. The father, who had every right to be furious with his son, embraces him and they are reconciled. Christians see the father in the story as a symbol of God's actions towards human beings. God prioritises forgiveness and reconciliation and Christians are encouraged to do likewise, however the refusal of the older son to join the celebration shows that reconciliation and forgiveness are not always easy.

The idea of reconciliation is particularly important in Catholicism which has a sacrament of reconciliation. This involves confession of sins through a priest who has the power to grant forgiveness for those sins. Catholics believe that this power was given to the Church by Jesus, hence a priest acting as representative of the Church can forgive sins committed against God and other people.

The impact of reconciliation on communities and society

Many Christians believe it is part of their Christian duty to work for reconciliation on a wider level in society. However, this is not something that is found in the Bible as the early Church, to whom

Sources of authority

'So he got up and went to his father. But while he was still a long way off, his father saw him and was filled with compassion for him; he ran to his son, threw his arms around him and kissed him.' (Luke 15:20)

'Therefore, if you are offering your gift at the altar and there remember that your brother or sister has something against you, leave your gift there in front of the altar. First go and be reconciled to them; then come and offer your gift.' (Matthew 5:23–24)

'The confession of sins even from a simply human point of view frees us and facilitates our reconciliation with others.' (Catechism of the Catholic Church 1455)

the Apostles were writing, did not have a great deal of influence in Roman society. Some evangelical Christians do not see reconciliation within society as a key aim of the Church. Instead, they prefer to prioritise what they see as more spiritual aspects of the Gospel such as an individual's relationship to God.

Most other Christians do see working for reconciliation within communities and societies as important. The Corrymeela Community in Northern Ireland (see page 69) and the Truth and Reconciliation Commission in South Africa are two examples where this has taken place.

The **Truth and Reconciliation Commission** was set up at the end of apartheid – a political system where black people lived in segregation and were discriminated against. The first black president of South Africa, Nelson Mandela, asked Archbishop Desmond Tutu to chair the commission. Over two years, the commission heard accounts from both victims and perpetrators from all sides of the community. Those who had carried out harmful actions were encouraged to be honest and confess their deeds and the commission was given the power to grant amnesty to those who appeared.

Analyse and evaluate

Should Christians always work for reconciliation?

Yes	No
It is the responsibility of individual Christians and the Church as a whole to carry on the work of Jesus in bringing forgiveness and reconciliation.	Reconciliation is a two-way process. There are times when it is not possible to pursue reconciliation as there is no repentance or desire to change from one of the parties.
Jesus commands Christians to prioritise reconciliation. They are to make sure they repair relationships before they offer gifts of worship to God.	In situations where abuse has occurred, the first priority has to be protection of the victim(s). Reconciliation may not be appropriate.

Activities

Review
1. What does the Parable of the Lost Son (Luke 15:11–32) show about forgiveness and reconciliation?
2. What does Jesus teach about the importance of reconciliation?

Develop
3. How do different Christians approach the idea of the Church bringing reconciliation in society?

Link
4. Look at spread 2.6 on sacraments. What is a sacrament and how does this help in understanding the sacrament of reconciliation?

Debate
5. Is bringing together the victim(s) of a crime with those who committed the crime a helpful approach? Discuss this issue and note down any arguments raised.

Stretch
6. Find out more about the Corrymeela Community or the Truth and Reconciliation Commission. How did this help achieve reconciliation?

7.10 Is it always necessary and possible to forgive?

Aim
To explore Christian ideas of forgiveness and consider some examples

Starter
'Unforgiveness is like drinking poison yourself and waiting for the other person to die' (Marianne Williamson (b.1952), American author and activist). What does this quote mean? Do you think that Marianne Williamson is right?

Key word
Forgiveness – a deliberate decision to no longer hold anger or resentment towards a person for their actions

Sources of authority
'For if you forgive other people when they sin against you, your heavenly Father will also forgive you.' (Matthew 6:14)

'Then Peter came to him and asked, "Lord, how often should I forgive someone who sins against me? Seven times?" "No, not seven times," Jesus replied, "but seventy times seven!"' (Matthew 18:21–22)

'Jesus said, "Father, forgive them, for they do not know what they are doing."' (Luke 23:34)

Top tip
It is important when answering questions on this topic to use the evidence from Christianity to argue a case rather than just expressing your personal opinion.

Christian beliefs about forgiveness

Christians see **forgiveness** as extremely important. It is a key part of both the teaching and example of Jesus. In the Lord's Prayer, Jesus taught his disciples to forgive other people just as God had forgiven them. Jesus seems to suggest that the forgiveness that Christians experience depends upon them forgiving others. This idea is also a key feature of the Parable of the Unforgiving Servant in Matthew 18, where a servant who has had a huge debt written off then attempts to extract a small sum of money that he is owed by a fellow servant. This reinforces the message that just as God forgives a Christian's sins, so they must forgive others.

The Parable of the Unforgiving Servant is told in response to a question from Peter. Peter asks if he is required to forgive someone who sins against him up to seven times. Jesus replies that seventy times seven is what is now expected. This shows how much more radical Jesus wants his followers to be. Jesus did not only teach about forgiveness – he modelled it by forgiving those who had crucified him.

While all Christians agree on the importance of forgiveness, some Christians argue that forgiveness may be dependent upon repentance. The Catechism of the Catholic Church (1451) suggests that those who attend Confession and seek forgiveness for their sins should at least be penitent – they should experience a sense of sorrow or remorse for their actions.

Examples of Christian forgiveness

There have been many remarkable examples of forgiveness from across a range of Christian denominations over the years. Three examples from more modern times are described below.

Example 1: Pope John Paul II

Pope John Paul II was Pope between 1978 and 2005. In 1981, he survived an assassination attempt by Mehmet Ali Ağca. Following the shooting, Pope John Paul II asked people to 'pray for my brother [Ağca], whom I have sincerely forgiven'. The Pope met Ağca in prison in 1983 and they exchanged letters over many years. The Pope was also in touch with Ağca's family. Ağca converted to Roman Catholicism and was released from prison in 2010.

Example 2: Ruby Bridges

In 1960, Ruby Bridges was the first African-American child to be allowed into an all-white school. The decision caused much anger and Ruby had to be protected on her way to school. White parents removed their children from the school and Ruby was educated alone. Even as a child, Ruby's Christian faith was important to her. She explained in later life that each day as she walked through the protesters she prayed for them, asking God to forgive and change them. In 2011, Ruby was invited to the White House to meet the first black president of the United States, Barack Obama, who told her that were it not for the brave actions of people like her, he would not have been in the position he was in.

Example 3: Gee Walker

In July 2005, 17-year-old Anthony Walker was walking home when he was racially abused by two men. Anthony walked away but the men, Michael Barton and Paul Taylor, followed him and attacked him with an axe in a park. Anthony died in hospital a few hours later. Barton and Taylor were sentenced to life imprisonment for racially aggravated murder with the recommendation that they are not released for at least 30 years. Anthony's mother, Gee Walker, and sister, Dominique, were committed Christians and spoke of the importance of forgiveness. After the court case, Gee Walker stated that 'I've got to forgive them. I still forgive them. My family and I still stand by what we believe: forgiveness.'

Analyse and evaluate

Should Christians always forgive, given that God forgives them?

Yes	No
The Bible commands Christians to forgive others. Jesus states that they should be prepared to forgive others many times.	God doesn't forgive everyone – they have to confess their sins. It is hard to forgive those who show no remorse.
As well as religious arguments, it is important to forgive and let go of past hurts as this helps our psychological wellbeing.	Although forgiveness is necessary, it is often not immediately possible where deep hurt has been caused.

Activities

Review
1. What does Jesus teach about forgiveness?
2. How does the crucifixion show Jesus' example of forgiveness?

Develop
3. How does the Parable of the Unforgiving Servant show Christian beliefs about forgiveness and unforgiveness?

Link
4. Review spread 1.12 on the crucifixion of Jesus and spread 1.14 on salvation. How do these help your understanding of Christian ideas of forgiveness?

Debate
5. Does forgiving someone who has killed someone we love disrespect the memory of that person? Discuss this issue and note down any arguments raised.

Stretch
6. Watch the BBC Bitesize video on Gee Walker's forgiveness of her son's killers (www.bbc.co.uk/bitesize/clips/zjt2fg8) and find out more about the Anthony Walker foundation (https://anthonywalkerfoundation.com/).

7.11 Christian beliefs about justice and injustice

Aim
To explore different Christian ideas about justice and injustice

Starter
Sports stars and musicians are often able to make a lot of money doing their job. As a result of this, they may end up paying a higher rate of tax than those who earn less than them. Is this fair or does it penalise them for being successful?

Key word
Justice – fairness, giving people what they deserve

Sources of authority
'O people, the Lord has told you what is good, and this is what he requires of you: to do what is right, to love mercy, and to walk humbly with your God.' (Micah 6:8)

'There is neither Jew nor Gentile, neither slave nor free, nor is there male and female, for you are all one in Christ Jesus.' (Galatians 3:28)

EQUALITY | EQUITY | LIBERATION

■ Justice can be described as fairness. What different understandings of fairness are conveyed in this image?

The idea of **justice** has already been mentioned in connection with its relationship to peace (see spread 7.7) and reconciliation (see spread 7.9). Yet justice is more than just ending conflict or forgiving those who have caused harm – it is about what is right and fair in society, and it considers what sort of society is ideal. When Christians think about justice, they also think about ideas of equality, hence beliefs about justice may lead Christians to take action on issues such as poverty and racial inequality.

Two views of justice

Christians are committed to justice but they may have differing understandings of what justice means. Often the view of justice that Christians take has as much to do with political beliefs as it does any religious beliefs.

- **Equality and merit:** this idea of justice centres around equality as the idea of treating all people the same. This might mean that everyone pays the same rate of tax or pays equally for any services, regardless of their wealth. Supporters of this view argue that those who are successful deserve to be rewarded because their achievements are on merit. For example, if a footballer earns thousands of pounds a week, they deserve to keep that money as their talent is what enables them to earn such a salary. Their talent is the reason why thousands of people are willing to pay to watch them play football.

- **Equality of opportunity:** this idea of justice revolves around equality of opportunity and addressing disadvantage in society. At present, there are groups that are disadvantaged and unable to do as well as others in society through no fault of their own. This view suggests that it is right to expect successful and privileged people to pay more to support those less well-off. Governments and other organisations should prioritise those who need most support.

Christianity and justice

Some Christians may support the idea that justice involves treating everyone the same. The Bible states in Galatians 3 that, for Christians, distinction of gender, race and social status (at that period of time this meant enslaved people and masters) do not matter. Some Christians may believe that there is a link between hard work and success and thus that there are occasions where poverty can be avoided. In his letters, Paul makes a distinction between those who are able to work and those who are unable to work – the church is only responsible for the latter group. Some evangelical Christians believe in an idea known as prosperity Gospel, which is partly based on an interpretation of 3 John. This states that wealth is a sign of God's blessing and that Christians should pray to be wealthier. This view has been influential among right-wing evangelical Christians in the United States.

Other Christians support the idea that justice involves working to address the imbalance in society. They argue that the principle of providing help to those who need it most is a Biblical principle. This ties in with the idea found in Matthew 7 that Christians should do for others what they would wish to have done for them. The Bible also contains a number of passages where concern for the poor is shown to be God's main concern.

Sources of authority

'So in everything, do to others what you would have them do to you, for this sums up the Law and the Prophets.' (Matthew 7:12)

'Beloved, I pray that you may prosper in all things and be in health, just as your soul prospers.' (3 John 2 (NKJV))

Analyse and evaluate

Does justice mean that everyone should get the same?

Yes	No
God loves all people equally. 'There is neither Jew nor Greek', so there is no place for favouritism.	God cares deeply about the poor. The Old Testament criticises those who cannot show justice or mercy to the poor.
In the story of the workers in the vineyard (Matthew 20:1–16), Jesus suggests that all his followers get the same rewards.	Society is unfair and a key role for Christians is to work for the kingdom of God. This involves helping **some people more** to reverse disadvantages.

While it could be argued that everyone deserves the same in terms of basic rights, it may be the case that some people require more support than others.

Activities

Review

1. What is meant by describing justice as being about equality and merit?
2. What is meant by describing justice as being about equality of opportunity?

Develop

3. Which view of justice seems to have the most support in the Bible?

Link

4. Review spread 7.3 on the links between peace and justice. What do St Augustine and St Thomas Aquinas say about justice?

Debate

5. Some people argue that entry grades for top universities should be lower for people from disadvantaged schools or areas. Is this right? Discuss the issue and note down any points relevant to the issues in this spread.

Stretch

6. The Sojourners Network is a Christian organisation in the USA which aims to encourage and support Christians working on issues related to justice. Find out about its work by visiting its website: https://sojo.net/

7.12 How Christians work for social justice

Aim
To explore how different Christians view injustice and how they work for social justice

Starter
Look at the graphic to the right which depicts the world as if it were a village of 100 people. Which of the statistics surprise you? Which might be described as being issues of justice or injustice?

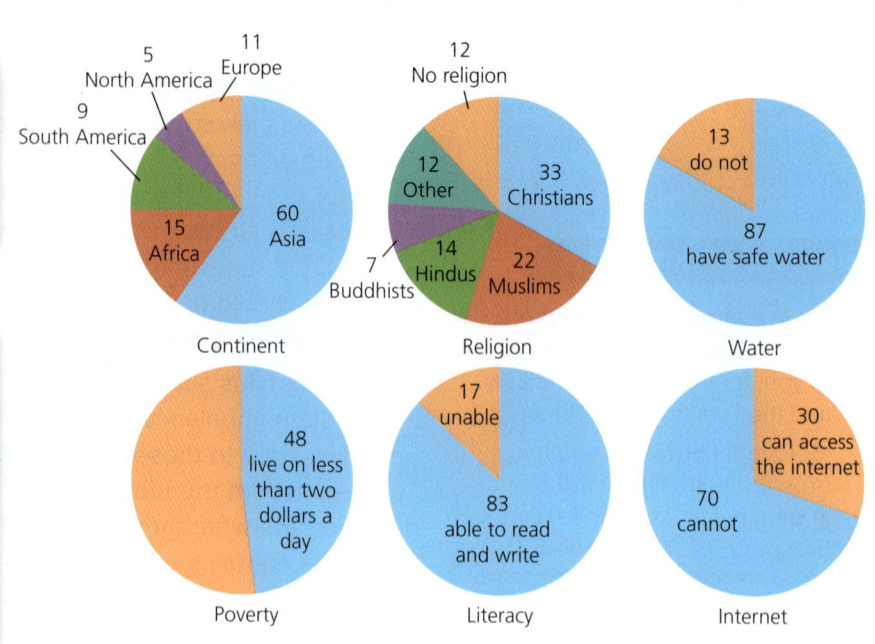

Continent: 60 Asia, 15 Africa, 9 South America, 5 North America, 11 Europe

Religion: 33 Christians, 22 Muslims, 14 Hindus, 7 Buddhists, 12 Other, 12 No religion

Water: 87 have safe water, 13 do not

Poverty: 48 live on less than two dollars a day

Literacy: 83 able to read and write, 17 unable

Internet: 30 can access the internet, 70 cannot

■ These diagrams represent the world as if it were a village of 100 people

Most Christians see working for social justice, and thus opposing injustice, as an important aspect of their faith. Their work addresses two main linked areas: poverty and rights.

Working for social justice – poverty

The Catholic Church states that 'the Church's love for the poor is a part of her constant tradition' (Catechism of the Catholic Church 2444) and this is derived from Jesus' own teachings about love for the poor. The Catholic Agency for Overseas Development (CAFOD) (see page 71) is a charity that works in many countries to bring relief from famine and support those who experience poverty or natural disasters. Its vision states that 'We believe that if one of us is hurt, hungry or abandoned, we all are hurt, hungry and abandoned. No one should be beyond the love and support they need to live a dignified life.' (https://cafod.org.uk/)

Protestant Christians are also active in addressing poverty both in the UK and overseas. It is estimated that almost two-thirds of food banks in the UK have some link to Christian churches or organisations. One of the largest organisations is the Trussell Trust, which aims to support people regardless of their background. The Trust is not explicitly Christian but is 'based on, shaped, and guided by Christian principles. These values have strong roots in the Christian teaching and practice.' Protestant organisations also work overseas with organisations such as Tearfund (see page 71). Well-known organisations, such as the Salvation Army, the YMCA and charities such as Barnardo's, also have strong Christian roots.

Sources of authority

'For the Lord is righteous, he loves justice; the upright will see his face.' (Psalm 11:7)

'Away with the noise of your songs! I will not listen to the music of your harps. But let justice roll on like a river, righteousness like a never-failing stream!' (Amos 5:23–24)

'In the same way, faith by itself, if it is not accompanied by action, is dead. But someone will say, "You have faith; I have deeds." Show me your faith without deeds, and I will show you my faith by my deeds.' (James 2:17–18)

Working for social justice – rights

The UN Declaration of Human Rights (UDHR) states that all people should be entitled to basic rights such as the right to life, work, education, medical care, the right to vote, fair wages and the right to a fair trial. These rights are often under threat in various parts of the world and Christians play a key part in campaigning for and supporting the oppressed. They are influenced by Biblical teachings, in particular the writings of some of the Old Testament prophets. In Amos 5, the prophet suggests that the noisy and enthusiastic songs of worship will be pointless if the worshippers forget justice and mistreat the poor.

Some Christians have also worked to bring about workers' rights. The modern trade union movement in Britain was, in part, inspired by the Methodist Church and individual Christians who were keen to see that the lives of workers should be better than what they currently experienced under harsh Victorian conditions. Other Christians prioritise the needs of animals or are motivated by concern for the environment. Organisations such as CreatureKind and the Green Christian movement work actively in these areas. However, not all Christians believe that these are important priorities; some argue that human beings are more important as they are made in the image of God.

Case against social justice

Some evangelical Christians do not think that social action should be a key priority for Christians. They believe that the key priority is to work to bring God's kingdom closer by sharing the message of Jesus so that as many people as possible can choose to follow him. However, this viewpoint is held by a minority of evangelical Christians. Most evangelical Christians note that Jesus addressed both physical and spiritual needs when he was on Earth and that Christians do not have to choose between either preaching the Gospel or social action. As the Apostle James states in his letter, faith and action go together.

Analyse and evaluate

Is social justice the most important aim for Christians?	
Yes	No
The book of Amos shows that God's priorities are justice and right action. If Christians are not committed to these then their worship is meaningless.	While social justice may be important, the message of Jesus is a spiritual message. It is about salvation and preparing people for heaven.
Jesus spent much of his time dealing with people's physical needs and helping the poor.	Focusing on social justice means that Christians get distracted from God's kingdom and focus on politics instead of matters of faith.
Social justice is part of the message of Jesus, who came to save the whole person – not just their soul. As the Apostle James says, faith without action is dead.	

Activities

Review
1. How do Christian organisations work to reduce poverty in the world?
2. According to the United Nations, what basic rights should people be entitled to?

Develop
3. Why do Christians differ on whether social justice should be a priority?

Link
4. Review spread 2.14 on the mission of the church on a worldwide scale. How do the organisations that you studied in that spread deal with the issues raised in this one?

Debate
5. It could be argued that the issues discussed in this spread should be the work of government, not the Church. Discuss this idea and note down any arguments raised.

Stretch
6. Find out more about the work of CreatureKind (www.becreaturekind.org) or the Green Christian movement (https://greenchristian.org.uk/).

Summary activities

CHECK YOUR NOTES

STAGE 1

Check that you have detailed notes that cover the following:

- [ ] How teachings about violence are understood by individual Christians and communities
- [ ] Christian attitudes to terrorism
- [ ] Different Christian attitudes to the ideas of just war and holy war
- [ ] Christian attitudes to modern warfare including technological warfare and apocalyptic warfare
- [ ] Christian teachings and beliefs about absolute and conditional pacificism
- [ ] How Christians work for peace and justice in situations and society
- [ ] Non-violent action
- [ ] The concepts of forgiveness and reconciliation; how Christians understand these concepts
- [ ] How Christians understand and work for social justice

GETTING READY

STAGE 2

Quick quiz

1. In the Sermon on the Mount, how does Jesus suggest that Christians should respond when they experience violence?
2. How is terrorism defined?
3. In the just war theory, what two criteria address how the war should be fought?
4. What type of warfare do CND and CCND campaign against?
5. What is the difference between absolute and conditional pacifism?
6. What term describes illegal protests such as strikes, marches or sit-ins that are held peacefully?
7. Define the term 'reconciliation'.
8. What was the role of the Truth and Reconciliation Commission in South Africa?
9. How does Jesus' crucifixion show his belief in forgiveness?
10. What does the Prophet Amos say about the importance of justice?

Quick quiz answers can be found online at www.hoddereducation.co.uk/ocr-gcse-rs-answers

ACTIVITIES

STAGE 3

1. Create a set of flashcards for the key technical terms in this topic. Each card should contain a definition, an explanation and, if appropriate, a link to a source of wisdom or authority.
2. P and P essay planning: one quick way to check whether you understand a topic without writing a full 15-mark essay is P and P essay planning.

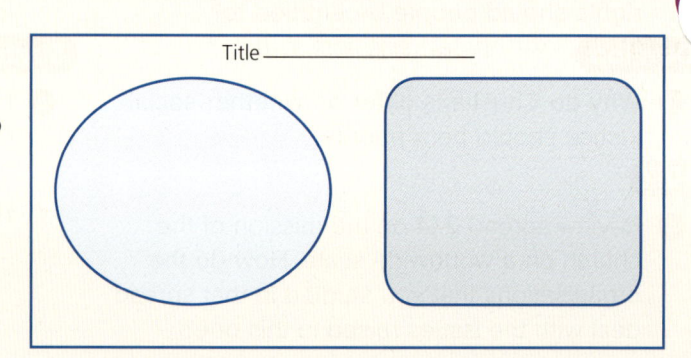

Title _____

- Step 1: Choose an exam question you wish to attempt
- Step 2: Use the circle to write an essay plan
- Step 3: Write out one of your paragraphs in full in the other box

GET PRACTISING

STAGE 3

Use this section to help you develop your understanding of how to answer questions on this topic.

Ask the Expert:

Benjamin is about to write an essay on whether Christians can ever go to war. The plan for the essay is below.

P1: Reasons for war

P2: Reasons against war

P3: Christian views

P4: My opinion

Expert Comment

This type of structure has the acronym FARM (**F**or, **A**gainst, **R**eligious View, **M**y view). It doesn't really work for all GCSE mark schemes. You will notice two things about the questions and mark schemes.

- Firstly, under each of the 15-mark questions on this paper are two bullet points asking you to discuss this within the context of Christianity. There is also a reference to Christian groups in the levels of response mark scheme – so this needs to be more than just a paragraph.
- Secondly, the mark scheme also asks you to evaluate ideas and reach a reasoned conclusion. One way of doing this is to think of yourself as writing a little bit like a lawyer.

Writing like a lawyer: planning backwards

Arguments have reasons and a conclusion — they attempt to persuade. Your 15-mark essay is an argument. In the planning stage, it may be useful to work backwards in the following manner:

- **Step 1:** What will you conclude? A judgement not a personal opinion.
- **Step 2:** What will your reasons be? Check that at least some of these reasons use evidence from Christianity.
- **Step 3:** What is the counterargument? Why might other Christians adopt a different view?
  You now have the starting points for each paragraph.
- **Step 4:** For higher levels — how strong is each of the arguments? How might each point be answered?

This will develop as you write each of the paragraphs.

Benjamin's improved plan

Intro: Christians can support war

P1: Catholics support the just war theory …

P2: Catholics support self-defence via double effect theory

P3: Duty of all Christians to 'give to Caesar what is Caesar's'

P3: Counterargument: Quakers and teachings of Jesus BUT this is for individuals not nations

C: So, on the whole Christians can sometimes support war

245

CHAPTER 8
Dialogue between religious and non-religious views

8.1 Christianity in British society

Aim
To understand the importance of Christian religious traditions in British society

Starter
What aspects of 'being British' can you identify as having Christian origins or links?

Key word
Established religion – the state religion of a country; a religion officially recognised by a country

Source of authority
'The Church [of England] has a duty to protect the free practice of all faiths in this country… [It] has created an environment for other faith communities and indeed people of no faith to live freely… [It] has helped to build a better society… for the common good…' (Queen Elizabeth II, speech at Lambeth Palace, 2012)

Christianity in Britain

This topic examines British society and the changing role of religion for British people. Christianity came to Britain in Roman times, nearly 2000 years ago. The country became Catholic and was under the leadership of the Pope until King Henry VIII made himself the head of the Church of England as part of the Reformation in England in 1534. Now, the monarch is the Supreme Governor of the Church, and British society and traditions clearly show the long links between Christianity and daily life. In law, the Church of England is the **established religion** – the official religion of England.

The monarch swears to protect the form of Christianity found in the Church of England as the established religion. One of their titles is 'Defender of the Faith'. At their coronation, they are anointed by the Archbishop of Canterbury and given an orb to indicate that their authority is God-given. The monarch appoints senior church leaders, opens sessions of the Church of England's governing body (the General Synod) and aims to lead a life in public that reflects their role.

However, many people, both Christian and non-Christian, question whether this is still a relevant situation to be in, given the changes in society. In the 2021 census for England and Wales, less than half the population described themselves as Christian (46.2 per cent) and, although 'Christian' was the biggest religious group, 'no religion' was the second biggest with 37.2 per cent. The numbers were very different to the 2011 census (revealing a 13.1 per cent decrease in the number of Christians) and because church attendance has not changed very much, it could be argued that fewer people identify themselves with the established religion now than in the past.

However, people turn to the Church for rites of passage, especially baptism, marriage and funerals. The Church believes it to be important to continue to support family life in this way. Christian morality also underpins much of what it is to be British; for example, the care for the most vulnerable in society that reflects the teaching of Jesus in the Parable of the Sheep and the Goats. Many food banks, as well as the hospice movement, come from Christian roots. Christian thought shapes the making of new laws and policies on issues such as medical ethics, ensuring that there is a balanced debate between freedom of practice and the issues concerning the value of human life.

Christianity plays a central role in public life in Britain, including:

Public holidays based on Christian celebrations	Christian services to mark key events	Bishops in the House of Lords
The biggest Christian feast days – Christmas and Easter – are the main holiday periods in the country, each with two public holidays. The late May bank holiday is traditionally linked to Pentecost (Whitsun). School terms also arranged around these festivals. Britain also enjoys the celebration of Shrove Tuesday (the day before Ash Wednesday), Hallowe'en (the day before All Saints' Day) and Valentine's Day (the celebration of a saint).	When there are key events in British public life, there are often Christian services to help mark these events. For example, on Remembrance Day, the public services are mainly Christian, even though they are welcoming to those of other faiths and no faith. Royal events (weddings, funerals and coronations, for example) all have a Christian focus and often take place in the great Christian buildings of the country, such as Westminster Abbey. It is an important part of British culture for there to be a spiritual element to these events and as the diversity of the country changes, there are more opportunities being taken to include the range of religions from British society. There is also an increase in the public participation in festivals and commemorations from other religions, for example, Diwali, Vaisakhi, Yom Kippur and Eid-ul-Fitr.	The House of Lords is the upper house of the British Parliament. The members (over 750 of them) bring a wealth of experience from different backgrounds. Twenty-six of the bishops of the Church of England are entitled to sit in the House of Lords as 'Lords Spiritual' (rather than 'Lords Temporal', who are often political figures). This means that they can have a significant impact on debates surrounding the passing of new laws and decisions which affect British society.

Analyse and evaluate

Should Church of England bishops be able to sit in the House of Lords?

Yes	No
As the Church of England is the established religion, bishops have a right to play more of a role in law making.	The bishops have not chosen to be politicians and they should focus on their work as religious leaders.
The bishops are exposed to a range of different life experiences and views and can bring that wisdom to the House of Lords.	Britain is no longer religious and so should not be governed in any way by religious people.
Some would argue that there should be Lords Spiritual from a range of faith backgrounds, to reflect modern British society.	

Activities

Review
1. What is meant by the idea of the Church of England being an established religion?
2. How is Christianity central to British public life?

Develop
3. Find current statistics on the make-up of different religions and different denominations of Christianity in British society. How do these statistics contribute to the discussion on these pages?

Link
4. Sunday trading laws currently restrict what shops are allowed to do on the Sabbath. Do you think this is appropriate? Why or why not?

Debate
5. Should one denomination of Christianity have more of a role in the public life of Britain than other denominations?

Stretch
6. Find out more about why British society has changed in its cultural and religious make-up and summarise the reasons for this change in 50 words.

8.2 Secularisation

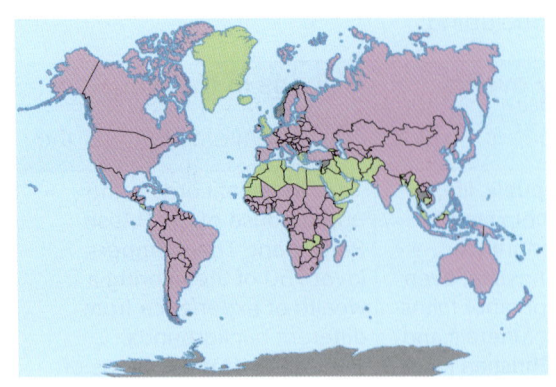

The green countries have established religions, the purple ones are secular states and ambiguous states are grey

The place of religion in a secular society

If a religious society is one where religion is the starting point for decision making and a **secular** society is one where non-religious values are the starting point, then **secularisation** can be said to be the process of a society moving from the first to the second. Many would argue that Britain (indeed, the Western world) is in the process of secularisation. Religion is becoming more of a private matter and it is more commonly felt that religious views should not influence laws, education or public life. One of the reasons for secularisation is a move towards the view that religion describes the supernatural and that everything can be explained without the need for a divine being to guide people's lives or to answer prayers.

The effects of secularisation on religion

Christians might say that secularisation undermines their beliefs and might also feel that their beliefs are not being respected. Alongside secular beliefs can come accusations that religious people are deluded or ignorant. Practising a faith can be seen as equivalent to a hobby, rather than a fundamental way of life. This means that Christians might feel they have to justify their beliefs more frequently and this could lead either to Christianity being quite hard line in its views and being seen in opposition to society or to Christian beliefs being watered-down, which some might see as a good thing and some might see as a negative move. For example, society saying that Sunday is not a special day might lead some Christians to want to reinforce the need to go to church to be a proper Christian and others to say that it is not necessary to attend church on a Sunday to be a Christian. Alongside the idea of freedom of expression comes the idea that all views are equally valid, which goes against any religious idea that one particular religion is 'true'.

Many Christians do not have a problem with the separation of Church and state. They believe that Christians can still live successfully within a secular society, as seen in countries such as the USA and France: secular societies where religion still plays an important role in daily life. These Christians still feel able to challenge policies they do not agree with and there is perhaps less pressure on them to adapt to 'modern' life.

The rise of humanism

Humanism is an approach to life that developed quickly in the twentieth century, although its roots were formed much earlier. While there are many different definitions of the term, it generally focuses

Aim
To explore the impact of secularisation on society

Starter
How would you say society has changed since you have been in secondary school? How would your teacher say it has changed since they were in secondary school?

Key words
Secular – not connected to religious ideas
Secularisation – the decline in the influence of religion over time
Humanism – an approach to life that focuses on humans (rather than a divine being) holding the potential to develop society

on the importance of human freedom, human wellbeing and a rejection of religion. It is not an organised group, although some humanists have come together to try to connect their ideas (for example, Humanists UK) and to develop society as a group. Generally, humanists aim for all-round happiness and fulfilment in life.

Humanism centres its view on celebrating the work of science and believes that:

- humans should try to live self-fulfilled lives
- good morals are at the centre of good society
- positive action makes a difference
- (most importantly) humans have the right to do all of the above.

Freedom and equality

With the changes described above, society has begun to reconsider what it means to talk about freedom and equality.

- **Tolerance:** the idea that different views need to be able to co-exist in society.
- **Freedom of belief:** the human right that all people are free to hold whatever religious or philosophical beliefs they want.
- **Freedom of expression:** the human right that all people should be able to express their views without government interference as long as they do so while respecting other people's rights.
- **Freedom of practice:** the right to practise any religious or non-religious belief someone might hold.

Source of authority

'Everyone has the right to freedom of thought, conscience and religion; this right includes freedom to change his religion or belief, and freedom, either alone or in community with others and in public or private, to manifest his religion or belief in teaching, practice, worship and observance.' (Article 18, United Nations Universal Declaration of Human Rights)

Analyse and evaluate

Does having an established religion reduce a person's freedom?	
Yes	No
A person cannot be a full member of society if they are not part of the established religion because they are always an outsider.	As long as there is an emphasis on tolerance for all, an individual person's freedom will not be restricted.
Politics and religion should be separated so that the views of the Church of England are not imposed on others.	Having an established religion does not affect a person's ability to reject that religion.
Some might point to the fact that Britain successfully tolerates the views of many but other states are perhaps not as tolerant and so it depends on the country being discussed.	

Activities

Review

1. What are the fundamental beliefs of humanism?
2. Write a paragraph explaining the possible effects of secularisation on a society. Use these words and phrases: tolerance, freedom of belief, freedom of expression, freedom of practice.

Develop

3. How might a Christian use the following Bible passages in the debate about secularisation: Matthew 5:16, Mark 12:17, Romans 13:1, 2 Timothy 3:1–5 and 1 John 2:15?

Link

4. How might secularisation affect a Christian's attitude to mission and evangelisation?

Debate

5. Can it be said that secularism has failed because it has not successfully solved the challenges in society (such as the environment, inequality and poverty)?

Stretch

6. Research what it is to be a Christian in either France or the USA and explain how Christians in Britain might learn from the experiences of Christians in these secular countries.

8.3 Religious and secular values in education

■ Should Christian practice feature in schools?

Aim

To explore the role of religious values in schools

Starter

What has been your experience of religion in school?

Source of authority

'Jesus answered, "I am the way and the truth and the life. No one comes to the Father except through me."' (John 14:6)

'The Catholic school forms part of the saving mission of the Church, especially for education in the faith.' (Sacred Congregation for Catholic Education, The Catholic School 9)

'A good education must promote life in all its fullness.' (Church of England Vision For Education)

Different values in schools

Most state-funded schools in England and Wales are required by law to teach Religious Education to all year groups as well as to hold daily collective worship. Usually, both of these must be 'mainly Christian'. For many, this continues to be appropriate because British values and traditions have their roots in Christianity. Others would argue that the values of not stealing or killing, of tolerance and individual liberty (for example) are universal values and not just Christian ones.

For many of those who disagree with the legal requirement, there are two issues:

- The religious diversity of the country has changed significantly – not only is it multi-faith, it is significantly non-religious. Therefore, there is no place for a 'mainly Christian' approach to school values or practice.
- Even if you accept the priority of Christianity, the law essentially allows Christianity to be 'pushed' onto children, which could be argued to be a form of brainwashing: religion is a private matter and not for schools or the state.

Many will approach this by saying that schools should expose children to the range of worldviews and lenses with which people view the world and they will value the role Religious Education has to play in this. Others might observe that the Church of England is the established religion in the country and therefore, whether or not non-Christians agree, it is the situation that we are in. Many might observe that it is possible to teach a mainly Christian curriculum and to teach religious values without pushing these onto young people. The starting point for a secular approach to this issue is often that all views are equally valid but, for Christians, the starting point is that their religion is true.

Faith schools

Around one-third of state-funded schools in the UK are faith schools. The vast majority of these are Church of England or Roman Catholic schools, though there are over twice as many Church of England schools than Catholic schools, as might be expected with an established religion. In rural areas, some families do not have any realistic choice about which school to send their child to and so they may be forced to send their child to a church school. Broadly speaking, there are four different viewpoints with regards to faith schools:

- For those who oppose religion having a role in schools, the presence of faith schools that are funded by the state makes the issues raised above even relevant.
- Some people have no issue with faith schools, as long as there is a choice of school.

- Many parents who are not religious are happy to send their children to a local Christian school because they agree with the aims and values of the school: the Christian values are not overly pushed onto the children and the values are universal.
- Parents who are religious may want their children to have religious values reinforced by schools. They might argue that it is important that schools teach that Christianity has relevance today in an ever-more secular state.

For many Christians, there are great advantages of church schools, such as:

- Children can grow in their faith alongside people their own age, which is especially important given the decline in young people attending church.
- Faith schools are countercultural because they value spirituality, reject the notion that material things alone provide meaning and challenge the sole importance of science as a way of thinking.
- Jesus challenged the assumptions of society when he worked with outcasts and sinners so why shouldn't Christians? The parable of the Good Samaritan (Luke 10:25–37) is a reminder to Christians to not simply 'go with the flow'.

Top tip

Remember that Christianity is only the established religion in England. The other countries in the UK do not have a state religion, although they have rich Christian traditions.

Analyse and evaluate

Should Christians always aim to send their children to church schools?

Yes	No
It is a valuable way for children to be brought up in the faith, surrounded by those of a like mind.	Bringing a child up in the faith is the role of the family, not the school.
With declining church attendance, it is important for practising Christians to maintain their community.	Children must learn to live within modern society and church schools are not reflective of this.

Some might argue that Christians can and should be lights to the world in whatever situation they find themselves in, so it does not really matter.

Activities

Review

1. Give two arguments for and two arguments against religion being a part of state-funded schools.
2. Choose the stronger argument for and against and write a counterargument to each.

Develop

3. Look up some primary and secondary Christian schools online and look at their values and/or mission statements. Is it fair to say that faith schools 'push' religion onto young people?

Link

4. What benefits and challenges might there be for members of a faith school worshipping together? Try to use some of the key phrases from spread 8.2 in your response.

Debate

5. 'Removing faith schools from the country would improve society in the next generation.' Discuss this view.

Stretch

6. Imagine it is the year 2100. Looking back on the twenty-first century, what contribution should Christianity have made to British society?

8.4 Marriage and equality

Aim
To examine potential clashes between religion, tradition and secular law in terms of marriage and equality

Starter
Where might Christianity disagree with secular ideas in terms of marriage and equality?

Top tip
Material on marriage from spreads 5.2–5.6 and on equality from spreads 5.11–5.13 will be directly relevant to this topic where the focus is on the relationship with society.

■ Some Christians allow women equal ministry to men but others believe Jesus intended that only men should be priests

Key words
Forced marriage – where one or both members of a couple are married without a choice
Arranged marriage – where the couple are introduced to each other by family members who see the marriage as a suitable or good match

Marriage

Religious views on issues to do with relationships are often different to those of wider society. Where society's focus may be on self-determination, freedom and tolerance, religious believers can be more prescriptive because of the laws that they follow. Some in secular society would argue that religious laws come not from a divine being but from the fact that religions are following traditions that are now outdated. Within Christianity, there are, of course, diverse views, depending on the denomination or lens through which the issues are seen. There are a number of specific areas within the topic of marriage which can lead to clashes with wider society.

- **Whether or not to get married:** Many Christians argue that marriage is the proper place for sexual relationships because of the link between sex and family life. While some Christians, such as Catholics, reject cohabitation, others are more tolerant, seeing living together before marriage as a step on the journey to marriage or the lesser of two evils when compared to divorce.

- **Divorce:** Catholics reject divorce on the grounds that marriage is a permanent vow made with God as well as with the other person; other Christians try to avoid it. Many Christians would argue that it is too 'easy' to get divorced and that perhaps more should be invested in relationship counselling. Others would argue that getting divorced should be an easy process in order to avoid abusive relationships.

- **Who to marry:** Many Christians reject same-sex marriage because they consider the definition of marriage to be an act between a man and a woman. Some Christians, such as the Church of England, allow same-sex civil partnerships but not marriage, and some liberal Christians allow same-sex marriage. Some feel unhappy that Churches are exempt from equality laws that require same-sex marriages to be treated the same as opposite-sex marriages.

- **Forced marriage:** Christians believe that the love between a married couple is a reflection of God's love and so reject all forms of **forced marriage**. The vows are designed to be an expression of free choice. Secular society agrees with this approach.

- **Arranged marriage:** Some cultures have a tradition of **arranged marriage** and facilitate introductions between couples – in Christian families as well as in those from other faiths. In this situation, Christians would want to be sure that love blossomed and that the couple were free to choose not to continue with the match. Sometimes, there might be pressure for an arranged match to become a marriage and Christians would challenge any situation where an arranged marriage became a forced marriage.

Equality

The Equality Act 2010 states that people must be treated equally when it comes to employment but some religious jobs are exempt from the law due to some Christian beliefs about female ministry and homosexuality. For some secularists, this is unacceptable but many would argue that members of religions have the right to freedom of practice and therefore to apply these restrictions.

Christians might also be affected by equality laws because there is no protection for the faith, despite being the established religion in England. People have the right to freedom of expression and therefore they have the right to express negative views about Christianity. Some might argue that the many years of special treatment that Christianity has enjoyed in British society should continue.

Some might argue that there is a difference between 'equal value' and 'equal status' which society does not always recognise. For example, Catholics, who reject divorce and do not allow divorced and remarried people full membership of the Church, would still say that remarried members of the Church are of equal value to others, even though they no longer have the same status as them.

Christians might also suggest that it is wrong to make decisions about equality based on ideas of individual freedom. Christians do not believe that we are individuals as much as we are a community, based on relationships with others. Ethical decisions should not be made in isolation from this understanding.

■ Why might Christian views on equality sometimes differ from those of others?

Analyse and evaluate

Are Christian attitudes to equality outdated?

Yes	No
Christian approaches to equality are usually based on the Bible, which reflects a very different society than today.	Just because society has changed, it does not mean that what is good, right and true has changed – so Christians' views are still relevant.
It is always wrong to deny people happiness, which is what would happen if (for example) there is not tolerance for members of the LGBTQ+ community.	Christian views on equality throughout the history of the religion have been groundbreaking. For example, in Biblical times enslaved people were allowed to become Christians.
When considering this question, some might point to the huge divergence within Christianity and especially to those Christians who try to practise their faith within the context of a changing society.	

Activities

Review
1. Why might marriage be an area of conflict between Christians and wider society?
2. What is the difference between forced and arranged marriages?

Develop
3. Look up and make a list of the 'protected characteristics' in law. What are different Christian views on each one and how might they clash with wider society?

Link
4. Use the material in Chapter 5 to add appropriate sources of authority to your notes for this topic.

Debate
5. 'Christians should always reject arranged marriages.' Debate this statement.

Stretch
6. Do you think the media helps or hinders Christianity's relationship with secular law and tradition?

8.5 Medical ethics: euthanasia and abortion

Aim

To examine potential clashes between religious teachings and scientific development in the context of euthanasia and abortion

Starter

What makes humans different to animals?

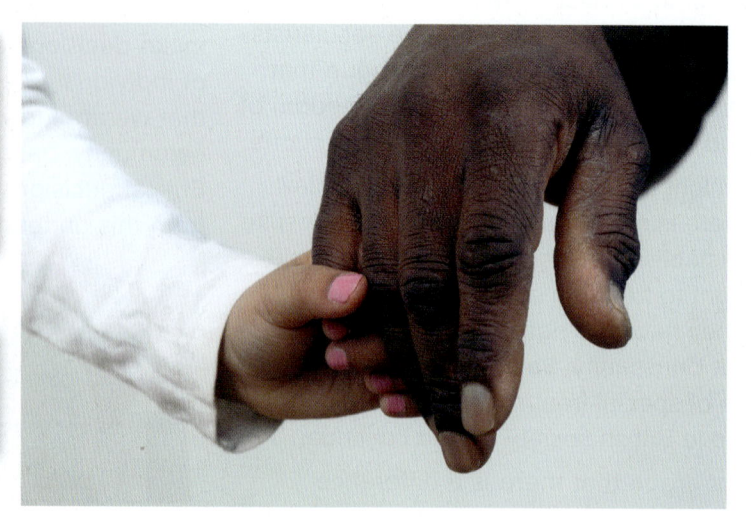

Christians believe that all human life is sacred

Key words

Sanctity of life – the belief that all human life is sacred
Sacred – set apart, holy
Euthanasia – literally 'a good death'; deliberately ending a person's life to relieve suffering
Abortion – deliberately terminating a pregnancy

Euthanasia and the right to die

Christians believe in the **sanctity of life** – the belief that human life is **sacred** from conception to natural death – and that all life is of equal value – so all people, from conception to death, have equal rights. These beliefs also mean that human life belongs to God and it is not up to us when it should begin or end.

An increasing number of countries permit different forms of **euthanasia** and, although it is illegal in the UK, people who have helped sick friends or relatives to die in other countries have not been prosecuted when they have returned home.

Christian arguments in favour of and against euthanasia	
For	• The idea that we have freedom over our own bodies, whether or not we are ill. • Euthanasia does not increase the overall number of people who die – but it does decrease the amount of suffering, allowing death with dignity, just like for animals. • Death is not something the state or a religion should be involved in – it is an intensely private matter. • Jesus believed in compassion and the relief of suffering as well as emphasising people's individual rights, so some Christians argue that he would have allowed euthanasia, had medical developments allowed it during his time.
Against	• It is not our decision when life should begin or end – and we do not always know if a recovery will come unexpectedly. • There are improving forms of pain relief available for end-of-life care. • Relationship with doctors will change because their role will no longer be focused on preserving life. • Allowing euthanasia in even the rarest of cases will end up allowing it more and more frequently. • Vulnerable people may feel under pressure from their families to opt for Euthanasia when it is not their choice.

Abortion

Abortion is legally permitted up to the 24th week of pregnancy in England, Wales and Scotland (and up to birth if the mother or baby

Source of authority

'Don't you know that you yourselves are God's temple and that God's spirit dwells in your midst? If anyone destroys God's temple, God will destroy that person.' (1 Corinthians 3:16–17)

Top tip

There are no direct Bible teachings on medical ethics so different Christian attitudes to the Bible might affect why Christians have different views on these issues.

would be at risk if the pregnancy were to continue). There are a number of conflicting rights at play in this debate, including:

- **The right of the child:** if the baby has equal rights from conception then surely the law should protect them.
- **The right of the mother:** many argue that the mother has greater rights than the child until such time as the baby is not physically dependent on the mother's body.

Christian beliefs may also be challenged as medical science develops. Doctors are becoming more accurate at analysing the foetus and can identify irregularities and complications during pregnancy. This might make people more likely to have an abortion and some Christians might need to weigh up whether the God-given blessing of scientific advancement is more relevant than their beliefs about abortion.

Not all Christians reject abortion completely. Those who do reject it, such as the Catholic Church, would argue that they are not saying 'no' but saying 'yes' to protecting an innocent baby.

Some Christians, such as some members of the Church of England, believe that where there is a clash between the rights of the baby and the rights of the mother, the lesser of two evil options may be to allow the abortion to take place.

Analyse and evaluate

Is abortion acceptable?

Yes	No
Abortion should be acceptable until a certain point in pregnancy (for example, first heartbeat or first brain function or until the baby can survive outside the womb).	Rather than women being allowed abortion, society should focus on better provision (for example, childcare, workplace laws, adoption options).
A woman who is pregnant as the result of rape should never be made to carry that baby to term.	Some would say abortion is not acceptable even after rape because to allow it would be to assume that the problem is that the woman is pregnant and not that the woman was raped in the first place.
Many would consider the difference between abortion 'on demand' and abortion where the mother's mental or physical health – or that of the unborn child – are at risk when thinking about this question.	

Activities

Review

1. Why are the debates about euthanasia and abortion often to do with the rights of different people?
2. Why might different Christians disagree with each other when it comes to the issue of abortion and/or euthanasia?

Develop

3. Find out the views of at least two different Christian denominations about abortion and euthanasia and add them to your notes.

Link

4. How might the secularisation of society affect issues to do with the sanctity of life?

Debate

5. Is it fair to say that the UK law on euthanasia will have to change?

Stretch

6. Find a news article about either abortion or euthanasia and analyse not only the issues that are covered but also how the situation was covered by the media.

8.6 Medical ethics: genetic manipulation and the creation of life

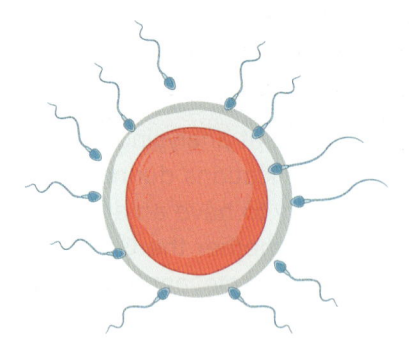

Scientific developments continue to proceed very quickly

Genetic manipulation

Genetic manipulation refers to any procedure that changes the natural development of genes. It can be used in the context of therapeutic cloning, where a cell is used to create an embryo which is genetically identical to the donor cell. That embryo is then used in research to understand and treat diseases. Genetic manipulation can also be used to create a 'designer baby', where genes in the sperm, egg or embryo are manipulated to ensure that the baby has or does not have certain characteristics.

Different Christian views

- For most Christians, such as Roman Catholics, this immediately goes against the idea of the sanctity of life or the idea that God is in control of creation – as seen in the Genesis creation accounts, for example. It is not the role of humans to 'play God'.
- However, some Christians might point to the good that can be done through genetic manipulation; for example, curing disease, or allowing someone with a hereditary illness to give birth naturally to a child. They might say that this is a sign of *agape* or observe that our intelligence is a God-given gift and we must be allowed to use it.
- Some Christians and non-Christians might be suspicious of genetic manipulation because of the possibilities of it going wrong in the future. For example, allowing some forms of it today might lead to many forms of it in the future – including 'designer babies' based on characteristics not linked to health, which could lead to a divided society where those who can afford to pay for genetic manipulation are separated from those who cannot.
- The Bible says nothing about genetic manipulation because it was not a concern at the time the Bible was written. Christians can only use general principles from the Bible to guide them in this area and it seems that sometimes these general principles could disagree with each other when applied to modern situations. For example, the general principle of helping a sick person might clash with that of not playing God when creating embryos for medical use. Christians might refer to their beliefs on abortion when considering whether an embryo, once created, has equal rights to all people, and when considering how spare embryos should be treated, including whether they are stored or destroyed if no longer needed.

Aim

To examine potential clashes between religious teachings and scientific development in the context of genetic manipulation and the creation of life

Starter

When is it wrong for people to 'play God'?

Key word

Genetic manipulation – using technology to change genes

Source of authority

'The LORD said: "Who is this that obscures my plans? ... Where were you when I laid the earth's foundation?"' (Job 38:2–4)

Top tip

The material in this spread and the previous one is a huge area for modern ethics and is fascinating to study. Do take time to find out more about the issues.

The creation of life

There are many different forms of fertility treatment. Some try to enhance the natural process (for example, through hormones) while others require medical intervention (such as artificial insemination or IVF – *in vitro* fertilisation). In some cases, a number of embryos are created (for example, in IVF) and a decision needs to be made about what to do with those that aren't used. Sometimes, the sperm and egg of the couple are used and sometimes donors are needed; sometimes a surrogate is needed to carry the baby. This raises ethical issues:

- Should a third party (such as a sperm or egg donor, or a surrogate) be introduced into the process? Some Christians would reject anything that goes beyond the couple in this way, arguing that it is unnatural or adulterous.
- Should any non-natural process be used? Some, such as Catholics, believe conception outside of the womb is unnatural; believe it can be justified as the lesser of two evils: allowing a non-natural process is better than the pain of not allowing a couple to have their own child.
- Are the created embryos human lives and can spare embryos be discarded or used for medical research?
- Should society encourage adoption more? There are many babies and children who cannot be raised in their birth family who would benefit from the love of those who cannot have their own children naturally.
- Should any person who wants a child of their own be denied it? What about single people?

The principles discussed above and in the previous spread are often relevant here: the sanctity of life, the importance of science, the rights of different people. As science develops, the success rate of different types of fertility treatment improves. While the Roman Catholic Church and many evangelical Christians reject the creation of spare embryos, and the Catholic Church believes that natural forms of conception are preferable, some Christians, such as the Church of England, allow the process because it is the lesser of two evils.

Analyse and evaluate

Should Christians accept scientific advances?

Yes	No
Scientific advances make life better for people who are infertile, unwell and so on. Christians should celebrate this.	Medical scientific advances challenge the idea that human life is a gift from God and ultimately belongs to God.
Science is a God-given ability and one of the most important achievements of the human race.	Scientific advances may be exciting when they are new but the future impact on society is not always clear.
Many would differentiate between good advances and bad ones. Many Christians, for example, would reject scientific advances that contribute to apocalyptic warfare.	

Activities

Review

1. Why might genetic manipulation be helpful to a person?
2. For each of the issues related to the creation of life above, use your knowledge to explain two different Christian responses.

Develop

3. Find out the views of at least two denominations about the issues covered in this spread and add them to your notes.

Link

4. Why might Christian teachings on God's goodness and creation challenge a couple who cannot conceive naturally? How might a Christian support an infertile couple in their community?

Debate

5. How true is it to suggest that 'designer babies' are inevitable in the future?

Stretch

6. One secular principle for making ethical decisions is always to try to bring about the most happiness and to reduce the amount of suffering for those concerned. How might this principle apply to issues concerned with the sanctity of life?

8.7 Is Christianity the only way to salvation?

Aim
To explore three different approaches to whether non-Christians can be saved

Starter
What is the definition of a religion?

Source of authority
'For God so loved the world that he gave his one and only Son, that whoever believes in him shall not perish but have eternal life.' (John 3:16)

Key words
Exclusivism – the belief that only Christians will be saved
Inclusivism – the belief that non-Christians can be saved because they are anonymous Christians
Anonymous Christians – living a Christian life without realising it

Source of authority
'God … accepts from every nation the one who fears him and does what is right.' (Acts 10:35)

Key word
Pluralism – the belief that many religions can lead to salvation

Exclusivism

The key focus for **exclusivism** is the sacrifice of Jesus and the decision of a Christian to accept the centrality of this in their lives. If you do not need to be an active Christian to go to heaven, then surely God could have saved the world in other ways? Jesus' sacrifice on the cross showed how he was a mediator between sinful humanity and perfect God and restored the gap between the two which had been created by the Fall.

Catholic exclusivists believe that only the work of the Catholic Church itself – through the sacraments, for example – brings people into contact with God's grace. Some Protestant exclusivists believe that it is only by accepting Jesus into their hearts that a person is saved.

Some Christians criticise exclusivism because it does not seem to be the message found in the Bible, such as in the Parable of the Sheep and the Goats (Matthew 25:31–46), where it is somebody's actions, not their faith, that is important. There is also the understanding that exclusivism suggests that a loving God rejects those who never had a chance to choose Christianity.

Inclusivism

Inclusivism rejects the narrow approach of exclusivism. Inclusivism believes there needs to be a balance between God's love and the centrality of Christ and some inclusivists understand this in terms of the idea that people can be **anonymous Christians**. An anonymous Christian is someone whose lifestyle or whose faith has a lot of overlap with Christianity and so that person could quite easily have been a 'good Christian' had they had the opportunity. Some inclusivists believe that a person who rejects Christianity after they have been exposed to it can no longer be considered an anonymous Christian and cannot be saved; others believe that there will be the chance to apply their lifestyle to the truth at the moment of judgement.

Some Christians reject inclusivism because it does not seem to place enough emphasis on the importance of having faith in Jesus, which is a central message of the Bible. It also seems to reject the role of being a Christian and being part of the work of the Church.

Pluralism

Pluralism is the belief that there are many different paths to being saved and members of other religions can be saved not because they are Christians without realising it, but because their religion

God's plan to save

Jesus bridges the gap

Sinful humanity — *Perfect God*

Broken relationship with God

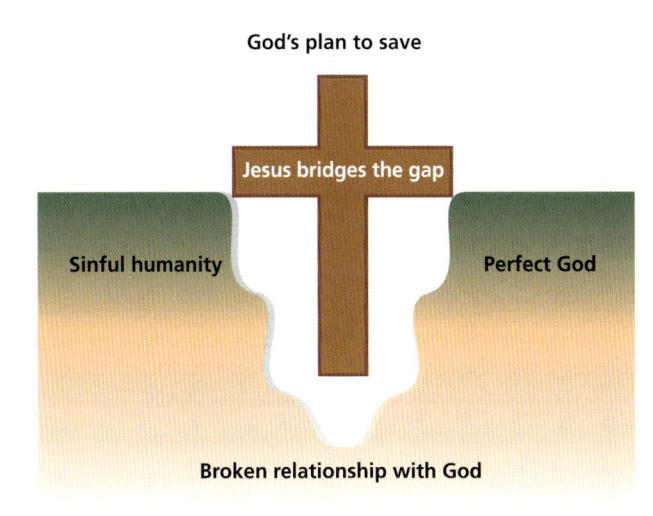

■ God's plan to save humanity from the effects of the Fall

is a valid way of journeying towards God. The idea here is that there are different worldviews and none should be seen as more or less valid than another. For Christian pluralists, the focus is on the benevolence of a God who would not wish to condemn any of creation to hell. The Parable of the Sheep and the Goats, for example, does not make any reference to religious belief and the general message of the Bible is about acceptance and *agape*.

Pluralists do not necessarily say that all people will be saved – some simply believe that different religious systems allow salvation because no human institution, like the Church, can be perfect, as some Christians might believe. However, to accept pluralism means that the role of Jesus is sidelined and that the Bible is no longer to be seen as such an important text. These two aspects make some Christians feel that pluralism simply cannot be true. These Christians might observe that God's love is not the same as God allowing all things and that some things are simply not true or correct.

Analyse and evaluate

Should a Christian definitely be an exclusivist?

Yes	No
There is little point in being a Christian if you are not going to 'buy in' to the centrality of Jesus' sacrifice.	To say that Jesus is the only way to salvation does not mean that Jesus does not save non-Christians.
It is possible to be an exclusivist but also to be humble enough to say that God might make decisions about salvation that are not for humans to discuss.	It is wrong to think that Jesus' sacrifice was so narrow that it did not save more than just those who are practising Christians.

Some might say that, although the Bible seems very clear and says that Jesus was the culmination of God's plan, the Bible may not be literally true.

Activities

Review

1. What are the key beliefs of exclusivists?
2. What are the similarities and differences between inclusivists and pluralists?

Develop

3. Look at the following passages and explain how each relates to the material in this spread: Matthew 7:21–23, John 14:1–9 and Acts 17:22–32.

Link

4. Look again at earlier work on God, salvation and grace (for example, spreads 1.3, 1.14 and 1.15). Does this material support or reject any of the three positions on these pages?

Debate

5. 'Going into a non-Christian place of worship, you cannot deny that the worship is as genuine as in a church.' Is this view valid and what is the impact on exclusivism?

Stretch

6. Look up how different people have defined 'religion' and try to make your own definition of what a religion *is* and what it *does*.

8.8 Dialogue between religious groups

Aim

To examine the importance of inter-faith dialogue to Christians

Starter

How could different religions together make a positive difference to society?

- What would be the impact of all religions working together for society?

Key word

Inter-faith dialogue – interactions between members of different religious groups

Inter-faith dialogue in twenty-first century Britain

In an increasingly multicultural society, which is also increasingly secular, many people would say that it is important for religions to work together to express their shared values, such as the importance of spirituality, charity work and relationships. '**Inter-faith dialogue**' is a term used to describe any interaction between different groups, although, of course, the emphasis is on positive encounters and co-operation. It is not limited to discussions about beliefs (although these are important in order to help understanding) but also includes action, such as charity work or work within society. There might be inter-faith representation at important events (for example, Remembrance Day) or school events and sometimes at religious worship.

Inter-faith dialogue seems necessary in twenty-first-century Britain because a lack of understanding about other faiths can lead to prejudice and discrimination. This can be seen after terrorist attacks, for example, when all members of a faith might be labelled as terrorists. Also, in an increasingly secular society where religion can be rejected because of its contribution to historic wars, there is a greater need for everyone to understand the positive things religions can bring to society.

Some examples of inter-faith dialogue in action include:

- **The Feast:** an organisation that seeks to bring together teenagers from different faiths to explore faith, create friendships and change lives. It is important that young people challenge the assumptions made by older generations about religion and its place in society. In 2021, a survey of adults in the UK found that 18–34-year-olds are twice as likely to pray as those aged 55 and over (source: Savanta ComRes).
- **The World Community for Christian Meditation:** a spiritual community focused on meditation that organises high-profile events which often involve famous guest speakers. It emphasises that in all religions there is a sense of mystery and a quest to develop spirituality and this is something that religions can explore together, because in many cases, religions use different vocabulary to describe the same things.
- **The Inter Faith Network for the United Kingdom:** an organisation that aims to promote understanding and co-operation through engagement, building relationships and communal action.

Christian views on inter-faith dialogue

All Christians believe that activities that promote peace and tolerance are good things – not only because all people are made in God's image and likeness (Genesis 1:26–27) but also because it

Source of authority

'You have heard that it was said, "Love your neighbour and hate your enemy." But I tell you, love your enemies and pray for those who persecute you, that you may be children of your Father in heaven.' (Matthew 5:43–44)

is not a human's place to judge others (Matthew 7:1). Pope Francis describes it as 'a necessary condition for peace in the world' (*Evangelii Gaudium*, 250) and the Church of England commits to participating in inter-faith dialogue.

For Christians, their approach to inter-faith dialogue will partly depend on their views about whether members of other religions can be saved:

- For pluralists, the focus of inter-faith work can be on joint participation and even joint worship. By believing that other faiths can be a road to salvation, Christian pluralists can focus on relationships and action.

- For exclusivists, the belief that the only true religion is Christianity means that they can participate as equals in charity work or work in society but dialogue to promote understanding might be seen as a step on the path to trying to convert someone. It is also important to recognise that the other faiths involved might well be thinking the same. This is one of the greatest barriers when it comes to further development of inter-faith work.

Analyse and evaluate

Is inter-faith dialogue important in twenty-first-century Britain?

Yes	No
Religions must stand together to oppose the increasing secularisation of society.	The focus for Christians should not be on dialogue as much as converting non-Christians.
It is only with understanding that we can prevent hatred and intolerance.	There are too many other issues within Christianity, like the fall in church attendance, to focus on inter-faith issues.

Some might say that a response to this question depends on what is meant or understood by 'dialogue'.

Activities

Review

1. What form might inter-faith dialogue take?
2. Explain two contrasting Christian approaches to inter-faith dialogue.

Develop

3. Research further an organisation that takes part in inter-faith dialogue activities and create a summary of its work and beliefs. You could use one of the organisations listed above or choose a different one.

Link

4. Find out about the work of local authority SACREs. How does their work contribute to both inter-faith dialogue and religion in schools?

Debate

5. Is it fair to say that inter-faith dialogue cannot be more effective because people might treat each other with respect but still think each other is wrong?

Stretch

6. Philosopher and theologian John Hick was a pluralist who wrote: 'As I spent time in mosques, synagogues, gurudwaras and temples as well as churches, something very important dawned on me ... the externals were different ... but at a deeper level ... essentially the same thing was going on' (*An Autobiography*, John Hick, 2002). Discuss this view.

8.9 Religion and wider society

Aim
To explore the importance of Christian values to individuals

Starter
What makes something British?

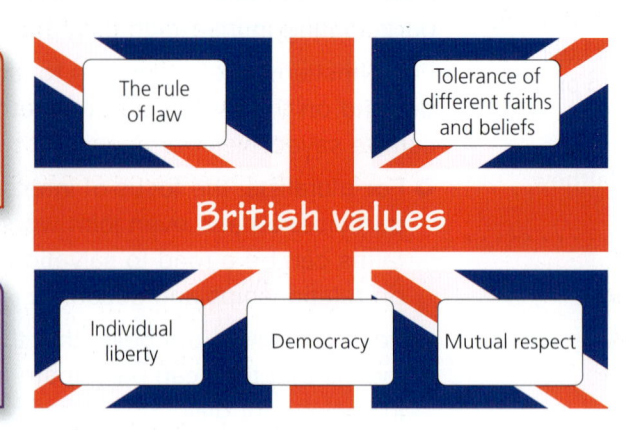

British values:
- The rule of law
- Tolerance of different faiths and beliefs
- Individual liberty
- Democracy
- Mutual respect

- Are the fundamental British values based on Christian values?

Source of authority

'Do not conform to the pattern of this world.' (Romans 12:2)

- The monarchy is perhaps the ultimate representation of British identity

- British identity changes with time

Key word

Proselytisation – the process of converting someone from one faith to another

Religion and national identity

National pride is evident at major events, such as sporting events and royal weddings, but British national identity has changed in recent years. It is more difficult to associate it with the more distant, traditional images of the past, which might include the Church of England as the established religion. It can also be argued that the media impacts what it means to be British because people are influenced by what they see as normal when they see things in the media. If the concept of the state is a group of ideas that represent the nation and its people, then we can see that the ideas that represent Britain today are different to those in the past – and Christianity is no longer a special part of this.

For some, too much focus on national identity can be dangerous, especially if the identity is centred around one particular idea. At the same time, studies have shown that too much focus on religion can make people feel less engaged with their nation. Many would argue that over the years, the Church of England has helped to define Britishness as well as being accepting of the changes in society.

Other denominations that are not so closely linked with Britishness, particularly the Roman Catholic Church, which is more global in outlook, see the link between religion and national identity differently. Some Christians might emphasise the importance of being *in* the world but not *of* the world. This means that Christians should remember that they are part of society alongside non-Christians but they should not let worldly things (for example, material things or non-Christian values) rule their lives. It is important for Christians to hold fast to their integrity in the face of outside pressures to go against their values.

Proselytisation

Proselytisation is the process of converting someone to another faith. Some might find the idea of Christians converting those of other faiths offensive because:

Source of authority

'Therefore go and make disciples of all nations, baptising them in the name of the Father and of the Son and of the Holy Spirit.' (Matthew 28:19)

The monarch is Supreme Governor of the Church of England

- diversity within society is important and consensus is not a necessity. Some Christians would reject this because they believe the Christian message is the truth that all need to follow
- freedom of expression must be protected and proselytisation gets in the way of this
- historically, British values, as well as the values of the Church of England, were spread with the British Empire, which is considered an outdated approach.

Christian approaches to proselytisation can vary:

- Some Christians emphasise the need to preach directly about the Christian message of God's love and offer of salvation.
- Others, such as the Church of England and the Catholic Church, believe that it is important to understand where other faiths are coming from and to engage with them at this level. Churches should also emphasise their own hospitality and not present themselves as being against others.
- Many Christians feel they should show others what Christianity is about through their actions and through being open about their faith and then leave the rest to God, praying that their example will have an impact.

Analyse and evaluate

Is British national identity today linked to Christianity?

Yes	No
Even though it is not explicitly linked, British values come from a long history of Christianity being at the centre of British life.	People do not listen to the teachings of the Church of England but there is still a clear British identity. The two are clearly no longer linked.
The Church of England is the established religion and successfully helps to define what it is to be British, even in broad terms.	Being British is about co-existing with people of many different faiths and no faith.

Some might say that being British is linked to the shared values of religions and that religions in Britain are, in the majority, Christian, so while national identity does not rely on Christianity specifically, it does rely on religion.

Activities

Review

1. Why might some say that national identity and religion should be kept separate?
2. Why is proselytisation a challenge for some people?

Develop

3. What might the views of exclusivists, inclusivists and pluralists be about proselytisation?

Link

4. Look back at spread 2.14 and explain the place of evangelism in twenty-first-century Britain for different Christians.

Debate

5. 'Society will never be in harmony if religious people try to convert others.' Do you think this is a fair view? What are the implications of agreeing or disagreeing?

Stretch

6. Based on all the material in this spread so far, what are the arguments for and against the idea that religion should be a completely private matter?

8.10 Christian attitudes towards each other

World Council of Churches

- Will ecumenism bring about a more peaceful society?

Aim
To examine Christian approaches to ecumenism

Starter
Choose two different Christian denominations. What are the similarities and differences between the two?

Key word
Intra-faith communication – examining your own faith in the context of inter-faith dialogue

Source of authority
'[Jesus prayed] may [they] be one as we are one – I in them and you in me – so that they may be brought to complete unity.' (John 17:22–23)

Ecumenism

The desire of Jesus was to establish one Church that brought together believers until the Parousia (Matthew 16:18). Some would say that the state of the Church today makes it very unappealing to potential converts because of both the in-fighting and the lack of clarity about what is true. For them, the purpose of ecumenism would be to unite the Church. Others would celebrate the diversity in expressions of worship and argue that freedom of expression is available within the Christian tradition. For them, ecumenism is about celebrating what people have in common.

For some Protestants, certain aspects of the Catholic Church make uniformity of belief too difficult. For example:

- the authority of the Church and its leaders. Catholics might respond that the Church is the way of Christians getting access to God's grace
- the focus on sacraments, saints and objects to help worship, instead of direct access to God. Catholics might respond that it is important to get all the help possible to come into relationship with a transcendent creator
- beliefs in transubstantiation and purgatory
- the lack of leadership roles for women, the treatment of remarried people and other ethical issues.

Catholics believe that only the Church holds the fullness of God's message. Other denominations are referred to as 'separated' brothers and sisters and reconciliation is considered the aim of all. Catholics believe that other denominations can have barriers to salvation for their followers.

Intra-faith communication

Intra-faith communication is part of the process of dialogue with others within Christianity. It is about understanding that dialogue with others leads a Christian to learn more about their own faith. It can encourage humility and empathy, as well as openness and hospitality, which are virtues that all Christians should be proud of.

Good intra-faith communication will cause a Christian community (or individual) to reflect on what their faith looks like to external eyes. They might reflect on the disunity in their own denomination or consider what it might feel like for someone to realise that Christians believe that they are wrong.

Christians might feel it is important to stress what different denominations have in common. They might draw on key beliefs (such as the sacrifice and resurrection of Christ) as well as passages from the Bible (such as the Good Samaritan). They might reflect on how far Christians have come in their acknowledgement of the need to work together and might reflect on the impact of a more secular society. Throughout history, there have been ups and downs when it comes to relationships between different denominations.

A World Council of Churches conference

Many Christian charities bring different denominations together

Analyse and evaluate

Will ecumenism ruin Christianity?

Yes	No
To allow different things to be true will simply water down Christian beliefs and it will be unclear what is true.	Christians agree on what matters. The remainder of Christian teachings are down to personal preference.
Focusing too much on other Christians will stop the important work of all Christians to preach the Gospel to those outside the Church.	Ecumenism should make Christians learn about other denominations in order to get closer to the truth, which has been lost in all the splits since the time of Jesus.
Some may point to the impact of intra-faith communication after ecumenical work. Anything that allows an individual Christian, a local community or a church as a whole to become more hospitable and open to others must be a good thing.	

Activities

Review

1. What issues might some Christians have with ecumenism?
2. Explain what is understood by intra-faith communication.

Develop

3. What impact might ecumenical work have on British society? Think about your local area as well as the country as a whole. You could research local groups to add to your notes.

Link

4. Look at spread 2.16 and add key points from it to your notes for this spread.

Debate

5. 'Intra-faith communication is just an excuse to ignore those around you that you disagree with.' How significant is this view?

Stretch

6. Find out about the debates that took place at the Lambeth Conference in 2022. What areas of similarity and divergence are found between different Anglican churches? Do they matter?

Dialogue between religious and non-religious views each other   8.10 Christian attitudes towards

8.11 Dialogue with atheism and agnosticism

Non-Christians might argue that it's impossible to believe in God and enjoy life

Aim
To explore the shared and differing values between atheists and agnostics and Christians

Starter
Should atheists try to convert Christians?

Key words
Atheism – the certainty that there is no God
Agnosticism – not believing nor disbelieving in a god or religion; being unsure about the existence of God

Top tip
Study this spread alongside the next two spreads.

Shared values

While many people who identify with the worldviews of **atheism** and **agnosticism** would relate to the groups to be studied in the next two spreads, it is important to consider the values and ideals of the wider groups. Just like with Christianity, it is important not to assume that all atheists or agnostics have the same lenses as each other.

Many would argue that it is important to keep an open mind about the world and to examine evidence that supports and also challenges our beliefs. For most of his career, the philosopher Antony Flew (1923–2010) was an atheist but he began to believe in the existence of a god (though not the God of most religions) later in his life. Christians believe that our ability to reason is God-given and Catholics, in particular, emphasise that reasoning helps us to come to God as much as our faith.

Some atheists and agnostics from Christian countries such as Britain reject the religious beliefs of Christianity but accept aspects of Christian morality. Even famous atheists agree that Jesus was a great moral teacher. Indeed, because atheism and agnosticism are not ways of life, there are no values attached to them and so an atheist or agnostic would need to identify their own values.

Disagreement and difference

Atheists, agnostics and Christians agree with the basic principles of fairness, freedom and the protection of the vulnerable in society but there are major areas of disagreement and difference.

Central authority

- A key area of disagreement is that Christians are likely to take their moral values from the belief that there is an authority that should be seen as central (for example, God or the Bible).
- Atheists or agnostics are more likely to look at the consequences of actions to decide if they are right or wrong.

Spiritual matters

Atheists and agnostics are likely to place different emphases on spiritual matters:

- Atheists will focus their attention on physical things. For them, spirituality refers to feelings such as awe and wonder.
- Agnostics might be more open to a type of spirituality that reflects the fact that they are undecided about their beliefs. For example, they might refer to 'the universe' as working in a particular way or the idea that there is more to the world than meets the eye.

- Christians tend to link all non-physical things to God or the divine spark in humans.

Trust in a higher power

Where atheists will most radically disagree with Christians is in the idea that we should place our trust in a higher power.

- Some atheists have described Christians as being deluded and said that parents who bring up their children as Christians are brainwashing them. Christians might respond by observing that their relationship with God helps them to 'just know' that it is true and want to share that with their own children.
- As atheists and agnostics do not experience God in the way that many Christians do, it is very difficult for dialogue between the two groups to be fruitful.

Design or first cause arguments

Christians might observe that reasoning can lead them to understand that God exists. They might point to the design argument or first cause argument to suggest that evidence from the universe leads to a belief in God. These might be rejected, of course, from other evidence in the world, such as evolution or suffering.

Analyse and evaluate

Is there any point in dialogue between Christians and agnostics?

Yes	No
With many shared values and the fact that they share and live in society together, dialogue is always important.	The differences will never be resolved and so dialogue may lead to tensions or clashes and so should be avoided.
Christians might argue that dialogue leads to shared values and this provides an opportunity for evangelism.	The principle of freedom of belief suggests that people should be left to believe what they want.

Some might question the sort of dialogue that should be shared and suggest that dialogue to do with morals or society is acceptable but should not touch on God's existence.

Activities

Review

1. In your view, what is the most significant similarity between atheists and Christians?
2. In terms of the relationship with Christianity, what is the difference between atheists and agnostics?

Develop

3. Which of Jesus' moral teachings need no belief in God to be relevant to people today?

Link

4. Look at spreads 6.12–6.14. How might Christians use some of these topic areas to engage with atheists and/or agnostics?

Debate

5. 'Atheists have made their decision so Christians should avoid dialogue with them.' How valid is this approach to evangelism?

Stretch

6. 'Faith is the great cop-out, the great excuse to evade the need to think and evaluate evidence' (Richard Dawkins, 1992). Find out more about Richard Dawkins and his relationship with religious belief and present a summary to the class.

8.12 Dialogue with humanism

Aim

To explore the shared and differing values between humanists and Christians

Starter

What is a human?

Sources of authority

'If you declare with your mouth, "Jesus is Lord," and believe in your heart that God raised him from the dead, you will be saved.' (Romans 10:9)

'Jesus said, "I have come that they may have life, and have it to the full."' (John 10:10)

What is humanism?

Humanism sees the world using reason, science and logic rather than the approach taken by religions. For humanists, only humans can decide the course of life, not God, and people can have a full and good life without God or religion. God does not provide moral authority – this is provided by reason and a concern for other people – and there is no afterlife to look forward to: the focus must be on human decisions searching for happiness in this world.

To be a humanist, a person does not have to be part of a group, nor do they have to hold a set of beliefs, although Humanists International records a list of typical beliefs in its Amsterdam Declaration, first set out in 1952 and updated in 2022.

Some of the principles of the Amsterdam Declaration are set out in the table on the opposite page, with possible Christian responses to them.

Analyse and evaluate

Do humanists and Christians have more in common than they have differences?

Yes	No
Both groups work for the good of humans and the natural world and keep that at the heart of their decision making.	When one group believes that the other is wrong and should convert to its views, the differences must be greater than the similarities.
Although for different reasons, both groups celebrate everything positive that humans have achieved.	That one group believes everything comes from God and another rejects this is too fundamental a difference to agree with the statement.

As there is no such thing as a typical humanist, some might argue that the question can never be fully answered.

Activities

Review

1. Use the 'Shared values and areas of disagreement' table to state and explain the main similarities between Christians and humanists.
2. State and explain the potential areas of disagreement and difference between Christians and humanists.

Develop

3. Look into the work of Humanists UK and add your findings to your notes.

Link

4. Look back on other material from Chapter 5 onwards. Where might there be other areas of shared values and potential disagreement?

Debate

5. Do you think that by having a list of opinions and by being a community, humanists are essentially just a form of religion?

Stretch

6. Do you think humanism has more in common with Christianity or with other faiths? Try to explain a range of responses to this question.

Shared values and areas of disagreement between humanists and Christians	
Amsterdam Declaration	**Christian response**
Humanists strive to be ethical.	Christians of all denominations would share this value.
Humanists believe that there are benefits to helping and not harming other living things.	Christians might point to the teachings of Jesus such as the Parable of the Good Samaritan (Luke 10:25–37) and the Parable of the Sheep and the Goats (Matthew 25:31–46) to agree with this point.
Humanists believe that ethics come from reason and compassion and need no source outside humanity.	Some, such as Catholic Christians, believe that reason is a valid way of coming to know God and a useful tool for people. All Christians believe that our ability to use reason is a God-given gift, which is in opposition to humanism, although disagreeing on the source of reason might not affect life significantly.
Humanists believe that individuals have worth and dignity.	Christians celebrate human life as being specially made and chosen by God (for example, Genesis 1:26–27). The idea of individual worth and dignity is a concept important to Christians.
Humanists believe that every human has complete freedom (as long as it is compatible with the rights of others).	Christians believe that God's gift of free will is central to the story of Christians. They would also agree that human freedom must not negatively impact others but where humanists decide what to do depending on how they impact others, Christians decide what they do by consulting their sources of authority, such as the Bible.
Humanists support peace, democracy, the rule of law and universal human rights.	Christians agree with these fundamental aspects of life. Passages such as the Beatitudes (Matthew 5:1–2) remind Christians that they have a duty to protect the vulnerable in society.
Humanists reject racism and prejudice and celebrate diversity.	Christians agree with this approach. Some Christians come into conflict in society where personal freedom and diversity seem to contradict traditional Christian views, especially in the area of sexual ethics.
Humanists believe that there is a responsibility to society, including future generations and other sentient beings and the natural world.	This links well with the Christian view of stewardship as Christians should look after the planet for future generations. However, Christian stewardship comes from the idea that the planet belongs to God.
Humanists celebrate reason.	Christians celebrate reason as coming from God but also believe that the use of faith to understand the world is important. For Christians, correct use of reason comes from having faith.
Humanists believe that science needs to be balanced by human values.	Christians celebrate scientific advances as gifts from God and would agree that ethical living needs to make sure that not all scientific advances are pursued (such as weaponry). Some Christians might not place as much emphasis on science and instead focus on what the Bible reveals. Although Christians would agree with this humanist belief, they would want to reflect God in the statement.
Humanists believe that human life is about fulfilment.	Christians agree with this but might see that fulfilment as coming in different ways. By Jesus reversing the effects of the Fall, Christians believe humans can be fully fulfilled.
Humanists treasure creativity and beauty.	In the eyes of Christians, both of these come from God. Just like humanists, they believe that the arts and the search for the sense of awe, wonder and peace are important uses of people's time.
Humanists do not believe there is one source of authority and this means that beliefs can develop over time.	All Christians believe there is one source of authority and so disagree with humanism here. Some Christians believe that this authority is fixed in the Bible and others with more liberal lenses believe that Christianity can and should develop over time.
Humanists do not wish to impose views on others.	Christianity is a missionary religion but many Christians believe that evangelism should be by example, rather than by imposition. Most Christians believe that being a Christian leads to salvation and so some would want to impose their views on others.
Humanists want to exchange ideas and co-operate with others.	Christianity celebrates dialogue with other faiths and those of no faith but ultimately, this co-operation should be linked to the desire of Christians for people to convert.
Humanism is an alternative to religion.	This is a key point of disagreement as Christians believe that humans are made by God in order to be religious and worship God with all their hearts (for example, John 4:24).

8.13 Dialogue with secularism

Aim

To explore the shared values and areas of disagreement between Christianity and secularism

Starter

Using your knowledge of secularism, predict what areas of agreement and disagreement there may be with Christianity.

- Should the state have anything at all to do with religion?

Top tip

Someone can support secularism and be a humanist and/or an atheist, so you should study these pages alongside the previous two spreads.

Source of authority

'Then Jesus said to them, "Give back to Caesar what is Caesar's and to God what is God's."' (Mark 12:17)

Shared values between Christianity and secularism

The National Secular Society identifies the main principles of secularism as:

1. Separation of religion and state.
2. Freedom of belief (or non-belief).
3. Equality of all to avoid some being advantaged or disadvantaged.

Shared values	
Secularism	**Christianity**
Secularists want to live peacefully within society and accept society's rules.	The Bible suggests that Christians should live peacefully within society and accept society's rules over them as well as God's rules over them. Some Christians would argue that this promotes the separation of Church and state.
Secularists reject religion within schools. They might argue that the home is the place for people to teach and practise religion.	The Bible assumes parents to be the first teachers of children and God's commandments should be 'impressed' onto children by their parents: 'talk about them when you sit at home and when you walk along the road' (Deuteronomy 6:7). Some Christians might accept this approach and be happy with the separation of Church and state.
Secularists reject the Church of England as the established Church.	Some Christians might also reject the Church of England as the established Church.
Secularists focus on equality and justice.	Some Christians might also agree with the secularist focus on equality and justice.

Areas of difference between Christianity and secularism

Areas of difference	
Secularism	**Christianity**
Secularists want to separate the Church and state.	In British society, some Christians, especially from the Church of England, might be nervous that separating Church and state would lead to lost opportunities for evangelism and also harm the British way of life.
For secularists, giving priority to one group over another can lead to disharmony in society and they would argue that it is wrong for laws or ways of life to be based on Christian principles when not everyone is a Christian.	Christians might reject this approach on the basis that the point of an established religion is to provide a framework for a nation's way of life. They might also argue that just because everyone isn't a Christian, it does not mean that Christianity is not right or true.
Secularists believe in freedom of belief (or non-belief).	For some Christians, the main issue with secularism is the way that some secularists are aggressively against religion. Christians feel that the positive experiences that so many people obtain from religion are ignored by the secularist agenda. Some Christians might feel that secularism weakens the moral position of society and undermines the sanctity of life or the value of marriage and so on.

Analyse and evaluate

Does religion have any role left in society?

Yes	No
The example religion sets in its works of justice and charity demonstrates the important role it has in society around the world.	As society becomes more secular, religion has more in common with a leisure activity than anything else. This shows that it has no further role in society.
Religion supports people through difficult times and helps people to mark key moments of life.	Even though Christianity is part of the fabric of Britain, laws are passed that Christians disagree with. This shows that religion has no further role.
Spirituality is very popular among people now even if religion is not. Religion simply needs to 'catch up' and modernise and then it will have a role in society.	

Activities

Review
1. State and explain areas where Christianity and secularism might agree.
2. How might Christianity and secularism disagree?

Develop
3. Look into the work of the National Secular Society and add to your notes on this topic.

Link
4. Use some of the earlier pages in Chapter 8 to explore the question of whether British society would be significantly different if Church and state were separate.

Debate
5. Could secularism harm society more than Christianity could?

Stretch
6. Find out about the idea of Catholic Social Teaching and the Joint Public Issues Team. How could the impact of these approaches contribute to the debate about the role of religion in society?

8.14 Christian views and attitudes

Religious and secular values

While it is clear that religious and non-religious values overlap in many ways, the ultimate area of difference is to do with the existence of God and the centrality of religion to life. In Matthew 13:44, Jesus tells the short parable of how the kingdom of heaven is like hidden treasure found in a field. When someone discovers it, they sell everything in order to buy the field. Jesus was teaching that finding faith is worth everything and this precious thing is something that Christians find it hard not to share with others.

Throughout the Bible, faith and good works sit side by side as the marks of true religious beliefs. Christians find it hard to separate the two if instructed by society. However, secular societies, such as France and the USA, exist happily where faith is central to daily life but the state is not officially religious. Many Christians fear the separation of Church and state because they imagine the closing down of religion but this is very different to the reality elsewhere.

Different Christian views

A Christian's views on pluralism, inclusivism and exclusivism will be key to determining their approach to dialogue with other worldviews.

- **Pluralists** might worry less about what others believe and so they might see dialogue with other worldviews as a good way to connect and work together. They believe diversity in expression and belief should be celebrated.
- **Inclusivists** might see good ways of life in others and even want to learn from others but ultimately would want to express the Christian message to those they encounter.
- **Exclusivists** aim for consensus because they believe that the Christian faith is truth and this must be shared so that people might be converted and saved. Dialogue is therefore not about compromise but a way to find out how other people view the world (their lens) in order to help them understand the Christian message better.

For some, the idea that religion is declining in society is the driving force behind the need to promote an agenda of secularisation. However, many would argue that religion is actually reviving, even though the traditional religious worldviews or lenses seem to be less relevant today. Some look for modern worship; other Christians have a liberal worldview that promotes freedom of expression. They might argue that Jesus looked after the marginalised and it is important that those on the edges of society today are recognised and welcomed.

Aim
To examine Christian approaches to issues to do with dialogue with other worldviews

Starter
Which group do you think is the greatest threat to Christianity in Britain: atheists, agnostics, humanists or secularists?

Source of authority
'Jesus replied, "Love the Lord your God ... love your neighbour as yourself. All the Law and the Prophets hang on these two commandments."' (Matthew 22:37–40)

Jesus' teaching often began with dialogue with those who disagreed with him

Pope Francis

Some Christians would argue that dialogue is the only way to exist in future society. Whatever their agendas, these Christians might observe that by the Church listening to the feelings and wishes of others, especially younger people, it might be able to be a Church that is welcoming to all. These Christians would argue that the teachings of the Bible and the way of life that Jesus promoted are timeless but need to be communicated appropriately to each new generation. Pope Francis emphasised the need to listen to all by involving young people from church communities and faith schools in a global shake-up of the Catholic way of life between 2021 and 2023.

Analyse and evaluate

Should Christians engage in dialogue with other worldviews?

Yes	No
It is never wrong for anyone to engage in dialogue with others who hold different views.	Peace is a shared value and so Christians should avoid conflict and allow those who disagree with them freedom of expression.
Exclusivists might argue that engaging with other worldviews is the only way to evangelise effectively.	Dialogue suggests compromise, not consensus, and Christians should never water down the truth of Jesus Christ.

Some might argue that for most Christians, daily life is not about dialogue but simply living life faithfully and developing their individual relationship with God. Dialogue is something undertaken by a small group of trained people.

Activities

Review

1. Why is the Christian faith something that Christians might want to share?
2. Why might it be an assumption to declare that people are moving away from Christianity?

Develop

3. Discuss how much of being a Christian in modern British society requires someone to be publicly open about their faith. How does this impact the discussion on this topic?

Link

4. Having completed the course, what do you think are the three most important aspects of being a Christian?

Debate

5. Is it acceptable for people to call themselves Christians if they don't regularly go to church?

Stretch

6. What do you think are the biggest challenges facing Christianity in the next 50 years?

8.14 Christian views and attitudes — Dialogue between religious and non-religious views

Summary activities

CHECK YOUR NOTES

STAGE 1

Check that you have detailed notes that cover the following:

- [ ] How Christianity can be seen as the established religion in the UK today
- [ ] The role that Christianity plays within public life: government, holidays, schools
- [ ] The concept of secularisation
- [ ] How religion and secular law may clash on views of equality
- [ ] How religion and science may clash on issues such as abortion, fertility, euthanasia and genetic manipulation
- [ ] Understand different beliefs and attitudes that Christians have to each other and to other faiths: exclusivism, inclusivism and pluralism
- [ ] Consider the importance of inter-faith dialogue
- [ ] The relationship between religion and national identity
- [ ] Christian attitudes towards non-religious ideas such as atheism, agnosticism, humanism and secularism
- [ ] Potential areas of agreement and disagreement between religious and secular ideas

GETTING READY

STAGE 2

Quick quiz

1. How is the monarch connected to Christianity in the UK?
2. State two ways that Christianity influences public life in the UK.
3. How might some Christians disagree with secular equality laws?
4. How might some Christians disagree with scientific developments in medical ethics?
5. What does the term 'exclusivism' mean?
6. What is ecumenism?
7. Give one reason why a Christian might engage in inter-faith dialogue.
8. What is proselytisation?
9. What is the main difference between atheists and agnostics?
10. Give two areas where humanists may disagree with Christian values.

Quick quiz answers can be found online at www.hoddereducation.co.uk/ocr-gcse-rs-answers

ACTIVITIES

STAGE 3

1. Create a mind map showing different issues where religious thought clashes with secular law and with science. Aim to illustrate each spoke with two to three development points.
2. **AO1 focus:** Key terms. Make a set of flashcards for the key terms used in this chapter. You should aim to have a definition and a development point on each card. Where appropriate you could add a source of wisdom or authority.

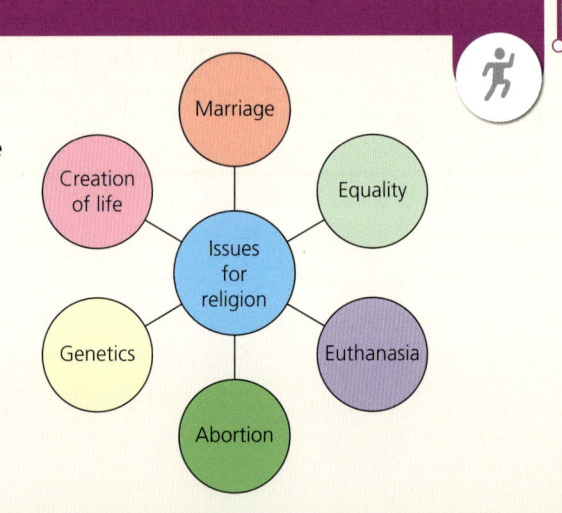

Issues for religion: Marriage, Equality, Euthanasia, Abortion, Genetics, Creation of life

GET PRACTISING

STAGE 3

Use this section to help you develop your understanding of how to answer questions on this topic.

Ask the expert

Khalil asks:

Although I spent a lot of time improving my planning on the longer essays, my marks are not improving by much. I find that I get through the things I plan to include quite quickly and often have time left over at the end. My teacher has talked about developing each point but I'm not too sure what she means.

Khalil's essay plan for an essay on euthanasia:

Intro: Euthanasia is a concern for Christians

P1: Catholic and Anglican statements reject euthanasia

P2: Euthanasia does not respect sanctity of life – image of God

P3: Bible is against euthanasia – do not kill

P4: Counterargument: quality of life, could be most loving thing

C: So allowing euthanasia would be a problem for Christians

The expert says:

Khalil's essay plan is reasonable enough, so the important thing for the higher levels will be the amount of depth he is able to get into each paragraph. He has to ensure that he does not just state arguments but evaluates them, weighing up how strong the point is. There are lots of different ways of doing this but one way is to use the acronym PACE.

- **P**–oint: The opening sentence states the argument
- **A**–nalyse: Elaborate upon the point explaining what it means and why it is relevant
- **C**–riticise: Offer a criticism of the original point if you are able
- **E**–valuate: Reach a judgement about the point in your opening sentence – does it defeat the criticism?

Khalil has attempted to use this technique in the paragraph below.

Khalil's sample paragraph:

One argument that some liberal Christians use to support euthanasia is to make reference to the quality of life (POINT). This takes into account the fact that for some people in the last stages of a terminal illness, their life may no longer be worth living as they may be unable to do anything for themselves and they may be in great pain. It would seem that allowing them to die under these circumstances could be an act of love (ANALYSE). However, many other Christians would have concerns about this type of approach as they worry that this is open to abuse. Some elderly people or people with disabilities might feel that they are a burden to their families and feel pressure to opt for euthanasia (CRITICISE). So the quality of life argument has to be used with caution and should only apply in very limited circumstances (EVALUATE).

Glossary

Abortion deliberately terminating a pregnancy

Absolute pacifists/pacifism the belief that it is never right to take part in war, even in self-defence

Adultery sex between a married person and someone else that they are not married to

Advent the season of preparation for Christmas

Agape Greek word for 'love' emphasising unconditional love; the Greek word used to describe God's love for the world

Agnostic someone who believes that we cannot know whether God exists

Agnosticism not believing nor disbelieving in a god or religion; being unsure about the existence of God

Akhirah belief in the afterlife and the Day of Judgement

Allah Arabic name for God

Al-Ashari a group that believe Allah is the cause and controller of everything

Al-Jannah heaven

Al-Nubuwwah prophethood

Al-Qadr predestination; belief that Allah is in control of the outcome of good and evil actions

Annulment a declaration that a marriage was invalid, so that legally it never properly existed

Anonymous Christians living a Christian life without knowing it

Anthropic principle the belief that the universe was created/allowed to evolve by God to bring about intelligent human life

Apocalyptic beliefs about the complete destruction of the world at the end of time

Apocalyptic warfare any form of warfare that can result in widespread and utter destruction of huge areas

Archangels higher-ranking angels

Arranged marriage where the couple are introduced to each other by family members who see the marriage as a suitable or good match

Ascension Jesus being taken up into heaven

Ashura Shi'a commemoration of Imam Hussain's martyrdom

Atheism the certainty that there is no God

Atheist someone who believes that God does not exist

Atonement repairing the relationship between God and humankind

Bada' Shi'a belief that Allah can change a person's destiny

Barzakh 'barrier'; the intermediate state between death and judgement, when the soul has left the body

Believer's baptism baptising someone who has decided for themselves to follow Jesus

Benevolent loving, compassionate, kindly

Celibacy abstaining from sex, particularly for religious reasons

Charismatic in Christianity, the idea that the Holy Spirit's gifts are in operation today

Charismatic worship worship that draws on the Holy Spirit's presence

Christmas the celebration of the Incarnation

Church spiritual the Church in heaven

Church temporal the Church on Earth

Civil partnership a legal relationship which can be registered by two people who aren't related to each other. Civil partnerships are now available to both same-sex couples and opposite-sex couples.

Clergy a religious leader such as a priest or vicar who is ordained/authorised to carry out religious duties

Cohabitation when a couple in a relationship live together without being married

Commendation the part of a funeral service where the person who has died is handed over (commended) to God's love

Committal the part of a funeral service where the person who has died is given (committed) to burial or cremation

Conditional pacifists/pacifism the belief that war and violence are wrong in principle, but there may be occasional circumstances where war may lead to less suffering than not going to war

Confirmation the service when someone takes on the responsibilities of their faith for themselves

Complementarian the belief that men and women, although equal in status, have different but complementary roles and responsibilities

Contraception use of various methods to avoid a woman becoming pregnant, particularly by artificial means

Cosmological argument an argument for the existence of God that claims that God has to be the cause or explanation of the world

Creed a statement of beliefs

Crucifixion the death of Jesus on the cross

Culture the ideas, customs and social behaviour of a particular people or society

Dedication a service that dedicates a baby to the church community

Denomination a group within a religion

Devotion a type of religious observance

Divine providence the protective care and provision of God

Divorce the legal dissolution or ending of a marriage

Dominion the idea that Christians are to rule and take control, in this case over animals and the natural world

Du'a a personal prayer or supplication

Easter the festival when Christians celebrate the resurrection

Ecumenism work for Christian unity

Egalitarian the principle that all people are equal and deserve equal rights and opportunities

Eid-ul-Adha festival of sacrifice

Eid-ul-Fitr festival marking the end of Ramadan

Eid-ul-Ghadeer Shi'a festival commemorating the choice of Ali as the Prophet Muhammad's successor

Embedded inequalities the idea that inequality or unfairness is built into the structure and working of society

Eschatology the aspect of belief to do with death, judgement and the afterlife

Established religion the state religion of a country; the religion officially recognised by a country

Eternal separate to or outside of time

Eucharist one of the central Christian church services where bread and wine are used to remember the body and blood of Jesus

Euthanasia literally 'a good death'; deliberately ending a person's life to relieve suffering

Evangelism the process of spreading the message of Christianity

Evil the opposite of good; something that brings suffering

Exclusivism the belief that only Christians will be saved

Extempore prayer using own words for prayer; prayer where the words are unplanned

Fidelity faithfulness to a cause or person

Five pillars of Islam the most important duties for Sunni Muslims

Forced marriage where one or both members of a couple are married without a choice

Forgiving able to move on from feeling angry or from wishing to punish

Forgiveness a deliberate decision to no longer hold anger or resentment towards a person for their actions

Free will the ability to make choices for ourselves

General revelation refers to knowledge of God that is acquired through natural means that are available to all humans

Genetic manipulation using technology to change genes

Good something that is approved of or is of a high standard

Good Friday the day in the year when Jesus' crucifixion is remembered

Gospel (Injil) scripture revealed to Isa

Grace the unconditional gift God gives of love

Greater Jihad spiritual or inner struggle

Heaven a place of eternal happiness and reward

Hell a place of eternal punishment or separation from God

Heterosexual being sexually attracted to members of the opposite sex

Holy war a war where the main cause or purpose of the war is religious OR a war that God has commanded

Holy Week the week before Easter, remembering Jesus' time in Jerusalem

Homosexual being sexually attracted to members of the same sex; in some contexts, the word can be intended as a slur

Humanism an approach to life that focuses on human beings (rather than a divine being) holding the potential to develop society

Ihram state of purity and dedication that Muslims must enter before performing Hajj; also, two pieces of white clothing worn by male pilgrims

Immanent part of everyday life; within the human universe

Incarnation the term used to describe God becoming a human being in Jesus

Inclusivism the belief that non-Christians can be saved because they are anonymous Christians

Inconsistent triad the idea that the goodness of God, the power of God and the existence of evil are incompatible

Infant baptism the baptism of babies

Informal worship worship that has no set structure
Intercessions prayers for others
Islam 'peace' and 'submission to Allah', Allah's chosen religion for humanity
I'tikaf retreat
Jahannam hell
Jihad struggle
Judge someone who has the authority to decide right from wrong or make decisions about a person
Just fair
Just war theory the belief that some wars are morally justifiable and that there are criteria for deciding whether to go to war and how that war should be fought
Justice fairness, giving people what they deserve
Kabaa cube-shaped building, first house of Allah in Makkah (Mecca)
Khalifah (Caliph) successor or leader after the Prophet Muhammad (PBUH); representative of Allah on Earth
Khutba sermon given on Friday and other major Islamic festivals such as on Eid days
Khums 20 per cent tax paid by Shi'a Muslims
Kutub holy books
Lay people church members who are not ordained
Laylat al Qadr Night of Power
Lent the period of preparation for Easter
Lesser Jihad removing evil from society with the aim of making the world an abode of peace
Liturgical prayer using prayers that are in set forms
Liturgical worship formal worship using set words, forms and processes
Liturgy a formula for formal public worship
Martyrdom dying or being killed for religious beliefs
Ma'ruf doing what is right
Merciful compassionate
Messiah the awaited Jewish promised one; anointed one
Metaphorical figurative or symbolic or not literally the case
Missionary someone who spreads the message of Christianity
Monotheistic the belief that there is only one God
Moral argument the idea that the existence of right and wrong provides evidence or proof of the existence of God
Moral evil evil that is a result of human free choices

Munkar doing what is wrong
Muslim a believer in Islam
Mu'tazillite a group that believed everyone has freewill and is responsible for their actions
Mystical experience a direct experience of God, or ultimate reality; a sense of the oneness of all things
Nabi prophet
Nativity the story of Jesus' birth
Natural evil evil that comes from nature or natural sources
Niyyah intention, made before prayer
Non-violent direct action protest techniques that go beyond normal lawful means but are peaceful in nature
Omniscient all-knowing; able to know everything there is to know
Omnipotent all powerful; able to do anything
Ordination/ordain a ceremony where someone is authorised to become a priest or vicar
Original sin the first sin of Adam and Eve that is passed on to humans
Parousia the second coming of Chris
Pauline referring to St Paul, an Apostle of Jesus who wrote many letters in the New Testament
Persecution bad treatment of a group, perhaps because of religious beliefs
Personal able to be related to as a person, not an invisible force
Pilgrimage a journey to a place of significance
Pinnacle the high point of something
Polytheism the idea that there are many gods
Prayer communicating with God in one of many different ways
Premarital sex sex that takes place before marriage
Prophet a person chosen by Allah to teach humans what is right and wrong
Proselytisation the process of converting someone from one faith to another
Psalms (Zabur) scripture revealed to Dawud
Purgatory a place of cleansing to prepare a soul for heaven
Qibla direction of prayer, towards Makkah (Mecca) in Saudi Arabia
Radicalisation the process by which an individual or group comes to support extreme views
Rak'ats cycles or sequences of actions during prayer
Ramadan the month of fasting for Muslims

Glossary

Rasul messenger

Reason the use of intelligence, philosophy and argument to reach a conclusion

Reconcile to restore a broken relationship, often as the step after forgiveness

Reconciliation the restoring of a good relationship after a conflict or disagreement

Remarriage where someone marries again after divorce or the death of their first husband/wife

Resurrection rising from the dead; having been completely dead and then coming back to life again

Revelation the idea that God shows truths about himself to human beings, for example, through the Bible or religious experience

Righteous morally good

Risalah 'message', referring to belief in prophets and messengers

Rite a formal religious action

Rite of passage a ceremony that marks the transition from one stage of life to the next

Ritual a series of rites brought together in a ceremony

Sabbath a day of rest and focus on God

Sacrament a Christian religious ceremony or ritual that is seen as a special way of accessing God's grace

Sacred set apart, holy

Sadaqah voluntary alms

Sahifah (Scrolls) scriptures revealed to Ibrahim and Musa

Salah/Salat Muslim prayer

Sanctity of life the belief that all human life is sacred

Sawm fasting

Secular not connected to religious ideas

Secularisation the decline in the influence of religion over time

Shahadah the Muslim declaration of faith

Shari'a linguistically means 'the way to water'; the Islamic legal system

Shirk setting up equals to or worshipping anyone other than Allah

Sifat a characteristic of Allah, for example foreknowledge

Sin actions against God's law

Six Articles of Faith the key beliefs of Sunni Muslims

Son of God title used to refer to Jesus being God

Soul-making the idea that one of God's purposes in allowing humans to experience good and evil is to allow the development of character

Special revelation the communication of truths about God that come to certain people at certain times, often through supernatural means

Steward someone who takes care of something

Stewardship the job of supervising or taking care of something for someone else, in this case looking after creation

Suffering pain or harm experienced as a result of evil

Surgical strike a military attack intended to damage only a legitimate military target, with no or minimal collateral damage

Tarawih voluntary night prayer during Ramadan

Tawhid the oneness of Allah

Technological warfare any form of warfare that uses advanced technology, for example, drones and AI (artificial intelligence)

Teleological argument the argument that the apparent design of the world is proof or evidence of God's existence

Ten Obligatory Acts the most important duties for Shi'a Muslims

Terrorism the unlawful use of violence and intimidation, especially against civilians, in the pursuit of ideological (political or religious) aims

The Fall the moment when Adam and Eve permanently broke the relationship with God

Torah (Tawrat) scripture revealed to Musa

Transcendent beyond everyday life; outside the human universe

Trinity the Christian concept of God as one God in three persons; Father, Son and Holy Spirit

Twelver Shi'a Muslims the largest group in Shi'a Islam who believe that there were 12 Imams after the death of Muhammad. Twelvers believe that the twelfth Imam is still alive somewhere on Earth and will one day make himself known and bring equality to all

Ummah worldwide community of Muslims

'Usul-ad-Din 'Principles of Faith', the key beliefs of Shi'a Muslims

Vision an experience of seeing something significant or supernatural

Vow a promise made at a wedding

Worship the expression of love and praise for God

Wudu ablution ritual before prayer

Zakah/Zakat 'purification' of wealth

Index

abortion 254–5
Adam 14–15, 17, 90, 94, 98–9
adoration 46
adultery 169
Advent 56–7
afterlife 33, 103, 106–9
agape 20–2, 30
agnosticism 266–7
Ahmadiyya Islam 76–7, 85, 91, 93
Akhirah 106
al-Jannah 108–9
Allah 76, 78–81, 98–9, 101
  communication with 117
  as creator 87
  judging humanity 78–9, 107
  nature of 84–7
almsgiving 58, 132–5
angels 98–9
annulment 168
anointing with oil 63
anthropic principle 186, 196–7
Apostles' Creed 9
Aquinas, Thomas 190, 192, 194–5, 219, 233
archangels 100–1
arranged marriage 252
ascension 27
Ash Wednesday 58
Ash'arites 104–5
Ashura 142–4
atheism 184, 190, 195, 266–7
Bada' 103
baptism 48–51
Baptist Church 3
barzakh 107
Beatitudes 23
benevolence 6, 84
Bible 3, 202–3
  Gospels 12, 24, 26–7, 29
  New Testament 27, 32
  Old Testament 18, 32, 184–5, 187
Big Bang 194–5
Bridges, Ruby 239
British identity 262–3
cafe church movement 66
CAFOD 71
Catholic Church *see* Roman Catholic Church
celibacy 164
charismatic experiences 209–10
charismatic worship 39, 41
charities 70–1, 135
Christian Aid 71
Christmas 56–7

Church of England 3, 163, 262–3
church planting 66
'Churches Together' movement 69
civil partnerships 167
cohabitation 162–3
community 62, 67, 176
complementarianism 178
confession 46
confirmation 62–3
contraception 164–5
conversion experiences 208–10
Corrymeela 69
cosmological argument 194–5
creation accounts 10–13, 178–9
creeds 9, 184
crucifixion 24–5, 58
Crusades 224–5
Darwin, Charles 192–3
Dawkins, Richard 174, 184, 190
Dawud (David) 91, 94
Day of Judgement 78–9, 107–9, 117
dedication service 51
Deism 184
denominations 2–3
design argument 192–3
discrimination 178
diversity 263
divine providence 186
divorce 168–9, 252
Easter 26, 59
ecumenism 68–9, 264–5
egalitarianism 178–9
Eid-ul-Adha 140–1, 144–5
Eid-ul-Fitr 141, 144–5
Eid-ul-Ghadeer 142–4
Epiphany 57
equality 176–81, 240–1, 249–53
Equality Act 2010 253
Eucharist 24, 40, 48–9, 52, 58–9
euthanasia 254
evangelical Christians 2–3, 16–17, 64–5, 157, 162–3, 169, 174, 187, 193, 195, 206, 221
Eve 14–15, 17
evil 16–17, 188–9
evolution 192–3
exclusivism 258, 272
extempore prayer 47
Fall, the 14–17, 29, 188
families
  Christian 62–3, 156–7, 164–5, 170–5
  gender roles 170–5
  non-nuclear 157

fasting 58, 113, 114, 136–9
fertility treatment 257
festivals 140–1
Five Pillars of Islam 112–13, 116, 123
five roots of 'Usul ad-Din 80–2, 106
forced marriage 252
forgiveness 6–7, 86, 109, 238–9
free will 14–15, 104–5, 188–9
funeral rites 61
gender equality 178–81
gender roles 170–5
Genesis 4, 6, 8, 10–11, 13, 14–15, 176, 178–9
genetic manipulation 256–7
God
  as creator 10, 186
  and morality 198–9
  nature of 4–7, 184
  proving existence of 190–215
  revelation 200–15
Good Friday 24, 59
goodness 14–15, 184–7
Gospels 12, 24, 26–7, 29
grace 30–1
Hajj 113, 114, 126–31
heaven and hell 34–5, 108–9
Holy Communion 40–1, 45, 52–3, 62, 176–7
Holy Spirit
  Christianity 8, 10, 26, 31, 59, 62–3, 209–10
  Islam 100
holy war 148, 224–5
Holy Week 58–9
homosexuality 164, 253
humanism 248–9, 268–9
Ibrahim (Abraham) 90, 140
immanence 4–5, 84, 87, 184
incarnation 18–19, 56
inclusivism 258, 272
informal worship 39
intercessions 46
inter-faith dialogue 260–1
intra-faith communication 264–5
Isa (Jesus) 91, 99
Islam, definition 76
Isma'il (Ishmael) 90
Israfil 101
Izra'il 100
Jahannam 108–9
Jerusalem 54
Jesus Christ
  ascension 27
  baptism 50

280

Index

crucifixion 24–5, 58
incarnation 18–19, 56
life of 20–2
as Messiah 18–19
resurrection 26–7
as saviour 24–5
second coming 32–3
as Son of God 18–19
as Word of God 203
Jibril 100–1
Jihad 146–51
Judaism 2, 22, 91, 136
judgement 6–7
just war theory 222
justice 240–3
King, Martin Luther 234–5
Last Supper 53, 58
Laylat al-Qadr 92
Lent 58
Lewis, C.S. 198, 208–9
liberal Christians 2, 16–17, 166, 169, 171, 187, 193, 194
life after death 106–9
liturgical worship 39–40, 47
Lord's Prayer 6–7, 42–3, 238
Lourdes 206
Luther, Martin 191
magisterium 204
Makkah (Mecca) 113, 114, 126–31
marriage 60–1, 158–61, 252–3
divorce and remarriage 168–9, 252
same-sex 166–7
martyrdom 108, 136, 143
Mary 18, 55
Mass 24, 39–40, 46, 52–3
meditation 46–7
Messiah 18–19
Messy Church worship 66–7
Methodist Church 3
Mika'il 100
miracles 205–7
mission 64–5
monotheism 4–5, 184
morality 198–9
mosques 120–1
Musa (Moses) 91
Mu'tazilite 104–5
nativity 56
New Testament 27, 32
Nicene Creed 9
non-violent action 234–5
Old Testament 18, 32, 184–5, 187
omnipotence 4, 84, 87, 102
omniscience 4, 84, 87, 107
Original Sin 14–15, 28–30, 50
pacifism 229–30

Paley, William 192–3
Palm Sunday 58
parables 7, 70, 236, 238
Parousia 32–3
Pentecost 26, 59
Pentecostal Church 3, 5, 206
persecution 70–1
pilgrimage 54–5, 113, 114, 126–31
pluralism 258–9, 272
polytheism 9, 86
Pope John Paul II 238
poverty 242
prayer
Christianity 42, 46–7, 58
Islam 112–14, 121, 124–5
Lord's Prayer 6–7, 42–3, 238
predestination 78, 102–5
premarital sex 162
Prophet Muhammad 76–7, 79, 83, 88, 92–3, 94, 96, 117, 120, 125, 129, 136–7, 142, 149
prophethood 88–93
proselytisation 262–3
Protestant Church 2–3, 7, 39, 48, 264
on the Eucharist 52–3
experiencing God 214–15
gender roles 170–3
on grace 31
on marriage 159
purgatory 35
Qur'an 77, 80–1, 83, 86, 94, 96–7, 108, 121, 136, 139
radicalisation 220–1
Ramadan 136–9
reconciliation 236–7
Reformation 3, 246
remarriage 168–9
resurrection 26–7
revelation 200–15
rites 40, 48
rites of passage 60–1
rituals 60
Roman Catholic Church 2–3, 7, 194, 264
on contraception 164
on evil 16–17
on evolution 193
and family and gender roles 156, 170, 172, 175
on grace 30
magisterium 204
on marriage 60–1, 159, 161, 163, 166–7, 168, 253
Mass 24, 39–40, 46, 52–3
sacraments 48–9, 214, 236
Sabbath 10

sacraments 48–9, 214–15, 236
sacrifice 140
Salah/Salat 117–21
salvation 28–9, 258–9
same-sex marriage 166–7, 252
schools 250–1
secularism 248, 250, 270–3
Sermon on the Mount 22–3
sex 162, 164, 252
shari'a 77
Shi'a Islam 76–7, 80–3, 85, 89–91, 93, 101, 103, 107, 114–16, 134, 142–5
shirk 86, 117
sin 14–15, 28–31, 50, 86
Six Articles of Faith 78–9, 82, 88, 101, 106
social justice 242–3
stewardship 106
suffering 16–17, 188–9
Sufis 76–7
Sunni Islam 76–9, 82–3, 85, 93, 100–1, 103, 107, 112–13, 116, 123, 134, 136–7
supplications 46
Swinburne, Richard 185, 190, 192, 196
Taizé 69
Tawhid 78–9, 86, 117
Ten Commandments 5, 15, 91, 186
Ten Obligatory Acts 114–16, 134
terrorism 220–1
Torah 94–5
transcendence 4–5, 84, 184
Trinity 8–9, 86, 184
Twelver Shi'a Muslims 76–7, 85, 89, 134
ummah 76
violence 218–19
visions 211–13
Walker, Gee 239
war and conflict
holy war 148, 224–5
just war theory 222–5
modern warfare 226–8
pacifism 229–31
violence 218–19
wealth inequality 181
World Council of Churches 68–9, 265
worship
Christianity 5, 24, 38–41, 44–6, 66
Islam 117–25
wudu 117–18
Yahweh 5
Zakah/Zakat 113, 114, 123, 132–5

Photo credits

The publishers would like to thank the following for permission to reproduce copyright material:

Christianity section opener © Marina/stock.adobe.com; p.2 © Balazs/stock.adobe.com; p.4 t © Marina/stock.adobe.com, b © Paul Quayle/Alamy Stock Photo; p.6 © Art Collection 2/Alamy Stock Photo; p.7 XXX; P.8 © PAINTING/Alamy Stock Photo; P.12 © Michelangelo; p.14 © Jorisvo/stock.adobe.com; p.16 © Matej Divizna/Getty Images; p.20 t © Zzvet/stock.adobe.com, b © Howgill/stock.adobe.com; p.22 © Renáta Sedmáková/stock.adobe.com; p.24 © Renáta Sedmáková/stock.adobe.com; p.26 © Artmedia/Alamy Stock Photo; p.30 © Fluenta/stock.adobe.com; p.32 © Fine Art Images/Heritage Images/Getty Images; p.34 © Jozef sedmak/Alamy Stock Photo; p.38 © Curtbauer/stock.adobe.com; p.40 © Pontino/Alamy Stock Photo; p.42 © Rawpixel.com/stock.adobe.com; p.44 © Liubomir/stock.adobe.com; p.46 © Music-Images/Lebrecht Music & Arts/Alamy Stock Photo; p.48 t © Nadia Koval/stock.adobe.com, b © Friedrich Stark/Alamy Stock Photo; p.50 © Matthew Chattle/Alamy Stock Photo; p.52 l © lightpoet/stock.adobe.com, r © Caralynn Scott/stock.adobe.com; p.54 l © MIKEL BILBAO GOROSTIAGA- TRAVELS/Alamy Stock Photo, table l © kirill4mula/stock.adobe.com, table r © Stripped Pixel/stock.adobe.com; p.55 l © Homer Sykes/Alamy Stock Photo, r © Vivida Photo PC/stock.adobe.com; p.56 © Vstock HC/Alamy Stock Photo; p.58 © Bernadett/stock.adobe.com; p.60 © David L/Peopleimages.com/stock.adobe.com; p.62 © John Leyba/Denver Post/Getty Images; p.64 © Jonathan Torgovnik/Getty Images; p.66 © DALLAS KILPONEN/The Sydney Morning Herald/Fairfax Media/Getty Images; p.68 © Abaca Press/Alamy Stock Photo; p.70 © Libby Welch/Alamy Stock Photo; p.71 l-r © Mark Boulton/Alamy Stock Photo, © Arlette Bazhizi/Tearfund, © Thom Flint/ CAFOD; Islam section opener © Aviator70/stock.adobe.com; p.78 © As-artmedia/stock.adobe.com; p.80 © Mansoreh Motamedi/Moment/Getty Images; p.86 © Mama Belle and the kids/Shutterstock.com; p.88 © Matteo Omied/Alamy Stock Photo; p.92 © Nurlan/stock.adobe.com; p.94 l © WavebreakMediaMicro/stock.adobe.com, r © Shalini Saran/IndiaPictures/Universal Images Group/Getty Image; p.96 tl © Malik Nalik/stock.adobe.com, bl © Meeko Media/stock.adobe.com, r © Godong/Alamy Stock Photo; p.98 © Petr/stock.adobe.com; p.100 t © SVRSLYIMAGES/stock.adobe.com, b © Mother/stock.adobe.com; p.102 t © Maximusdn/stock.adobe.com, b © Bargais/stock.adobe.com; p.104 © Diane/stock.adobe.com; p.106 © Ilya Batkovich/stock.adobe.com; p.108 t © Lucky-photo/stock.adobe.com, b © DiKiYaqua/stock.adobe.com; p.112 © Rick Henzel/stock.adobe.com; p.117 © Meeko Media/stock.adobe.com; p.118 © A travel images/Shutterstock.com; p.120 t © Lee Thomas/Alamy Stock Photo, b © Rawpixel.com/stock.adobe.com; p.122 t © Dr_pad/Shutterstock.com; p.123 © Amorn/stock.adobe.com; p.124 t © Bangkok Click Studio/stock.adobe.com, b © Leo Lintang/stock.adobe.com; p.126 © Aviator70 - stock.adobe.com; p.127 © Zurijeta/Shutterstock.com, p.130 t-b © Youcef/stock.adobe.com, © Hasan hatrash/Alamy Stock Photo, © Ayman Ali/Anadolu Agency/Getty Images, © ASHRAF AMRA/EPA-EFE/Shutterstock; p.132 t © MohamadFaizal/stock.adobe.com, b © ROMEO GACAD/AFP/Getty Images; p.134 © Supreme Leader Press Office/Handout/Anadolu Agency/Getty Images; p.136 t © ArkReligion.com/Art Directors & TRIP/Alamy Stock Photo, b © Aisylu/stock.adobe.com; p.138 t © Gulsina/stock.adobe.com, b © Imageplotter/Alamy Stock Photo; p.140 t © Bobi/stock.adobe.com, b © Queenmoonlite Studio/stock.adobe.com; p.142 © Morteza Nikoubazl/NurPhoto/Shutterstock; p.143 © Matthew Chattle/Shutterstock; p.146 © Puhhha/stock.adobe.com; p.147 © Daniel Vrabec/Alamy Stock Photo; p.148 © Meysam Azarneshin/stock.adobe.com; p.150 © Mintaha Neslihan Eroglu/Anadolu Agency/Getty Images; Ethics section opener © Alfazet Chronicles/stock.adobe.com; p.156 © DragonImages/stock.adobe.com; p.158 © Monkey Business/stock.adobe.com; p.162 © Nenetus/stock.adobe.com; p.166 © Svitlana/stock.adobe.com; p.170 © Inti St. Clair/stock.adobe.com; p.172 © Ken McKay/ITV/Shutterstock.com; p.174 © Jeff Morgan 02/Alamy Stock Photo; p.176 © KS JAY/Shutterstock.com; p.178 © UPI/Alamy Stock Photo; p.186 © Jacob Lund/stock.adobe.com; p.192 © Alfazet Chronicles/stock.adobe.com; p.198 © KEYSTONE Pictures USA/ZUMAPRESS/Alamy Stock Photo; p.205 XXX; p.208 © Renáta Sedmáková/stock.adobe.com; p.211 © Vlastimil Šesták/stock.adobe.com; p.212 © Chronicle/Alamy Stock Photo; p.214 t-b © VividaPhotoPC/Alamy Stock Photo, © Jantanee/stock.adobe.com, © Fitz/stock.adobe.com; p.220 © Sebastian Portillo/Shutterstock.com; p.222 © SOPA Images Limited/Alamy Stock Photo; p.224 © jorisvo/stock.adobe.com; p.226 © Operation 2022/Alamy Stock Photo; p.227 © Photo Researchers/Science History Images/Alamy Stock Photo; p.229 © Ddukang/stock.adobe.com; p.232 © Zac Hancock/Shutterstock.com; p.233 © Amer ghazzal/Alamy Stock Photo; p.234 t © Bettmann/Getty Images, b © Bettmann/Getty Images; p.236 © Julio Etchart/Alamy Stock Photo; p.238 © Franco Origlia/Hulton Archive/Getty Images, p.239 t National Park Service, Uncredited Public Domain, b © Phil Noble/PA Images/Alamy Stock Photo; p.240 © KS JAY/Shutterstock.com; p.250 © Angela Hampton Picture Library/Alamy Stock Photo; p.252 © Tim Moore/Alamy Stock Photo; p.254 © Photosaint/stock.adobe.com; p.262 tl © WPA Pool/Shutterstock.com, bl © Daniel Vernon/Alamy Stock Photo; p.263 © Vibrant Pictures/Alamy Stock Photo; p.264 © World Council of Churches; P.265 l Photo by Mike DuBose/WCC, r Amanda Cattini and João Tavares at the London Marathon 2021 for Christian Aid, used by permission of Christian Aid, p.266 © Anthony Devlin/PA Images/Alamy Stock Photo; p.270 © VICTORIA JONES/POOL/EPA-EFE/Shutterstock.com; p.272 © Renáta Sedmáková/stock.adobe.com; p.273 © Independent Photo Agency Srl/Alamy Stock Photo